MERCY, MERCY ME

Race and American Culture

Arnold Rampersad and Shelley Fisher Fishkin
General Editors

MERCY, MERCY ME

AFRICAN-AMERICAN CULTURE

AND THE AMERICAN SIXTIES

JAMES C. HALL

OXFORD
UNIVERSITY PRESS
2001

OXFORD

UNIVERSITY PRESS

Oxford   New York

Athens   Auckland   Bangkok   Bogotá   Buenos Aires   Cape Town
Chennai   Dar es Salaam   Delhi   Florence   Hong Kong   Istanbul   Karachi
Kolkata   Kuala Lumpur   Madrid   Melbourne   Mexico City   Mumbai   Nairobi
Paris   São Paulo   Shanghai   Singapore   Taipei   Tokyo   Toronto   Warsaw

and associated companies in
Berlin   Ibadan

Published by Oxford University Press, Inc.
198 Madison Avenue, New York, New York 10016

Oxford is a registered trademark of Oxford University Press.

Library of Congress Cataloging-in-Publication Data
Hall, James C., 1960–
Mercy, mercy me : African-American culture and the American sixties / James C. Hall
p. cm. — (Race and American culture)
Includes bibliographical references and index.
ISBN 0-19-509609-6
1. Afro-Americans—Intellectual life—20th century.   2. Afro-American arts—
History—20th century.   3. Afro-Americans—Social life and customs—20th century.
4. Modernism (Art)—United States—History—20th century.   5. Modernism
(Literature)—United States—History—20th century.   6. United States—History—1961–1969.
7. United States—Social life and customs—1945–1970.   8. United States—
Intellectual life—20th century.   I. Title.   II. Series.
E185.61 .H1972 2001
973'.0496073—dc21   00-055774

1 3 5 7 9 8 6 4 2

Printed in the United States of America
on acid-free paper

In memory of my dad,
Stanley Hall (1931–1992)

There is a moment in the history of every nation, when, proceeding out of this brute youth, the perceptive powers reach their ripeness and have not yet become microscopic: so that man, at that instant, extends across the entire scale, and, with his feet still planted on the immense forces of night, converses by his eyes and brain with solar and stellar creation. That is the moment of adult health, the culmination of power.

RALPH WALDO EMERSON, *Representative Men*

Teach us, Forever Dead, there is no Dream but Deed, there is no Deed but Memory.

The Autobiography of W.E.B. Du Bois

Systematic healthy-mindedness, failing as it does to accord to sorrow, pain, and death any positive and active attention whatever, is formally less complete than systems that try at least to include these elements in their scope.

WILLIAM JAMES, *Varieties of Religious Experience*

Mercy, mercy me,
Things ain't what they used to be. . . .

MARVIN GAYE

PREFACE

> To articulate the past historically does not mean to recognize it "the
> way it really was." It means to seize hold of a memory as it flashes up
> at a moment of danger. . .
>
> WALTER BENJAMIN

In the 1960s a diverse group of African-American artists and intellectuals forcefully asserted their vision of the limitations and restrictions of contemporary American life. Their concerns grew out of not only the fervor of the civil rights revolution, but also a sense that American culture was sterile, secular, and disturbingly immune to the tragic lessons of history. In response, these artists—sometimes individually, sometimes collectively—reflected openly about the effects of this modern America on their sense of self and community. This book explores the character of this antimodern sentiment and, further, its viability as an interpretive historical paradigm for understanding the shape and development of African-American culture in the "Second Black Renaissance."

This project is different from attempts at retelling the story of the Harlem Renaissance of the 1920s. While comprehensive institutional histories are necessary to our gaining a better understanding of African-American culture and the 1960s, it seems unlikely that there can ever be a satisfactory retelling that is as capacious as, say, David Levering Lewis's *When Harlem Was in Vogue*. The Second Black Renaissance—if that is the proper designation for the outpouring of African-American creativity in the 1960s—was an incredibly diffuse phenomenon both geographically and ideologically and may at bottom be fundamentally inchoate. On the other hand, certain folkloric conceptions as to the meaning of black creativity in the 1960s do seem to have become authoritative. Too often I hear students (and colleagues) confidently reflect either nostalgically or with a certain scorn about the character of African-American culture in the 1960s. This version of the 1960s—oft repeated in certain diagnoses of all that is supposedly wrong with American culture in the 1990s—too often lacks depth and distinction.

A reading of 1960s African-American cultural history through the lens of "antimodernism" (not anti-literary modernism, but, rather, a protest against or rejection of modernity) shifts attention from an understanding of the period which places primacy upon the playing out of a series of social dramas between "militants" and "liberals," "radicals" and "compromisers," "authentic Blacks" and "Toms." This book revises the picture of African-American cultural accomplishment in the 1960s away from a vision of intra- and intercultural war about the shape of correct cultural representation and toward that of a dynamic challenge to the hegemony of a naive faith in progressive and good American life. The cultural actors described herein hold to a complex politics of race and nation. They are cosmopolitan in outlook and critical of a culture of congratulation. African-American antimodernists—W.E.B. Du Bois, Robert Hayden, Paule Marshall, William Demby, John Coltrane, Romare Bearden, and many others—make important contributions to American culture by noting that culture's limitations. In particular, they highlight the close relationship between slavery and the construction of American citizenship, "manifest destiny" and black "social death." In general, they document the destructive advances upon the self by consumer capitalism, technology, and ritualized violence. These artists lament, memorialize, conjure, condemn, and celebrate. Ironically, they seek to provide hope against hope, seeing in creative remembrance potential resistance to the belief that "everything will be all right."

I HAVE MANY debts to acknowledge. This work began in the very supportive and engaging environment of the American Studies Program at the University of Iowa. George Barlow, Mary Lou Emery, Ed Folsom, Bruce Goebel, Mae Henderson, Richard Horwitz, Tom Lutz, James Marshall, Mary Janell Metzger, Peter Nazareth, Pat Nunnally, Dale Rigby, Al Roberts, Alan Spring, and William Welburn were all incredibly supportive and each contributed in quite specific ways to my intellectual growth. Darwin T. Turner and Jonathan Walton both passed away during my years at Iowa; I could not have had better teachers of African-American culture and history and it is my great regret that they did not live to see this work completed. Albert E. Stone was not only the most important intellectual influence on this project but was—and is—a supportive friend and mentor too.

I have also been lucky to find a supportive academic community at the University of Illinois at Chicago. Joe Alter, Ike Balbus, Eva Bednarowicz, Cynthia Blair, Ginger Brent, Preston Browning, Franz Burnier, Katrina Caldwell, Luisa Cariño, Nancy Cirillo, Jennifer Cohen, Chiquita Collins, Cathy Colton, George Courts, Dan Dale, Jamie Daniel, Mike Davros, Terri de Langis, Susan Edgerton, Julie Moody-Freeman, Judy Gardiner, Gwynne Gertz, Bridget Harris, Darnell Hawkins, Annette Henry, John Huntington, Robert Jagers, Lansiné Kaba, Dawn Kelly, Javelin Lawrence, Donald Marshall, Mildred McGinnis, Chris Messenger, Charles Mills, Erica Myles, Kaine Osburn, Tom Philion, Sterling Plumpp, Barbara Ransby, Stephanie Riger, Phil Royster, Tricia Rowe, Kim Ruffin, Chris Shannon, Jim Sosnoski, Terri Thorkildsen,

Shirley Turner, Deborah Um'Rani, Steve Warner, Jeanne Weiland, Virginia Wexman, Dave Zauhar, and Daniel Zellman all get my thanks for the multiple ways they have provided support and encouragement. Eric Arnesen and Peg Strobel have been colleagues, friends, and mentors above and beyond the call and duty and have my undying respect.

Academic life is, of course, also very much a process of cultivating friendships and working collaborations from afar. Once again I have been lucky. I am thankful for the support, conversation, and challenges of Linda Dahl, Kathryn Earle, John Gennari, Heather Hathaway, Bill Kenney, Tom and Carol Montgomery-Fate, Joycelyn Moody, Geraldine Murphy, Xavier Nicholas, Nigel Rothfels, Suzanne Smith, Alan Wald, and Tim Waples. While our contacts have been unfortunately brief I need also to acknowledge the thoughtfulness and support of Michael Dyson, Gerald Graff, Nathaniel Mackey, Nellie McKay, David Lionel Smith, and Mary Helen Washington. William Demby and Paule Marshall have graciously answered all my queries. I hope the great respect I have for their lives and work is made most clear in these pages.

One individual must be singled out: James Miller has been an exemplary mentor and friend. Every junior scholar should be so lucky as to have such a thoughtful guide to and interpreter of the profession. While it is a cliché to acknowledge that teaching gets short shrift in our profession, it is a painful truth to note that such thoughtful *friendship*—itself substantial work—is never acknowledged as perhaps the most crucial contribution a scholar can make. I do want to acknowledge publicly this important work and express my great appreciation for his help and guidance.

While all of these friends and acquaintances graciously gave their time and assistance, it is, of course, my family who has paid the greatest price for the completion of this book. Walter performed the disarmingly crucial function of ritually but sincerely saying to me, "Tell me about your day, Dad." Just as ritually—and I suspect just as sincerely—Rebecca engaged and amused Walt at strategic moments. Calum is perhaps luckiest in that he was born too late to fully observe the book's false starts and their effect on his father. Given that, in many ways, this book is about the restoration of meaningful public life, their patience and love come to me as the very best teaching and cause for hope and persistence.

I GRAVITATED TOWARD American Studies out of a need to find an institutional location which possesses a rich tradition and breadth of vision, and in which my interest in social transformation might be acknowledged. This book, certainly a product of my encounter with that tradition, has modest extrahistorical goals. It is meant to be cultural criticism as well as cultural history, an attempt to situate antimodern sentiment in the modern university, fully conscious, I hope, of all the ironies inherent in that act.

Perhaps one odd characteristic of my intellectual autobiography is my loyalty to many of the creative intellectuals studied here. By loyalty I mean not an uncritical acceptance of all actions and statements, but, rather, a commitment to publicize their significant accomplishments, regardless of whether or not critical consensus perceives them to be "major" or "minor" contributors to our culture. Whether or not this complicates credibility, my book means to address the subjective issue of what it means to be a student of African-American culture. I can say for certain that I have been studying African-American literature and culture for fully a third of my life; it is inevitable that I have been greatly influenced by the struggles of these individuals to make sense of the world in which they found themselves. My encounter with these thinkers has immeasurably enriched my existence. It goes without saying, however, that this world is not strictly my own. Nevertheless, I hope that I have used my privilege carefully, as should we all.

CREDITS

Excerpt from "64 Like a Mirror in a Darkroom, 63 Like a Mirror in a House Afire," in *The Beautiful Days*, (New York: Poets Press, 1965). Courtesy of A. B. Spellman.

William Demby, selections from *The Catacombs*, courtesy of William Demby.

W.E.B. Du Bois, selections from *The Autobiography of W.E.B. Du Bois*, 12–13, 57–58, 61, 63, 92, 143, 148, 156, 181, 193, 222, 253, 277, 279–280, 283, 285, 337, 339, 392–393, 400–401, 409, 412–414, 417, 422–423, reprinted with permission of International Publishers Co., New York.

Richard Farina, 1964, *Birmingham Sunday*, Universal—Songs of PolyGram Intl., Inc. International copyright secured, all rights reserved.

Marvin Gaye, 1971, *Mercy, Mercy Me (The Ecology)*, Jobete Music Co., Inc. All rights controlled and administered by EMI April Music Inc. All rights reserved. International copyright secured. Used by permission.

Marvin Gaye and James Nyx, 1971, *Inner City Blues (Makes Me Wanna Holler)*, Jobete Music Co., Inc. All rights controlled and administered by EMI April Music Inc. All rights reserved. International copyright secured. Used by permission.

Robert Hayden, selections from the correspondence of Robert Hayden, Robert Hayden Papers, National Bahá'í Archives, Wilmette, IL.

Robert Hayden, selections from *Collected Prose*, courtesy of Maia Patillo.

Robert Hayden, selections from "Frederick Douglass," in *Collected Poems of Robert Hayden*, edited by Frederick Glaysher (New York: Liveright Publishing Corp., 1966). Courtesy of Liveright Publishers.

Paule Marshall, selections from *The Chosen Place, The Timeless People*, material used with the permission of the author.

CONTENTS

MERCY, MERCY ME

CHAPTER ONE

AFRICAN–AMERICAN ANTIMODERNISM AND THE AMERICAN SIXTIES

Come round by my side and I'll sing you a song
I'll sing it so softly, it'll do no one wrong
On Birmingham Sunday the blood ran like wine
and the choirs kept singing of Freedom
"Birmingham Sunday," LYRIC BY RICHARD FARIÑA[1]

Imagine, if you can, the morning of Monday, September 16, 1963. You are ready to work. Your typewriter is at the ready. You have coffee, maybe cigarettes. No distractions. But there is still an edginess, the pressure to produce, the commitment that words on paper entails. So you delay and retrieve the newspaper at your door. The *New York Times* headline: "Birmingham Bomb Kills 4 Negro Girls in Church; Riots Flare; 2 Boys Slain." Continue working? Four children—Denise McNair, age 11, and Carole Robertson, Addie Mae Collins, Cynthia Wesley, each age 14—killed just prior to a worship service at the Sixteenth Street Baptist Church in Birmingham, Alabama. Later that day, James Robinson, age 16, is shot in the back by police trying to break up rock throwing between white and black teenagers. And, finally, Virgil Ware, age 13, is shot by a white teenager (an Eagle Scout) who had spent the afternoon at a white supremacist rally. Five hundred National Guardsmen and three hundred state troopers had taken control of the streets. Six black *children* slain, killed by *men*, by representatives of the state, by other children. Continue working? Prior to the explosion, the girls killed at the church had heard the completion of Ella Demand's Sunday School lesson, "The Love That Forgives." That same day, President Kennedy had stated in an address that "a new national awareness of discriminatory practices against Negroes was bringing progress toward the goal of equal opportunity."[2] Forgiveness? Progress? Continue working?[3]

Or, perhaps more importantly, just what might constitute work, especially intellectual or artistic work, at this particular historical moment? If one is an artist how should one respond to this brave new world? What strategies of representation might possibly be up to the task of expressing one's outrage and sorrow? Regardless of how one has experienced the disruptions of modernism, whether one is committed to a strictly mimetic art or is more likely to embrace fragmentation, collage, or dissonance, the question of a modus operandi seems likely to be overwhelmed by a boundless despondency, or perhaps a dramatic stupefaction. How can this be happening? A mere nineteen days after the triumph of the march on Washington. What is one to make of this simultaneity of agony and ecstasy, civilization and barbarism? This synchronicity would certainly have been felt by African-American artists and thinkers at other "modern moments," but there is something unique about this historical juncture. The mobilization of students, churchgoers, labor unions and intellectuals engaged in nonviolent civil disobedience, concrete judicial and legislative gains in civil rights coincident with intractable poverty (the "other America," in Michael Harrington's apt phrase), and mundane, epidemic race violence is a complex existential situation. The bombing of the Sixteenth Street Baptist Church in Birmingham is but a single manifestation of this crisis, although somehow more than typical. It is fitting to begin with Birmingham as there is something about the violation of childhood (and perhaps of worship) and what can be called without exaggeration an attendant reaction of horror that best introduces this decade of radical questioning.[4] For many African-American creative intellectuals, there was a turn toward a fundamental disbelief in the inherent goodness of the offerings of modernity, indeed, an antimodernism. The stunning presence of murderous violence in a supposedly advanced, progressive society suggested to many African-American artists that the Enlightenment project was, if not fully compromised, in need of careful reexamination.

The cultural mainstream of the nation is an empty street, full of bright lights that try to glamorize the cultural wreckage and flotsam of our times. Over this deranged, tormented cultural wasteland reigns a social stratum—a white cultural elite of America, the soured cream of our creative and aesthetic intelligentsia, that dominates nevertheless to the roar of prestigious acclaim. This elite has become intellectually bloated, dull, unoriginal, critically tongue-tied, smug (or downright scared), time-serving, and societally dishonest. . . . And during all these years of gradual descent from its own Parnassus, it worshipped at the altar of the white Anglo-Saxon ideal. Thereby, it collaborated spiritually in spreading the pall of debased and unprocreative white middle-class cultural values that shroud America today.

HAROLD CRUSE, *The Crisis of the Negro Intellectual* (1967)[5]

In the 1960s an incredibly diverse range of African-American artists decried the character of American modernity. In jeremiads and stories, in new and old forms, they called American culture "out of its name." Larry Neal wrote that "it is clear that the question of human survival is at the core of contemporary experience. The black artist must address himself to this reality in the strongest terms possible. In a context of world upheaval, ethics and aesthetics must interact positively and be consistent with the demands for a more spiritual world."[6] In further evaluating this "contemporary experience," James Baldwin reflected that "the American dream has . . . become something much more closely resembling a nightmare, on the private, domestic, and international levels. . . . Behind what we think of as the Russian menace lies what we do not wish to face, and what white Americans do not face when they regard a Negro reality—the fact that life is tragic."[7] This pessimistic assessment was seemingly advanced even by Ralph Ellison: "Today we are an affluent society and yet we're very unhappy. We no longer know what truth is. We no longer recognize heroism when it's demonstrated to us. . . . We don't seem to know where we are."[8] For June Jordan, "identity of person has been pursued through the acquisition of material clues admittedly irrelevant to the achievement of happiness. Identity has been secured among watery objects ceaselessly changing value. Worse, the marketplace has vanquished the workable concept of homeground, or as the children say in their games, home-safe."[9]

These cultural critiques are exemplary of the way in which African-American art in the 1960s claimed for itself an expansive social capacity. These diagnoses were standard practice, a kind of repertory philosophic grounding, across more specific ideological boundaries. In thinking about African-American creativity and the 1960s, these challenges have been too often ignored as rhetorical or ceremonial. In a rush to take sides in specific debates about representation, the nature of tradition, or the role or character of black folk or vernacular expression, critics and historians have ignored a vital consensus. The paradigmatic battle fought to determine what would be the aesthetic currency of protest made clear, for instance, that there was a way in which the problem could be identified, discussed, lamented, and experienced without agreement as to how it would be represented. Means were not so much the issue as were ends. A stunning number of African-American creative intellectuals emphatically asserted the pervasiveness of historical insensitivity, secularized personal and community life, and the bankruptcy of American morality. They sought refuge from this malaise in a variety of ways. They investigated the possibilities within an African past and present, both recognizable and invented. They considered numerous possibilities of religious revitalization, both within and outside the tradition of Euro-Christianity. They sought out sites for collective discussion and possibilities for alternative institutional structures for their artistic endeavors. Experimentation, nationalistic and avant-garde, resulted in many African-American artists radically challenging the accepted boundaries of their art form. Most significantly, African-American artists of the 1960s attempted to assert cultural identity itself as necessary resistance to despair. Harking back to W.E.B. Du Bois's singling out of double consciousness and double vision as the identifying marks of African-American experience in the United States, artists and intellectuals in the 1960s embraced the ambiguity of that "two-ness."

Most of our contemporary discussions of the character, scope, and trajectory of modernity have resolutely distanced themselves from the Enlightenment's entanglement with slavery. Paul Gilroy has elegantly detailed the tendency in writers like Marshall Berman and Jürgen Habermas to suggest that "an all-encompassing modernity affects everyone in a uniform and essentially similar way."[10] Following Gilroy, my book attempts to reveal a "primal history of modernity . . . reconstructed from the slave's point of view" (55). Most countermodern critiques remain immanently situated in the Enlightenment and retain (often enthusiastically) "such central categories . . . as the idea of universality, the fixity of meaning, the coherence of the subject, and, of course, the foundational ethnocentrism in which these have all tended to be anchored" (55). By taking seriously the history of African-American artistry in the 1960s, an artistic practice "inescapably both inside and outside the dubious protection modernity offers" (58), there is an opportunity to significantly expand a repertoire of strategies of resistance and to reevaluate—perhaps most especially on the political left—narratives of liberation which have never fully contended with slavery as a central factor in determining New World social relations.

African-American creative intellectuals' "double talk" brings the historical experience of betrayal to a variety of critiques of modernity. It is speech that expresses skepticism, doubt, even dismay and despair. In the 1960s, often in opposition to both the traditional political right and left, they declared an interest in a radical moral awakening and cultural revolution. Somewhat like the religious revivals of the Seventeenth and Eighteenth centuries, individuals as diverse as Martin Luther King, Jr., James Baldwin, Amiri Baraka, Audre Lorde, and many others demanded that Americans face up to a deteriorating social order. Sometimes Calvinist, sometimes Africanist, these individuals noted personal sinfulness and the fragility of community. Sometimes vitalist, sometimes evangelical, these thinkers called for new forms of conversion and devotion. In the embrace of a broad religious feeling (sometimes called "soul," sometimes "spirituality," sometimes "memory"), these artists challenged definitions of modernity (and countermodernity) in which religious world views are superseded and, in the words of Paul Gilroy, "the process of cultural rationalization whereby science, morality, and art are separated into autonomous spheres, each governed by its own epistemological rules and procedures of validation" (50). *Talk* by no means should be seen as superseding other forms of experience (organizing, demonstrating, taking up arms, etc.) but there is certainly a substantive legacy left to us by this sixties generation of informed reflection through fiction, poetry, painting, autobiography, and music toward the displacement of an untenable modernity.

AFRICAN-AMERICAN ANTIMODERNISM

In describing the central figures in this historical reconstruction as "antimodernists," specific allusion is made to the work of the cultural historian Jackson Lears who in his book *No Place of Grace: Antimodernism and the Transformation of American Culture, 1880–1920*[11] considered a eclectic band of cultural resisters and their relationship to the coalescence of American modernity. Lears defined antimodernism as a reaction to the feeling of "helplessness." It is:

> transatlantic in scope and sources [and draws] on venerable traditions as well as contemporary cultural currents: republican moralism, which promoted suspicion of urban "luxury"; romantic literary convention, which elevated simple and childlike rusticity over the artificial amenities of civilization; a revolt against positivism . . . which rejected all static intellectual and moral systems, often in the name of a vitalist cult of energy and process; and a parallel recovery of the primal, irrational forces in the human psyche, forces which have been obscured by the evasive banality of modern culture. (57)

Lears examined the Arts and Crafts movement, medievalism, the martial ideal, Anglo-Catholicism, and more generalized "religious protest" as elements of an American nervousness about the meaning of modernity; his dramatis personae included Charles Eliot Norton, Ralph Adams Cram, George Cabot Lodge, and Henry Adams. A reading of African-American cultural conditions in the 1960s can be offered that profoundly resonates with Lears's characterization (and characters) of this earlier period. The readings offered in the following pages are an attempt to suggest a provocative affinity. As important, however, are motives shared with Lears and scholarly goals that are more distinct. My own critical sentiment, like Lears's, shares the antimodernists' "discontent with modern culture: its crackpot obsession with efficiency, its humanist hubris, its complacent creed of progress" (xx). African-American studies remains, however, an academic discourse often denigrated as "particularist" and, as such, *Mercy, Mercy Me* is further interested in reminding commentators on modernity, in general, and the contemporary American scene, in particular, about the centrality of African-American or, in Gilroy's parlance, Black Atlantic cultural reflection to these debates and histories.

While my work might be seen as parasitic, it attempts to validate the continued existence of "antimodern sentiment" and hopefully complicates matters. Lears has been understandably restrained in making too much of the contemporary significance of his work and of the transferability of the paradigm of antimodernism despite wishing to add some historical depth to an often ineffectual and feeble debate about public life. *Mercy, Mercy Me* is little concerned with why African-American antimodernism might have occurred at the historical moment in which it does and even less with any direct intellectual connection between Lears and its own cast of characters. (In other words, it is not necessary that readers know the specifics of Lears's argument.) Unlike their nineteenth and twentieth century WASP ancestors, African-American antimodernists were not so interested in the maintenance of a certain kind of cultural hegemony, or motivated by the fear of the "emergent masses." Instead they were faced with confronting an entrenched consumer culture, the legacy of institutional and internalized racism, an ascendant therapeutic ethos, and the cold war demonization of almost all forms of progressive social criticism, all of which contributed to a kind of national procrastination in the process of instituting interracial democracy. Much of their challenge grew naturally out of the contemporary discourse of civil rights; part of the challenge was clearly participation in a long African-American tradition of asserting the immorality of American culture and intellectual life, especially in periods of its most virulent racism.[12] Like their WASP ancestors, African-American resisters were indicative of the paradoxical character of much American counterculture. They were unable to anticipate ways in which their own lamentation might contribute to the continuance of the very hegemonic discourse they wished to challenge. Lears's description and documentation of this paradox suggests that the situation of African-American intellectuals in the 1960s might be even more provocative still for the analysis of the efficacy of contemporary oppositional discourses in this country. Lears states: "Preoccupied with authentic experience as a means of revitalizing a fragmented personal identity, dissenters have often been unable to sustain larger loyalties outside the self. Their criticism has frequently dissolved into therapeutic quests for self-realization, easily accommodated to the dominant culture of our bureaucratic corporate state" (xix). The fragmentation of African-American oppositional discourse—conceived of as, say, the decline of a nationally visible civil rights movement or media promotion of generalized intracultural dispute, like mid-1980s debates on African-American gender relations—suggests an even more complicated process at work. Even when communal or nonindividual structures of meaning are preserved, such as those some might ascribe to post–World War II African-American fiction, the critical edge may be lost. It might be argued that a sinister development of postmodernity or late capitalism is the ability of the marketplace to make even politically conscious and historically accurate memory nonthreatening. Of what oppositional value is a heightened historical consciousness in these United States?

What is important then about the borrowing of "antimodernism" as a descriptor of African-American intellectual production in the 1960s? The term describes a response to modernity that is related to but strategically different from that body of thought and action known as "modernism." No doubt many readers will find it fundamentally counterintuitive to work with "antimodernism," especially as by just about any measure most of the central figures here—Romare Bearden, William Demby, Robert Hayden, and John Coltrane most especially—will seem to be "classic" modernists. And yet, as Houston Baker has argued most forcefully, most critical accounts of modernism have resolutely ignored black contributions to the transformation of twentieth-century aesthetics.[13] Baker has taken this absence as the cue for the construction of a striking filial interpretive paradigm which has transformed the critical gaze upon the 1920s and the Harlem Renaissance. While this new approach to the first quarter of the twentieth century is much welcome, it also flirts somewhat with an old-style nationalism, not so dangerous as a potential reduction of complexity, but very much so as an invitation to dismiss its insights as simply racial counterstatement. Antimodernism seems worth exploring insofar as it is both declarative of signal black difference and suggestive of affinities with multiple traditions of reflection, including those both inside and outside of the domain of modern Western thought. Importantly, unlike Baker's "renaissancism," antimodernism is not necessarily triumphalist. In suggesting its potential connectedness to a variety of modes of resistance, it is necessarily the case that the shortcomings of a sustained opposition are inevitably detailed.

Rarely initiating a complex analysis of the difficulties of class and especially gender, many African-American creative intellectuals of the sixties often engaged in the inscription of individualized ailments instead of the development of an engaged cultural criticism. Often the "romance" of resistance and challenge was sexist; it relied upon the rediscovery and celebration of black manhood, and delighted in the ceremony of warrior postures. Moreover, few artists of the period were able to translate their prophesies of inevitable apocalypse into a concrete recipe for reform, nor were they able to step back and consider the privilege of their positions, no matter how restricted they might be. On the other hand, the most effective of the antimodernists—including the figures upon which this book will focus, Robert Hayden, Paule Marshall, William Demby, John Coltrane, Romare Bearden, and W.E.B. Du Bois—developed a complex ethnoracial consciousness, at once able to critique naive quests for race authenticity and to recognize the need for strategic thought and action around the question of African-American culture. Culture became a means to restore some sense of agency, some sense of viable selfhood, against the process of reification.

Despite the significant accomplishments of these exemplars, the totality and long-term prospects of this cultural critique were seriously flawed: it was neither pragmatic enough to be clear about the efficacy of (or how to make permanent) such a consciousness, nor did it sufficiently direct us toward recognizing the totality of a capitalist world system. But African-American antimodernism is a vital contribution to American cultural discourse. Although it is difficult to measure, the African-American antimodernism of the sixties helped to pave the way for contemporary reexaminations of our basic categories of classification; that is, it provided much of the impetus for rethinking canons, and it changed the shape of our artistic landscape, asserting the values of pluralism and radical democracy. Most dramatically, African-American antimodernists preserved the social-critical function of art throughout the cold war and critical formalism, and consistently (if sometimes reluctantly) noted the inseparability of artists and the world in which they live and work. It made sure that we were never completely comfortable with depoliticized art or its criticism; more generally, for its audience, it assured that they too would never become comfortable with what Jackson Lears has called a "national chorus of self-congratulation" (xvi).[14]

Obviously, in a period of great countercultural activity, it would be chauvinistic (and stupid) to assert that only African-Americans engaged in challenges to the status quo. Challenges to the "goodness" of modernity were obviously not undertaken only by African-Americans, nor, for that matter, are they articulated only by intellectuals on the margins. African-American antimodernism, however, is especially valuable for its interrogation of (and longing for) community. By considering the relationship between the dominant disposition of American modernity and continued promises of full citizenship from the state, African-American resisters proffered a compelling meditation on the value and resilience of the bonds of nation, race, and family. (For me the systematic and informal reflections of sixties African-American creative intellectuals continue to resonate much more strongly than, say, the Port Huron Statement. One of the goals of this book is to explain and investigate this continued power.) The urgency with which African-American antimodernists directed themselves to our malaise—and the psychic cost of their resistance—makes them an important special case. It is also worth considering, as Lezlek Kolakowski has pointed out,[15] that the debate over modernity and its discontents is not limited to the twentieth century. The intellectual, spiritual, and emotional *hesitation* felt by individuals and communities in the face of calls to novelty, change, and progress may be best described as an acknowledgment of the human desire for a paradoxical grounding in the transcendent. The articulation of this desire may represent an attempt to reveal some real deep structure of human consciousness—all the more reason, then, to consider African-American creativity, an unusual and compelling intersection of the universal and particular.

PREFACE TO THE SIXTIES

To fully present the paradigmatic experience of this antimodern consciousness and its social sources requires a brief examination of the situation of post–World War II African-American creative intellectuals. Increasing interest of late in the sixties should direct our attention more forcefully to the period beginning in late 1945 through to an interregnum of the years 1957 through 1962. (A more detailed discussion of periodization will be found below.) There is a tendency in historicizing African-American cultural traditions (most especially in literature, less so in music) to move rapidly from the

Harlem Renaissance to the Black Arts Movement, too easily dismissing the complex politics of the intervening decades. Part of this myopia is a product of a cold war ideology which has framed considerations of postwar American culture in a largely self-congratulatory fashion; part may be attributed to the disarming complexity of the period. Sketched here, then, is the contested terrain of the postwar years and an attempt to suggest the ways in which it is the compelling source of the coalescence of an antimodern consciousness, and implicitly to argue for a more sustained historical reevaluation of cultural questions in the period—to see the late 1940s and 1950s as more than just the calm before the storm.

In the post–World War II period, as preface to the sixties and a cohesive and substantial antimodernism, there is a complex and dynamic *motion* and, more concretely, significant clusters of dramatic self-transformations and conversions. The metamorphoses of African-American creative intellectuals are at times strictly or conventionally religious, but at times it is *motion* itself—rather than, say, a distinctive metanoia—that is most revealing. Motion means here both geographic displacement (expatriation, emigration, eviction, return) but also a turning from the no-longer-worthy to some site of possibility. (These sites would include new faiths, institutions, styles, genres, personal relationships, even sexualities.) Compelling as a preface to the sixties are profound and paradoxical losses and gains: the failure of prevailing and pedestrian religious belief and (yet) the ebbing of secularism too; the abandonment of the United States (and its stories) and at the same time the discovery of its abiding, inescapable influence; returns to ancestral homelands but neocolonial disappointments; critiques of the decadence of a distended modernism and still a renewed commitment to experimentation. This is not so much circular as it is an extended liminality; as such, it suggests difficulty in reaggregation and the enforcement of ambiguity. In Arnold Van Gennep's terminology (through Victor Turner), what is missing for the creative intellectual, then, is "a relatively stable state . . . and . . . rights and obligations vis-à-vis others of a clearly defined and "structural" type."[16] Harold Cruse writes:

> World War II shattered a world irrevocably. But people who thought as I did were called upon in 1945 to treat the postwar era with intellectual and critical tools more applicable to the vanished world of the thirties —a world we had never had time to understand as we lived it. I spent the years from 1945 to about 1952 wrestling with this perplexity.[17]

The product of such a lack of social and cultural clarity is in many cases the emergence of a tangible anxiety which manifests itself in both psychic disturbance and institutional instability.

This perpetual motion has as its intellectual and spiritual source the belief that one can always start anew. Despite the deadening effects of modernity—and despite the horrors of recent history—one can begin again, reshape a life, reclaim a self. The nihilism potentially associated with a hostility to modernity or commitment to perpetual motion is displaced by this pattern of recognizing, to borrow from George Lamming, the "pleasures of exile."[18] William James has described these monumental shifts, displacements, and transformations as the process "by which a self hitherto divided, and consciously wrong inferior and unhappy, becomes unified and consciously right superior and happy."[19] This transformation or retooling is arguably the most important legacy of this generation of creative intellectuals. Demonstrating (often at significant personal cost) that integrity in living is the primary means by which one resists the etherealness of modern life, many African-American intellectuals in the immediate post–World War II period challenged the status quo by rejecting both the promises of change and the hegemonic image of an anointed American empire, or what James called "natural good." The particular character of this therapeutic motion is represented, experienced, or enacted, however, in a number of different ways.

The significant move of African-American intellectuals to Europe (especially Paris) in the late 1940s was a dramatic collective demonstration of dissatisfaction, if not disaffection. Michel Fabre describes Richard Wright's first half-decade in Europe as "an intense spiritual life" in which he was "each day removing himself from purely American preoccupations by acquiring a more European, more global view of his situation in particular, of the black situation in general and of the situation of contemporary man." It was, Fabre suggests, Wright's "second maturation."[20] Wright was followed or joined by a virtual who's who of the post-war African-American creative intelligentsia: Samuel Allen, James Baldwin, Romare Bearden, Beauford Delaney, William Demby (in Rome), Ollie Harrington, Chester Himes, Albert Murray, Myron O'Higgins, William Gardner Smith, Donald Byrd, Kenny Clarke, Don Byas, Gordon Heath, Maya Angelou, Vincent Carter, Conrad Kent Rivers, and many others.[21] Even Ralph Ellison, arguably the most optimistic thinker of this postwar generation, eventually made his way to Rome for an extended furlough. Not all of these individuals went to Europe with some sense of despair and escape. Many certainly went with very specific educational goals in mind. A broad comparative reading suggests, however, that their experience was often an education in the sense offered up by Henry Adams; inevitably it extended beyond the boundaries of any particular educational institution, even the Sorbonne, in a curious mixture of insight, memory, and an encounter with history. From the perspective of the cultural and intellectual historian, what is most important is the way this displacement of intellectuals and artists resulted in an intermingling of African-American thought with that of the emergent colonial world (George Padmore, C.L.R. James, Aimé Cesaire, Franz Fanon, Leopold Senghor) and unsettled Europe (Albert Camus, Jean Paul Sartre, Simone de Beauvoir, Jean Genet). As Paul Gilroy has pointed out, this entanglement is not novel. African-American intellectual existence has always been diasporic.

There is, however, an unusual intensity to this intermixture as a result of the important Pan-Africanist writers' conferences of Paris and Rome, the appearance of the important intellectual journal *Présence Africaine* (1947), the formal onset of decolonization in the Gold Coast (1957), and the nascent (and inchoate) nonaligned movement represented by the Bandung Conference (1956). From this intercultural cauldron emerge, to mention but a few examples, Richard Wright's *Black Power* (1954), *The Color Curtain* (1956) and *Pagan Spain* (1957); the Paris essays of James Baldwin; the musician John Lewis's Venice compositions (1957); Miles Davis's *Sketches of Spain* (1960); the novels of William Gardner Smith; and the sculpture of Richard Hunt. Despite the richness of this work and the commitment to a diasporic and cosmopolitan perspective, certainly part of the intensity of the experience was the common refrain that the more the African-American artist ran from the United States the more likely it was that he (or she) would discover their Americanness. Baldwin wrote that "exile saved my life. . . . What Europe still gives an American . . . is the sanction, if one can accept it, to become oneself. No artist can survive without this acceptance. But rare indeed is the American artist who achieved this without first becoming a wanderer, and then, upon his return to his own country, the loneliest and most blackly distrusted of men."[22] Upon a quest to discover individuality and cultural specificity, the African-American artist is but partially rewarded, and the costs, Baldwin suggest, are real and substantial.

Not only Europe was of interest, of course. The visual artist Elizabeth Catlett relocated permanently to Mexico, and Robert Hayden was greatly influenced by his time there. The critic Saunders Redding and Martin Luther King, Jr. traveled to India; Paule Marshall's work as a magazine writer took her to Brazil, which led to an important novella and an enduring impact upon her work. Josephine Baker maintained France as a home base, but traveled extensively and was significantly influenced by her travels in Latin America. Harlan Jackson's late 1940s trip to Haiti permanently shaped his painting, just as Dizzy Gillespie's encounter with Cuba redirected much of his music. Certainly, the poet Frank Marshall Davis's move to Hawaii deserves inclusion here, as might the many persons like pianist Hampton Hawes who served in the Korean war and developed some interest in Asian cultures. In this mode, one would certainly have to include the move of W.E.B. Du Bois to Ghana near the end of his life as perhaps the most dramatic and emotionally charged example. Du Bois's leaving seemed to suggest that (although this was not necessarily his intention) one did not have to remain forever committed to struggle in the United States. Less dramatically, and in summary, this internationalization of the African-American consciousness meant an increasing hostility to provincialism, a heightened awareness of world politics and nuclear proliferation, and, sometimes, a familiarity with the situation of the masses of the world's citizens living in conditions largely unimaginable to most Americans.

Within the context of the United States, the continued reorganization of African-American life through the ongoing migration from the largely rural South to the urban North impacted cultural production in ways somewhat contrary to those suggested by the more international and exilic trends. Most famously, wholly new genres of African-American music appeared: Muddy Waters's emigration to Chicago from Mississippi (and an audience and music with him) continued the transformation of the blues from a folk music to a product readily associated with the mass urban culture of the North; Louis Jordan's transformation of a regional music (Kansas City jump blues) into a national (if racially proscribed) phenomenon—rhythm and blues—was also directly related to the Great Migration in its appeal to and reliance upon new audience formations. That both of these musics relied heavily upon folk sources (forms and consciousness in the case of Waters; style and attitude in the case of Jordan) is at one level seemingly in contradistinction to certain international and universalist trends. More significant, perhaps, regardless of its impact upon the music, this emigration must be considered as a crucial motion in its own right, one that impacted both the consciousness of the average African-American and broad trends in social organization. The complex social contract of rural southern communities, designed to deal with the exigencies of the threat of race violence and as a means of preserving unique cultural values, was inadequate (or at least inappropriate) to the demands of the urban ghetto. Certain institutions survived—most notably the Baptist and Pentecostal churches—but still needed to adjust their vision and outreach. While this understates its accomplishment somewhat, James Baldwin's first novel *Go Tell It on the Mountain* (largely written in a Swiss village retreat) deals with the situation of this urban church and its confrontation with racism, urban mores, and widespread poverty. John Grimes's struggles with his stepfather are largely a result of the family's vexatious poverty and the father's struggle to replace himself in the new urban environment. Consistent with the story this book is trying to tell about the postwar environment, it is not surprising that Baldwin articulates this crisis in specifically metaphysical terms. While readers might remain skeptical, it makes perfect sense that John Grimes's solution to his problem is a vigorous religious conversion. Baldwin's ambiguous, but longing, gaze at the lost Southern landscape in the novel hints at the imminent importance of cultural memory for the decade to come, and suggests the ways in which high cultural angst and popular cultural veneration might be reconciled. While it would be a mistake to level too enthusiastically, say, the distance between the Roy Decarava and Langston Hughes collaboration *Sweet Flypaper of Life* and Ralph Ellison's *Invisible Man*, or, say, between Howlin' Wolf and the Modern Jazz Quartet, it is not unreasonable to attribute much of their power to a kind of generalized homelessness. Richard J. Powell has elegantly described the odd distance in postwar African-American visual arts between a "folk cult" and the emergence of a number of black abstract expressionists. While Powell does not speculate much about this multiplicity, it can be argued that this distance is less a result of fundamentally different ideological commitments and more a case of choosing different strategies—often those most immediately at hand—to deal with a generalized alienation.[23]

The arguably belated impact of high modernism upon African-American artistic practice in jazz, poetry, fiction, and painting might also be thought of in terms of motion or as a series of (often ambiguous) turns. Again, the publication of Ralph Ellison's *Invisible Man* comes most obviously to mind. Ellison's epic tale, rich with allusion to European, American, and African-American traditions, is arguably the most important American novel of the postwar era. While this is too easily overplayed, Ellison himself became skilled at (and indeed seemed to spend a great deal of his intellectual energy) describing the shift in aesthetic philosophy marked by his novel. This shift is, of course, specifically a repudiation of the naturalism (and philosophic realism too) of Richard Wright.[24] Similar alterations can be seen in the biographies of 1950s African-American visual artists. A turn to abstraction by a Norman Lewis or Romare Bearden was both an attempt to contend with the critical preeminence of the New York school and a sincere belief that in a post-Hiroshima universe traditional strategies of representation had run their course. The well-known jazz musical revolution at Minton's Playhouse, led by Charlie Parker and Dizzy Gillespie, had social implications as significant as its aesthetic transformation of American popular music. (Eric Lott has suggestively documented a political dimension to bebop and its subculture.[25]) Certainly any simplistic association of bebop with modernism is imprudent. "Jazz rhythms" and jazz culture are present in European high modernism much prior to this early 1940s shift. What is important here is not so much the description of an incontestable genealogy but rather the notion of a controversial break from a previous musical orthodoxy.[26] Interestingly, by the early 1950s and successful experiments with long forms by Mary Lou Williams, Duke Ellington, and Dizzy Gillespie, among others, and with an increasing dissatisfaction with the generic designation of "jazz," many musicians in this idiom developed an interest in the musical modernism of the Western art tradition, especially Hindemith, Schoenberg, and Stravinsky. The shifts in African-American poetry were more complex still. While Melvin Tolson, Robert Hayden, and Gwendolyn Brooks solidified their reputations as masters of the modern language and style, younger poets, especially LeRoi Jones and Bob Kaufman, had already fallen in with (and helped to shape) groups from which the next disruptions of the broad American poetic tradition would come. In a very diffuse manner, Kaufman and Jones absorbed the lessons of the Black Mountain and San Francisco schools, whose interest in American vernaculars and general rebelliousness certainly presaged the African-American poetries of the late sixties. The narrative of 1950s African-American poetry, then—like that of fiction, painting, and music—is subject to numerous breaks. The rather bland designation by the editors of the recent *Norton Anthology of African American Literature*[27] of the 1940–1960 period as "Realism, Naturalism, Modernism" is suggestive of not so much a paradigm shift as paradigm ambiguity. The designation's weakness is that it does not adequately communicate the political and psychological turmoil associated with this aesthetic hesitation. These breaks often come at great personal cost.

The most important examples of "motion," in many ways nicely synec-dochic of all of the above, are the specific ideological conversions, secular and religious, of a number of African-American creative intellectuals (that is, mo-tion from one set of ideas toward another): the turn to Roman Catholicism by Claude McKay and Mary Lou Williams; the conservative turn by Zora Neale Hurston and George Schuyler; W.E.B. Du Bois's turn to the Commu-nist Party U.S.A.; Ollie Harrington's permanent move to East Germany; the unconventional religious conversions of Robert Hayden and Margaret Dan-ner (both to Baha'ism), Malcolm X (Nation of Islam), Bob Kaufman (Bud-dhism), Yusef Lateef (Islam) and others. While it is certainly true that the ma-jority of these transformations are overdetermined, it is still reasonable to connect these personal turns to a collective postwar dissatisfaction with the inherited status quo. Comparatively speaking, and to state the obvious, there is more than a little political and theological variance in these turns. In the preface to the sixties, however, it is more important to point to an aggregate exhaustion with received forms than it is to identify the immediate postwar period with a cohesive politics. These conversions are significant *across ideo-logical barriers* in the way in which they point toward an emerging sympathy, if not desire, for real and imagined pasts. These alterations of faith are cer-tainly indicative of the ways in which previously held cosmologies cease to produce comfort. Collectively, however, they are emblematic of a more gen-eral dis-ease or disappointment with American culture and the resources, both material and spiritual, that that culture provides to the black artist. Conversion is a rich means of organizing the self in which a sense of alien-ation from modernity often resides.

While framing this preface to the sixties largely in terms of a kind of mood, there is, of course, a specific sociocultural context to be described, a product and a producer of the displacements already sketched. World War II itself was a contradictory and enigmatic experience for African-Americans. As in the case of World War I, any optimism associated with the possibility that black heroism might translate into concrete reform in the American apartheid system was offset by the frustrating encounters of black service-men and women with segregated facilities and sometimes with violent at-tacks. The disturbance in Harlem in early August 1943 had certainly given clear indication of the tenuousness of any lasting peace on the home front without a direct confrontation with racially determined economic dispar-ity.[28] The character of the period can be captured by considering the disso-nance created by the existence of an expanding economy, the beginnings of a liberalization as regards civil rights, and a tentative commitment to disman-tle segregation at the same time as the McCarthyist attack on civil liberties, the establishment of the surveillance state, and nuclear proliferation. The difficulty is—to put it mildly—that this synchronicity generates an interpre-tive knot.

Very brief consideration of two standard works of African-American lit-erary history will be useful here to understand how misapprehension of the postwar period makes misinterpretation of the character of African-American culture and the sixties inevitable. Robert Bone's much maligned *The Negro Novel in America*, first published in 1958, is quite accomplished in its extended evaluation of the social context of African-American literature. In evaluating the postwar environment, Bone notes the establishment of the Fair Employment Practices Commission and important Supreme Court decisions in interstate travel, housing, family law, and voting rights; at the same time he grants that "these are legal and formal victories, which have yet to be validated in the popular consciousness."[29] Quite optimistically he writes, "the historical trend is unmistakable: the edifice of white supremacy is crumbling in every important cultural area" (162). He then adds some quite striking remarks:

> The all important matter of interpretation remains: why, in a few short years, were such immense strides made in the field of civil rights when, for example, the situation in regard to civil liberties was steadily deteriorating? Official liberalism maintains, in a mood of self-congratulation, that the democratic conscience of America has at last become aroused. Those who, in the light of the hysterical legislation of the McCarthy period, view the democratic conscience of America with some misgivings will prefer to seek a more substantial explanation. (162)

This is a significant piece of cultural analysis, especially so for 1958. What is unusual, then, is the conclusion that Bone decides to draw for African-American art:

> A guarded optimism, which recognizes the roots and therefore the limitations of the present trend, seems the best attitude to adopt. But whatever one's appraisal of the objective situation, the subjective impact of these events on the Negro literary world is clear. The recent gains have led to an upsurge of assimilationism, a revolt against the protest novel, and, in some instances, a conscious abandonment of the materials of Negro life. (162–63)

Why is the character of 1950s African-American art and literature to be a product of the *gains* of the period rather than a response to the "deterioration of civil liberties?" Once conditions and responses have been arranged in this way, "guarded optimism" becomes a kind of evaluative hermeneutic that eliminates much of the range of novelistic expression of the period: Lloyd Brown's *Iron City* is a "propaganda piece"; William Gardner Smith's drawing of parallels between the postwar United States and Nazi Germany in *Last of the Conquerors* is a "crude equation."[30]

A generation later, but in related fashion, Bernard Bell, in his *The Afro-American Novel and Its Tradition* (1987), opens his chapter on the 1950s with a very nice paragraph which appropriately complicates (perhaps inadvertently) efforts at interpreting the period.[31] While the paragraph ostensibly means to document the "acceleration" of "integration," it also reveals a contradictory impulse: "One of the dubious honors for black Americans as a result of the climate fostered by the recommendations of President Truman's interracial committees on civil rights and integration is that blacks constituted 30 percent of the United States forces in the Korean War (1950–51) but were only 10 percent of the general population" (188). Furthermore, toward the end of the paragraph, as a way of qualifying the impact of decolonization, he notes: "In 1961 political and military intrigue by imperialist countries, following the independence of the Congo, resulted in the execution of Premier Patrice Lumumba" (189). Largely consistent with my argument in this chapter, Bell then writes:

> From 1952 to 1962 two parallel movements in the tradition of the Afro-American novel can be observed: a movement away from naturalism and nonracial themes, and a movement toward the rediscovery and revitalization of myth, legend, and ritual as appropriate sign systems for expressing the double-consciousness, socialized ambivalence, and double vision of the modern black experience. (189)

Bell is certainly on track and prescient to note the "rediscovery and revitalization of myth, legend, and ritual"; there is also in Bell (and in Bone) an unwillingness to fully contend with the hostility of the political and cultural landscape. Bell's picture of the decade is one in which Ellison and Baldwin take center stage, largely on New Critical terms; once again, novelists who see as a necessity the more direct representation of political injustice—Lloyd Brown, Frank London Brown, William Gardner Smith, Ann Petry, W.E.B. Du Bois—tend to be shifted to the margins.

There is unfair advantage, of course, in reading with the benefit of significant hindsight. Bone's text was written before the great violent disruptions of the sixties, and perhaps it made sense to articulate an optimistic critical paradigm positive. And insofar as my book is a post–cold war document it is not wholly unsurprising that its perspective on the 1950s might differ from that of Bernard Bell;[32] there is much more historical urgency to account for the wreckage of the period, and I am less compelled than scholars of the previous generation to engage in the identification of major and minor writers and artists. Too much effective and valuable African-American cultural discourse of the period (certainly novels, but poems, plays, music, and painting too) has been set aside, however, so as to make straightforward a celebration of Ellison, Baldwin, and a few others, whose style lent themselves to the valorization of both the New Critical establishment and bourgeois literary intellectualism.[33] (It can be argued further that the repression of the political in Ellison and Baldwin has unquestionably and negatively distorted our understanding of the *breadth* of their accomplishments.) Again, neither Bone nor Bell deserves abuse—this study is certainly indebted to both, especially to their willingness to think historically; what remains true, however, is that no adequate history of post–World War II African-American cultural accomplishment can be undertaken without a full accounting of the psychic, political, and other costs of the cold war. Despite the tendency of some commentators to separate the broad geohistorical struggle between the United States and the Soviet Union and the domestic and international struggle for racial justice, these events are intimately connected. The celebration of conformity from roughly 1947 through at least the late 1950s made the articulation of any explicit critique of American mores difficult. Stephen Whitfield quotes Albert Canwell, the chair of the Washington State Legislative Fact-Finding Committee on Un-American Activities as saying: "If someone insists that there is discrimination against Negroes in this country, or that there is inequality of wealth, there is every reason to believe that person is a Communist."[34] The well-documented and relatively well-known experiences of Paul Robeson and W.E.B. Du Bois alone might be cited here so as to document the psychic and political costs of speaking out in this kind of political and cultural context. The work of scholars like Mary Dudziak, Gerald Horne, Brenda Plummer, and Penny Von Eschen has begun to fill out our understanding of the relationship between the ideology of the cold war and the trajectory of gains in civil rights.[35] It is not the task or intention of this chapter to extensively document this connection; it is, however, crucial to the account of the sixties to come that readers not carry with them a picture of the preceding decades as benign or sanguine.

Somewhat ironically, the personal transformations, conversions, or "movements" that are a prime response to a hostile cultural vista were often mediated by formations that are direct products of the very ideological landscape often deemed reprehensible. The G.I. Bill, for instance, made it possible for African-American creative intellectuals like Romare Bearden and William Demby to study and live in Paris and Rome respectively. In whatever ways that 1950s African-American creative intellectuals felt a kind of hangover from the war, this is certainly one positive development of its aftermath. Christopher Lasch, among many others, has documented that much funding of journals, books, institutes, and the like can be directly related to Cold War paranoia.[36] State Department sponsored jazz tours, the promotion of African cultures within the United States, writers' conferences and the granting of fellowships, even the desegregation of educational institutions, all bear somewhat the tinge of this global ideological warfare. Indeed, even some technological developments (in television, in satellite communications) with implications for the arts might be described with regard to their ties to an obsession with competitiveness. The question of blackness and modernity, then, is by no means transparent. African-American creative intellectuals did benefit from the "permanent war economy," described and prophesied by C. Wright Mills, and from real and fabled abundance within American culture. This book will continue to assert, however, that any convincing narrative of the period must seriously consider the significant cultural ruins. Part of the advantage of an interdisciplinary perspective lies in the ways in which it moves our interpretations beyond a cataloguing of merely formal change within the confines of a single tradition. (Any celebration of Ralph Ellison's arrival, for instance, should have to deal with the untimely "departure" of Charlie Parker.) Unquestionably, positive represen- tations of the immediate postwar period rely upon a teleological under- standing of black consciousness in which the internationalization of black cultural expression, the emergence of "major" cultural figures vis-à-vis es- tablished and recognizable American traditions, and a fuller encounter with modernisms, are seen as signs of cultural maturity. As prefaces to accounts of the sixties they inevitably foreground narratives of either betrayal ("na- tionalist demigods subvert the telos") or pure freedom ("second-generation inheritors occupy a newly opened cultural space").

An alternative model of post–World War II African-American culture might profitably be described by noting the existence of a costly "dialectic of Enlightenment." The strategy of sustained assault upon the legal instru- ments of segregation pursued by the NAACP, labor unions, and other mis- cellaneous individuals and organizations generated important successes by the mid-1950s. There was, however, a serious (and just as well-organized) counterstrategy pursued by government and other organizations to curtail black challenges to the U.S. status quo. Black left activists like W.E.B. Du Bois, Paul Robeson, and Josephine Baker had their speech curtailed or made difficult. (Even African-American creative intellectuals of a clearly centrist persuasion found themselves the targets of FBI surveillance.) Random vio- lence remained a significant part of the landscape of the South and chal- lenges to the conventions and hierarchy of black-white social relations were especially dangerous. Sexism and homophobia continued to seriously con- strain the dreams, ambitions, and accomplishment of a significant portion of the African-American community. On the one hand, African-American creative intellectuals could not help but be impressed by the concrete results of decades of organizational struggle, largely on the terms of the liberal democratic state. Appeals to and for "equality" seemed to be paying off. A centuries-long investment in the rhetoric and values of the Enlightenment project might one day concretely bring justice to black peoples. Modernity's displacement of feudal and other strictly hierarchical forms of social organ- ization might be extended to include false race hierarchies too. On the other hand, expressions of white rage and the inability of the state to adequately respond in defense of black citizens would inevitably temper or confuse that enthusiasm. (Numerous critics and historians have noted, for instance, the impact of the Emmett Till case, in particular, upon the African-American artistic consciousness.[37]) The resilience of the Ku Klux Klan and other agents of race terror, the use of state power against black intellectuals, and the con- tinued apartheid of educational and cultural institutions obviously compli- cated enthusiastic black assessments of modernity. More specifically, as regards culture, the contemporary world must have seemed full of contra- dictions. Sartre's "Black Orpheus" (1948) found in the writings of the theo- rists of Negritude a new and vital universalism; the filmmaker Marcel Camus's *Black Orpheus* (1959) (resituating Sartre's important essay) successfully subverted nominal expectations of the site of the universal by transporting the Greek myth of love (and death) to "Africa-America" and grounding it with an unrelenting samba.[38] There was, however, an important countertendency in Louis Simpson's infamous review of Gwendolyn Brooks's *Selected Poems* (1962): "I am not sure it is possible for a Negro to write well without making us aware he is a Negro; on the other hand, if being a Negro is the only subject, the writing is not important . . ."[39] A further illustration of this dichotomy might be the establishment of courses in jazz studies at North Texas State University (1946), or the establishment of the Newport Jazz Festival (1954), and the decision by the Pulitzer Prize committee (1966) to refuse an award to Duke Ellington. As African-American cultural expression becomes more fully institutionalized within the context of any number of world cultural systems, consciousness is raised, somewhat ironically, about its disturbing incongruousness and, to some extent, its partial resistance to assimilation.

This incongruity manifests itself throughout the cultural period in a consistent pattern of dispersal or abandonment, that is, attempts to complete or pursue the Enlightenment dialectic. This may be a conventional religious conversion but may take more esoteric or subtle forms too. We find dramatic reversals from commitment to a particular artistic form or style. We find intense reevaluations of cultural identity, either in whole or in part. We find a preponderance of dramatic physical journeys. We also find significant repetitions of action or statement which are also themselves indicative of crisis or obsession, the abandonment of vicissitude. This picture of the immediate postwar period, then, is significantly more sober than the more benign designation of a decade marked by the "poetics of integration." Bernard Gendron's essays on post-swing jazz have drawn attention to the ways in which the reception of the music was dramatically affected by commentators who used discursive frameworks largely imported from the criticism of European high modernism—without qualification—to explain importance and meaning.[40] Part of the continuing significance of race within American cultural history is the necessity of drawing attention to the insufficiency of those frameworks and to make clear the challenging particularity of black cultural experience. Eagerly (and not wholly inappropriately) cultural historians have described a double assault on the racial behemoth, sociopolitical and cultural battles, a popular historiography of presence: Ralph Bunche, Jackie Robinson, Marian Anderson, Ralph Ellison, James Baldwin, and Nat Cole among others assume center stage. What may be lost, however, is an awareness of African-American culture as fundamentally a negation of accepted truths. An obsession with integration as the guts of this historiography of presence is a dangerous enthusiasm.

Indeed, the briefest comparative biographical study of the postwar, cold war environment suggests that the "psychology of disintegration" may be a more accurate rendering. Within the jazz community the loss of Charlie Parker, Billie Holiday, Fats Navarro and many others from drug use is largely misunderstood and unstudied. We celebrate Jackie Robinson, but have no adequate framework to understand the loss of Josh Gibson. What should we make of struggles with depression (and even more destructive mental illness) by Robert Hayden, Romare Bearden, Charles Mingus, Bud Powell, and others? The black religious experience—rather than become a relic of the pre-modern, pre-Enlightenment world—continued to shape central intellectual disputes. African-Americans continued to articulate identity struggles with specifically spiritual language: John Coltrane, Mary Lou Williams, Phillipa Schuyler, and, despite his attempts to distance himself from orthodox Christianity, James Baldwin, among many others already mentioned, connected the specific situation of a segregated America to questions of salvation. Perhaps more than the experience of any one individual, the consolidation of the Nation of Islam in the 1950s should give pause to any commentator who would assert that the narrative of postwar African-American culture be structured around the increasing accommodation of black life to modernity and/or the increasing accommodation of modernity to blackness.

While not all of the above can be described or explained by reference to the contemporary social world (and certainly there is room for discussion of particularity, the unique, and the idiosyncratic) neither can such dis-ease and disturbance be ignored. We must, of course, take personal weakness into consideration, but we must also resist attempts to suggest that deviation from norms of participation in the modern world is by *necessity* failure. By strategic utilization of the paradigm of antimodernism my book seeks to recover attempts to negate domination, enthusiastic and self-conscious deviation from the mainstream, and recognition of the virulent entanglement of myth and power. What may appear from the perspective of hegemonic liberalism as defect may be a determined effort to reveal that "natural" ideological position as serving the interests of Enlightenment as will-to-power. Too much black creativity in the postwar period has been rejected as deviant, provincial, "natural," improvised, racist, deluded, intolerant, difficult, simplistic, etc., without regard for its commitment to change the way we understand truth, beauty, or justice, without recognizing its rejection of a concept of progress that could not include blacks.

There is no need to underplay the concrete gains of the period. They are substantial and meritorious. But if the sociologist Anthony Giddens is correct when he suggests that the character of modernity is best described through a discussion of risk and trust relationships, then urgent and resilient African-American ambivalence is hardly difficult to understand.[41] "The nature of modern institutions is deeply bound up with the mechanisms of trust in abstract systems," he writes (83). The sometimes questionable trustworthiness of the judiciary, the education system, and even the institution of literary criticism, place individuals in situations of "high-risk." The violation of this necessary relationship in the modern world is ultimately a psychological violation, an attack on "ontological security."

However "mistrust" is too weak a term to express the antithesis of *basic* trust, the focal element in a generalized set of relations to the social and physical environment. The forging of trust here is the very condition of acknowledging the clear identity of objects and persons. If basic trust is not developed or its inherent ambivalence not contained, the outcome is persistent existential anxiety. In its most profound sense, the antithesis of trust is thus a state of mind which could best be summed up as existential *angst* or *dread*. (99–100)

Without confidence in the nature of "rational systems of communication," in aesthetic "standards," or even "rights," African-American creative intellectuals often had to dissent to preserve individual and communal psychic health. Du Bois-ian "double-consciousness" had to become a kind of "super-vision" and not schizophrenia.[42]

Theodor Adorno and Max Horkheimer's dialectic—locating barbarism and civilization in a single locale—had (and has) significant (and unique) psychic costs for the African-American creative intellectual who is denied the opportunity to safely observe the dialectic at work. The psychic cost of this skewed dialectic is a politics and poetics of the precipice. For African-American artists and writers of the postwar generation, there was a feeling that the edge has been reached. Unable to fully enjoy the experience of full selfhood, agency, and citizenship, or the clarifying counterstance of absolute outsidership, many African-American creative intellectuals were forced to radically reevaluate their relationship to nation, race, and even mode of living. By the 1960s, this sense of being at the precipice became, for some, a necessary, sweeping antimodernism, a provocative counterstatement. In response to this anxiety, these artists and writers would call upon cultural memory and identity (both essential and socially constructed) as the most productive means of articulating a radical critique of modernity.

Adorno and Horkheimer are not invoked here lightly. While many African-American creative intellectuals of the 1950s and 1960s would not have accepted the Frankfurt School's critique of the bourgeois subject, there was tangible shared concern. In many respects, African-American creative intellectuals functioned, as did this group of European Jewish intellectuals, in exile. More importantly, there is common anxiety about their relationship to the modern bureaucratic state—in particular, as to how the group might have their very existence threatened by the workings of the state. Within both groups there is an urgent pursuit of a total critique of society cognizant of the disposition of twentieth-century history. Neither group is satisfied with the orientation (or conventional use) of the major critiques of Enlightenment, Marxism or psychoanalysis. There is an attempt to replace these critiques with a more ideologically flexible and interdisciplinary assault on the status quo. The most significant divergence between the two "schools" (other than on the question of the status of the bourgeois subject) would most likely be concerning mass culture. African-American creative intellectuals would concede the distorting impact of the culture industry on, say, the quality and direction of jazz, but would not wholly disallow the possibilities of resistance within the field. (Adorno, Horkheimer, and others, were simply not situated so as to understand the political potential of repetition.[43]) More important, however, than an attempt to mark what Nathaniel Mackey would call the "discrepant engagement" of black and Jewish intellectuals in the postwar period is to insist upon recognition of the scope of black intellectual ambition.[44] It remains unfortunately commonplace to encounter perspectives on African-American intellectual and cultural history in which their development is seen to be primarily a side conversation to the Western tradition.

To return once again to a ritual structure: the character of African-American intellectual life at midcentury was marked by an increasingly disruptive ambivalence, a liminality, a "betwixt-and-between-ness." This state cannot be maintained indefinitely. The character of African-American intellectual life (and, to a certain extent, much more expansively, culture) in the American sixties can be profitably be described relative to a sweeping critique of modernity meant to generate (counter to the liminal state) a form of revitalization and regeneration. Is this a "rage for order?" The emergence of a certain kind of cultural conservatism—Afrocentrism, in particular, but varieties of black poststructuralism too—is clearly pertinent here, as is a legacy fairly described as a "rage for justice," the insistence that a practice emerge that restores self-consciousness to the Enlightenment project.[45] Sixties African-American antimodernists asserted the incommensurability of black subjection and progress. They loudly declared the presence of decay. Unlike Huxley, Ortega y Gasset, T. S. Eliot, and others, however, African-American creative intellectuals had little interest in, say, the *decline* of the West (as concept), and instead insisted upon a present and fundamental injustice that belied any simplistic valorization of principles of Enlightenment.

Self-consciously, there is a kind of crude Hegelianism to this argument. The totality claimed for African-American artistic expression of the sixties smacks of a certain messianic urge. A partial response is "So be it." At its worst, then, it would only exist in contradistinction to demonizing arguments that locate in the decade and often within black cultural expression the end of an imaginary golden age of cultural consensus. Less combatively, however, within the totalizing gesture significant ideological, methodological, even theological variation exists, such that the messianic urge is transformed into something more appropriately dialectical. A focus on biographic formation of six exemplars will invite the drawing of distinctions such that "African-American antimodernism" will appear to be less some untenable *Geist* and more a complex nexus of social, cultural, and interpersonal relations suggestive of a number of tentative critical formations.

AFRICAN-AMERICAN CREATIVITY AND
THE AMERICAN SIXTIES

> History is eliminated in oneself and others out of a fear that it may remind the individual of the degeneration of his own existence — which itself continues. The respect for something which has no market value and runs contrary to all feelings is experienced most sharply by the person in mourning, in whose case not even the psychological restoration of labor power is possible. It becomes a wound in civilization, asocial sentimentality, showing that it has still not been possible to compel men to indulge solely in purposeful behavior. That is why mourning is watered down more than anything else and consciously turned into social formality; indeed the beautiful corpse has always been a mere formality for the hardened survivors. . . . In reality, the dead suffer a fate which the Jews in olden days considered the worst possible curse: they are expunged from the memory of those who live on. Men have ceased to consider their own purpose and fate; they work their despair out on the dead.
>
> THEODOR ADORNO AND MAX HORKHEIMER,
> *Dialectic of Enlightenment* (1972)[46]

> I Shine say there is a putrid wind
> blowing through those sockets
> I say we hear the death din
> as well as the cooing song
> of the lovers among the summer grasses
>
> LARRY NEAL,
> "Shine Touched by Death's Whisper"[47]

The interrelationship of artistic practice, text, and certain habits of mind within the context of African-American culture and the American sixties indicates a response to profound historical "inconsistency" and personal dissatisfaction. This interrelationship is indicative of an outlook on the world that can be designated as antimodern. More specifically, however, careful consideration of this outlook reveals the emanation of a remarkable elegiac mode. As articulated in the sixties, African-American antimodernism is above all an attempt to insist upon the impossibility of (to echo Ernest Becker) the denial of death. The withdrawals, reemergences, transformations, conversions, and mourning I will describe intend to make plain the secret of modernity. The only progress that is assured is the "sickness unto death." To acknowledge the studied avoidance of this truth is the most provocative challenge to modernity's promise of the inevitable transcendence of myth. Sixties African-American antimodernists articulated the real limits to this *hope* by documenting the despairing clarity of race hatred. Denial can be nothing but folly in the face of Watts, the assassinations of King and Malcolm and Medgar Evers, of Vietnam, of Birmingham. In place of denial, however, mourning asserts *virtues* patently premodern—the need to address the void, the value and potential of a grieving community, the bond of consciousness with nature—even as the particular character of the assertion is explicitly affected by modernity's transformation of our understanding and experience.

Again, the elegy, or, more correctly, the elegiac, is a useful organizing principle, a means of limiting the disorder suggested by such broad cultural gestures and arguments. Recent scholarship on the twentieth-century elegy has made clear the ways in which as a unique poetic form it is irrevocably transformed by modernity's intellectual accomplishments; often cynical, despondent, unable to find solace in orthodox religious formations, inclined to commemorate scoundrels as well as saints, the modern elegy, as Jahan Ramazani argues, is much more likely to be immersed in melancholy than to perform a substitution for loss. Not all of the texts under consideration in subsequent chapters are conventional elegies, however (nor are literary texts to be the only subjects), and so my engagement with this literary critical shift will be slight.[48] (Thinking of an elegiac *mode* is appropriate, as it can be utilized for both for its literary and musical allusions.) What is crucial is the appearance within a variety of African-American texts of a broad consideration of death and culture. Although awareness of specific formal considerations is useful, it is not primary; the elegiac mode is important for the way it directs us to broader cultural instincts and commitments. This elegiac mode communicates not so much an interest in the modern technology of death or commemorative artifice but rather in death's challenge to history; African-American culture of the sixties produces a "mourning text," a reminder of the past (or more strongly an assertion of the past's "presence") and a concomitant insistence upon human limits. It is a response not unaware of the epistemological uncertainty characteristic of much twentieth century grieving, but it is rarely narrowly theological in orientation. Unlike traditional elegies, the nature of the black mourning text is neither compensatory nor consoling.[49] It is, instead, profoundly declarative, an attempt to articulate that, yes, something is gone, irretrievable. The black elegiac mode is antimodern, not only insofar as it valorizes cultural memory, but also as it tends toward lamentation and jeremiad. While it may be direct or explicit like Archie Shepp's "The Funeral" or Dudley Randall and Margaret Burroughs's collection of elegies for Malcolm X, it is more often than not indirect and embracing of the culture at large.[50] This is not to say, of course, that the African-American elegiac mode is always public. As it relates to the explication of the role of African-American culture within American culture, however, less interesting is an intracultural funerary logic and more central a kind of mourning dialogue.[51] By documenting this compelling cultural phenomenon, better understanding of the African-American creative intellectual's ability to negate, to challenge commonplace hopeful shared understanding, to undermine the normative capability of American culture, might be achieved.

A. B. Spellman's stunning (and largely unknown) poem "'64 like a mirror in a darkroom. '63 like a mirror in a house afire" nicely illustrates this possibility. After noting that this is a "new year's day poem," he writes:

> the newly dead silly
> my best sentiments by an absence
> more vital than memory. how
> write for them except say the difference
> in potency between a.b. & the newly
> dead is barely measurable.[52]

The onset of the new year brings on an anxiety for the poet as to his intense awareness of the short distance between life and death. Yet, while the poem allows for an interpretation that is fundamentally autobiographical, it also invites a broader cultural interpretation. The poet is dumbstruck at the problem of reconciling writing and commemoration of the dead, alerting us not only to personal difficulty in marking loss, but also to a more collective failure to recognize the frailty of life. After providing us with an accounting of the death of a number of friends over the past year, he concludes:

> that's '63 backwards: a passage of names
> into graves: one man i knew by his mind's seminal
> flutter; another by the way he kept himself alive.
> i want to care about each longer than it takes
> to write & correct these lines.
>
> if i can care for the newly dead as far as from here/
> to here/
> i may be thought not to be among them.

The growing awareness of the "barely measurable" distance between life and death and the necessity of remembrance and consecration is the poet's burden and responsibility, and potentially his salvation. That Spellman chooses to shape the poem around the death of close friends, somewhat anonymous historically, rather than, say, John Kennedy or Medgar Evers, makes clear for us that the struggle is somewhat different than simply the construction of monuments. Instead, he alerts us to the folly of our immature future orientation, our cultural confidence, while we are surrounded by an experience more tentative in its goodness.

This assessment of the relationship of death to life—really the sacralization of life—is not only pursued through the specific commemoration of the passing of individuals. The elegiac mode is significantly broad in its religious feeling; indeed "religion" may be too narrow and problematic to do full justice to this cultural mode. From John Coltrane's dirge "Alabama" to Michael Harper's commemorations of the death of his child, this vocalization of antimodern sentiment engages and attempts to resurrect humanistic virtues. From Otis Redding's "My Lover's Prayer" to Albert Ayler's "Spiritual Unity," an incredible range of African-American art attempted to found within the cultural space of the American sixties a just response to the offenses of modernity, regardless of whether or not those transgressions were racially determined. From the masses of Mary Lou Williams to the ritual dramas of Ed Bullins and Amiri Baraka, these creative intellectuals structured encounters with the fragility of both human concord and individual existence. This forceful combination of a faith-seeking humanism and ordered consideration of past and present injustice — the establishment of a mourning ethic — foregrounds the possibility of conversion as it has been broadly conceived here, foregrounds, then, a possible continued relationship between art and social transformation.

It also *attempts* to ground a distinct response to Enlightenment. The elegiac mode, then, is a response to and uniquely skeptical of modernity's dismissal of the past. Placed between Spellman's two mirrors — one a distorted hellish past, the other a future nothingness, useless knowledge — anxiousness about individual and social death is transformed by the ordering mechanism of the elegiac into something potentially heuristic. Readers will likely have little immediate objection to the description of the thematic urge portrayed here in which order, hierarchy, are both overturned and reinscribed. More complex, and somewhat vexing, however, is the history of African-American artistic forms in the American sixties, perhaps, especially Spellman's own poetics. How do we reconcile this ordering and sorting with a popular understanding of the decade as one of overturning and iconoclasm? Experimental fictions, "free" jazz, vernacular poetries, abstract painting: how do these formal innovations accord with a thematic (and sometimes moral) conservatism? Part of the explanation has to do with the ways in which African-American artistry is simultaneously involved in a confrontation with modernity and with inherited (and normative) Eurocentric traditions of response. One may feel the urge to reconstruct a real or imagined past and dispose of burdensome "traditions" of response, that is, to concurrently challenge modernity's etherealism and ethnocentrism. There is no easy way to sort out this conflation of political and artistic perspectives. Robert Hayden's commitment to poetic form does seem connected in some subtle way to his religious belief and his interest in black history. At the same time, Clarence Major's experimentalism in a book like *Reflex and Bone Structure* (1967) reads a stunningly moral document. Anthony Braxton's musical adventurism is less transparently culture-critical (and historically grounded), than, say, that of Albert Ayler or Archie Shepp.[53] Ray Charles's wonderful *Modern Sounds in Country and Western Music* (1963) — surely a title crying out for deconstruction — is hardly a fond celebration of racist rural agrarianism, although certainly respectful of a dynamic body of American music. While there is a danger here of too easily equating experimentalism with a disregard for form (and conservatism with craftsmanship), the general point holds. Regardless of the choices that individual artists made as how to best advance their craft, there was significant agreement (if not serenity) among sixties African-American creative intellectuals as to the character of American modernity. This

issue is absolutely crucial to the development of adequate histories of the period. There does not seem to be any simplistically predicative means of identifying artistic allegiance or genus. Narratives that mean to document the accomplishment of African-American creative intellectuals in the American
sixties will have to rely on more than surface characteristics (presence of the
vernacular, abandonment of "tradition," rhetorical gestures against whiteness) to suggest order and pattern.

WHAT ARE THE AMERICAN SIXTIES?

> Nothing in America can last more than 10 years. . . .
>
> PHILIP RAHV (1964)

These commitments cannot only be explained simply by the invocation of a
pure history of ideas, an imagined conceptualization, without some consideration of multiple world trends definitive of "sixties-ness." First off, some
comment should be made about the use of "sixties" as a kind of demarca-
tion, and "American sixties," in particular.[54] It should be clear by now that it
is an attempt to distinguish the period from nostalgic considerations. Frederic Jameson, in his seminal article "Periodizing the 60's," writes:

> Nostalgic commemoration of the glories of the 60's or abject public
> confession of the decade's many failures and missed opportunities are
> two errors which cannot be avoided by some middle path that threads
> its way in between. . . . History is necessity. . . . The 60's had to happen
> the way it did and . . . its opportunities and failures were inextricably
> intertwined, marked by the objective constraints and openings of a de-
> terminate historical situation.[55]

This is good advice, and should discourage the tendency—perhaps understandable in a cultural and political environment in which any and all things
can be blamed on the 1960s—to romanticize this past. Jameson goes on to
add that to "think in terms of historical periods" is currently "unfashion-
able." In response he reminds us that it is "surely only against a certain conception of what is historically dominant or hegemonic that the full value of
the exceptional . . . can be assessed." I share with Jameson the opinion that a
period may be

> understood not as some omnipresent and uniform shared style or way
> of thinking and acting, but rather as the sharing of a common objec-
> tive situation, to which a whole range of varied responses and creative
> innovations is then possible, but always within that situation's struc-
> tural limits. (178)

(To this suggestion it can be added that possible responses might be seen as
a "partially shared subjective situation," a pattern of belief and idiosyncrasy.
Jameson's attempt to counter the desire for "expressive unification" is to

focus on the *breaks* within a historical narrative. Hopefully *Mercy, Mercy Me* breaks from organic notions of history by taking seriously the individuality of its "figures.") None of this, one might argue, still clarifies what exactly the sixties were. Following Jameson once more:

> The simplest yet most universal formulation surely remains the widely shared feeling that in the 60's for a time, everything was possible: that this period, in other words, was a moment of universal liberation, a global unbinding of energies. . . . We have described the 60's as a moment in which the enlargement of capitalism of a global scale simultaneously produced an immense freeing or unbinding of social energies, a prodigious release of untheorized new forces: the ethnic forces of black and "minority" or third world movements everywhere, regionalisms, the development of new and militant bearers of "surplus consciousness" in the student and women's movements, as well as in a host of struggles of other kinds. (207–208)

This is a succinct summing up and, even if a little abstract, likely to be recognized and confirmed by most observers, even those potentially hostile to its political perspective. African-American antimodernism is a part of this general phenomenon; it was, however, unconventionally conservative and not simplistically optimistic, yet it remained involved in the liberatory "unbinding of energies."[56]

Whatever the clarity (and limitations) of such a formulation, it is certainly likely that the general, popular understanding of the period is more of an obstruction. Perhaps it is the image of a clenched fist or black power salute, maybe Tommie Smith and John Carlos on the medal stand at the 1968 Olympics in Mexico City. Certainly it includes images and an assessment of the outbreaks of rage in Watts, Detroit, Chicago, Newark, and numerous other cities throughout the decade. On the more obviously cultural front, images of dashikis, Afros, and posters of Malcolm and Huey dominate the popular imagination. As is most often the case, such images are important reminders of primal scenes. They reveal something about our most compelling and dangerous passions. On the other hand, as memories, they are always incomplete and are often implicated in the active repression of some other historical truth. These experiences (closely akin to the primal scene) and the intensity of such experiences ensure that the American sixties will likely never be simply a problem of historical reconstruction. For the time being, at least, the American sixties is simultaneously a problem of reconstruction, interpretation, and desire. And, to state the obvious, *Mercy, Mercy Me* is not desire-free.

The American sixties to be described, then, exists at the intersection of the experiences of a group of exemplary African-American antimodernists and broader trends, discourses, and idealizations, including those alluded to by Jameson. An adequate description of this meeting point will constitute a suggestive reordering of the character of African-American cultural thought within the period and also a challenge to monolithic constructions of sixties-ness, whether inside or outside the academy. The individuals included here are representative of antimodern protest and exhibit a profound ambiva-lence about their personal relationship to American culture. Perhaps as ex-pected, these figures express dismay at the continued vigor of race discrimi-nation and find hope in the moral fervor of the civil rights revolution. Perhaps unexpectedly, they also seem heavily invested in a more general cri-tique of American culture. Robert Hayden battled with his very conception of self, as black man in a racist society, but also as a poet in a society that seemed to little value his art. The creative work of Paule Marshall and William Demby was distinctly international in scope and ambition. It ambi-tiously pursued an *explanation* for nuclear proliferation, the regularization of violence, and our surprising ability to cope. John Coltrane constantly reex-amined his relationship to musical traditions, a quest certainly shaped by the impact of race on the reception of jazz, but he chose to explain his question-ing in terms of a search for spiritual insight. For Romare Bearden, the 1960s marked the reinvention of his very method of creating art, a necessary recen-tering brought about by the simultaneity of social upheaval and his contin-ued disciplined aesthetic inquiry. Finally, my version of the American sixties will conclude with an examination of W.E.B. Du Bois's commemoration, once again, of modernity's troubling relation to the color line, through the ordering of his experience in autobiography. Ambivalence—or, to put it more strongly, angst—emerges when the creative intellectual is unable to de-termine what his or her relationship is to the "mainstream," and is in the pre-carious position of not recognizing whether one's relationship to the domi-nant culture is primarily synecdochal or metonymic. It is to contain and articulate this anxiety—and in vigorous pursuit of a dynamic critique of the peculiar character of American modernity—that collective and individual cultural memory is enthusiastically celebrated.

The specific sociohistorical context that provokes, frames, counters, and supports these individual experiences is complex. I would highlight, how-ever, four components of a potential historical narrative as crucial to the temperament or posture: first, a deterioration of the urban race compact; second, the complex synchronicity of decolonization and civil rights; third, unresolved global tensions, particularly as they led to nuclear proliferation, the commonplace use of torture as a political tool, and, in the most specific way, the Vietnam War; and, finally, the particular character of American con-sumer culture. The overarching historical master narrative that I would offer —if *Mercy, Mercy Me* were seeking to impose such a picture—would be, then, some combination of the insights of the Kerner Commission Report, the Bandung Conference, and Christopher Lasch's *Culture of Narcissism*. All of this, of course, exists amidst the inherited cold war terrain—which is to say that to fully confront these components is to place oneself in a mode of chal-lenging official American optimism and self-congratulation.

Working in a quasi-biographical mode could be seen as a quaint anachronism, or a remnant of a criticism that portrayed subjects as transparently whole and uncontested. An informed biographical method, however, leads to the highlighting of those very elements of identity that, from the perspective of the postmodern, are so significantly fragile. Most importantly, for the purposes of this project and the documentation of a broad culture-critical mode among sixties African-American creative intellectuals, a biographical perspective reinforces some of the central concerns of the creative intellectuals themselves: the question of moral agency, the frailty of the body and mind, and the individual's confrontation with history. In the strongest sense, the following chapters should be seen as profiles. Richard Bernstein suggests that

> a profile is a partial view that highlights the features of a figure, typically a face. We know from the history of art that there are not only many different styles of drawing a profile, but that a profile can draw out what is visible and invisible, what is revealed and concealed. . . . In studying profiles we frequently learn as much about what is being portrayed as we do about the perspective from which it is seen.[57]

The strategic value of the profile is its ability to show the relationship between the production of culture, individual inspiration, and consumption. The profile, at its best, immediately situates the creative intellectual such that we see him or her negotiate the demands of critics, editors, and audiences, all the while struggling to articulate a personal vision. Collectively, a set of profiles has the tendency to complicate long-held notions about a period, an important selling point when trying to disrupt dismissive accounts of the American sixties. As the basis for a method, the profiles combine with the insights of the antimodern perspective to form a hermeneutic that disrupts convention. By not focusing upon a historically constituted school or institution or geographical location, there is the real opportunity to see something completely anew. Together the profiles suggest a kind of family album. Suggestive of forgotten and repressed stories, they encourage an especially active mode of reading. Indeed, they require the acknowledgment of the many ways in which we are entangled. No mean biology can tell the tale.

CLASS, GENDER, AND THE POLITICS OF AUTHENTICITY

There is, of course, a cost to any method. The profiles do surrender at some level to a kind of individualism, and questions of social class, as such, are somewhat elided. The difficulty is not that such tensions and anxieties do not exist in the decade—a reading of Amiri Baraka's career alone, for instance, would make this very clear—but rather the way in which the historical actors approached the problem. Frustrated cultural ambition proved to be just as profound a catalyst to insurgent intellectual activity as was economic anxiety. Many of the profiles reveal quests for cultural status and authority, articulated in terms not strictly related to an increase in economic power, or toward the disruption of the hegemony of a privileged class. For whatever reasons, the language of class solidarity never seemed to become an especially central dimension of African-American cultural critique in the sixties.[58] The combination of a shift from Old to New Left rhetorical strategies and the necessity of relentless confrontation with racial categories meant a shift — perhaps intended to be only temporary — to a more generalized language of justice and liberation. Again, this does not mean that class anxiety was not a major motivating factor in the emergence of this antimodern critique; what is acknowledged is that the focus on profiles is not likely to adequately excavate its existence. Insofar as the majority of the figures considered here are male, the same complication must be identified in attempting to do adequate justice to gender difference. In a post-Sixties setting, Michelle Wallace has quite effectively articulated a feminist critique of the whole period, yet perhaps not so destructively as to counter the standard (i.e., male) reading of the decade.[59] This effort follows hers somewhat, presuming the romanticization of black (and white) male warrior postures. There is no question that a major weakness of some African-American cultural thought in the sixties is its complacency toward patriarchy. Once again, this study is somewhat cornered: aware of this significant weakness, and yet convinced that this largely male dramatis personae is the most effective means to initiate the necessary rereading of the decade.[60]

What is gained from this strategic decision to bracket questions of class and gender is a vantage point from which to effectively critique theories of the sixties that rely upon or seek out "authentic blackness." More direct than the commentary on class and gender, this reading of African-American antimodernism is an attempt to interrogate the construction of race and racial identity in the United States. If there is a direct correlation to be made between the antimodernism of turn-of-the-century America and that of the sixties it is certainly their common interest in the cult of "authentic experience." African-American antimodernism can be seen, to paraphrase Ralph Ellison's famous preacher, as an exploration of "the blackness of blackness." Turn-of-the-century figures immersed themselves in medieval cultures, Catholic ritual, and a "vigorous masculinity" to recover "real experience."[61] In the 1960s, African-American artists explored the resistance of black identity to assimilatory modernity, the "whitewashing" of African-American selfhood.[62] As asserted earlier, the most skilled practitioners of this kind of recovery work were not naive essentialists. Anticipating recent work on diasporic black cultures, however, Hayden, Demby, Marshall, Coltrane, Bearden might still be associated with a strong Pan-Africanist model, tending toward internationalism, rather than, say, the strategic battles fought by Ralph Ellison and Albert Murray on "mulatto" culture.

Much has appropriately been written about the importance of anthropology, and in particular Franz Boas and Zora Neale Hurston, to the consolidation of cultural consciousness in the Harlem Renaissance.[63] It is most unfortunate that anthropological theory had a much more marginal relationship to the formulation of the African-American cultural consciousness in the 1960s. In many ways, the psychoanalytic (and sociopolitical) musings of Franz Fanon superseded anthropological perspectives, especially as anthropology, as a discipline, came to be associated with colonial hegemony and intellectual imperialism. There is no question about Fanon's importance and value in the cultivation of a dynamic vision of counterstatement, sober reflections on the meaning of violence, and insight into global geopolitics. Still, the absence of overt cooperation between anthropological theory and the black cultural vanguard[64] meant that it was easy for some members of that vanguard to inscribe constructions of blackness and African-American culture that flirted with, or enthusiastically embraced, a vulgar essentialism.

The exemplars of African-American antimodernism considered here were supremely aware of this drift and attempted to expose its dangerous pretensions even as they acknowledged that it was the weightlessness of much of modern life that brought it about or made it attractive. The non-essentialist approach to modernity, practiced by these exemplars, focused upon the reconstruction of black history. The racialist approach was largely to move that history toward countermyth, oftentimes very valuable and revealing countermyth. (And, again, it is important to not ignore shared interest. While focusing upon exemplars, "antimodernism" is appropriately descriptive of much of the counterstatement of both reconstructionists and racialists.) Within this context, the profiles perform, then, a dual function. On the one hand, they bring to the forefront the objections of the exemplars; on the other hand, by drawing the reader's attention to the very significant differences between the subjects, the profiles themselves make constructions of any essential blackness (and indeed any monolithic construction of African-American culture) increasingly difficult to swallow.

INVENTING AFRICAN-AMERICAN CULTURE AND THE AMERICAN SIXTIES

The historiographic goals of this book are twofold. First, *Mercy, Mercy Me* seeks to offer an accurate, full, and challenging picture of its subject and to describe African-American cultural life in the sixties as assiduously as possible. Insofar as is possible within the confines of a single book, the goal is to provide some indication of the depth of African-American artistic and critical reflection and the complexity of the social matrix within which it existed. Despite the popular media image of an academia overrun with "sixties radicals," only preliminary historiographic groundwork has been done.[65] Because of the curious relationship that this period has to many current disputes about the shape and nature of a liberal education, this history is increasingly crucial, and must be painstakingly undertaken to assure that "folkloric" versions of this past do not take precedence. On both the political right and left, commentators maintain with confidence that they remember clearly who was a hero and who a villain. This simply does not do justice to the enigmatic and often mysterious ambivalence among cultural actors that I have identified. Second, in a somewhat more limited fashion, *Mercy, Mercy Me* seeks to challenge American cultural and intellectual history to catch up with labor and social history in the evaluation of African-American experience. This involves not only "canon-busting," but also the initiation of a theoretical endeavor to contemplate the relationships of "minority" traditions within a plural society beyond that of margin to center.[66] There have been very specific calls to this work. In Darwin T. Turner's introduction to a special issue of the *Black Scholar* on the "Second Black Renaissance," he suggests, "It is important that we consider cultural issues of the period. Too often the attention given to the 1960's has focused only on political or economic activities. No satisfactory cultural history has been written of this era . . ."[67] Another call comes from David Lionel Smith: "Though the literary output by black writers of the 1960s and early 1970s was substantial, there is a paucity of scholarly literature on this body of work. . . . By "paucity" I do not mean that the scholarly literature is weak or that there simply needs to be more of it. I mean, rather, that even the most rudimentary work in this area is yet to be done."[68] Neither of these calls has been forcefully addressed. African-American cultural and intellectual history of the sixties deserves close scrutiny.[69]

While I describe this work as initiating a series of my largely theoretical endeavors, it is also meant to be initiatory of institutional histories. Ultimately, and perhaps ironically, the viability of this reading of African-American culture during this period may only be affirmed (although it can certainly be challenged now) when we have carefully delineated histories of some central African-American organizations and institutions of the period. It is imperative that we try to preserve the catalytic work of organizations like the Black Arts Repertory Theatre, Broadside Press, Southern Free Theatre, Stax Records, US, Africobra, Spiral, OBAC, AMSAC, Third World Press, the Umbra Poets, and numerous less well known organizations of varied ideological perspectives. The decentralized character of this renaissance has resulted in incomplete documentation and preservation by our libraries. (It is ironic, for instance, that many research libraries have more complete editions of *The North Star* than they do of *Negro Digest, Liberator,* or *The Journal of Black Poetry*.)

There have been at least two recent attempts to deal with the intersection of African-American life and the American sixties. In his recent book on the Watts riots, *The Fire This Time: The Watts Uprising and the 1960s*, Gerald Horne accomplishes one of the more substantive reads of black cultural formation in the sixties that have so far been attempted.[70] After documenting the destruction of leftist organizations in Los Angeles by McCarthyist legislative, judicial, and intelligence activities, Horne argues that the decline in a tradition of substantive interracial grassroots organizing, especially around issues of class, left a void in African-American political life that was filled by the rise of cultural nationalism, which was ultimately decadent in orientation. There is a great deal of truth in this observation, although it also suggests a tendency to dismiss culture in order to restore politics. The trick is to pursue both at once. At the other end of the spectrum, perhaps, is William Van Deburg's *New Day in Babylon: Black Power and American Culture*, a marvelously documented account of political and cultural nationalism, but which seems to actively displace criticism of his subject matter. Transplanting the "culturalist" model of slavery scholarship to the study of the sixties, Van Deburg implicitly argues that because of the continued existence of a racist social order any African-American cultural formation is unique, justified, and to be celebrated. While certainly only speculative, there seems to be at the center of both approaches a kind of nervousness about the contemporary political terrain.[71] There is no way, however, to avoid the messiness that writing about the sixties currently seems to generate.

IN MARCH 1959, Lorraine Hansberry addressed the first conference of Negro writers, sponsored by the American Society for African Culture.[72] The title of her talk, "The Negro Writer and His Roots: Toward a New Romanticism," was not meant to be ironic.[73] This was a willing reembrace of 1930s style radicalism, on the one hand, while, on the other, it was superbly prophetic of New Left ambitiousness for a total critique of American culture. Not surprisingly, given its ambition, the talk was rangy, loose, and often witty. Clearly a manifesto, but, despite some shared ideological commitment and shared insight into the situation of African-American artistry, it was also clearly distinct from Richard Wright's twenty-year-old "Blueprint for Negro Writing" and Langston Hughes's seminal "The Negro Artist and the Racial Mountain." Hansberry's sermon imagined a vital and expansive role for the writer. The Negro writer must recognize the central task of the artist:

> There is a desperate need in our time for the Negro writer to assume a partisanship in what I believe has been the traditional battleground of writers of stature for centuries, namely the war against the illusions of one's time and culture. (131)

Hansberry offered up a long and funny laundry list of cultural illusions that assessed not only American culture's racism but also its sexism, its provincialism, and its anti-intellectualism. The source of such illusions was perfectly clear:

> I say that foremost are the villainous and often ridiculous money values that spill over from the dominant culture and often make us ludicrous in pursuit of that which has its own inherently ludicrous nature: acquisition for the sake of acquisition. (137)

Rejecting the pretensions of agitprop, however, she insisted that what she was after was recognition of the inseparability of beauty and truth. Her critique—deserving of the status granted to the statements by Wright and

Hughes—sought a substantive African-American (and American) art, cosmopolitan *and* Pan-Africanist, relentless in its deconstruction of the myths of America's popular culture.

Working from the perspective of significant nuclear anxiety and seeking to answer those who were unclear about the necessity of human survival, Hansberry's reflections resist the closure of modernity's dialectic of power:

> . . . it is *still* the dark ages. And because now, at last, on the upward ladder toward human enlightenment, we find that man's relationship to man seems by far the most precarious, the most dangerous, and in that sense the newest of our terrors, we fear for the future itself. (141)

The strategy to be pursued was clear: "The work of the Negro artist is cut out for him: the vast task of cultural and historical reclamation—to reclaim the past if we would reclaim the future" (136). (Significantly, Hansberry notes, this role for the artist is somewhat distant from more sensationalist constructions of black difference suggested by other 1950s perspectives. She complained of Norman Mailer and the Beats that "they do not hear as yet the tempo of an impatient and questioning people" [135].) This antimodernism suggests the ways in which such counterstatement is, at its most productive, dialectically entangled with the perseverance of Enlightenment. The overall effect of Hansberry's manifesto is quite startling; it is virtually unimaginable that it might be written today.

Hansberry's anticipation of a "new romanticism" was prescient. For W.E.B. Du Bois, a new romanticism would be at some level a restating of an old one. The "souls" of black folk had a distinct historical role to play, a crucial philosophic counterweight to the confidence of Enlightenment. Romare Bearden discovered a kind of Wordsworthian dimension to the ordering of physical and psychic space and came to find that reordering a distinctly useful resistance to modernity's forgetfulness. John Coltrane recognized the falsehood of material perpetuity and sought to replace that crude faith with an expansive spirituality. William Demby and Paule Marshall considered revolution—in all senses of the word—and their work was marked by the anxiety that such possibility must raise. Hansberry's anxious enthusiasm, then, was met by a decade's worth of artistic and intellectual work of important substance and ambition. The "new romanticism"—or antimodernism—was a vital prophetic mode within American culture.

Robert Hayden also felt strongly the need for "historical reclamation" and he had, by the 1960s, been at it perhaps longer than any other African-American creative intellectual, with the exception of Du Bois. Hayden's straightforward commitment to the dynamic pursuit of black history (the unfortunately, but revealingly, named "Black Spear" project) did not, however, simplistically relieve his anxiety with the modern world. Indeed, his pursuit of "recovery" suggested that African-American antimodernism had a strange way of folding in upon itself. What if no one was interested in your work? If its effective criticism made it difficult to distribute? What if your commitment to speak to all Americans came to be seen as weakness, as a lack of commitment to the African-American community in particular? Ironically, Hayden's heroic pursuit of some way to retreat from the precipice seemed to imprison him, and, on occasion, send him into a kind of free fall. Hayden tried to assert the meaningfulness of cultural identity in order to transcend it; at fleeting moments, when the beauty of that juggling act was clear and sustainable, he elegized our losses and revealed the possibility of our future.

CHAPTER TWO

Mourning Song

ROBERT HAYDEN AND THE POLITICS OF MEMORY

The power to impose a shape upon oneself is an aspect of the more general power to control identity — that of others at least as much as one's own.

STEPHEN GREENBLATT, *Renaissance Self-Fashioning*[1]

What is always torn off, as it were, to construct a public, believable discourse? . . . The "tearing off," Nietzsche reminds us, is simultaneously an act of censorship *and* of meaning creation, a suppression of incoherence and contradiction.

JAMES CLIFFORD, "On Ethnographic Self-Fashioning"[2]

To be a good liar you got to have a good remembrance.

ROBERT HAYDEN[3]

In a recent essay,[4] Kimberly Benston argues that the predominant critical schools of "blackness" and "universality" have led us to an intellectual dead end.

> Unless we shift the ground from underneath a criticism erected on such contraries, locating our discussions at some *juncture* of ideological and aesthetic concerns . . . we will fail to perceive the poetry's own dynamic lesson of its upheaval, that it is not an inevitable object but rather a motivated, constructed, corrosive, and productive process. (167)

The subversion we stand to lose, Benston suggests, is the parodic potential of a tradition which dramatizes attempts to limit notions of African-American and American selfhood. African-American poetry is "a performative activity that sees itself in struggle with other practices" (182). Critics should avoid the false choice between "schools" (or between aesthetics and ideology) and instead direct their energy toward the literature's ability to complicate our understanding of self and society. "African-American poetry"—both the creative activity of poets and the ordering activity of critics—is often radically reflexive and reveals much about contemporary American reality. It exposes contradictory desires for autonomous selfhood and definitive community, for unlimited possibility and comforting continuity, and, as such, inevitably complicates claims as to what exactly makes up a self. This critique of subjectivity complicates both simplistic nationalisms and the impulse toward or imposition of assimilation.

C.W.E. Bigsby, among many others, has noted the symbolic role of the poet in African-American literary and intellectual history.[5] From Phillis Wheatley through Paul Laurence Dunbar,[6] and Langston Hughes through Audre Lorde, the African-American poet has often been the focus of attention in a volatile interrogation of African-American selfhood, and especially questions of artistic practice and responsibility to the community. It is also important to note that African-American poetry has always been coded and, despite occasional charges of mimicry and "parroting," has never been a transparent exercise. Like all artistic practices, it simultaneously speaks to the conditions of its own creation and, more covertly, to the status of its creator. African-American poetry demands careful attention to the dominant social order, the aesthetic object, *and* a contested self, both public and private. Poetry—and the African-American poet—is, then, an appropriate place to begin an interdisciplinary rumination on, and analysis of, the relationship between sixties African-American artistic discourse and antimodern sentiment.

Benston also suggests that the historiographical and critical starting point for this reorientation of our contemporary critical inquiry into African-American poetics is a determination of "the continuing meaning of the Black Arts movement of the 1960's and 1970's."

> On what terms shall we calculate its aims, achievements, and legacy? For our current disputes in the late 1980's over, on the one hand, the propriety of extra-textual criteria, and, on the other hand, the political motivations of various neoformalisms, should be seen as displacements or extensions of an earlier inquisition of the "poetic" as a valid category of value. . . . The tactics we employ in decoding and recoding black poetry still turn in some measure on our interpretation of the ferment which stands now at a generation's remove, on our attitude toward the programmatic declarations and practical performances which carry the Black Arts movement's freight of aesthetic, ontological and political visions. (167)

Benston's identification of the legacy of the Black Arts movement as an "inquisition" is apt. It was, in hindsight, among other things, an inquisition into the values and practices of the "objective" New Criticism and the academic poetry to which it gave rise. The Black Arts revolution directed attention, in very pragmatic fashion, toward the relationship of art and community, as opposed somewhat to poststructuralism and postmodernism's questioning of traditional meaning-making practices, themselves at odds with the New Criticism. It is important to emphasize, however, that the efficacy and range of "Black Arts" can only be fully understood and revealed through an acknowledgment of the diversity of African-American poetics in the decade. African-American modernist poets, for instance, could never accept the segregation of poetic and political value as advocated by the most extreme New Critics. Rather than facilitate the construction of an aesthetic retreat from the social, African-American poetic modernism (and the best of its critics) emphasized aesthetic value over and against more consumerist constructions of meaning, even as it struggled to make sense of the role and function of the poet. In this regard, African-American poetry is (somewhat) continuously antimodernist and is thus a strong challenge to constructions of a sixties African-American culture which rely upon some assertion of "hostile camps." In Benston's terms, a useful "destabilization" of contemporary confidence about the character of African-American cultural tradition is to be found within the conflicts that made up sixties African-American poetic discourse.

Benston chooses as tactic a qualified neoformalism of his own which, he readily admits, is *a* reading of *a* problem; this chapter will invoke as tactic a biographically oriented cultural history in an attempt to reveal the limitations of any one particular orthodoxy concerning African-American poetry and the American sixties. If the performance of blackness should increasingly be our concern, a historical reconstruction of a crucial social drama, one paradigmatic in discussions around the question of "authenticity," should prove interesting. This very partial reconstruction—a single element in a comparative study of an artistic discourse—is an attempt to restore the unpredictability of recognizable human agency and the meaningfulness of historical coincidence and connectedness. More specifically, poetic identity—in particular that of Robert Hayden—and demands for an authentic black voice are considered in the light of an entanglement of competing and complementary intra- and inter-cultural claims on selfhood.

Attention to this "authenticity drama" reveals the complexity of antimodern sentiment. It is not transparently resistance to the status quo, nor, for that matter, a demand for assimilation. Ultimately, this emergent consciousness involves a complex negotiation between the self and various social contexts. Recognition of the ways in which identity issues play a part in sixties discourse foregrounds contemporary nervousness about the shallowness of identity politics. In other words, rather than simplistically celebrate African-American resistance, the recovery of the breadth of black artistic discourse and its insistence on the value of cultural memory requires some willingness to acknowledge its limitations.

Robert Hayden can reasonably be seen as the inheritor of the assaults on "failed" black poesis, next in line after Phillis Wheatley and Paul Laurence Dunbar. Possessing a contemplative sensibility in a period that celebrated ecstatic experience, Hayden attempted to shape his identity toward the reunion of art and morality. More interested in the nature of redemptive history than in rapture, Hayden reconstructed an African-American past toward adequate understanding of the nature of suffering and the permeability of the individual. Despite the charges of his antagonists that his insistence that his poetry be considered nonracially and that his poetic identity be thought of nonracially was regressive and a betrayal, Hayden was far from being interested in preserving a repressive social order. Perhaps no figure within the decade was so shaken by the unwillingness of the nation to make real its democratic vision. For Hayden, the struggle to retain the right to impose a shape upon himself was itself an attempt to determine a particular relationship between beauty and justice, and thus enter into the social fray in the most credible way possible. Evaluating Hayden's legacy—his cultural accomplishment, certainly, but also the stories woven by contemporary critics and writers to describe his sixties experience—is key to any satisfying attempt to locate the meaning of the intersection of African-American culture and the American sixties.

Hayden's great African-American modernist peers, Melvin Tolson and Gwendolyn Brooks, both concerned with the banality of modern American life and skeptical of liberal assurances of gradual change, articulated their understanding of self in a somewhat different fashion. These differences led, on one occasion at least, to a very public dispute between Hayden and Tolson, and in retrospect have contributed to the establishment of a loose "consensus narrative" as to the shape of sixties African American poetry. The first task of this chapter is to describe this performative multiplicity, and ultimately to make clear the unity within diversity, what the critic Henry Taylor has called—in reference to the continuity of Brooks's career—its "essential sanity." African-American poetry as performative practice has both synecdochal and metonymic relations with American literature and within its own boundaries. This is to say that the practice of its poetry—a charged and volatile conversation in the American sixties—paradoxically manages to contain that which does not fit. It is to this disputation and its associated tales that we must go, but first a brief digression suggesting a connection between antimodernism and authenticity.

For African-Americanists, the term "authenticity" is entangled within a tradition of what Henry Louis Gates, Jr. calls "prefaces to blackness."[7] It is a tradition of literary and cultural gestures by white patrons, readers, and critics attesting to the relationship between the text at hand and the authorship and creativity of its signatory. Within the slave-narrative tradition, such gestures affirm that the events so represented have a basis in reality, that "this is what slavery is really like." They also, however, perform the function of mediating the resistance of readers who are skeptical about the ability of blacks to produce their own texts, and thus call the author into being. Insofar as such resistance (racism) might be seen as a central element of an ideology that is part of, or necessary to, the rise of modernity within the context of the Western European and the "New" worlds, any evaluation of African-American challenges to that legacy must contend with the inevitably acrimonious debates about "real blackness."[8] To suggest resonances between this racial discourse and approaches to authenticity within other modern discourses is, however, more complex—and potentially more provocative. In Jackson Lears's reconstruction of Anglo-American antimodernism at the turn of the twentieth century, for instance, the search for the "authentic" self was part of the process of "revitalization," a protest against "feminization," banality, and spiritual sterility.[9] More generally, social theorists have located in the term "identity" an attempt to come to terms with the modern assault on the notion of a unified subject.[10] To clearly identify the contours of a sixties discourse of black authenticity,[11] and implicitly comment upon related uses of "vitalist" conceptions of the self, is an attempt to extend the contemporary philosopher Charles Taylor's concern with the "politics of recognition." There is more to be made of these difficult sixties quarrels than to lament "counter-racism" (Crow Jim, in jazz discourse) or lack of intellectual substance. The discourse of racial authenticity must be examined along with other endeavors to counteract the corroding effects of modernity upon the self.

Identity dramas for African-Americans in the sixties were complex and ambivalent encounters with the particularity and universality of African-American history. African-American artists and intellectuals approached these encounters with a comprehensive and matter-of-course angst about the difficulties faced by all speaking subjects, while further burdened with internalized and institutionalized mediations of black intellectual accomplishment by outsiders. All this proceeded as they attempted to speak authoritatively, like their Anglo-American predecessors, about decay and disillusionment. The writers' conference—while not originating in the sixties, yet certainly quite ubiquitous—becomes a hopeful and fragile site of speaking. It gives evidence of both "critical black difference" and sustainable black selfhood.

RITUAL, CEREMONY AND AFRICAN-AMERICAN LITERARY COMMUNITY

Central to the intellectual landscape of African-American cultural discourse of the sixties were announcements of and the proceedings from the writers' conferences.[12] Writers, artists, and activists had gathered at Berkeley, California, and at the New School for Social Research in New York, Rockford College of Illinois, Fairleigh Dickinson University, and Alabama A&M University, to name but a few locations, to discuss their work and mission. These public presentations hovered painfully between the work of ceremony and the work of ritual. For the James Baldwins and Ralph Ellisons the conferences functioned to reemphasize their status as "artist." Celebratory in tone, the conference was communal confirmation of shared accomplishment. For others, like Alice Childress, William Melvin Kelley, Mari Evans, or Zack Gilbert, for whom entry was not complete and status undetermined, they were rites of passage, often individual demands for respect and attention.

The coexistence of such liminal and (pre)determined space meant much tension. The demands of rites of passage—separation, trial, impartment of knowledge—were not directly compatible with the demands of ceremony—confirmation, celebration, renewal. Such tensions were heightened when the very boundaries of community were confused and complicated. Who was doing the confirming? Who would determine the trials? Who would determine which knowledge was important for communal self-definition or cultural "health"? The writers' conference demanded the negotiation of its very terms of invitation and inclusion. What made the writer? What is art? What is the role of the artist?

Such questions are, of course, prime cocktail party fodder. But for the African-American writer in sixties America such gatherings meant confronting the "authority" in authorship. The real or imagined incursions of white critics like Leslie Fiedler, Richard Gilman, Irving Howe, Robert Bone, Harvey Swados, or Nat Hentoff signaled the negotiation of cultural authority from the outside. Similarly, the presence of Saunders Redding, Arna Bontemps, Sterling Brown, Ralph Ellison, John Killens, or James Baldwin resulted in singular attempts from the inside to indicate the required shape of African-American creative expression.[13] This two-pronged aggression did not limit itself to the general task of inventing tradition. Its full power was mandated in the attempt to determine or shape individual identity. The writers' conference stage was the site of self-presentation—racial, vocational, and political. The American drama of assimilation, the paradox of individuality within community, was acted out in the context of literary investigation and appreciation, and often brought about (or solved) personal crisis or transition. Furthermore, this "drama" is central to the emergence of a *pattern* of antimodern resistance. African-American resistance in the sixties is not inscribed in the discourse of African-American poetry by the "victory" of any one individual, but is, rather, a product of collective participation in a volatile conversation about what might constitute the most authentic (and efficacious) intervention into American culture. This interrogation of African-American identity made clear the value of nonmainstream identity formations in displacing homogenization and, more ambivalently and paradoxically, Americanization.

The coincidence of dramas of consensus and liminality made clear the personal cost involved in negotiating between an ephemeral communitas and a necessary local politics of compromise. On the one hand, there were the demands of a constructed genealogy and an invented tradition. A matrix of reputation and status had to be reinforced through explication and celebration. It was necessary to determine and designate influence, patronship, caste, and rank. Such process might be agonistic and require ritual patricide and matricide or it might reflect on the nature of a particular absence and require a jeremiad against "sinners." On the other hand, constant awareness of an influential cultural "mainstream" meant that a confrontational rhetoric had to be developed so that individuals might declare allegiance to the resistance. Community could be identified beyond essentialist denotations by outlining dominant "values" and the stagnancy of the status quo and then celebrating the vibrancy of countercultural expression.

Not surprisingly, the end result was an interesting but bewildering mix of assertions and performances. The awareness of concrete power (provincial cultural gatekeepers and racist institutional barriers) ironically framed all new attempts at "building"—keeping barely submerged questions of imitation or repetition—and made difficult, for instance, productive conversations about what might be useful within Western and American traditions. But the decision to perform, to proceed anyway, was the only chance at addressing that power. The seminal African-American literary critic George Kent ruminated that

> much thinking went into the expressions of roles of the writers, the building of appropriate institutions, and the struggle simply to create freshly or in a revolutionary way. In the process, there was an increase in the authority of blacks to influence black writings and a corresponding reduction of the authority of the white liberal consensus. . . .[14]

The chipping away at this consensus may be the central legacy of the conferences. It can be seen as a direct accomplishment of "gathering together," the recognition and extended development of a community of interest. What was less well understood was the diversity of the resistance that was set in motion.

Again, the sixties saw a number of these functions. In August of 1964, African American and White writers and critics gathered at Asilomar, near Monterey, under the auspices of the University of California to discuss the "Negro Writer in America." The conference was directed by the NAACP Labor Secretary Herbert Hill. It was a visible gathering significant enough to be covered by *Newsweek* : "Now, in the summer of 1964, the subject of the Negro Writer in America has explosive and far-reaching implications."[15] *Negro Digest* reported that "Literary feuds aside, the conference . . . turned out to be, more or less, an occasion for airing the intricacies and implications of the civil rights struggle."[16] The literary feuds, including the white critic Robert Bone's attack on James Baldwin in his absence, could also have been shaped as "civil rights commentary." The following year, in New York, at the New School for Social Research, a similar gathering was held. The conference was co-organized by the School and the Harlem Writers' Guild. "It . . . had all of New York City outside the New School auditorium, a less cozy atmosphere, and some extremely rude people masquerading as militants."[17] Richard Gilman initiated controversy by stating that "art" requires consideration of the nature of being, and therefore, since "Negroes" are seeking to *establish* being, "Negroes" cannot produce art. While Gilman was grandstanding somewhat—as he would do again in his call for a moratorium on white commentary on black writing—his insistence that "being" was the fundamental subject of these public negotiations was prescient.[18]

Less volatile gatherings were held at Alabama A&M University and Rockford College of Illinois. The Alabama A&M ("The Negro Writer in Our Time") conference, the first on a traditionally black campus, was organized by the visiting scholar Rosey Poole, a white Dutch woman, an important anthologist of African-American poetry. Hoyt Fuller happily reported no "wandering into political waters . . . hassling with black nationalists intent on disruption," although Robert Hayden's frustration over a panel considering African-American drama clearly foreshadowed difficulties to come: "And Mr. Hayden, all but livid with silent rage, later expressed exasperation with critics who ignore the pertinent facts about plays to concentrate on such relative irrelevancies as language and subject matter. 'Blues for Mister Charlie and Dutchman are just bad plays!,' he asserted."[19]

That Hayden expressed his reservations "later" rather than on the panel itself implies that a certain kind of protocol was being maintained. The protocol suggested that one separated, as best one could, the idea from the individual. But a series of gatherings held at Fisk University in Nashville beginning in 1966 somewhat changed the rules. Fisk's history would seem to demand such prominent revisionary status. Founded in 1866, as part of the American Missionary Association's program to develop institutions of liberal and vocational education, it was home to the Fisk Jubilee Singers, who were central to an emergent mythos of black/white cultural relations. Singing hymns and "traditional" spirituals, the choir toured much of the country raising money for the university's construction costs and the hiring of teachers. It was said of Jubilee Hall, the site of most conference activities, that "its bricks were red with the blood and dust of toil." W.E.B. Du Bois was Fisk's most famous graduate (in 1888), while Charles S. Johnson and James Weldon Johnson would also achieve fame.

Within this history and context was created the First Fisk Black Writers' Conference in 1966. Organized by John Killens, whom the university had specifically brought in for the task, its stature was similar to that of the First World Festival of Negro Arts in Dakar, Senegal. Reminiscent of any number of Harlem Renaissance endeavors, the conference was to quickly become a kind of objective correlative for the emergent cultural revival. As had become the pattern, Ralph Ellison was unlikely to attend, and James Baldwin's schedule did not provide for his presence either, but still it promised to be the most significant gathering of African-American writers ever. The tangible change in American race relations—between the Asilomar and the Fisk conferences came the long summers of 1964 and 1965, the assassination of Malcolm X, and the Mississippi civil rights campaigns—meant that this conference held a new urgency. Reporting for *Negro Digest*, David Llorens captured some of the accompanying expectation:

> One attends a writers' conference anticipating new ideas, pertinent criticisms, enhanced perspective—a touch of the inexplicable as well as

the profound — but one also secretly hopes for that person who will rise to the occasion and provide the emotional stimulus that transforms writers' conferences into good old "down home" Baptist conventions — for at least a little while.[20]

This desire for a "revival" meeting nicely alludes, of course, to the revitalizing component of the antimodern attitude. Rightly or wrongly, African-American writers saw themselves immersed in a struggle to provide or capture in the aesthetic realm what students and ministers had delivered in the political and social. Increasingly, many felt the desire to generate the energy needed to reorient American culture. The conference was an attempt to claim an appropriate liminal space, an area of possibility in which face-to-face relations might be engaged toward some concrete social change.[21]

It is not insignificant that two African-American poets would provide the impetus so that the conference might enter the realm of the liminal. For the African-American poet, more than the playwright or novelist, felt, perhaps, the pressure of such public trials and performances. Arguably, through the spirituals and blues, if not the historical accomplishments of Phillis Wheatley, Paul Laurence Dunbar, Countee Cullen, Langston Hughes, and others, poetry was at the center of African-American literary accomplishment. The poet felt the demands of a kind of artistic correctness and was less susceptible to the demands of the marketplace — if only, of course, because the marketplace was likely to ignore them regardless of what they did. The cultural capital associated with poetic forms from folk tradition meant that the poet was subject to special demands, especially as the ritual enactment of many of these forms was a vehicle for the negotiation of identity. This is not to construct the modern African-American poet as some kind of pseudoshaman. African-American poets were fully aware of and engaged by modern American poetry's investment in social critique. And ironically, some of the most interesting and challenging movements in American poetry in the 1950s had turned enthusiastically toward African-American culture for inspiration.

This spotlight — and burden — was intensified because of significant transitions in the business of African-American poetry. Dudley Randall's Broadside Press conceived of cheap editions of timely poetry accessible to all and was a response to both the obscurity of African-American poets and a sense of their latent possibility. Numerous anthologies were produced in America and abroad, edited by, among others, Robert Hayden and Rosey Poole. Furthermore, *Negro Digest* attested to the growing popularity and vigor of African-American poetry with the publication of its annual "poetry portfolio." The portfolios were designed to mix the old with the new, the established with the emergent. While Aldon Nielsen has recently and convincingly documented the existence of dynamic communities of support for black poetic activity from the Second World War through the sixties, it remains reasonable to assert a relationship between the popularizing described above and the emergent cultural nationalist consciousness — the "Black Arts movement."[22] Black Arts poets and critics recentered poetry in discussions of the direction of African-American literature. A dismissal of many modernist conventions (while secretly embracing others), the celebration of the urban vernacular, cultivation of Black Pride, and the development of a populist sensibility were central to this ostensible literary revolution. Poetry suddenly seemed the ideal genre for the dispersal and development of new cultural and aesthetic ideas. Easy to produce and a more direct representation of African-American language use (or so it was thought), this literary tradition was easily and widely utilized in the search for an authentic black voice.

At the First Black Writer's Conference at Fisk University in 1966 were Robert Hayden and Melvin B. Tolson. The distinguished poets represented the dual inheritance of high American modernism and the Harlem Renaissance. Hayden had recently won the grand prize for poetry at the First World Festival of Negro Arts in Dakar, while Tolson sorted out the mixed responses to his epic *Harlem Gallery, Vol. 1, "The Curator."* Both had "establishment" connections: Hayden with W. H. Auden, and Tolson with Allen Tate and Karl Shapiro. These connections undoubtedly brought both fame and suspicion. Part of the fame meant that they were known in mainstream literary circles; they had earned some kind of imprimatur and partial entry into the academy. The accompanying suspicion was that they must have sacrificed some element of blackness in order to gain that entry.

John Killens opened the conference: "For too long we have looked into the eyes of the white master for an image of ourselves," and later continued, "The Negro revolt is part and parcel of a worldwide revolution. Our literature should have social relevance to the world struggle, and especially to the struggle of black Americans."[23] Killens's open embrace of an art/propaganda meetingplace summarized in *tone* the Black Arts revolution. Questions of accountability would move to the forefront. Killens made no mention of aesthetics: the contours (and content) of a literary *art* would have to be subject to the needs of ideology. It is also worth noting, however, that a different kind of political commitment was at least implied by Killens's presence and engagement with the audience. Killens, who had shepherded the Harlem Writers' Guild in the early 1950s, had impeccable leftwing activist credentials. While accounts of the African-American literary battles of the sixties often appropriately detail attitudes towards cultural nationalism and black power, too often cold war (and prior) ideological orientations are placed to one side.

An African-American literary critic from a previous generation (and with a distinctly different set of credentials from the cold war), Saunders Redding, suggested a similar tone for the conference, as David Llorens reported: "He cited the value of Negritude, calling it 'a relatively inexplicable mystique,' and drew a loud burst of applause with his suggestion that the 'literary mainstream resembles a sewer.'" (55) Response to Redding's presentation on African-American fiction, however, guaranteed that there would be no clear boundary lines between camps. Llorens reported of Redding's argument: "'Preoccupation with repossessing a heritage has led to distortion of values and reality in some cases,' said Redding in a preface to accusing some Negro writers of 'making heroes out of heels'" (55). Pressed by the audience, Redding is said to have responded, "Oh Lord, I don't want to argue." Redding's discomfort with the situation, despite setting such a confrontational tone himself, suggests that he was surprised to find himself placed in the "sewery" mainstream. Redding's status, and thus his statements, had likely never been challenged in a public forum.

The white writers Bert Gilden and Margaret Halsey preserved the mode of challenge by suggesting that whites were primarily guilty of "unconscious sinning." George Kent later wrote that "Gilden's statement that blacks were without self-hatred was met by advice that he not try creating Negro characters 'until you find out something about Negroes.'"[24] Of the whole exchange, Llorens suggested: "By this time, the enormous gap between the way white and black Americans view the world was revealing itself both in and out of the 'official' conference sessions" (58). Of course, Llorens might also have mentioned the emerging gap between the way black (or white) Americans viewed the world among themselves. Descriptions of Gilden and Halsey show them as bewildered, seemingly shocked at the disappearance of goodwill toward liberal whites.

But the high point of controversy—indeed the occasion by which the conference is most often recalled—was an exchange between Robert Hayden and Melvin Tolson. Their panel was entitled "Poetry from the Negro Renaissance until Today," and featured Arna Bontemps, Margaret Walker, Hayden, and Tolson. This seemingly benign topic immediately produced contention. Bontemps began with a reference to Hayden's recent award at Dakar and Hayden, seemingly without provocation, started in:

> "I have said this until I almost think I'll choke and fall over backwards," thus began a visibly disturbed Robert Hayden, addressing himself to the argument as to whether one is a Negro poet or, as Hayden insists, "a poet who happens to be Negro." Reading lines from Yeats, Hayden solemnly commented, "I didn't have to be Irish to love those lines." . . . "Let's quit saying we're black writers writing to black folks—it has been given importance it should not have." Hayden's anticipation of opposition gave way to a slight stutter. "I don't think we're trying to escape." (60)

Hayden's decision to "draw fire" may have been a conscious acknowledgment that the atmosphere had changed significantly enough that there would be no ignoring the issue. The questions he raises in quick fashion are not insignificant: ethnicity, social class and poetry's readership ("black folks"), and art's social utility. The "we" of "I don't think we're trying to escape" is brilliant and devious. While appearing alone, he has at least planted the seed with his audience that perhaps there are others of like mind, and that the task of enforcing consensus is a hopeless one. By raising of the question of "love" (and implicitly "understanding") he holds true to the faith that there is some concrete meaning to be found, if not some truth that is unchanging and undeniable. His inflammatory continuation, however, is quite extraordinary, and partially undoes the work of his initial assertions. He proceeded to define poetry as "the beauty of perception given form . . . the art of saying the impossible," and concluded on the matter of identity, addressing the opposition, suggesting that if they didn't agree with him, "Baby, that's your problem, not mine" (62).

Hayden's concluding note, a slip into the vernacular, is striking for its audacity. Ostensibly challenging essentialist constructions of African-American culture, he at the same time seemingly invokes a ritual language game rooted in that culture. It was a cultural cue that few audience members would have missed. Tolson had first chance to participate. He dramatically began: "Nobody writes in a vacuum or out of a vacuum—when a man writes, he tells me which way he went in society." Llorens reported:

> The audience, now spellbound, listened as the man who might affectionately be called the grandfather of the conference spoke of the tridimensionality of man: "A man has his biology, his sociology, and his psychology—and then he becomes a poet. . . ." (62)

The "spellbound" audience is more important here than is Tolson's reference to the obscure "tridimensionality." Tolson continued by ridiculing Hayden's use of "happens to be":

> "Hap, hap . . . let me see, hap means accident. Is someone going to make M. B. Tolson an accident? You'll never make me an accident," and by this time his voice was blazing to the rafters as he exclaimed: "I'm a black poet, an African-American poet, a Negro poet. I'm no accident—and I don't give a tinker's damn what you think." (63)

By centering in on the "accidental," Tolson centers in on the desire for purposeful birth and identity. The "you" in the final sentence works against Hayden's "we," and contributes to a process of ostracization.

Tolson continued by discoursing on the downfall of Western civilization, through a discussion of LeRoi Jones's *The Toilet*:

> Everyone thinks he was talking about a toilet in Harlem; he wasn't talking about a toilet in Harlem—he was talking about an entire civilization that has become a commode. When the intellectuals and the artists condemn a civilization, that doesn't mean that the civilization is in trouble—it means it's on its way out! (63)

Tolson's talk had clearly moved beyond Hayden's initial challenge. This was now the camp meeting that David Llorens had hoped for. While the message is not irrelevant, performance has somewhat pushed content to the periphery. It is also the case, however, that Tolson's challenge to Hayden is not easily reducible to a stereotypic nationalism. As Tolson's biographer notes, he "responded to the question of racial identity that Hayden raised by reiterating his longstanding belief in nurture over nature, and in capitalism being responsible for the world's race problem."[25]

Hayden's ordeal, however, was not finished with Tolson's summing up. James Forman, fresh from civil rights battles, asserted himself from the audience: "I think that the question of whether or not one identifies himself as a Negro writer has bearing on the choice of material one writes about." Forman initiated a discussion of the relationship of the writer to the "movement." Llorens commented on the next speaker, identified as an "activist":

> The speaker, obviously impatient with the inability of his voice to keep pace with his thoughts, next addressed himself to Hayden: "Mr. Hayden, I don't think that Jim Forman is questioning your ability to identify yourself as a Negro. You said that you didn't think you were consciously trying to escape, but is it not true that perhaps you are unconsciously trying . . ." But before he could finish, Hayden interrupted, saying that he was tired of being attacked at every writers' conference. (64)

The unnamed questioner who speaks of *"Mr.* Hayden" and "Jim" is clearly participating in a process of identity formation. The tone and structure of the address suggests not respect but a familial tie that Hayden is about to be denied.

> Insisting that he have his say, the speaker asserted: "The question of whether or not you identify yourself as a poet who happens to be Negro or as a Negro poet does have effect on the students who come in contact with you at this University. It is a fact that many young black people leave Fisk terribly deluded, and someone is responsible for their delusion. I am suggesting that you do have a responsibility to them, a responsibility to help them understand that they will become black poets, black teachers, or what have you—and whether you like it or not, that is your problem, baby." (64)

At one level, the speaker has here begun a process of scapegoating and ostracization.[26] Or, perhaps more accurately, Hayden will certainly *feel* shunned. He will leave Fisk within a year.

Ossie Davis, as he had done on other occasions, ritually closed the conference by eulogizing Malcolm X and

> giving a rousing call for the development of a new language and a new image through which blacks must overcome being made the expendables of America. In the process, the artist would eschew the images of the dead Uncle Tom and Honorary White Man and create those having relationship to the man in the gutter and capable of appealing to him. (Llorens 64)

The conference had taken care of the Honorary White Man through the decentering of white voices on the program, and Hayden was dangerously close to being designated as Uncle Tom. Davis's conclusion is a nice benediction to the communal process of identity negotiation.

With the exception of the central place given Llorens's account of the conference in *Negro Digest* and, perhaps, the speed with which the second conference at Fisk was announced, contemporary response to the conference has been difficult to measure. Tolson's biographer, Robert Farnsworth, draws attention to two interesting texts. Dudley Randall wrote to Tolson to tell him that David Llorens (the *Negro Digest* reporter) "was very taken with you. He wrote me, 'Tolson, not Cassius, is the Greatest'" (Farnsworth 298). The reference is somewhat ironic, and the comment itself raises questions about Llorens's "objective report." The African-American novelist William Melvin Kelley's letter to Tolson, in response to his performance at Fisk, is more helpful:

> I have only known you for a short time, but already I feel as if we have known each other for 300 years now, all our years in bondage. You are part of my proud past—the past that my white man's education kept from me. You are a great man. And that word MAN is a very heavy word. Somehow in the James Baldwins and the Leroi Joneses I have never been able to find that MAN, and I didn't expect to find one at Fisk either, and I am moved that I did. (298)

Kelley's letter provides some interesting clues to the stakes in the encounter at Fisk. It is noteworthy that no mention is made of the substance of the Hayden/Tolson dispute. The emphasis on "re-education" and "masculinity" suggests that the issue was in fact self-presentation and self-understanding. It reveals an important subtext (if not pretext) surrounding the re-claiming of black masculinity.[27]

What is the nature of this interesting historical moment? The central elements here are culturally specific performance, the negotiation of racial, gender, and sexual identities, and the silence of the female voice. (Why was Margaret Walker silent during this exchange, or did David Llorens not think to record her words, given that he saw this as a debate about masculinity?) Most importantly: Is the event what it seems to be? Is Tolson the recognizable and appropriate defender of blackness against Hayden's universalizing? If this is the conclusion to be drawn, it is highly ironic.

Melvin Tolson's tussle with Hayden was partially a function of his history as performer.[28] A long time debater, actor, and theater director, Tolson, sensing the drama of the moment, would have had a difficult time resisting the clear challenge—especially in the way in which it was presented by Hayden. Tolson the orator took over, with little or no regard for a careful consideration of Hayden's argument. Indeed, the "tri-dimensionality of being"—psychology, biology, and sociology—could be seen as a variation on Hayden's "history," and was not especially convincing intellectually. But, more importantly, if one part of the legacy of the Fisk conference is the "designation" of Robert Hayden, Tolson should not be seen as "ritually clean." If, as Mary

Douglas suggests, the notion of pollution is a central categorical tool in social organization,[29] Tolson himself had engaged the taboo. His history as
writer was perhaps even more complicated than Hayden's. The phrase often
used to discuss Tolson's difficult location as writer, as articulated by John
Ciardi, was "the vertical audience." His fascination with the most complex
forms of literary modernism, his reading of T. S. Eliot, and his love of obscure allusion to both classical European and African culture, made him
largely unreadable to the average American of whatever descent.[30] To understand the significance of this event it is important to challenge the notion of
Tolson as "pure product." A close reading here of Tolson's *Harlem Gallery* is
not necessary (though that is clearly what readers who want to understand
Tolson's "place" in the American sixties will need to do for themselves) in
order to recognize that Tolson can in no simple way be construed as being in
direct dispute with Hayden despite the nature of their exchange. Indeed, it
is more accurate to suggest that Tolson and Hayden cooperate to provide the
community an opportunity to restate the importance they attach to the investigation and interrogation of "selfhood." In this sense, the antimodernism
that they *share* is a refusal to be discarded.

   In the lives of Hayden *and* Tolson (and, to a lesser extent, in the life of
Gwendolyn Brooks[31]) there are narratives of tryst at work. Narratives of tryst
are patterns of implication which question and subvert any realm of purity
or authenticity. Within the narrative, the "authentic black voice" is a mediated and negotiated statement of belonging which relies upon a number of
communal and personal signifiers: race, history, geography, gender, vocation, faith. Narratives of tryst reveal the inability of the individual to walk a
straight line between the "inside" and "outside." They question, as the "romantic" connotation might suggest, the desire for the culturally ascetic, by
preventing the individual from not becoming involved. More negatively, they
may also demand competitive and costly ceremonies of designation and rituals of passage. These jumbled "concerns"—masculinity, identity, blackness,
community, poetry, and art—are the elements, I would argue, of a protest
that is invoked communally, yet not necessarily with ideological consensus.
Recognizing that narratives of tryst are at work means that the oppositional
character of black speech in American culture cannot be seen as straightforward and transparent. It can never be a question of resisting assimilation (or
despiritualization) through the strong assertion of authentic blackness. The
Hayden/Tolson exchange at Fisk University suggests that blackness and antimodernism are the products of a complex cultural performance. And corollary to that cultural performance is a contemporary desire to misremember
that Hayden was attacked by "militants."

   This complexity has been treated much too reductively in most critical
treatments of Hayden, especially the major monographs: John Hatcher's
From the Auroral Darkness: The Life and Poetry of Robert Hayden, Pontheolla T.
Williams's *Robert Hayden: A Critical Analysis of His Poetry*, and Fred Fetrow's
Robert Hayden.[32] Each reading of Hayden and the sixties is overly influenced

by Hayden's own critical position, which each author explicitly endorses. Each writer's presumptive commitment to Hayden's aesthetic reinforces the notion that Hayden was wronged and ultimately distorts history. Hatcher relates that at Fisk "Hayden was severely attacked by some participants. The background to this humiliation and to the conference itself was the progressive faltering in the civil rights movement. . . . The result was an ostensibly spontaneous outburst of militancy. . . . To those attending the conference Hayden was an easy target" (36–37). Williams writes that Hayden "was severely attacked by a group of militant black nationalists who had convened at Fisk. . . . They espoused the Maoist-inspired philosophy, decreed by Ron Karenga and other black nationalists, that black literature should be didactic and propagandistic for the purpose of indoctrinating the masses in their revolutionary cause" (30–31). Both characterizations are radical simplifications that ignore Tolson's own modernist credentials and distort both personal and cultural context. (Williams's mention of Karenga—who will never be confused with James Forman—seems especially to suggest a form of critical mythmaking at work.) Fred Fetrow argues that "several participants took vociferous issue with Hayden's assertion that there should be no difference in the criteria for judging art, whether the artists be black, white, or whatever" (25). Fetrow's "vociferous" is accurate, but he too makes Hayden out to be transparently heroic, making a last stand to hold off the barbarians at the gate. The construction of a Hayden beleaguered by militants mishandles a central paradox: the poet is seemingly under siege at the very moment that he is receiving long-desired recognition for his work. This contradiction makes ironic Hayden's own position of a nonracial poesis. As the culture becomes increasingly interested in African-American creativity, Hayden has been offered the chance to become a cultural authority, and to enhance his own status as poet.

Much of Hayden's *anxiety* is rooted far from intracultural disputes about poetics and aesthetics. He is obsessed with his own texts, constantly revising and tinkering, to the point at which he begins to disavow some of his earliest work. Hayden was an overworked and underpaid teacher, and no doubt part of his struggle with "self" was a product of family difficulties, crises of faith, and perhaps his sexuality, a set of struggles arguably much more significant and heroic than his combativeness about questions of race and poetry. The central component of Hayden's anxiety—and often our anxiety about Hayden as critics—is agitation as to when, or if, he would be discovered. This consideration in particular should complicate singular assertions about authenticity and preface a more historically satisfying evaluation of Hayden's contribution to sixties American culture. The cost of misapprehending the meaning of Hayden's sixties experience is the displacement of his substantive and sharp critique of that culture. There is little of lasting value to be gained in making Hayden a weak emblem of liberal humanism.

The matter at hand is not to decide on the correctness of Robert Hayden's conception of his blackness or its relation to the understanding of poetry.

The issue is not to measure authenticity (or to reject one conception for another, likely equally frivolous) but to certainly grant it its due as a significant theme in his life and career. Hayden's antimodernism does surface in the struggle to make identity or "lived life" complex, a permanent and costly struggle. (It is important to note that it was rare for Hayden to identify provincialism in his combatants and antagonists and more common for him to assert the importance of his own responsibilities.) To remember Hayden as "antimodernist," however, is to fundamentally displace the myth that he had no involvement with a complex cultural nationalism or that his career was primarily about declaring the wrongness of other African-Americans. A reorientation of attitudes toward Hayden's experience sets the groundwork for narratives of the sixties and African-American culture that are more focused upon social critique and aesthetic accomplishment than intracultural dispute.

ROBERT HAYDEN AND THE AMERICAN SIXTIES

Hayden, in his late 40s, enters the sixties as an instructor at a black college in a provincial and segregated city. In his first thirteen years at Fisk, he had mentored some important black writers to be—most notably William Demby and Julius Lester—and had authored a striking poetic manifesto.[33] Somewhat simultaneously, he came to loath Fisk's middle-class pretentiousness, while struggling to achieve some of his own bourgeois-like stability: a home, comfortable family life, and a little disposable income to travel. Neither he nor his wife, Erma, had ever lived in the South, and they agonized about educating their daughter, Maia, in a segregated school environment. Most troublingly, he had difficulty in following up his first collection, *Heart Shape in the Dust* (1940), with a full selection of his more mature work. After study with W. H. Auden at the University of Michigan, a major poetry prize, publication in *Poetry* magazine and two significant anthologies of black writing, Hayden could reasonably have expected more than to be bogged down with a teaching load that was a minimum of fifteen class hours per week and more often than not included at least two sections of Introductory Composition. If measured only in terms of publication, the 1950s were noteworthy for, if not stagnation, then certainly a kind of extended pause in the development of his poetic career. Hayden's understanding of himself as writer, however, and his commitment to writing as craft was extraordinarily strong. He would survive this banishment to thrive and be acknowledged as an important contributor to American culture.

While much of his sixties experience can indeed be foregrounded with reference to those conscious decisions he made about his artistic identity, there are other commonly acknowledged biographical details that extend our understanding, and further the suggestion that there is something of particular importance about Hayden's experience. There was, for instance, certainly the problem of names and naming. For Hayden the notion of identity as vexed or fragmented was not especially abstract. Born "Asa Sheffey," "Robert Hayden" was the name given him by his adoptive parents, a discovery he did not make until relatively late in his life. While he maintained an important relationship with his birth mother, and was able to resolve much enmity toward his adoptive father through his poetry (especially "Those Winter Sundays"), Hayden often felt emotionally adrift and unclear about his place in the world. Growing awareness of homoerotic desire complicated that sense of place even further. Through the turmoil with parents and discovery of his past, he had become somewhat anchored by sincerely adopting and pursuing the role of father and husband. If Hayden flirts with real despair, it is understandable. While his increasingly incisive religious vision no doubt brought real comfort, there remained significant moments of doubt and fear. His newly adopted Baha'i faith (or, for that matter, the faith of his Baptist forebears) was not especially tolerant of bisexuality.

Despite the clearly political turmoil of the sixties, for the poet and artist the question of racial (and, for that matter, national) identity was complicated by other aspects of the personal.[34] The opportunity to choose—indeed, insist upon—a specific identity no doubt became increasingly important to the sensitive Hayden. Poetic meditations upon communal history might illuminate complex family relationships, but not so much that one would predominate or "solve" the other. Hayden comes to the sixties still, no doubt, in the process of inventing himself. Without displacing the sincerity of his assertions about poetic identity—or dismissing the credibility of his argument—it seems necessary to take seriously the *act* of identity creation itself as perhaps primary.

In similar fashion, while critics and literary historians have noted correctly that the designation "black poet" is at the crux of understanding Hayden's career, perhaps not nearly enough attention has been directed to the "poet" part of the claim. It is not likely that even if Hayden were to have somehow won the debate about the appropriateness of a racially qualified sense of literary vocation—whatever that might have meant—it would have brought the onset of a great calm around his choice of a literary life. Hayden reflected often on the loneliness of the American poet. The cultural currency of poetry was minimal and Hayden could be straightforwardly bitter about this characteristic of American existence. Still, Hayden had since 1947 functioned as the unofficial writer-in-residence at Fisk and mentored numerous aspiring writers.[35] William Demby has noted how crucial Hayden was as a role model and described the Hayden home as "an oasis of civility." This kind of acknowledgment mattered greatly to Hayden, and served to temper the experience of his otherwise minimal cultural authority, and make living in Nashville worthwhile.[36] As fragile as his life in the institution actually was, as a writer he had much invested in Fisk. The University's decision to bring in John Killens as official writer-in-residence, whose first task was to organize the Black Writers Conference, no doubt heightened Hayden's anxiousness about his status and authority. In reflecting on his commitment to the

Baha'i faith and its radical dedication to the oneness of mankind—not a popular theme among radicals, liberals, or conservatives in the mid-sixties— it becomes clear to contemporary readers (and no doubt to Hayden in 1966) that his small piece of hard-earned cultural status was indeed fragile. Regardless, then, of how one places oneself within the context of this particular aesthetic and political debate, it is easy to extend sympathy to a Hayden who was talented, largely unrecognized, and who had concrete struggles with the question of "Who am I?"

Once again, however, sympathy for this beleaguered and often heroic individual should not become the occasion for hagiography. If the despicable image of Uncle Tom is an inappropriate designation of Hayden, so too is that of martyr. It is an intriguing and attractive myth, but the cost is high. The formation most often produced by the myth is that Hayden was apolitical and had no significant investment in any kind of cultural nationalism; this is unsustainable. (The myth likely reveals much more about our own contemporary struggles with cultural pluralism than it does any real truth about the sixties.) Just as a close reading of the Fisk conference suggests something other than a Manichean literary history, so too do other details of his personal and professional life reveal something much more complex. The clarity of his social criticism needs to be rescued from that set of vigorous desires about Hayden that constitute the myth.

One step toward demythologization is to consider the prefaces and introductions that Hayden wrote to a variety of literary projects in the late sixties and early seventies. In these documents Hayden further articulated his by now familiar aesthetic position, and, to some extent, his ambivalence about contemporary African-American life. While these documents are readily offered up by critics as further evidence of the absolute clarity of his aesthetics, rarely is enough attention directed toward the scope of his inquiry. For instance, in a textbook introduction published in 1973, entitled "Twentieth-Century American Poetry,"[37] Hayden unapologetically presents movements in African-American poetry as central to American tradition. If mainstream criticism still readily marginalized black poetic accomplishment, Hayden was willing to be more effusive about both its prospects and past. Of the "black aesthetic" school, he suggests:

> Not yet satisfactorily defined, this term, originating in the sixties, may be interpreted as a sense of the spiritual and artistic values of blackness. It is, perhaps, a logical (some would say "chauvinistic") reaction to negative American racial attitudes. Perhaps the concept is summarized best by the slogan "Black is beautiful." Those who accept this point of view regard Negro subject matter as their exclusive domain, feeling that only those who have shared "black experience" can articulate it. (53)

Hayden's demand for clarity is clearly different than rejection or ridicule. One suspects that his mention of "spiritual and artistic values" suggests the seeking out of some kind of critical and personal common ground.[38] His attempt to represent the "black aesthetic" fairly or objectively—note the use of the passive voice and third person—must, in and of itself, complicate the notion of the Fisk exchange as somehow obvious or self-evident. Most importantly, however, Hayden's attempt to center African-American poetry, to educate the American audience as to the richness of black expressive culture, should be as much a part of his legacy as his palatable identity politics.

The most troubling blindspot, however, is in the failure to emphasize that Hayden was gaining significant cultural authority through his knowledge of and ability to present a black poetic tradition, and that strategically, if not with great epistemological confidence, Hayden spoke often of such a tradition. Ironically, Hayden was having significant success in the creation or stewardship of products anxiously desired by stalwart cultural nationalists. Despite the high idealism of much of the Counterpoise manifesto as an introduction to the establishment of a poetry series under Hayden's direction, it is most notable for its attention to the marginalization of black poetry. There is real anger in his challenge "to having [African American poetry] misinterpreted . . . by coterie editors, reviewers, anthologists who refuse to use encouragement or critical guidance because we deal with realities we find it neither possible nor desirable to ignore." Hayden's idealism never displaced the hard lessons of American history and culture . . . not even for himself.

In 1967, Hayden edited an anthology called *Kaleidoscope: Poems by American Negro Poets*. In his introduction, he suggests:

> It has come to be expected of all Negro poets that they will address themselves to the race question—and that they will all say nearly the same things about it. Such 'group unity' is more apparent than real. Differences in vision and emphasis, fundamental differences in approach to the art of poetry itself, modify and give diversity to the writing of these poets, even when they employ similar themes. And certainly there is no agreement among them as to what the much-debated role of the Negro poet should be. (59)

Hayden defends the community's ability to make meaning in a variety of ways. Again, he somewhat distances himself from the debate and recognizes the logical necessity (and paradox) of his making room for a position that may negate his own. His subsequent questioning of the desire or need for consensus also seems prudent, and should act as a guide to our contemporary historiographic attempts.

Unlike many of his supporters, however, Hayden confronts the most difficult of contradictions:

> Perhaps it would be amiss to say in conclusion that neither the editor nor his publisher should be understood as necessarily endorsing the long-established custom of segregating the work of Negro poets within the covers of a separate anthology. Yet where, except in a collection

such as the present one, is the student to gather any impression of the nature and scope of the Negro's contribution to American poetry?[39]

Hayden's response to his own participation in "chauvinism" is appropriately evasive, although hardly satisfactory. Can he consistently ask the question of the "Negro contribution" given his hostility to the designation? In his concluding line, he acknowledges the relations of power which his sixties critics continuously insisted that he did not understand or recognize. This was no doubt a painful acknowledgment to make and a complex reality to negotiate. But it was negotiated, and, arguably, the audience for American literature is much better for it. Again, the truth is that the rise of his reputation as a poet is simultaneous with his increased productivity as an anthologist, critic, and commentator. Blackness may be an obstruction for Hayden, but it is also a vehicle that he utilizes to obtain some cultural power.

Perhaps Hayden's most interesting sixties prose is to be found in his interpretation of a seminal work from African-American cultural history. In 1968 Hayden wrote an introduction to a reprint of Alain Locke's *The New Negro*. It is especially significant because of the role of Locke's text in the communal and intercultural process of identity negotiation. This collection of poetry, fiction, art, and essays, which commented upon an African past and American present, was one that questioned the authentic but legitimized the negotiated and impure product. The bottom line for Hayden is made clear:

> The main thrust of *The New Negro* is clearly integrationist, not separatist. Dr. Locke and most of his collaborators thought of race consciousness and race pride as positive forces making the Negro aware of the true worth of his contributions to American society and helping him to achieve his rightful place in it. His task was interpreted as being twofold: He must be, in Dr. Locke's words, "a collaborator and participant in American civilization," and he must at the same time preserve and implement his own racial traditions.[40]

Hayden's desire for American life to have a particular shape demonstrates how clearly he saw his life as poet and teacher entangled with his life as citizen. He must also have recognized the irony in Locke's pre-World War II use of the term "collaborator," and preserved it knowing that his critics would say "exactly." Of course, to make too much of a potential betrayal on Hayden's part is to dismiss the seriousness of his final words, and the irony of the text's contemporary (re)production in the "second *black* renaissance."

The adjustment in perspective that needs to be demanded, then, from critics who would continue to reject Hayden in knee-jerk fashion, is recognition that for Hayden to emphasize the aesthetic was simply not an abandonment of struggle. Gwendolyn Brooks thoughtfully describes Hayden's position and situation in her review of his *Selected Poems*:

We need the poet who "lives in life," mixes with mud, rolls in rot, claws the scoundrels, bleeds and bloodies, and, grasping in the field, writes right there, his wounds like faucets above his page, at once besmirching and ennobling it. We need, also, the poet who finds life always interesting, sometimes appalling, sometimes appealing, but consistently amenable to a clarifying enchantment via the powers of art. His reverence for the word Art is what chiefly distinguishes him from Poet I. Poet II, moreover, may postpone composition until he is off the field, rid of the fray's insignia, and has had a bath.[41]

It is important to note that in some real way Poet I and Poet II are so intimately related so as to be indistinguishable.[42] While Poet II presents him or herself as clearly (or denotatively) "antimodern," Poet I never ceases to be a poet. Brooks's use of the imagery of "cleanliness" is significant, as is her recognition of the need for both "partners."

In a brief pamphlet from 1967, Hayden movingly summarized his struggles and ambition. The difficulty of his journey was made explicit: "I have been writing for many years now, but my development as a poet has been slow and tortuous, and my failures are more numerous than my successes, owing partly to the fact that I have had to work in defiance of limitations imposed from without while fighting personal demons within."[43] Once again acknowledging the paradox of his position, he notes that "Though I eschew the didactic, I admit to being a poet 'with a purpose.'" Hayden goes on to describe that purpose in specifically religious terms and to note his increasing interest in the "personal." His affirmation of black cultural context is once again apt: "I hope to add to the poems I have already published on themes from Negro history and folklore, because this material interests me and is untarnished from overuse, and because it gives me the chance to reaffirm the Negro struggle as part of the long human struggle toward freedom." Once again Hayden attempts to suspend the self between a transcendent, and often explicitly religious, idealism, and the inevitability of "living in life" and the encounter with sin and imperfection.

Hayden's various critical writings, then, complicate the image of him as the stately defender of a New Critical sensibility within the African-American tradition; neither is he easily a knight errant, a black Quixote charging nationalist windmills. That a public Hayden acknowledged with significant regularity "limitations imposed from without" makes even more striking the tendency towards critical myth. Other components of his biography, accessible through his unpublished papers and evidence from a somewhat more private self, are suggestive of further means of challenging the Hayden myth. For instance, the notion that Hayden's faith required that he wholly distance himself from "politics" needs significant qualification. While not an active member of any political party—and certainly invested in traditionally Baha'i notions of "world citizenship"—Hayden did not sit idly by during the civil rights revolution. He wrote to legislators in support of civil rights legislation, participated in educational forums on civil rights topics, and supported his students who sought conscientious objector status.[44] While it is certainly true that such activities pale when placed beside a more dynamic activist politics, it remains a politics nonetheless, evidence again of Hayden's dissatisfaction with the status quo. Neither can Hayden be easily charged with unconditionally courting white critical approval. Hayden perceived quite clearly, for instance, how condescendingly he was treated in David Littlejohn's *Black on White: A Critical Survey of Writing by American Negroes*, and he responded angrily.[45] It is also difficult to sustain the idea that Hayden was ostracized during the decade in any totalizing way. He was in great demand as a speaker, and letters attest to his popularity among students, scholars, and activists.[46]

There is also evidence, of course, of real wear and tear on his psyche. He was hospitalized—the diagnosis not completely clear—only a few months after the Fisk conference. An attempt to *qualify* the construction of a Hayden in direct and absolute battle with nationalist thinkers and writers should not mean disregard of his real disdain for all forms of absolutism and the depth of his suffering. In a striking letter to Rosey Poole in October of 1967—perhaps his most revealing letter—he wrote:

> I am sick to the point of nausea of all this race business—*from both sides*. The Black Power gang wants to regiment all of us, and after hearing Carmichael I have no illusions about the fascist propensities of the so-called black "revolutionaries." The only revolutionist I'll follow is Baha'u'llah. But for the Faith I should want to cut my wrists and get out of this mess, feeling, as I do, caught between black chauvinism on the one hand and white bigotry on the other.[47]

Again, however, it seems crucial not to lose that sense of "caught between." The Hayden remembered by contemporary critics and historians has become mainly one who rejected nationalist overstatement and prejudice.

Hayden's own recollection of the events at Fisk was unusual. Pontheolla Williams's report that "he was severely attacked by a group of militant black nationalists who had convened at Fisk University for the first Black Writers' Conference"[48] was based upon a personal conversation with Hayden himself. But, as we have seen, the primary opponent was a poet of Hayden's own generation, an academic who had been involved and entangled with the likes of Allen Tate, Karl Shapiro, and John Ciardi.[49] While Hayden cannot be accused of self-martyrdom, he did seem to participate in a process of mythologization. He created a "challenged self," which is, in many respects, what he had always understood himself to be.

THE MOST USEFUL picture of Hayden is that of a mediated, invented, and conjuncted self. This argument rests first on the performance of that self in the context of moments of institutional validation (writers' conferences, "introductions," "prefaces," anthologies, "collections") although the character of his poetic accomplishment can certainly be put toward this conclusion too. Critics of all stripes readily acknowledge Hayden's striking black history poems, especially those focused upon black "heroes."[50] (And neither did Hayden's symbolist technique place him comfortably in any kind of [white] poetic mainstream. Hayden's style was radically different than that of Amiri Baraka, but it was not that of John Ashbery either.) "History" was a person's prime "entanglement." His poems celebrating Frederick Douglass, Nat Turner, the middle passage, Harriet Tubman, and so on, were forthright in their black pride. But more important to Hayden, history was the artist's material. Hayden could no more think of escaping his "blackness" than he could his difficult family background.

Perhaps the best example, however, of Hayden's poetic representation of self and culture can be found in his poem "A Ballad of Remembrance,"[51] which is also the title of the 1962 book that signals his arrival. As an emblem of his poetic relation to the world, *Ballad*, the book, is presented twice, in 1962 and 1966. Despite the significant changes in American society between these years, there is an appropriateness in it as a compromise designation of who, what, and where he was as a poet and as an African-American. The title poem grew out of an attempt to make sense of his first trip to the deep South, to New Orleans in 1947, and his inevitable first encounters with overt and crass discrimination. The poem is set in Mardi Gras, a powerful representation of liminal space in our cultural life. We are introduced to:

> Quadroon mermaids, Afro angels, black saints
> balanced upon the switchblades of that air
> and sang. (lines 1–3)

and also the "Zulu King," and the "gun-metal priestess." This tableau of individuals both masked and "mulatto" are the aesthetic and political context of the poet attempting to buy coffee. The poem, like many Hayden works, is based upon ornate and erudite readings of the social and historical materials. Less grand than Mardi Gras itself, the simple economic and social transaction of attempting to purchase a drink is still a dramatic point of departure:

> What will you have? she inquired, the sallow vendeuse
> of prepared tarnishes and jokes of nacre and ormolu,
> what but those gleamings, oldrose graces,
> manners like scented gloves? Contrived ghosts
> rapped to metronome clack of lavalieres. (10–14)

The disruption is grotesque, but the choices he is offered are real and recognizable to us. "Accommodate," suggests the Zulu king, as the saints, angels, and mermaids chime love. Most dramatically, the gun-metal priestess "shrieks" hate. And despite the withdrawal of the priestess, "the dance continued."

The conclusion of the poem gets Hayden into trouble with later critics, in particular those of nationalist orientation:

Then you arrived, meditative, ironic,
richly human; and your presence was shore where I rested
released from the hoodoo of that dance, where I spoke
with my true voice again.

And therefore this is not only a ballad of remembrance
for the down-South arcane city with death
in its jaws like gold teeth and archaic cusswords;
not only a token for the troubled generous friends
held in the fists of that schizoid city like flowers,
but also, Mark Van Doren,
a poem of remembrance, a gift, a souvenir for you. (34–44)

Some have read this conclusion as a straightforward "moral," and more troubling, as the equation of moral authority with the presence of the white (and canonical) poet. Yet the poem's strength relies upon the willingness of the reader to submit to the inchoateness of its first two-thirds as well as its more ordered ending. Resolution can only be engaged alongside disruption. The Zulu king (a masked figure, a parody of blackness), the gun-metal priestess (an allusion to the "cultic" and secret background of New Orleans) and the "saints" are a simultaneity, a disruption of chronos. It might also be allowed that such a "souvenir" has either little value or only kitsch value, or, that, if taken seriously, such a "ballad of remembrance" demands responsibility of Van Doren as much as it identifies or grants authority.

Pontheolla Williams initially suggests that the poem might be conceived of as a surrealist experiment,[52] the dredging of a nightmare, yet she recoils from this reading because of the appearance of a moral, and the poem's commitment to a time-sequence structure. But that straightforward moral is called into question by the poet who is unable to enter one of the "metaphorical doors" presented to him by the "collection" of speakers. The poet is suspended betwixt and between, forced to deal with this dilemma on its own terms, both political and aesthetic. If we are offered "tokens" they are multiple, if not indeterminate, signs. "Ballad of Remembrance" is, then, emblematic of a strategy for confronting the world as it is. Indeed, Hayden referred to the whole of his poetic output as his ballads of remembrance.

Of course, the argument here is not that Hayden is a *postmodernist*. There is little evidence that Hayden would ever have appreciated that designation. Indeed, the argument in this chapter has been that Hayden is thoroughly *antimodernist*. As such, this balancing or juggling of identity choices is not an end in itself. Such identity work is only useful insofar as it prepares oneself—protects the self—such that it can give prophetic witness to a world gone wrong. An extended reading of one of the great masterpieces of sixties America, Hayden's *Words in the Mourning Time*, should illustrate this critical difference.

WORDS IN THE MOURNING TIME AND
THE ELEGIAC MODE

Words in the Mourning Time appeared in the Fall of 1970.[53] Like nearly everything else in Hayden's poetic career, there was a significant delay involved.[54] Even allowing for that delay, however, there is no mistaking the book for anything other than a sixties text. Certainly its subject matter makes it so — poems on Vietnam, political assassinations, student unrest, and the like — but, much more interestingly, it is harrowing in its investigation of the difficulty of living ethically and healthily in the midst of cultural and political turmoil. Its commitment to a distinct and direct cultural criticism is obvious. While it is philosophically invested in the particular perspective of the Baha'i faith and, more generally, in a radically extended tradition of American transcendentalist writing, it is timely, engaged, despairing, and hopeful.

As was Hayden's pattern — it would remain so for the rest of his life — the book included both new poems and a few that had appeared in previous collections or chapbooks and now stood revised. *Words* revisited three poems from *Figure of Time* (1955), one from *The Lion and the Archer* (1948), and one from *Ballad of Remembrance* (1962), while introducing fifteen new compositions. This general atmosphere of revisiting and remembrance is confirmed by the book's dedication to Marie Alice Hanson — the Detroit librarian from Hayden's childhood who encouraged his poetry — and Louis Martin — who gave Hayden a job writing for the *Michigan Chronicle* and also published his first book of poetry, *Heart-Shape in the Dust*, around 1940. While only two poems ("The Dream" and "El-Hajj Malik El-Shabazz") are obviously in the "historicist" mode that had brought him some fame, the act of memory, of looking backward and inward, is still of crucial importance to Hayden.

The book is divided into four sections. The first section, seven poems in total, is built around the question of the identity search in the midst of the perplexing difficulty of African-American history. The second section, five poems, can loosely be referred to as poems of "place." The third section, two poems, is fully and strikingly elegiac, while the final section, six poems, is constructively redemptive. More broadly still: sections one and two describe the American dilemma, section three is a prayer for its survival, while section four is thoughtfully forward-looking.

The opening poem, "Sphinx," seems especially well-placed and intriguing regardless of whether or not we are able to aptly discover the particularity of the riddle or its answer.

> If he could solve the riddle,
> she would not leap
>   from those gaunt rocks to her death,
> but devour him instead.
>
>   It pleasures her to hold
> him captive there —

> to keep him in the reach of her
> blood-matted paws. (lines 1–8)

The reader's task is less to solve the riddle than to identify it. All we know is that the "he" of the poem is seemingly doomed. The sphinx informs her prey that it is

> your fate to live
> at the mercy of my
>
> conundrum, which, in truth,
> is only a kind
> of psychic joke. No, you shall
> not leave this place.
>
> (Consider anyway the view from
> here.) (lines 11–17)

While the parenthetical remark is ostensibly a continuation of the Sphinx's remarks, its separation marks the possibility that "he"—or the poet—is directing the reader's attention to his "fate." This suspension between two possibilities, neither especially palatable, is a nice description indeed of Hayden's sixties dilemma. One reasonable reading of the riddle is to designate it as Hayden's coming to terms with his odd position in American letters. Part of his notoriety has to do with his resistance to a kind of racial chauvinism; on the other hand, that notoriety is certainly invested with its own chauvinism. It is crucial, after all, that he is a black man resisting absolute categories.

> In time,
> you will come to regard my questioning
> with a certain pained
>
> amusement; in time, get so
> you would hardly find
> it possible to live without
> my joke and me. (lines 17–23)

The smugness of the Sphinx's voice should caution, of course, that "he" has or will come to the resignation that is here designated as inevitable.

There are other possible identifications of the riddle, some as compelling as the identification of "questioning" with the Fisk drama and the sixties experience more generally. It can also be argued, for instance, that the poem is strategically placed as an introduction to more explicit and public attempts on the part of the poet to deal more openly with his sexuality. Or it can be asserted that the poem is distinctly metaphysical in tone and does not depend on the placement of the poet near the "blood-matted paws" of the Sphinx, but rather seeks to place the reader there and substantively put before us questions of ultimate things. And yet the more provincial reading—the poem as an attempt by Hayden to unravel his unusual agonistic relations with American and African-American culture—has real emotional power. Most commentators on the poem have noted appropriately that the mythic Sphinx's riddle ("What has one voice and walks on four legs in the morning, two at noon, and three in the evening?") effectively establishes the theme of identity. What has not generally been commented upon is that the Sphinx exists as both an African monument and a Greek myth (thus describing nicely Hayden's difficult crossroads) or for that matter the Sphinx's own "in-betweenness," half man and half animal. Extending the reading in this way is suggestive not only of "identity" as theme but also of the search for some ironic resignation to the bruising ideological battle. If there is some give here—toward acknowledging fate and the permanence of this dilemma— Hayden effectively maintains a mode of questioning. If none of the rest of the poems in the first section deal specifically with riddles, they do center the necessity of quest and interpretation. Pivotal words and phrases in the next six poems include: "puzzle," "dream," "theorem," "mirage," "stranger," "un-finished," "mysteria," and "pondering the logic."

More specifically, from a somewhat illusive and abstract "Sphinx," there is a move to a more direct exploration of the question of identity. Notably, identity seems to be not only knowledge of kin (or blood or roots), but also some evaluation of human frailty and the perplexing difficulty of black history. "The Dream (1863)" alternates the narration of a dying black slavewoman's relative indifference at the coming of the Jubilee with letter(s) from a Civil War soldier.[55] Certainly part of the poem's value, as Pontheolla Williams asserts, is its portrayal of a black soldier's determination and courage:

> and hope when these few lines reaches your hand they
> will fine you well. I am tired some but it is war you
> know and old jeff Davis muss be ketch an hung to a sour
> apple tree like it says in the song I see some akshun
> but that is what I listed for not to see the sights ha ha (lines 11–15)

But that is primarily a surface reading. What is crucial, as John Hatcher intuits, is the crisis between Sinda's "dream expectation" and the reality of freedom.

> The quarters now were lonely-still in willow dusk
> after the morning's ragged jubilo,
>   when laughing crying singing the folks went off
> with Marse Lincum's soldier boys.
>   But Sinda hiding would not follow them: those Buckras
> with their ornery
>   funning, cussed commands, oh they were not
> the hosts the dream had promised her. (lines 3–10)

Sinda's vaguely millennialist hope—the restoration (or resurrection) of the trinity "Cal and Joe / and Charlie sold to the ricefields oh sold away / a-many and a-many a long year ago" (23–25)—is dubious. The postemancipation reality is "ornery funning, cussed commands." While the poem taunts the reader somewhat with its measured sentimentalism—the "fevered, gasping" Sinda, who in falling mutters "Hep me Jesus," potentially straight out of *Gone With the Wind*—empathy is never abandoned. Cal's engaging vernacular balances the real with the possible and while Sinda is never ridiculed, her messianic urge, her desire for an improbable restoration is made suspect.

"Improbable restoration" is somewhat the topic too of "'Mystery Boy' Looks for Kin in Nashville." A direct meditation upon his anxiety about "naming," the poem is troubling memory work.

> Puzzle faces in the dying elms
> promise him treats if he will stay.
> Sometimes they hiss and spit at him
> like varmints caught
> in a thicket of butterflies. (lines 1–5)

This poem's possibility is exemplary of the quality of Hayden's judgment in insisting upon the mystery of some "private poems." One interpretive strategy is to deal with the poem as a somewhat direct representation of the anxiety generated by discovering the truth of his birth name. The title suggests (as might "hiss and spit") his Writer's Conference experience where, too, Hayden felt some difficulty in finding kin. Equally as compelling, however, is the suggestion that the lost name here has more to do with normative masculinity:

> From the road beyond the creepered walls
> they call to him now and then,
> and he'll take off in spite of the angry trees,
> hearing like the loudening of his heart
> the name he never can he never can repeat.
>
> And when he gets to where the voices were—
> Don't cry, his dollbaby wife implores;
> I know where they are, don't cry.
> We'll go and find them, we'll go
> and ask them for your name again. (lines 11–20)

The name here, Pontheolla Williams smartly suggests, may be "husband,"[56] although the comfort offered in the final stanza seems somewhat implausible, so that Fred Fetrow's suggestion that the poem is honorific of Erma Hayden's love and support seems unlikely. More than anything else the reader is left with a strong sense of the understandable psychic fragility of "mystery boy" and that "looking for kin" is not the simple reconstructive act that one might expect.

This reading sets up nicely "The Broken Dark," which focuses on a hospital stay in which Hayden found himself rooming with a dying man. Appro-

priately surreal and fragmented, it is also Hayden's first direct statement of
faith.

> Sleepless, I stare
> from the dark hospital room
> at shadows of a flower and its leaves
> the nightlight fixes like a blotto
> on the corridor wall. Shadow-plays
> of Bali—demons move to the left,
> gods, in their frangipani crowns
> and gold, to the right.
> Ah and my life
> in the shadow of God's laser light—
> shadow of deformed homunculus? (lines 1–11)

Hayden's despair (or that of the "I" persona) is life's indeterminacy. It is potentially just shadow-play or puppetry, or, more devastatingly, a "fool's er-
rand." "Son, go fetch a pint of pigeon's milk/ from the drugstore and be
quick." (l.12-14) The observation and meditation is concluded, however:

> Free of pain, my own death still
> a theorem to be proved.
> Alláh' u' Abbhá. O Healing Spirit,
> Thy nearness our forgiving cure. (lines 23–26)

John Hatcher points out that the last two lines are a clear paraphrase of a Baha'i prayer for healing, and that this is not an exclamation and instead quite
controlled. No commentator has pointed out, however, that "my own death
still a theorem to be proved" is strikingly close to Hayden's report of W. H.
Auden's injunction that good poetry is like "solving for x."

Metaphysical, personal, and historical anxiousness established by these
first four poems is temporarily put off by the relative clarity of the next two
in their dismissal of false paths. The figurative openness of "The Mirages,"
another private poem, is contrasted at some level with the explicitness of the
title and its repetition within the poem itself. A desert "stranger" relates an
irresistible temptation: "I knew what they were / yet often / changed my
course / and followed them" (lines 8–11). The relief is straightforward—
"Less lonely, less / lonely then" (12–13)—but they remain mirages just the
same. In similar fashion, "Soledad" rejects a more "material" option. The
poem relates the "blinded room" of an individual who chooses to be "cradled
by drugs." The poet's suspicion of this particular choice should not, however,
be framed in Puritan terms. Instead, more useful clues are to be found in
"Miles Davis coolly blows for him" and the poem's title. It is the insularity of
the persona portrayed that it is most important to challenge.[57]

The concluding poem of section I holds off chaos but does nothing to
put off the Sphinx's fateful questioning. In "Aunt Jemima of the Ocean
Waves" the poet is visited by a woman, formerly the "Sepia High Stepper,"

now a mere carnival freak. The poet feels that they are confederates, those who are "Enacting someone's notion of themselves / (and me)" (lines 1–2). What is crucial to this poem's effect is the restraint and articulation of the woman who finds herself in such odd straits. "So here I am, so here I am, / fake mammy to God's mistakes. / And that's the beauty part, / I mean ain't that the beauty part" (ll. 42–45). Most important in terms of her exchange with the poet is that when she laughs, he does "not, knowing what / her laughter shields. And mocks" (ll. 46–47). This poem is also important as a reminder of the not-so-fragile Hayden who was capable of effective work in an ironic mode.

The first section of *Words* nicely inscribes, then, the central components of Hayden's antimodern attitude. As John Hatcher insists, all readers must come to terms with Hayden's "religious feeling" (298). Hayden forthrightly makes his statement of faith and it clearly guards against despair while critiquing American culture's short-sightedness. And yet there is also the clear sense that systematic theological explanations are not up to the task, unaided, of measuring and relieving the difficult work of self-placement. What is most striking about this first group of poems, and indeed the book as a whole, is Hayden's skillful *intermixing* of the sacred and the secular. Its overall effect is toward reenchantment without being sectarian, and it certainly fiddles a bit around the question of teleological fixity.[58]

Section II continues to outline Hayden's worries. Much more focused now on questions of place—although identity questions are never far beneath the surface—Hayden is much more direct in his confrontation with American culture and history. The confident, knowing persona who can "gaze beyond the clutter" is more in control here. Hayden's public prophetic ambitions are nicely and effectively on display. "Locus" and "On Lookout Mountain" both utilize the landscape of the American South, and, in particular, striking resonances of both the Indian removal and the Civil War, to set up more contemporary allusions to violence and war. If "Locus" emphasizes the cyclical character of violence, "On Lookout Mountain" both points to the contemporary conflict in Vietnam and, more crucially, rebukes an idle and vain version of historical memory: "Sunday alpinists / pick views and souvenirs. . . . Behold how bright / upon the mountain the gadget feet / of trivia shine."(lines 13–14, 20–23) "Kodachromes of the Islands" also functions in this mode but instead relies upon images of Third World poverty as the starting point toward a radical reorientation. What a waste this history and practice of violence, the poet suggests; there is so much that is truly pressing to be done. "Zeus Over Redeye"—about the Redstone Nuclear Arsenal—is suggestive of how Hayden's symbolist technique and growing interest in classical mythology might be put toward a compelling cultural criticism. "I feel as though invisible fuses were / burning all around us burning all / around us. Heat-quiverings twitch danger's hypersensitive skin. / The very sunlight here seems flammable. And shadows give us no relieving shade" (26–32).

"Unidentified Flying Object" concludes this section and is quite interesting for the ways it has tripped up critics who struggle to identify its tone. The poem recounts the disappearance of a black woman, a cook, Mattie Lee. Will—who imagines her "every teasing brown / he's ever wanted—tries to convince a neighbor that she has escaped to a space ship. Pontheolla Williams describes this as the book's "light moment" and John Hatcher as a "humorous anecdotal narrative" (170). If this is a joke it is an evil joke. The extended description of the escape is at some level an escape fantasy, emphasized by Mattie Lee's "sunflower hat," the sunflower being for Hayden a symbol of hope. And the "space" theme is one that Hayden will come back to over and over in the 1970s, imagined space travel and moon walks the substitute on occasion for real relief from a violent culture. But perhaps more important is that this is "Will's tale," or even, perhaps, "the will's tale," indicative of the absurd lies by which the reality of violence is repressed within the culture at large.

To this point there is significant poetic accomplishment, but it is, in some ways, mere set-up for a powerful third section. The two striking elegies that make up this section are fundamental to any appreciation of African-American culture and the American sixties. "El-Hajj Malik El-Shabazz" is, as is often pointed out, perhaps the most accomplished of the many memorializations of the life and death of Malcolm X. This assertion is not without some danger. Hayden's emphasis upon Malcolm's hejira as completion can be seen as ideologically dishonest, just as it can be seen as aesthetically (and ideologically) satisfying. And insofar as Hayden chooses to repeat the now familiar naming associated with the chapter titles from *The Autobiography of Malcolm X*—Homeboy, Detroit Red, Satan—it can come dangerously close to feeling programmatic. Hayden resists this closure by insightfully unpacking Malcolm's life *before* his final metamorphosis. There is nothing but clarity in the condemnation of "The icy evil that struck his father down / and ravished his mother into madness / trapped him in violence of a punished self / struggling to be free (I, lines 1–4). (Worth noting too is the irony in "a racist Allah pledged to wrest him from / the hellward-thrusting hands of Calvin's Christ" [II. 9–10] as related to Hayden's escape from the Baptist faith to that of the Baha'i.) Later Hayden asserts that in "becoming his people's anger" Malcolm attempted a separation from whiteness, but, he says: "Rejecting Ahab, he was of Ahab's tribe. / 'Strike through the mask!'" (III. 8–9). Hayden treats fairly Malcolm's struggle and, if his sympathies are foregone conclusions, asserts real complexity.

The second elegy, "Words in the Mourning Time," begins conventionally as grieving for and meditation upon the lives of Martin Luther King and Robert Kennedy. There is immediate resonance with Walt Whitman's "When Lilacs Last in the Dooryard Bloom'd." Like Whitman, Hayden struggles to resolve his personal ethos and faith with the emerging reality of American life. If however, Whitman chooses to radically allegorize his attempts at resolution, Hayden chooses to remain fully engaged with the public sphere, and in

some ways—regardless of whether or not one accepts the Baha'i understanding of history—his encounter with America's self-destructiveness is
more complete. Whitman's symbolic structure is not so much indeterminate
as inconsistent; Hayden strikingly descends toward the chaos that Whitman
dares not approach. This disorder is at least partially captured through the
poem's varied formal structure. The poem is made up of ten sections that
differ greatly in their length, meter, and placement on the page. Section two,
for instance, states simply: "Killing people to save, to free them? / With na-
palm lighting routes to the future?" (II. 1–2), whereas section ten—which begins, reminiscent of Whitman's "Song of Myself," "And all the atoms cry
aloud"—consists of eleven triplets. What is consistent in sections two through
nine is a set of challenges to the "process, major means whereby, / oh dread-
fully, our humanness must be achieved" (I. 11–12).

These challenges take the forms of horrific specters of war ("flamed-out
eyes, / their sockets dripping. The nightmare mouth" [III. 2–3]). and personal meditations on how war may and has come home. Of special importance, Hayden reflects on his own students doing the killing and, quite
provocatively, connects this vision to a previous obsession with his own
death. Increasingly, as the poem evolves, even in the midst of chaos ("Lord
Riot") he becomes more capable of direct statement. "We hate kill destroy /
in the name of human good / our killing and our hate destroy" (V. 6–8). In
the wilderness, he discovers a redeeming voice: "Oh, master now love's instruments— /complex and not for the fearful, / simple and not for the fool-
ish. / Master now love's instruments" (VII. 8–11). In some sense, the challenge to impose order becomes more difficult:

> As the gook woman howls
> for her boy in the smouldering,
> as the expendable Clean-Cut Boys
> From Decent American Homes
> are slashing off enemy ears for keepsakes; . . . (IX. 1–4)
>
> what can I say
> but this, this:
>
> We must not be frightened nor cajoled
> into accepting evil as deliverance from evil. (IX. 7–10)

The final section is a Baha'i prayer. John Hatcher (171–74) insists upon an
orthodox Baha'i interpretation of the whole poem, and yet the quality of
Hayden's representation throughout the poem is so strong that certainties
upon which to insist are increasingly difficult to sustain. Hayden concludes:
"towards Him our history in its disastrous quest / for meaning is impelled"
(X. 33–34).

These two elegies are striking in their commitment to humanistic transformation and their willingness to "call America out of its name." Hayden
affirms Malcolm's pain and his transformation; he rejects the "monsters of

abstraction" and killing done by "Clean-Cut Boys." Identity-work is put aside, and yet the confidence with which Hayden is able to confront the horror he observes seems clearly a product of his continued insistence upon the necessity of his ability to name the self and thus hold fast to a deeply felt set of values.

The first five of the final six poems, in the fourth section, seek to offer comfort to both poet and readers overwhelmed by the "disastrous quest." Art itself in "Monet's Waterlilies" and, to a lesser extent, "The Return" is, not surprisingly, a source for survival. "October" is the most interesting of the poems as it juggles a set of seasonal, religious, historic, and personal allusions: the period of dying (and implied rebirth), the birth of the Báb, one of the two founders of the Baha'i faith, and the birth of the Hayden's daughter, Maia. (Less likely intended by Hayden but, of course, available to the reader is the association of October with revolution.) These poems do indeed provide comfort and significantly not by abandoning history. The first words of Part IV are "Today as the news from Selma and Saigon / poisons the air like fallout" ("Monet's Waterlilies," lines 1–2). If this is a celebration of the aesthetic, it is not fearful of struggle. At another level, however, these poems feel "occasional." The meaning quest is more fully implicated in the two elegies themselves, and Hayden's closing poem, an elegy too perhaps, is certainly fully in an elegiac mode.

But those who are judged to have lived a life of surpassing holiness — these are they who are released and set free from confinement in these regions of the earth, and passing upward to their pure abode, make their dwelling upon the earth's surface. And of these such as have purified themselves sufficiently by philosophy live thereafter altogether without bodies, and reach habitations even more beautiful, which it is not easy to portray — nor is there time to do so now. But the reasons which we have already described provide ground enough, as you can see, Simmias, for leaving nothing undone to attain during life some measure of goodness and wisdom, for the prize is glorious and the hope great.

SOCRATES IN PLATO'S *Phaedo*[59]

The final poem in *Words in the Mourning Time*, "A Plague of Starlings," is a disturbing vision. The poem's subtitle, "Fisk Campus," and the work that Hayden wishes the poem to do in "summing up" the sixties bring back to our attention the "primal scene" of the First Black Writers Conference. The poem tells the story of an infestation of the campus with starlings sometime during the mid-sixties. Campus staff had to resort to killing the birds one by one, and the campus was haunted by gunfire throughout the night: "Evenings I hear / the workmen fire / into the stiff / magnolia leaves, / routing the starlings / gathered noisy and / befouling there" (lines 1–7). Hayden's poetic representation of the "event" is some kind of "aftermath": images of avoiding, stepping around, bodies, is as evil a vision as can be imagined. Most disturbing to the knowledgeable reader is that starlings are a vibrantly black bird, but no one's favorite. They are infamous for laying their eggs in the nest of another bird, and then driving the bird from its home. Yet Hayden's poem does not so much judge their actions as portray (with a kind of dispassion that betrays a horror) the systematic killing of the "intruders" by "workers." If Hayden is shaken by the disturbance they have generated—by their "defouling"—he is equally disturbed by their inhuman disposal and execution. It might bring to mind images of troops in Detroit, FBI agents in Chicago, and even U.S. forces in Vietnam "clearing" a village. "Spoiled trees" are the result of gunfire as much as they are of the plague of misguided birds. Moreover, we must recognize, "The spared return, / when the guns are through, / to the spoiled trees / like choiceless poor / to a dangerous dwelling place, / chitter and quarrel / in the piercing dark / above the killed" (16–24). Where else are they to go?

Hayden consciously, and perhaps desperately, clings to the Socratic vision of holiness and immortality.

> Mornings, I pick
> my way past death's
> black droppings:
> on campus lawns and streets
> the troublesome
> starlings
> frost-salted lie,
> troublesome still.
>
> And if not careful
> I shall tread
> upon carcasses
> carcasses when I
> go mornings now
> to lecture on
> what Socrates,
> the hemlock hour nigh,
> told sorrowing
> Phaedo and the rest
> about the migratory
> habits of the soul (lines 25–45)

Surely, in the midst of all this violence, this must still be a possibility. But the hemlock, like the cancer beginning in Hayden's body that will torment him throughout the 1970s, makes of this an urgency as well as a hope. The poem's end is not so much an affirmation of timeless and universal art as it is an acknowledgment of all "ends." For Hayden, the continued "troublesome-ness" of the birds is a mark of similarity, a sign of kinship.

While the Fisk identity drama is crucial to an understanding of Hayden's accomplishment as poet and public intellectual, less than careful readings of it lead to the loss of its most interesting dynamic. From these readings, Hayden is either a "universalist" (and thus heroic and martyred) or "Euro-centric" (and thus tragic and duped). This binary construction, an aesthetic and cultural trench warfare, divests Hayden of a great deal of complexity. What makes Hayden such an interesting culture critic and what at least partially defines his antimodern outlook is his creative suspension between these two poles. *Words in the Mourning Time*, Hayden's most important collection of poetry, cannot adequately be interpreted with either simplification. While Hayden certainly continues to articulate his discomfort with the cultural nationalist ethos, too little attention paid to Hayden's challenge to and confrontation with white racism (and its counterpart white provincialism) foregrounds the possible use of his poetry by reactionary forces. The fundamental paradox in our understanding of Hayden's place in the American and African-American literary canon (and the status of *Words*, in particular) has been the assertion on the one hand of Hayden's universalism, while on the other hand noting admiringly his poetic reconstruction of African-American history.

At some level this must remain a paradox. Hayden's Baha'i faith certainly complicates matters by placing between himself and audiences a kind of comprehensive explanatory device, a shortcut of sorts, that often divests him of the responsibility of explaining carefully his understanding of events. On the other hand, Hayden's "religious feeling" is an obvious part of his dismissal of a despiritualized nation and its propensity to violence. In a similar fashion, Hayden's own ready and much repeated invocation of lessons learned from W. H. Auden and William Butler Yeats also tends to obfuscate; he oversimplifies Auden's own struggle to come to a full understanding of the relationship between poetry and politics and Yeats's commitment to "Irish-ness." (Nowhere does Hayden articulate in any depth his encounter with either man's life or career.) Somehow, however, *Words in the Mourning Time* transcends this kind of silencing. Hayden successfully articulates the myopic limitations of an impermeable nationalism. Any knee-jerk rejection of identity politics as not poetry's subject, however, is confused by Hayden's own obsession with the self. Admittedly, this self is not only racialized: Hayden writes about the body, sexuality, family, religion, being a poet, and being an adopted son. *Words in the Mourning Time* is successful because of the ways in which the negation of accepted truths is always the primary task. At the precipice, Hayden's dread in the face of our barbarity is tempered by the integrity of his search. The obvious but still elegant pun in the book and poem's title speaks to the contingency and possibility of hope.

STRUCTURE AND SATURATION: THE LEGACY OF AFRICAN-AMERICAN POETICS AND THE AMERICAN SIXTIES

> Sometimes a poet in his effort at self-revelation moves outside of
> the immediate concerns of the Black community. Some of the
> poems of Mari Evans, Gwendolyn Brooks, and Robert Hayden ap-
> pear to do this. Nevertheless, our mere awareness of them as Black
> persons helps to shape our response to the poem, and this is so
> whether or not the poet wants us to consider him as other than a
> poet pure and simple, or for that matter pure and complex. The fact
> of the matter is that the Black community does not intend to give
> up any of its beautiful singers, whether Countee Cullen or Melvin
> Tolson or Robert Hayden. We may quarrel with them sometimes,
> but ain't never gonna say good-bye.
>
> STEPHEN HENDERSON, *Understanding the New Black Poetry* (1973)[60]

Margaret Danner's defense of the African-American modernists at the Second Fisk Conference reemphasized the importance of history, and the necessity of resisting constructions of sixties accomplishment as simplistically
"revolutionary." Questions of tradition and authenticity are best worked out
within the context of a historical dialectic that constantly constructs and deconstructs itself. In "The Forms of Things Unknown," Stephen Henderson's
introduction to his seminal anthology *Understanding the New Black Poetry*
(1973), an attempt was made to demonstrate the formal basis of an African-
American poetic tradition. For Henderson it is crucial that "an attempt
should be made in which the *continuity* and the *wholeness* of the Black poetic
tradition in the United States are suggested (3). Kimberly Benston noted an
"absence of reading" and suggested a re/placing of critical debate and poetic
tradition that saw the reading of texts as enacting the structural dialogism.
Part of my argument has been to suggest that "re/placing" debate may not
require abandoning the discourse of "blackness" at all. As Henderson suggests:

> For Blacks the celebration of Blackness is an undertaking which makes
> value judgments, some of which certainly many American whites
> would reject. Nonetheless, if a Black celebratory poem is to be *under-
> stood* on the most elementary level it must be on these terms. There are
> none others that are valid. (66)

It is that process of "value judgment" and its relationship that I have been
trying to isolate—and, not incidentally, to suggest that such a *process* has
significant culture-critical potential. Between structure and essence may lie
the biographically peculiar, the ways that individuals are drawn into various
discourses both in and beyond their control.

In terms of understanding the legacy of African-American poetry in the
sixties, Houston Baker has effectively documented the ways in which this dis-

course chronicles a "paradigmatic shift," in Thomas Kuhn's sense.[61] "Black-ness"—a critical and complex blackness, not necessarily chauvinistic, related (in a familial way) to that of Hawthorne, Poe, and Melville—makes its last stand during the decade. Still, there seems to be a "plural unity" within African-American poetic production itself.[62] The issue is not the way in which late African-American poetic modernism holds out against the black aesthetic, but rather the way in which the conditions of African-American in-tellectual life are shared. The "militant" Stephen Henderson has suggested:

> Ultimately, the "beautiful" is bound up with the truth of a people's his-tory (as they perceive it themselves), and if their vision is clear, its recording just, others may perceive that justness too; and, if they bring to it the proper sympathy and humility, they may even share in the general energy, if not the specific content of that vision. (4)

The attempt here has been to assign to history—as did Hayden himself—the greatest of importance by assigning it the greatest of complexity.

> What most of the militants are asking is not separation, but to be included in—not as supplicants, but as owners, as entrepreneurs—to have a share of the wealth and a piece of the action. And this is precisely what the Federal central target of the new approach ought to be. It ought to be oriented toward more black ownership, for from this can flow the rest—black pride, black jobs, black opportu-nity and yes, black power.
>
> RICHARD NIXON (1968)[63]

> So Black Power is now a part of the nomenclature of the national community. To some it is abhorrent, to others dynamic; to some it is repugnant, to others exhilarating; to some it is destructive; to oth-ers it is useful. Since Black Power means different things to different people and indeed, being essentially an emotional concept, can mean different things to the same people on differing occasions, it is impossible to attribute its ultimate meaning to any single indi-vidual or organization. One must look beyond personal styles, ver-bal flourishes, and the hysteria of the mass media to assess its val-ues, its assets and liabilities honestly.
>
> MARTIN LUTHER KING, JR. (1967)[64]

The day after the infamous panel at Fisk, Hayden read his poetry. David Llorens reported that Hayden "masterfully engaged his audience." This is not so much a truce or reintegration or even contradiction as it is the commu-nity's ability to effectively maintain two or more discourses of challenge and appreciation simultaneously. The "reclaiming" of Robert Hayden demon-strates unity in the commitment to resist the homogenizing, banalizing tendencies within contemporary American culture, even as there is disagreement as to strategies, disguises, and the attestation of aesthetic value. This is similar to saying that ragtime and bebop are different ways of improvising, different ways of being within and without African-American culture.

The stakes involved in the kind of storytelling undertaken in this chapter are, however, significant. In William Rice's *New Criterion* essay "The Example of Robert Hayden," it is suggested that:

> Robert Hayden's achievement is all the more admirable for the courage he showed when circumstances required. . . . To a surprising degree, those circumstances are still with us. The militants of the 1960's gain little notice now in the culture at large, but in the academy a self-interested critic or poet may find it hard to resist the fashion that relates art and vision insistently to race, class, and gender. . . . If the new academic fashion widens Robert Hayden's readership, it will be mainly for the wrong reason—the isolated fact of his skin color. . . .[67]

In their history of American literature, Richard Ruland and Malcolm Bradbury suggest that the "work of Robert Hayden stands as an implicit rejoinder to Baraka and a powerful argument for a more fully formed—and informed—vision."[66] The neoconservative appropriation of Hayden as a prophet of the universal is such a partial picture as to be a radical distortion. More importantly, it dismisses the complexity that was at the core of Hayden's art and public persona, and imagines African-American literature as being primarily about one group of black folk correcting another.

James Clifford's question "What is torn off to make public discourse believable?" is especially pertinent when dealing with matters of cultural boundaries and identities. Richard Nixon's endorsement of Black Power suggests ways in which discourses can be compromised. The necessary tearing may be to remove cultural doubt within dramas of self-presentation; an alternative is a strategy of familial conversion that suggests a commitment based upon the preservation of conversation and exchange. Hayden's response—as a challenge to the continual fragmentation of the self in the face of modernity—is hopefully as valuable to us as is Melvin Tolson's tricksterism, or Gwendolyn Brooks's conversion. We should not, however, see Hayden's experience in the sixties as tragic. History is necessity here too. To be a good "liar"—in the African-American sense of the word—you do need a good remembrance. Perhaps there is no better commentary on the ways in which we have problematized questions of moral responsibility in our embrace of indeterminacy. Hayden could juggle self-images[67] *and* write the most enduring and powerful body of African-American historical poems that we may ever see.[68]

CHAPTER THREE

MODERN DOUBT TO ANTIMODERN COMMITMENT

PAULE MARSHALL AND WILLIAM DEMBY

The American writer inhabits a country at once the dream of Europe and a fact of history; he lives on the last horizon of an endlessly retreating vision of innocence—on the "frontier," which is to say, the margin where the theory of original goodness and the fact of original sin come face to face. To express this "blackness ten times black" and to live by it in a society in which, since the decline of orthodox Puritanism, optimism has become the chief effective religion, is a complex and difficult task.

LESLIE FIEDLER, *Love and Death in the American Novel* (1960)[1]

If we wish to reply to the expectations of the people of Europe, it is no good sending them back a reflection, even an ideal reflection, of their society and their thought with which from time to time they feel immeasurably sickened. . . . For Europe, for ourselves, and for humanity, comrades, we must turn over a new leaf, we must work out new concepts, and try to set afoot a new man.

FRANZ FANON, *The Wretched of the Earth* (1961)[2]

It is typical to invoke in accounts of sixties American cultural history the moral devastation of the Vietnam War. This is appropriate given the great rift in American life it created, the range of imaginative responses it elicited, and the significant investment of intellectual energy it demanded. But the Vietnam War does not represent the whole of the imaginative encounter with wars of decolonization in the sixties. Not surprisingly, wars of liberation fought on the African continent were of great concern to African-American artists and intellectuals. While W.E.B. Du Bois's dreams for a grand Pan-African coalition were never realized, the process by which African nations organized and fought for their independence from the imperial powers inspired a wide range of black creative intellectuals in the United States

78

to rethink accepted strategies of gradual acceptance into the Enlightenment inspired American polity.

There is both popular and high cultural evidence of this encounter and enthusiasm. Fifties and early sixties jazz was greatly influenced by this emergent consciousness of decolonization. Album titles and the names of individual songs were peppered with the evidence of this awakening: John Coltrane's *Africa/Brass* and *Dakar*, Dizzy Gillespie's "Tunisian Fantasy," Max Roach's "Tears for Johannesburg," or Sonny Rollins's "Airegin" ("Nigeria" backwards), to name just a few. The development of African-American literary and cultural institutions was increasingly shaped by and connected to knowledge of anticolonial battles. The American Society for African Culture organized the first "Negro Writers Conference" in 1959; it set up a number of centers in major American cities for conversations about U.S.-African cultural relations. *Negro Digest* regularly carried accounts of developments in Africa and published a number of articles about the interrelationship of African-American and African literatures. In general, while not all was done with great depth, and while there was still an awareness of real cultural distance, the African-American creative intellectual looked at these international developments admiringly, and perhaps with a certain amount of envy.[3]

Some battles outside continental Africa (but not necessarily outside the African diaspora) also caught the imagination of black creative intellectuals. No small number of African-American writers were impacted by the Cuban revolution. LeRoi Jones's famous essay "Cuba Libre" was his response to the optimism of the revolution as he experienced it in June and July of 1960; indeed, in many ways, the revolution was Jones's political awakening.[4] African-Americans became very much a part of the solidarity with Cuba movement and no doubt its geographic proximity increased hopefulness about imminent change in the United States. More important than the advancement of any particular version of left wing politics, what was most striking about the Cuban struggle to African-Americans was the idea that things could be dramatically overturned. And violence was not necessarily negative. A columnist for the *Afro Magazine*, Ralph Matthews, wrote:

> Every white man who cuffs, beats, deprives and abuses even the lowest colored person, simply because he is white and the other colored, should have seared upon his consciousness the fact that it is possible for the tables to be turned. Castro has proved it in our time.[5]

The idea of revolution functioned in a fashion similar to that of "conversion." It suggested—oftentimes with little or no ideological specificity—the possibility of starting anew.

One might make the argument, however, that it was the Algerian revolution, in particular, that had the greatest long-term impact on African-American intellectual life. On November 1, 1954, the Front de Libération Nationale (FLN), frustrated with the pace of change and dissatisfied with the parliamentary assembly set up by the Algerian Organic Statute (1947), began a series of attacks on government buildings and military posts; by 1956 the war had spread to the city of Algiers, and the use of terrorism was common. Random attacks on schools, cafés, and businesses were meant to demoralize the French colons. This effort was certainly successful, although it brought about a fierce counterterrorism. Eventually 400,000 French troops were stationed in Algeria; as many French men fought in Algeria as did Americans in Vietnam—representing, however, a much higher proportion of the eligible population. The French government—perhaps humiliated by the recent defeat at Dien Bien Phu—gave the military incredible latitude in conducting war on the FLN. The state effectively sanctioned the use of torture and refused to condemn the indiscriminate killing of Muslim civilians. The Algerian conflict and the response of the French intelligentsia was prophetic of the kinds of panic invoked in modern Western states confronted with a new kind of total war. When the fighting reached Algiers, an urban environment shaped by unjust racial economies, and panic ensued—indeed, the very existence of the French state was threatened—European public intellectuals were faced with their most challenging dilemma since the beginning of World War II. Very quickly Algeria became "une bataille de l'écrit."[6]

Algeria also brought to prominence the Martiniquan psychiatrist Franz Fanon and established him as the major theorist of "post-coloniality." While Fanon is not the only anticolonial intellectual and statesman to become part of the African-American consciousness—Amilcar Cabral, Aimé Cesaire, Kenneth Kaunda, Jomo Kenyatta, Patrice Lumumba, Tom Mboya, Kwame Nkrumah, Leopold Senghor, and, to a much lesser extent, C.L.R. James, Norman Manley, and George Padmore all had some impact—he resonated strongly with African-American sensibilities and traditions. *Black Skin, White Masks* extends in interesting ways the psychologizing of the "black experience" as pursued by W.E.B. Du Bois in *The Souls of Black Folk*. "Like the African-American," writes Lewis Gordon, "Fanon finds himself inextricably linked to the society that not only rejects him, but also tries to deny his existence as a legitimate point of view. . . ."[7]

For the purposes of this book, what is worth recounting, if only in passing, is the comprehensiveness of Fanon's critique. Lewis Gordon argues that Fanon's writing is best understood as a "critique of European Man," confronting the "nightmare of racist reason." Fanon insists that everyone must acknowledge how the Enlightenment project is infected by the negation of black existence. He insists that we recognize the ways in which "white man"/"white culture" has implicitly stood for humankind.[8] This attempt to insist upon a strategy that is simultaneously humanist and one that is "negating of accepted truths" is nicely descriptive of the antimodern ethos. While it is certainly true that his name would be invoked by many more individuals than had, perhaps, actually read his work, Fanon remains an important emblem of the total critique of the West in the American sixties.

The Algerian War is an important, if indirect, historical background to two sixties novels, Paule Marshall's *The Chosen Place, The Timeless People* and William Demby's *The Catacombs*. It serves to connect each writer across geographical space, but, more importantly, it is a catalyst for reflection if not the shaping of a particular world view. The North African conflagration, more than any other war of liberation, served to set the terms for ruthless confrontations with imperial power and equally ruthless counterinsurgencies. The FLN's challenge to the European settler culture and political control from Paris through the establishment of terror tactics is suggestive of the ways in which subject peoples had come to increasingly reject modernity's promise of reason-based political progress. As important was the limited ability of both the French Left and Right to conduct sustained protest against the state-sanctioned use of torture. The anxiety invoked or instigated by this difficulty with attention span raised questions about the very ability of "writing" to respond adequately to the modern world. John Talbott describes this as the onset of "a sort of moral numbness which made even death, torture, and humiliation seem boring."[9] Simone de Beauvoir complained of suffering in "this sinister month of December 1961, like many of my fellow men . . . from a kind of tetanus of the imagination." Marshall's and Demby's books can be read as responses to this paralysis.

Algeria is compelling evidence of the dialectic of enlightenment: on the one hand, it is the will to liberation, while on the other it is irrationality masking as reason. African-American fiction of the American Sixties has been too rarely read in the context of this international crisis of faith and the will to power.

DESPITE THE NOTORIOUS character of a few texts published toward the end of the decade, the sixties African-American novel has an amorphous quality. After the dramatic statement of Ralph Ellison's *Invisible Man* (1952) and James Baldwin's *Go Tell It on the Mountain* (1953), novelistic development meanders.[10] The publication of texts like Cecil Brown's *The Life and Loves of Mr. Jiveass Nigger* (1969), Sam Greenlee's *The Spook Who Sat by the Door* (1969), Clarence Major's *All Night Visitors* (1969), and Ishmael Reed's *The Freelance Pallbearers* (1967) were clearly indicative of discomfort with the "respectability" still demanded of African-American letters, but these novels never coalesced into a cohesive counterstatement. Major, Reed, and Brown, in particular, drew upon the tradition of "modernist black humor"—that is, they seem to have read carefully Joseph Heller, Thomas Pynchon, and Norman Mailer, as carefully as Richard Wright, James Baldwin, and Ralph Ellison— but no consensus emerged about the direction of the novel, nor the role of the African-American novelist in the context of American culture. The novelists are simultaneously alienated from the emergent Black Arts ethos, from the "direct" statement, and from an emergent postmodernism, "the literature of exhaustion,"[11] and its various chimeras, labyrinths, and funhouses.

The decade was not without some dramatic successes: William Melvin

Kelley's *A Different Drummer* (1962), John A. Williams's *Sissie* (1963), and *The Man Who Cried I Am* (1967), Hal Bennett's *The Wilderness of Vines* (1967), and the above mentioned Major and Reed texts received well-deserved critical attention. These texts were variously formally inventive, astute in their culture criticism, or elegant in conception and execution. They were, in other words, provocative. More indicative, however, of the decade were the numerous contributions of other writers, both extremely skilled and less so, that seemed to attempt to negotiate the moral politics of the fifties (or earlier) in the critical terrain of the sixties. Writers like Kristin Hunter, Ronald Fair, Ernest Gaines, Margaret Walker, Gordon Parks, and John Killens wrote personal, if not historically idiosyncratic, texts that attempted to refigure the significance of narrative within the emerging universe of Black Power and Black Arts.[12] Realism was by no means passé, but it was as if the very *location* of their written acts (within a nexus of Euro-generated novelistic convention) conspired against the emergence of a coherent voice that would be both transgressive and beautiful. If the "new Black poetry" (and theater and music) could rely upon a kind of guerrilla warfare against American culture, could "attack" orthodoxy and expectation, the novelist was tripped up by form, and the commitment it represented.[13] Whether conceived of as an extended consideration of sensibility and consciousness, or as the analysis of society, the novel guarded against the establishment of a cultural revolution. Ironically, the great sixties African-American novel(s) could be negotiated from outside the real and symbolic geography of the United States. The expression of discomfort with the "official religion" of optimism required complexity, and, as such, the short, sharp statement, the fictive equivalent of Black Arts poetry, would not be sufficient.

Consistent with this dilemma, there are few manifestos about the black novel similar to those numerous documents which tried to articulate the shape of an authentic black poetry. Exceptions might include some of Ishmael Reed's *Yardbird* writing, but these pieces, while contentious and meant to irritate the most committed of Black Arts followers, were usually focused on general questions of aesthetics, rather than the development of the novel as a specific genre. More importantly, his approach was to emphasize the flexibility of generic boundaries and criticize all conceptions of authenticity.[14] Larry Neal's influential essays on Richard Wright, Ralph Ellison, and James Baldwin, printed in a series as "The Role of the Black Writer," while clearly a more pointed attempt to talk about the paradigmatic power of blackness, rarely spoke to the specifics of the novel as form.[15] Indeed, Neal seemed to suspect that the form itself was irredeemable; it was too Western, too distant from the "community." Arthur Davis and Melvin and Margaret Wade surveyed the terrain of the decade but either saw things as inchoate, or utilized a loose Black Arts critical vocabulary to speculate on the novelistic tradition as the playing out of a specific set of themes.[16] No one felt confident enough to speak in any kind of extended fashion about the "new Black novel," the "Black Arts novel," or the "Black Power novel."

Other trends and developments, however, mitigated against the abandonment of the novel as a productive cultural enterprise. In contrast to the lack of aesthetic manifestos, there was a large amount of scholarly writing about African-American fiction that came to the fore. Much of it was limited in insight and somewhat opportunistic, but as part of a general cultural awakening to the richness of African-American culture, seminal works of African-American criticism from the past were reprinted, and a few new works were truly innovative. While attention is often drawn to the work of David Littlejohn, Edward Margolies, and Robert Bone, all white scholars — writing within what now feel like limited critical frameworks — it should not be overlooked that pioneering texts in African-American literary criticism by Hugh Gloster, Benjamin Brawley, and Vernon Loggins were also reprinted within this period.[17]

The controversy surrounding William Styron's *The Confessions of Nat Turner* demonstrated that the novel still had the ability to focus public attention on matters of central cultural concern. Indeed, much of the debate surrounding the *writing* and reception of that text might be seen as a result of the ascendancy of a combative historicism and its metaphors of memory and recovery. If the novel was not the best place to inscribe and perform the elements of a new Black aesthetic, it was still a significant symbol of cultural power, an emblem of authority, and a useful vehicle for the negotiation of cultural values. In support of this book's reinterpretation of sixties African-American culture, it is important to note the ways in which that controversy was linked directly to questions of memory, if not variant philosophies of history and "retellings." While few individuals comfortably articulated the commonplace assertion of previous generations — that accomplishments in the arts and the recovery of the past would lead to the concrete improvement of the conditions of black life — challenges to Styron's particular ideological perspective and the efficacy of his historical recovery suggest that memory was recognized as a fundamental site for the negotiation of cultural authority.

Of course, we would be well instructed to take seriously here the cautionary words of Warner Berthoff, who has described all of post-1945 American literature as "without qualities."[18] If the tradition of the American novel is decentered, it may have been indicative of powerful changes within the culture at large, and a profound ambivalence about the shape and direction of the novel in post-Sputnik, post-Kennedy, post-Watts America. The contemporary American novel may indeed be less likely to be explicitly oppositional. Moreover, in an age with a short attention span, questions of canon construction may soon become moot. Granting the slippery character of the boundaries of particular American cultural traditions should not, however, preclude critical attempts to evaluate the disruptive accomplishment of individual novels. Neither should it put an end to the articulation of arguments for the centrality of particular books in the African-American or American literary canons. Given a radically plural cultural milieu, it may be an error to abandon the task of discussing what is best. It is, after all is said and done, the opportunity to describe a more accurate picture of American cultural accomplishment. A commitment to this kind of narrative provides the opportunity (and demands the responsibility) to give testimony to the dynamism of the very pluralism that complicates our task.

First and foremost, then, the task of this chapter is to make an argument for the accomplishment of two writers, Paule Marshall and William Demby, who work, in many respects, in exile. These writers not only reflect the cultural dilemmas described above, but suggest compelling, if tentative, solutions. As is always the case, by articulating a different interpretive paradigm or starting point—antimodernism—there are new opportunities to reconsider consensus narratives around questions of canon formation, and in this case to bring about a kind of repatriation.

It is from the position of transnationality[19] that both Marshall and Demby develop an "antimodern voice." A critical voice is articulated, not so much in the discovery of perspective, but in the establishment of a ritual space in which history can be relived and change imagined. It can be convincingly argued that rather than seeing these writers through one of the dominant critical categories of the day—the poetics of integration—they be considered instead as authors of dis-integration. Such a refocus not only allows for an ideological reconsideration, but also clarifies the two writers' experiments with form. Ironically, Marshall's *The Chosen Place, The Timeless People* and Demby's *The Catacombs* have themselves, like their creators, existed in a kind of critical banishment.[20] Neither has received much attention, in either the celebration of black feminism or the discovery of African-American postmodernism. In addition to identifying each text and author as exemplary of African-American antimodernism, the question of the reputation of each text and the authors' culture criticism deserves to be reopened.

The fundamental starting point of this chapter is that Demby and Marshall's consciousness is not false—in the sense that their works do not bluntly mimic (or reject) the emergent rhetoric of black power—but is instead invested with a significant and thoughtful "indirection." Both writers insistently speak to the relationship of text and context, such that cultural critical questions can never be dismissed or displaced in favor of the aesthetic. They are suggestive of grounds for action, even responsibility, as existing in the space somewhere *between* their literary dystopias and the hegemonic ideology of progress. As we might expect, the result has been the marginalization of these efforts—and writers—as they did not readily conform to either the mainstream or those sixties writing practices considered potentially of most resistance. Their response to "late capitalism"[21] is neither neoentrepreneurialism, racial chauvinism, nor vulgar Marxism. Rather, it is closer to what Cornel West calls prophetic pragmatism, a paradoxical desire for a transformative conservatism. The difference *between* Demby and Marshall, as to narrative strategy and the meaning of historical recovery, however, is again suggestive of the scope of African-American antimodernism as a way of talking about literature and culture. There is significant ideological and philosophic agreement between the two writers, an agreement that substantively distances them from "official optimism."

INNOVATIVE LIVING: MARSHALL'S *THE CHOSEN PLACE, THE TIMELESS PEOPLE*

> A thing is at the same time its opposite, and . . . the contradictions make up the whole.
>
> PAULE MARSHALL, "The Poets in the Kitchen"[22]

> The curious extremity of ambivalent rebellion in *The Chosen Place, The Timeless People*, touches a "point" that allows us to chart a parallel to Poe's *Pym* and the succession of abortive mutinies against captain(s) block. In Paule Marshall's novel, the ground of failed mutiny is less obvious, the hierarchy of block commanders of the globe less sensational or immediately apparent. The emphasis upon commander and commanded actually shifts into a disequilibrium between commanding, material culture (associated with the rich, Western world) and commanded, subject crew (associated with ex-slave, colonial world). That shift adorns itself in the mechanics of the age, machinery, technology, into which is fed a Bournehills Icarus falling in the sky of civilization.
>
> WILSON HARRIS, *The Womb of Space*[23]

If two general tasks (among many) of this book have been to raise questions about issues of intercultural entanglement and the necessity of making oneself anew in an America haunted by race then Paule Marshall's novel, *The Chosen Place, The Timeless People*, is a useful point of discussion. Perhaps no imaginative work of literature in the sixties demonstrates such a demanding allegiance to pluralism (locating in "multiplicity" the desire to consolidate) *and* difference (the continuous frustration of that desire). Her dramatis personae is multifarious; it inscribes difference in numerous ways. Readers struggle not only with the challenges of race, but also with gender, class, nationality, vocation, sexuality, and, most importantly, the nature and interpretation of history. Barbara Christian suggests that:

> Because her major characters represent all aspects of the Western world, black and white, male and female, Jew and Anglo-Saxon, upper, middle, and working classes, natives and outsiders, Marshall creates a microcosm representative not only of Bournehills but also of other "underdeveloped" societies in the Third World, held captive both psychologically and economically by the metropolises of the West, yet somehow possessing their own visions of possibility.[24]

In forcing readers to grapple with the paradox of possibility within captivity, Marshall demands of readers a commitment unusual for texts of the sixties. The "puzzle" to be solved is not like John Barth's "funhouse" nor even John

Williams's "conspiracy." Readers must have the courage and resolve to deal with the fundamental paradoxes of human history and spirituality, and, no less problematic, some dire prophecies about the future of projects of liberal reform.

The nature of Marshall's own political commitment and participation in discussions of the sixties is difficult but not impossible to chronicle.[25] The general silence about the role of women in African-American literary culture, and the often aggressive sexism of the Black Arts and civil rights movements (which is, of course, not to single out race-centered reform movements; black men obviously held no monopoly on sexism in the sixties), has left us with an inadequate record of deeds, critical or otherwise. Harold Cruse includes her as a major figure within the "intellectual class" and, of special interest, he notes her participation in the June 1964 New York Town Hall debate on "The Black Revolution and the White Backlash." Cruse's account of her comments at that event would suggest that she was increasingly uncomfortable with the liberal approach to civil rights and other issues; he saw her as someone willing to ask difficult questions and challenge the status quo of American life and protest politics. While Marshall was associated with the Harlem Writers Guild in the 1950s, and has spoken directly of her connection to the Association of Artists for Freedom (both John Killens-sponsored groups), she is not easily seen as inseparable from any particular American literary or political movement.

Marshall can also be placed as a participant at important conferences like that at the New School for Social Research, and, in particular, on a panel devoted to "Women and Literature."[26] This particular prophetic gesture, foreshadowing the critical commitments of the forthcoming decade, is indicative of her analytic prescience. The unique nexus of identity questions, often used to limit or partition her work, leads Marshall to become a crucial mediating figure in the related but potentially hostile worlds of black feminism, black arts, postcoloniality, civil rights, and anticapitalism. Despite the resistance of some of her contemporary readers (or perhaps because of the resistance of her contemporary readers) Marshall can be read as one of the most effectively political writers in the American sixties. It is perhaps her between-ness that has made Marshall somewhat reticent about the particulars of this explicitly political past. In terms of cultural politics, she has no natural allies.

Her superb essay "Shaping the World of My Art" does, however, trace the contours of her political commitments. As she had explained in "The Poets in the Kitchen," most fundamentally her consciousness of the idea that she might be someone who could artfully manipulate words came from the exchanges between her mother and her friends in their Brooklyn brownstone. Despite their relative powerlessness, these women commented enthusiastically and with great adroitness on the world around them. Perhaps somewhat surprisingly, Marshall points to the figure of Marcus Garvey, who through her mother's talk became for her a generalized symbol of heroic black resistance. In other ways, however, this is perfectly in line with the great

cosmopolitanism of her outlook. In support of her arguments about the necessary and simultaneous tasks of creating credible stories and a viable political consciousness, she quotes from Baraka, Larry Neal, Ralph Ellison, Carlos
Fuentes, Esther Jackson, Franz Fanon, and the lyrics of the blues and ca-
lypso. It is hard to imagine any other African-American intellectual of the period working so comfortably across such contested terrain. But for Marshall
this kind of breadth of vision is a necessary pre-step to the recovery of a revolutionary intuition.

The writer's task, she suggests, is "to make use of the rich body of folk and
historical material that is there; and . . . to interpret that past in heroic terms,
in recognition of the fact of our history, as Ellison has described it, is "one of
the great triumphs of the human spirit" (108). As Marshall gains control
over this responsibility, she begins to pursue the more general "theme of the
emerging third world and a moribund West" (110). While she is increasingly
invested in a vision of the past in support of this theme, it is, she insists, distinct from nostalgia. In particular, she becomes interested in the idea of a return to the motherland.

> I am not really talking so much about an actual return, although it is
> couched in those terms. I don't know if that is really possible, or even
> necessary. The physical return described in the novels is a metaphor for
> the psychological and spiritual return back over history, which I am
> convinced Black people in this part of the world must undertake if we
> are to have a sense of our total experience and to mold for ourselves a
> more truthful identity. (107)

Not surprisingly, some critics have rejected this vision as overly romantic and
not truly engaged.

Marshall herself has stated, however, that she understood her early work
to be "political" even if those around her did not. Her first novel, *Browngirl,
Brownstones* (1959), a book about the distance between the promise and reality of the immigrant experience, and the effect of that distance on a second
generation Barbadian-American woman, was often rejected by *praising* it as
an interesting "coming of age story" or a "tale about a young girl."[27] Such
damning praise persisted even as she herself has talked of the novel's core
being an attempt to "articulate feelings . . . about the acquisitive nature of
the society and . . . its devastating impact on human relationships."[28] At any
rate, the possibility of any African-American artist pursuing "non-political"
work during the late 1950s and sixties may seem slim indeed. Darwin Turner
dramatically points out events within American political culture that would
have shaped her education at Brooklyn and Hunter Colleges in New York
City: Hiroshima, McCarthyism, Brown vs. Board of Education, and especially
the early civil rights movement.[29] As a black woman, the child of immigrants,
attempting—with little or no support—to make a career as a writer and journalist, her political initiation would be intense and risky.[30] If *Browngirl,
Brownstones* (1959), *Soul Clap Hands and Sing* (1961), and her sixties magazine

short fiction[31]—or for that matter her *Praisesong for the Widow* (1984) and *Daughters* (1992)—express their politics quietly, respecting a set of conservative conventions for narrative fiction, they do so with the author's conviction about "the importance of truly confronting the past, both in personal and historic terms, and the necessity of reversing the present order."[32]

While Marshall seems to experience no conversion so dramatic as that of Amiri Baraka, it is fair to characterize her intellectual commitments and inquiries in the sixties as dynamic. Again, however, it is her encounter with the work of Ralph Ellison *and* Franz Fanon that would seem to lead to a complex personal stance and outlook. Through her reading of, and response to, Ellison, she acknowledges the rich array of attitudes, manners, practices, accomplishments, ideas, and desires that make up African-American culture broadly conceived. It allows her to aggressively dismiss those who would ignore such a cultural presence, and, more importantly, allows her, like James Baldwin, to explore the subtleties of consciousness. In Fanon, however, she discovers a devastating critique of colonial and neocolonial mentalities and an explanation of the role of violence in liberation struggles. Marshall's inclusive embrace is of special interest here. During a decade in which Fanon and Ellison were lionized and scapegoated respectively, Marshall is revealed as a uniquely independent intellect. Marshall would seem to contribute to the problem of categorizing her own work as "West Indian" or "African-American"; she does not fall naturally into any camp. She is at once always possibly, but never only, protofeminist, post- or anticolonialist, anticapitalist, nationalist, internationalist, Pan-Africanist, and American.

What can be said with confidence is that Marshall's *The Chosen Place, The Timeless People* (1968) is a seminal contribution to sixties American culture. Its Caribbean location, its interracial cast of characters, its length and epic intent, and, most importantly, its political sensibility make it a serious challenge to the worldview and expectation of the reader. A few perceptive reviewers of the book contemporary to its release noted its culture critical function, its impressive and convincing portrayal of a class of people often either romanticized or ignored, and the "majestic" narrative. Of course, there was also something strangely anachronistic about this text: Who, in 1969, had time for a five-hundred-page historical novel?[33] Did Marshall not realize that the most respected fictional repertoire of the day was limited to cynical novels of manners (Evan Connell, *Mr. Bridge*), soft-sold ethnicities (Bernard Malamud, *Pictures of Fidelman*), word puzzles and narrative pyrotechnics (John Barth, *Lost in the Funhouse*; Kurt Vonnegut, *Slaughterhouse Five*; Robert Coover, *Pricksongs and Descants*), or the occasional lament at spiritual decay (Philip Roth, *Portnoy's Complaint*; John Cheever, *Bullet Park*). The most widely talked about black writing was blunt and sensationalist (H. Rap Brown, *Die, Nigger, Die*; Eldridge Cleaver, *Soul on Ice*).[34] What reader, or community of readers, would follow Marshall on her ambitious journey?

Bourne Island is the central site of action, and may indeed be seen as a character. It has a mystical presence—as all islands do, suggests Marshall—

an unexplained phenomenon in the middle of nowhere, an attempt to separate the Atlantic Ocean from the Caribbean sea and the "new world." In some
sense it is an interesting historical accident, and, as literary allusion, surely
conjures up Shakespeare's *The Tempest.* The appearance of a team of anthro-
pologists upon the island initiates a drama of attempted consensus building
and individual interaction and coming to knowledge. The cast of characters
is a made up of Saul Amron, a Jewish anthropologist; his wife Harriet, a
white American woman with connections to mainline Philadelphia and
Northeast corporations that implicate her in the island's colonial and neocolonial exploitation; and Allen Fuso, also an anthropologist, who has been
on Bourne before and has felt compelled to return. Representatives of the
Center for Applied Social Research, they are here to investigate the possibility of new development schemes and improvement projects.[35] This group of
intruders interacts with a group of "natives"; the term can be used decon-
structively with confidence as it includes a diverse group of individuals—former colonial administrators, North American tourists, representatives of European and American companies that control the production of cane fields,
and more centrally, descendants of African slaves, who themselves are differ-
entiated into a variety of occupational and class categories.

Merle Kinbona is conventionally the novel's protagonist, but much more
too. Her name is etymologically interesting: a merle is a kind of European
blackbird—representing her mixed heritage—and Kinbona, her married African name, literally unravels as "good kin." (Or perhaps "kin and bones.")
This, however, only begins to suggest her literal and figurative power. For
Merle's (and the reader's) dilemma is to come to terms with her disrupted
past and her complicated travels. As the unacknowledged daughter of a
white landowner and as the "kept woman" of a rich white woman while
studying in England, her history parallels and resonates with that of the island. She is entangled with colonialism, and, to put it crudely, also its product. We first meet Merle during her attempt to pick up the incoming group
of strangers at the airport, but, as is typical on Bourne, the road (described as
a slow spiraling descent) is washed away. Marshall's description is stirring:

> All this: the dress with its startling print, the strange but beautiful ear-
> rings that had been given to her years ago in England by the woman
> who had been, some said, her benefactress; others, her lover; the noisy
> bracelets, the shoes—all this could be easily taken as an attempt on her
> part to make herself out to be younger than she was. But there was
> more to it than that, one sensed. She had donned this somewhat
> bizarre outfit, each item of which stood opposed to, at war even, with
> the other, to express rather a diversity and disunity within herself, and
> her attempt, unconscious probably, to reconcile these opposing parts
> and make of them a whole.[36]

It is through Merle Kinbona, a self-described Obeah woman, that we face up
to the twin tasks of recovery and understanding. As introduced to us, Merle

embodies the past in the present, the attempt to deny that past, and, most provocatively, the paradox of the one and the many. This act of conjure should be taken with utmost seriousness for, as Marshall has suggested:

> Merle remains the most alive of my characters. Indeed, it seems to me she has escaped the pages of the novel altogether and is abroad in the world. I envision her striding restlessly up and down the hemisphere from Argentina to Canada, and back and forth across the Atlantic between here and Africa, all the while speaking her mind in the same forthright way as in the book. She can be heard condemning all forms of exploitation, injustice and greed. . . . I hear her inveighing constantly against the arms race, the Bomb, against a technology run amok. . . . On a personal level, she's still trying to come to terms with her life and history as a black woman, still seeking to reconcile all the conflicting elements to form a viable self. . . . She's the most passionate and political of my heroines. A Third World revolutionary spirit. And I love her.[37]

Critics usually look skeptically at this type of portrayal and remembrance. While holding back cynical snickers, we like to assert that it has much more to do with the assertion of a special kind of marketing talk than possessing any basis in "reality." There is, however, a sincere attempt to redefine the relationship between the literary text and its social context. Not only relying upon a Coleridge-like "suspension," the text (and its author) demands a collaborative attempt at meaning-making *and* a collaborative undertaking of concrete social action.

Merle maintains a close attachment to the inhabitants of Bournehills. It is the lowest of the low, an agricultural area of a small Caribbean island which is described as permanently backward and resistant to change, which has either sabotaged or looked at with disinterest previous attempts at "development." Despite Merle's "possessions" and "status" she chooses to maintain—that is, to acknowledge—her connection with what she calls "the little fella." She is a point of contact, a juncture or crossroads, although not an untroubled or transparent one. At numerous points within the story she becomes catatonic and is unable to face up to the intrusion of her past in the present, or the cycle within which the community seems to be trapped. Repeatedly readers are encouraged to see her as a significant figure for the condition of a neocolonial society. Wilson Harris aptly identifies her as the island's "queen." She must ultimately be seen as an emblem of humanity, as potential and as limitation. Merle's emblematic or incarnational capacity is crucial to negotiating and foregrounding special readerly involvement. Being both of and outside this "world" is crucial to the manufacture of responsibility. Through Merle all careful readers recognize their relationship to the island and to a world-system of economic and political exploitation.

Structurally the novel depends upon the suggestion of implication and the potential for self-understanding in the first half of the novel, and then the instigation of a belief in potential resolution and the collapse of that hope through the holy/days of Carnival and Whitsun, the subject of the novel's second half. In the first half of the novel, characters reveal and have revealed their various motivations and attachments to Bourne; these may be vocational, as in the case of Saul, compulsion as in the case of Allen, or need, as in the case of Harriet. More importantly, there is clear potential for lasting and significant change: Saul begins to see patterns of connection between Third World environments, Allen develops a significant friendship with Vere, and even Harriet is able to enter into the everyday life of Bournehills residents by setting up a regular pattern of visiting and interaction with the marginalized. "Atonement" is a distinct possibility.

We are also introduced to the primary resistance and historical consciousness of Bournehills society: their insistence on constantly retelling the story of Cuffee Ned and his brilliant yet ultimately unsuccessful slave revolt. As the source of communal consciousness, it is a paradox. If the revolt was so glorious and so brilliant, why did it fail? While retellings tend toward myth rather than history, readers can be tempted to straightforwardly connect the rebellion's failure and the present condition of the community.[38] Marshall, however, directs our attention away from the surface of the tale—whether or not, for instance, Cuffee held out for one or six months, a detail the barroom men like to argue over—and focuses our attention on its deeper structure and significance:

> They were singing, it was true, of Bryam, Cuffee and Pyre Hill, of a particular event, place, and people, simply telling their story as they did each year. Yet, as those fused voices continued to mount the air, shaking the old town at its mooring on the bay, it didn't seem they were singing only of themselves and Bournehills, but of people like them everywhere. The struggle on the hill which had seen Cuffee triumphant and Bryam brought low was, their insistent voices seemed to be saying, but the experience through which any people who find themselves illused, dispossessed, at the mercy of the powerful, must pass. . . . *"They had worked together!"*—and as if, in their eyes, this had been the greatest achievement, the thing of which they were proudest, the voices rose to a stunning crescendo that visibly jarred the blue dome of sky. Under Cuffee, they sang, a man had not lived for himself alone, but for his neighbor also. "If we had lived selfish, we couldn't have lived at all." They half-spoke, half-sung the words. They had trusted one another, had set aside their differences and stood as one against their enemies. *They had been a People!* (286–87)

Ultimately skeptical about interpretations of history which focus on narrow outcomes, Marshall seems to argue that we should be attuned instead to historical process.

The narrative builds toward, and the most dramatic retelling of Cuffee's tale takes place during, carnival—that important liminal period of the reduction of difference, of radical democratic leveling. For Marshall, results are always mixed: Carnival is experienced by Harriet Amron, for instance, as the self-awareness that her attempts to interact, to understand, have been failures. Her story always remains one of gaining and maintaining control. Ultimately, she is unable to see Bournehills except as totally other. For Merle and Saul, the carnival is convenient, but perhaps an insignificant factor, in the encounter which leads to the free telling of their stories—of Merle's England experience, and her African husband's taking of her daughter having discovered her previous liaisons, and of the death of Saul's first wife while on field work in Honduras—a spiritual and emotional dialogue that leads to sexual encounter. For Vere, Allen's friend and Bournehills native, returned from work as an itinerant agricultural worker in America, who, upon his return, has attempted to hide in the conquest of technology, through the rebuilding of an automobile—he is the Icarus figure mentioned in the Harris epigraph—it becomes an occasion to challenge the mother of his dead child and to humiliate her own attempt at escape and repression.

Even given warning signs about the consistency and depth of some individuals' experience, the reader is generally pleased with the state of things at the end of carnival. Allen has come to terms (if only negatively and through a conscious repression[39]) with his nonconformist sexuality, Saul and Merle have completed a movement toward each other, and Bournehills, most importantly, has made its recurrent historical statement. Insofar as Marshall utilizes some conventions of the popular romance, at this point, well prior to the end of the novel, she allows readers some sense of completion. But this temporary closure is undone in the section entitled Whitsun, traditionally the appearance of the Holy Spirit on the fiftieth day after Easter, but, ironically, on the island the time of the annual automobile race.

Vere's death in the automobile race, a betrayal of the technological escape he hoped for and nurtured, is followed by the news that the cane plant will be shut down before the processing of the cane from the individual plots of Bournehills residents, their only guarantee of a meager profit and, as a sign of individuality and nascent entrepreneurialism, the event which marks the short but important distance of their lives from slavery, as history and practice. Although they are able to band together to find a solution to their cultural and economic crisis, the optimistic framework of the novel has disintegrated. We have been reminded of what we should have known all along, that the "will to power" is active and omnipresent. In the aftermath, Harriet discovers Saul's infidelity, and attempts, in a direct effort at reemphasizing "colonial control," if not enslavement, to buy Merle, to pay her way to Europe. This crude intrusion, a reminder and replay of the economics and ethics of slavery, is the only statement that can bring Merle out of her catatonia, what Hortense Spillers calls her participation in a "neurasthenic constellation." Her verbal rebuttal of Harriet's crude proposal is not so important as the "ugly anguished scream torn from the very top of her voice."

And she let it come. Her head arching back against the wooden slats
that made up the backrest of the chair, bracing herself on the posts, she
forced it out, sounding like a woman in labor with a stillborn child,
who screams to rid herself of that dead weight. Merle might have also
been trying to rid herself of something dead inside her, that face perhaps which had attached itself like an incubus to her mind, sapping
her strength and purpose over the years, debauching her will. In what
seemed some ancient exorcistic rite she gave vent to the laugh, and as it
rose in a shrill steady line the sea beyond the railing appeared to fall
silent in deference to its greater power. (439–40)

As Harriet disintegrates—her desire for control now being expressed in the
crudest racism, letting surface her fear of the "black horde"—it will be the
sea, a mythic and geographic force in Marshall's novel, that will "swallow
her."

Her will gone . . . she continued on her way to the sea. And as always
she heard it—the sea—long before it came into view. The massive det-
onation set off by the breakers on the reef. And then the spray rising in
the dazzling white toadstool of a cloud. (459)

The spray that rises to mark Harriet's demise, the image of our potential destruction through an immoral technology, is no sentimental memorial;
rather, it suggests the historical cost of attempting to evade history. Interestingly, this conclusion—strangely reminiscent of Kate Chopin's *The Awakening* and the death of Virginia Woolf—is not without some sympathy for
Harriet. Writing around the time of the twentieth anniversary of the Hiroshima and Nagasaki bombings, Marshall alludes to the latent cost of not
confronting the urge to domination. The novelist critically acknowledges
and turns on its head the military logic of "mutually assured destruction."

Marshall concludes *The Chosen Place, The Timeless People* with an interesting
signature. She inscribes "Grenada, West Indies. New York. Yaddo., 1963–
1968." This marking is no accidental or incidental description of location
and chronos. Indeed, this revisionary signature suspends readerly expectation of authorial designation, and suggests a cultural matrix within which to
understand her literary accomplishment. This triangular relationship, paro-
dying the so-called triangular trade of human cargo as and for natural resources between Europe, West Africa, and the New World, draws readerly attention to the coexistence of contemporary acts of individual agents with the
historical experience of "peoples." The Caribbean island, Grenada (which obviously has its own interesting post-1968 resonance), the birthplace, Brooklyn, and, ironically, the "writers' colony" define the space of creation and the
site of reading. This matrix is suggestive of the complex mediation inherent
in African-American artistic activity, a consciousness more convoluted perhaps than that posited by W.E.B. Du Bois in the *Souls of Black Folk*, and also

the necessary suspension of that disunity. It also designates a dismissiveness about national identities, or at least those produced through the imperialist venture. To desire to reconstruct what it was like to *be a people* is not necessarily a crude nationalism; it is, instead, an attempt to figure out the relationship, as Marshall herself puts it, between our "past" and the "overturning of the present order."[40] Marshall's collectivism is rooted in a confrontation with history; her potential community of readers is designated neither by bourgeois commitment to the civilizing capacity of literature nor weak biological or cultural constructions of race identity.

The second part of her signature could also not be more significant. It seems difficult to imagine a more intense historical period in African-American social and cultural history. For 1963–1968 is a strikingly disruptive moment in American cultural and political history: it covers the deaths of John and Robert Kennedy and Malcolm X and Martin Luther King; it covers the intensification of the Vietnam war and the passing of the Civil Rights Act; it covers the explosions of Watts and many of the disappointments of the movement's work in the North. If the creation of *Browngirl, Brownstones* is marked by the experience of the 1950s and attempts at resisting demands leading toward assimilation and ideological conformity, *The Chosen Place, The Timeless People* would seem to be the second product of a complex political baptism. It is during this period that questions are raised about the limits of liberal consensus and the need to alter the national sense of what would constitute adequate participatory democracy. One product of this disillusionment is the heterogeneous and difficult discourse of black power. Part of the argument, however, of this chapter is that this disillusionment is anticipated by a number of African-American thinkers (and Marshall is an exemplar of this group) whose views, commitments, and texts can be revealingly and productively framed as antimodern.

One would expect that a text so embedded within the "present," a text that would seem to document and describe both hegemonic and counterhegemonic discourse, would find for itself a ready and enthusiastic audience. Despite some initial reactions that hailed the text as "epic" and "monumental," Marshall's second novel has not received the critical attention of her first or of her most recent work, nor has *The Chosen Place, The Timeless People* been canonized like other texts of her contemporaries, especially, for example, Morrison's *Sula* and Walker's *The Color Purple*.[41] On the one hand, the text seems to disrupt the preferred mode of a uniquely black feminist revision of female bildungsroman, a revision that Marshall herself undertook brilliantly in her novel *Browngirl, Brownstones*.[42] On the other, perhaps more important, hand, the text seems ideologically out of step for its historical occurrence—it is radically interracial, intercultural, and, not secondarily, international—for there is very little discussion of "blackness" per se. It seems less interested in the establishment of community boundaries than it is in the difficult task of interrogating some rules for living. Suggestive of another context for reading Marshall, Susan Willis's essay, "Eruptions of Funk: Historicizing Toni Morrison," is useful to explain the novelist's disruption.[43] Willis attempts to encourage a reading of Morrison's work that celebrates the coexistence of a mythic consciousness with concrete historical exploration and investigation. An "eruption of funk" is confrontation with bourgeois convention. In Morrison's work this is usually accomplished by the surfacing of repressed black female sexuality. To Willis, Morrison's corpus is especially valuable for the documentation of the assault of consumer capitalism on the nature of black and American selfhood. This can be extended to assert that the value of Marshall's "eruption of funk" is the shattering of the "rainbow sign," the exposure of the residue of colonialism in contemporary society, documenting the limits of good will and liberal consensus in the skirmish with cultural difference. This eruption challenges the poles of unassailable cultural difference, at one end, and notions of universality and consensus at the other. This disruption, this eruption of funk, is crucial to an attempt to center Marshall's novel in any reconstructed American or African-American literary canon of the sixties.

The Chosen Place, The Timeless People, then, is a novel which attempts to come to terms with the inadequacy of gesture, the necessity *and* limits of ritual, and the potential for redemption. Unlike her previous novel, *Browngirl, Brownstones*, which focused on a single character, Selina Boyce, and — to draw from Barbara Christian — made most clear the interdependency of culture and character, this second novel relies upon a complex cast of characters — interracial and intercultural, of varying class, gender, and educational backgrounds — each of whom relives their own repressed past through the present site. Not insignificantly, the book is "difficult." Although it is mimetic and provides us with a trustworthy narrator, it is also long and structurally complex. This difficulty, effectively described by Hortense Spillers as the simultaneity of myth, history, ritual, and ontology, makes the text in many ways a counterpoint to the iconoclasm of Amiri Baraka and the new poets. The novel's relationship to the tradition of social realism, or better still, American naturalism, however, is at best ambivalent. We are given a novel concerned with history but not strictly a historical novel. Marshall revels in the disruptive character of myth; the telos of realism is replaced with the circumambience of sin and human limitation. Once again, Marshall (and her text) challenges conventional strategies of categorization.

A relative outsider has noticed the exceptional character of her text. In an all too brief discussion of *The Chosen Place, The Timeless People*, the brilliant and evasive Guyanese critic and novelist Wilson Harris celebrates the book for its (unconscious?) appropriation of a particular Carib myth. This myth is called by Harris "the phallic-rainbow bridge." It tells of a hero who struggles to transcend the inconveniences of a profane earth toward a heavenly space marked by the sexual and cosmic absorption of elements, colors, and cultures. The bridge providing "transport" always collapses at the moment of climax, the moment of crossing or completion. With the collapse of the bridge, the hero literally comes crashing to earth, and the hero's discoverers come to see the body as a magical corpse, which, although inanimate, seems to signify necessary change. For Harris, whose own fiction celebrates alchemy and syncretism, this bewitchment of onlookers confirms the prerequisite, necessary quest for cross-cultural understanding, despite its paradoxical conclusion. Harris suggests that the "living dead" (a mythic *and* historical categorization in Paule Marshall's novel) demand "innovative living." The death of Vere, Marshall's Caribbean Anansi/Icarus, in his fire-red car in the Whitsun automobile race, shatters the transformative and transgressional nature of the carnivalesque, the structured hopefulness of *The Chosen Place, The Timeless People's* multicultural and multiracial narrative. Marshall writes:

> The car seemed to fall completely apart around him, *disintegrating* [my emphasis], all of it, into so many separate parts, the wheels moving out from their axle, the steering device becoming unhinged from its mooring under the dashboard, all the bolts and nuts and screws which he had so painstakingly and with such love secured over the months coming loose at once. The collapse was so total it seemed deliberate, planned, personally intended. . . . Or perhaps it had nothing to do with Vere. The collapse taking place around him, which he was helpless to stop, flowed perhaps out of a profoundly self-destructive impulse within the machine itself, and Vere, in foolishly allowing himself to be taken in by what he had believed was its promise of power, was simply a hapless victim. (366–67)

The communal gaze upon Vere's lifeless/life-full body disrupts progression, dialogue, understanding, and completion.

> With something of his smile lingering and his eyes open, he was staring like Seifert at the almshouse straight up into the sun through the fern-like leaves of the tamarind. Beside him in the dust, holding his head with its broken neck between her hands knelt a distraught, loudly weeping Merle. (368)

Harris's mythic conceptualization seems to fit nicely with the Tiv proverb that acts as epigraph for Paule Marshall's text: "Once a great wrong has been done, it never dies. People speak the words of peace, but their hearts do not forgive. Generations perform ceremonies of reconciliation but there is no end." Marshall's novel may be a needed guide to innovative living, but it is useless and perplexing unless one develops the appropriate gaze and stance. As complement to its aesthetic richness, Marshall's text survives (or should survive) as an incisive critique of a benignly inchoate sixties and, in particular, of a liberal politics that seeks to repress complexity and dissonance. For Paule Marshall, history and memory cannot be discarded nor ignored. Furthermore, the novel's critique of dialogic models of reading and understanding raises interesting questions about the direction of our contemporary critical undertakings.[44]

Ultimately the novel is about the always becoming. It is, paradoxically, history in the subjunctive mood. Merle begins her journey abroad (like Selina in *Browngirl, Brownstones* and Avey in *Praisesong for the Widow*) to find the past she has forgotten or repressed, to return to Africa to engage in a search for the daughter taken from her years ago, through Marshall's acknowledgment of the presence of Mr. Douglin, the "faithful keeper of the grave," and the road which has once again washed away. Merle cannot go with Saul to the place where "you read in the newspaper sometime back how they bombed a church killing four children, four little girls now the age of my daughter" (469). Most powerful of all, a predominant image toward the end of the book is that of an unborn child. Bournehills resident "Gwen" asserts, against the technical knowledge of the outsiders, that the child will appear when it is good and ready. The (re)birth of Bournehills is not a subject of scientific knowledge; it is, more complexly, enmeshed within the discovery of the nature of subjectivity itself.

It is also worth investigating, however, whether or not this text can effectively mediate the complex relationships it desires to illustrate. What role can a novel play in the achievement of such goals? To return to Harris:

> I find *The Chosen Place, The Timeless People* to be a work that confirms what is implicit in the thrust of an inquiry through cross-cultural extremity in several strangely parallel fictions; namely, the accent upon "negative capability" in dead-end realism, a realism made narrow by egocentric histories that need to be creatively disrupted by pressures of infinity within the womb of space if that realism is to yield insight into "inverted" metamorphoses as threshold to a higher aesthetic factor in pawns of the spirit.[45]

Harris's concern might be translated into an interest as to the existence of an audience sympathetic enough (i.e., adequately distant from "egocentric histories") to make "critical sense" of Marshall's cultural disruption. It may not be possible to sign off yet on the question of Marshall's accomplishment, but Harris's inquiry does provide a useful transition to a consideration of William Demby's *The Catacombs,* a book surely distant from "dead-end realism."

MEANING AND NOTHINGNESS: THE SERIOUSNESS OF DEMBY'S *THE CATACOMBS*

> The black writer is . . . the only one who will be giving voice to . . . black people. . . . The novel is a new thing [for blacks], and so it's useless to pretend that you're in some kind of universal tradition when, in reality, you are not. You're excluded from that, and so that is always at the back of your mind as you write. You are one of the very few among the family of your people who are putting things down in this form.
>
> WILLIAM DEMBY (1971)[46]

The expatriate writing of William Demby, and most especially his novel *The Catacombs* (1965), is an interesting companion statement to Paule Marshall's intercultural carnival and "dis-integration."[47] Unlike Marshall, who relied upon a mythically charged realism to offer up her diagnosis of American cultural sickness, Demby, like Wilson Harris, was skeptical of the transformative and representational power of narrative itself. The cause of truth-telling was not adequately served at this particular historical moment, in Demby's mind, by a narrowly mimetic literary practice. If Marshall offers up a "talking cure," Demby inundates the reader with fragments. Meaning is a product of the reader's recognition of homologous and analogous connections and co-incidences across various fields. The Algerian War, the making of the Hollywood epic *Cleopatra*, Italian filmmaking, the Second Vatican Council, political assassinations, McCluhanesque prophecies, the suicide of Marilyn Monroe, and many other events, ideas, and texts are all offered up as revealing (and disguising) the nature of a common dilemma. Demby tells us that this is a Gothic age, a special time, foreshadowing or revealing in palimpsest the postmodern age, and to some extent its preferred modes and forms.[48]

It can be reasonably inferred that Demby's expatriate experience is directly related to this "gothic" age. The same energy that directed writers to escape the disappointment of America after each of two world wars places William Demby in residence in Italy at the height of the civil rights movement. Demby's attachment to Rome, while not as celebrated or perhaps as glamorous as that of Richard Wright, James Baldwin, or William Gardner Smith to Paris, still provides a dynamic creative geography within which a complex psychological and artistic drama might be worked out. While Demby, like Baldwin, will eventually return to the United States, Italy becomes not so much a neutral site as a highly unique vantage point from which to write his version of the world. This singular world experience is, not surprisingly, especially conducive to the development of a distinct and spirited culture criticism. As with my treatment of Marshall, the task here is twofold. How can Demby's lucid culture criticism be placed within the general framework of African-American antimodernism? Can a compelling argument be made for the central placement of his novel *The Catacombs* within reconstructed African-American and American literary canons?

Born in 1922 in Pittsburgh, Demby grew up first in that city and later in West Virginia. His education at West Virginia State College (where he was a student of Margaret Walker's) was halted by the beginning of the Second World War. While stationed in Italy, he wrote for *Stars and Stripes*, a job that led him to take seriously the possibility of making a career as a writer. Immediately following the war he sought out feature writing opportunities with a number of Italian and American magazines, opportunities that led him to Ethiopia, the Middle East, and Japan. These writing experiences, and his enrollment at Fisk University where he became a student of Robert Hayden's, contributed to his confident first novel *Beetlecreek* (1950), loosely based upon his West Virginia experiences, and especially the desolation of the landscape and lack of social choices within a rural and provincial environment. Demby took some writing courses with Hayden, and designed and wrote for the student magazine to which Hayden was adviser. Demby's tour of duty in Europe and Africa, his writing experience, and his age might make it an overstatement to suggest that their relationship was one of mentor and initiate. More interesting, perhaps, is Demby's attraction to Italy and Hayden's attraction to Mexico, suggesting a shared "Latin-ism" or nascent "catholic" sympathy worth considering as part of a similarly shared culture-critical worldview.[49] At this early point in his career as a writer, Demby had already expressed his discomfort with naturalism and the literary paradigm of "protest," and, as such, his literary independence. Nathan Scott notes *Beetlecreek*'s relation to Sherwood Anderson's *Winesburg, Ohio*, which designates it as both "modern" and regional, but most importantly distances it somewhat from explanatory naturalism of the variety of either Richard Wright or Theodore Dreiser.

Demby returned to Rome in 1947, where he studied art history at the University of Rome. He began to make a living translating Italian films into English, and vice versa; he also wrote occasionally for Italian television. More importantly, he found himself living amongst an incredibly diverse group of artists, matched only, perhaps, by the perplexing diversity of Italian politics. Despite his immersion in Italian and European culture, Demby's expatriate experience—like that of Paule Marshall and James Baldwin—is always transitory and ambivalent. Demby argues: "You've been there for twenty years . . . but you haven't changed your language, you haven't changed your personal history."[50] This sense that one can leave and yet not be gone is echoed throughout Paule Marshall's work and biography. Like Baldwin, Marshall and Demby seem to be on a quest for a sustainable concept of "presence." The most significant ties that an individual possesses are those to his or her past, but the modern world disrupts and works to sever such an affinity.[51] There is a complex hermeneutic of suspicion at work here. On the one hand, Demby appears suspicious of romantic nationalism and equally of romantic expatriation, while, on the other hand, he occasionally posits a potentially romantic attachment to heritage or "personal history." As in the career of Marshall and Baldwin, there is a sense of a frustration at those categorizations (racial, national, literary) which serve to limit the achievement of full selfhood, while at the same time a recognition that the denial of limits has meant the sentimentalization of American culture.

An awareness of Demby's challenge to "protest realism" (as opposed to Marshall's dramatic or mythic realism)—arguably the most rigid artistic categorization and limit inherited by the African-American novelist—and of his general cosmopolitanism[52] in no way prepares the reader for *The Catacombs* (1965). Demby's dismissal of traditional narrative in that novel serves to generate a great readerly frustration. *The Catacombs* is alternately "meaningless" and, it might be said, "overdetermined." The "plot" centers upon a African-American expatriate writer living in Italy, who happens to have the name Bill

Demby. The character Bill Demby is writing a novel about Doris, the daughter of a woman he was in love with in while in college in the United States, who is involved with, among others, a man who seems suspiciously like Bill Demby. The text is even more challenging than simply requiring us to have a copy of *Facts on File* from each of the years in the early sixties in order to decode it. It demands that we recognize that it is the result of several causes *and* that its elements may be understood as operating (as having *significance*) at different levels.[53] Demby's self-consciousness with regard to the text being mediated by language (similar to Marshall's consciousness about "ritual") leads to a most challenging and perplexing composition.

Nathan Scott, in an introduction to the 1991 edition of the novel, has asserted the pessimistic outlook of the text. In response to earlier readings of the novel which simplistically took the Christian referential universe upon which the book seems to rely to suggest a redemptive vision, Scott instead perceives the beginnings of an African-American literary postmodernism.[54] Langston Hughes's "dream" metaphor for African-American creativity has not been made a nightmare or unlikelihood (à la Hansberry's *Raisin in the Sun*) so much as it is made to conform to a dream logic. More specifically, Scott has identified the aesthetic of the text as one of "cubism and pointillism," which creates a unique feeling of *simultaneity*, the ability to at once see an object (or text) from all perspectives, or, more powerfully, to be within and outside of a particular situation.[55] This special viewpoint duplicates the "dream experience" as it replaces "I have a dream." It is also important to point out that Demby has noted a more obviously vernacular explanation for his technique and goals. By manipulating literary chronology and readers' abilities to accurately regard "reality," Demby sought to duplicate the "experiments with time" pursued by the professional improvising jazz musician.

Regardless of the source of this special viewpoint, it can only make one aware of "prospects for our time"; it does not necessarily provide the reader with access to the knowledge of how to act. "Death"—and loss and alienation—is the all-encompassing "fact" of the novel. We are dealing with the "catacombs," after all. While being interrogated by her lover Raffaele:

Doris raises her eyebrows and assumes a comical air of innocence: "Oh, was I pensive? I wasn't aware of being particularly pensive. I thought I was being composed—*decomposed!*" She breaks out laughing, and somehow her dream-secret Negro laughter seems sacrilegious here in this country trattoria on the ancient Appian Way, and the Catacombs with their layers and layers of bone-powder death just across the street. "What I mean is—if you really had to take me sightseeing—and the good Lord knows I have enough sightseeing to my credit to have earned at least five Mortician degrees—why bring me to the Catacombs? Isn't there anything else to see in Rome except churches and tombs?[56]

Despite her "dream-secret Negro laughter," Doris's questions have the utmost seriousness, and the novelist (inside and outside) struggles to answer them. William Demby located "limitation" at the center of his art. He shares with Paule Marshall a concern for displacing belief in inevitable progress. They wrote "resistant fictions" thoroughly African-American and profoundly antimodernist. Their seriousness is in the way in which they wish to redefine our moral universe.

> Typical post-modernist questions bear either on the ontology of the literary text itself or on the ontology of the world which it projects, for instance: What is a world? What kinds of world are there, how are they constituted, and how do they differ? What happens when different kinds of world are placed in confrontation, or when boundaries between worlds are violated? What is the mode of existence of a text, and what is the mode of existence of the world (or worlds) it projects? How is a projected world structured? And so on.
> BRIAN McHALE, *Postmodernist Fiction*[57]

The "Bill Demby" who, as character, addresses the reader has an ambiguous relationship to the modern world. As readers, we know that he is a novelist; we know he is working on a novel whose central character is also a character in "our" novel. Our situation is multiple but not necessarily duplicitous. This ambiguity about the "modern world" can be critically unraveled as an inquiry into the relationship of worlds (racial, national, fictional, ideological), or, more complexly, about the nature of "world-ness." While he has ambitions to "say something important," his most effective mode of interaction is that of observer or voyeur.

> My warmest, most secretly perverse pleasure comes from observing (and vicariously participating in—alas, my trade is that of a writer) the seeming mutations, the illusory motion, the dreamlike sense of progression and progress which occur when the sun's rays shift on the eternal and timeless, the static, the sacredly silk-threaded tapestry of lives. (4)

He relates to a fellow writer who resides in Alabama—again alluding to the horrific bombing—the great difficulty that "seriousness" presents for the contemporary author. If we were truly serious would we not spend our time pragmatically engaging the world instead of writing? Despite the condition of Alabama—indeed, of the world in 1962—Bill Demby is skeptical of the ability of the writer to be effective in a referential or reverential way. This "cruel and gothic time" demands of the writer an appropriate response, but Bill Demby feels more comfortable in a retreat to observation. The text—understood as a novel, despite autobiographical overtones—suggests that its own existence is surprising, enigmatic, and perhaps anachronistic. It demands courageous moral reflection.

His daily ritual of reading fifteen newspapers is noteworthy for his attraction to accounts of the Algerian war; enticed and repelled by the experiences and writing of a correspondent covering the war, Bill Demby's reading challenges his own skeptical and cynical accounts of his writing philosophy. This paradox continues despite his attempts to escape: "Suddenly sick of the world, sick of the poisonous potion of anxiety and anguish filtered through row after monotonous row of identical typeface, I pick up my copy of Viking Press's *Portable Walt Whitman* and read from his Civil War Diary" (9). Even Whitman's "I" leads him back to the violence. More significantly, history itself has a fluid and reflexive character. The American Civil War blends with the Algerian War, and all texts enter into dialogue with explicit and implicit commentary. Although it is "just" a fragment, it is also the paradigmatic war of decolonization, despite Demby's (author or character-author) unwillingness to force feed us the significance of this "African world."

Again, the novel continues to provide ironic commentary on its own intentions. Despite the skeptical seriousness of its introduction, the text attempts to reassert (for "nervous" readers) its conventionality. The narrator seems to ask the reader if, perhaps, the text at hand is a romance? "Doris" is thus introduced as Bill Demby's subject and his "Beatrice." She disrupts his observational life: ". . . the atomic balance of my dusty book-lined studio is upset: my inner ear hears the crackling of minute magnetic explosions, my inner eye sees colorless flames shimmering around her body" (11). Her presence causes an interesting reaction:

> I am suddenly filled with an almost overwhelming desire (ancestral?) to escape the uncomfortable present and take to the forest (how much memory, how many billions of years of ancestral memory, can the human machine endure before vital action become imperative?) take to the forest and hunt and be hunted, abandon this dusty cowardly retreat, abandon the typeface and the sterile and deathly purity of paper, take to the forest and hunt and be hunted, and let history rest in peace, let history remain unwritten and unrecorded, let history (man's feeble scratching on the eternally shifting sands of the desert) ferment and through the never-to-be-solved mystery of memory at long last (alchemy of sacred wine) free and intoxicate the imprisoned human mind. . . .
> (12)

Whether this forest is a premodern existence, or is, more specifically, Hester Prynne's ground cannot be determined. It is the antimodern perspective at its most romantic, yet its critical voice is difficult to ignore. Doris is also a black expatriate in Italy. She is an actress and model, and at the time of their first meeting is working as an extra in the production of the movie *Cleopatra*, a "modern" production that seems to have everything and nothing to do with "blackness." Although the character Demby is married, he falls in love with her. The conventional (and readily interpretable) is contained within the inchoate whole. The novel seems to offer readers an out. If they are unwilling to deal with the full implications of the modern world they might still take refuge in a story of betrayal. Both tales are of sinfulness and limitation; take your pick.

We discover that Doris is engaged in an affair with Raffaele, an Italian count (also married), who works for a British airline. Their relationship is highlighted by discussions of the mythology of interracial sexuality. It is suggested that the count is made potent by the quality of her "otherness," and is reminded of "black Byzantine madonnas, amulets, and incensed prayers" (20) when in her presence. Similarly, Doris's allegiance to the count is at least partly explained by his status and its symbols. Doris is engaged by his aristocratic designation and affluence, as much as personal attraction. The relative affluence of the "black actors" in this novel, and their sometimes "bourgeois" concerns, itself pokes fun at the critical misrepresentation of the African-American novel as little more than ghetto ethnography.

The central dialectic that the text explores is that of death and resurrection. In particular the death of Laura, the "Creole beauty," commands a great deal of attention in the text. Laura had been part of a group of African-American expatriates that shared discussions about their common situation. Laura's death is associated with multiple images of religious sacrifice—as is literally played out in the life of Robert Hayden, Demby wishes to highlight the vitality of sixties discourses around sacrifice and scapegoating. Laura's death deconstructs the notion of Europe as a safe haven, as Merle Kinbona could also well reinforce it. (Doris writes home: "Maybe that's why Bill Demby is so weird. I mean he thought he was coming to a civilized country in Europe and suddenly discovered that in reality he was back in a kind of Africa his grandmother in Pittsburgh had tried to make him forget" [102].) It also speaks, however, to the violation of a dynamic feminine principle within culture (and more specifically within religion). Demby's maid responds to the story of Laura's death, and, in particular, to the silence of Laura's lover at the funeral: "Oh, no! Not *them! They* never suffer! *They* never suffer remorse! We're the ones who have to pay! It's we women who suffer in the end!" (55).

Another part of the textual collage is a newspaper column about Laura's death. The writer talks about the interracial relationship (and indirectly about Laura's lover's vocation as poet):

> They had all the ingredients of the modern couple, that is to say, the apparent attributes of the emancipated couple, the first of which is true love. . . . And yet I feel that it was just their emancipation that killed them. . . . The freedom, the emancipation of the woman, the equal rights between man and woman, are all phases in a glass of water when the social-economic system is capitalist. These principles create victims. The first victims . . . are the women. . . . The bourgeois male, no longer "King," suffers from so-called complexes and neuroses: it occasionally happens and with ever more frequency that the bourgeois

woman works and it is then that the famous crisis of the male whose
crown has been taken away occurs. . . . Sadism, today, they call "mental cruelty." In reality it is a slow and subtle form of killing one's
woman and becoming "King" once again. . . . My dear friend committed suicide. But we all know that she had been slowly led to suicide,
drop by drop. . . . Laura once again became the slave and he the "King."
(60–64)

Like other "texts" Demby lets this passage speak for itself. In some sense, the
sociological argument, like the Marxist rhetoric elsewhere in the article, is
not his preference in cultural analysis. Demby himself seems to be more ex-
cited by the almost coincident suicide of Marilyn Monroe, or at least lets it
continue to reveal similar cultural questions. Tired of Bill Demby's smug
masculinity and easy moralizing, Doris suggests:

What's so funny about Marilyn Monroe being Christ? I mean she made
people sit up and take notice. She made people feel something about
women. . . . Making people think what a *woman* is. . . . You men know
what a man is because you got Christ, or Adam crucified. But what
about Eve? . . . I'm religious, and I don't care who knows it. Marilyn
Monroe got herself crucified so everybody'd start thinking what a
woman is. . . . I don't feel sorry for her. I revere her! (70–71)

Demby has invoked an unusual "Mary-ology," or, in this case, "Marilyn-
ology." He reveals within the African-American antimodern perspective an
uncertainty, although not necessarily (in this case) hostility, about feminin-
ity (and feminism). It is unclear whether his use of this imagery is only
crassly symbolic (and thus romantic) or whether he is legitimately imagining
a means of discussing social power.

    This ambivalence becomes ever more important as the central controversy
of the novel is revealed to us. The novel's specific crisis, and the partial completion of the dialectic of death and redemption, is Doris's pregnancy. She
is unsure if she has been impregnated by the count or by Bill Demby, and
this indeterminacy is less interesting in terms of plot—as we have seen, plot
is a problematic concept at best—than in terms of emphasizing the idea of
moral responsibility. The death of Laura, and the subsequent analysis, discussion, and overlapping of related texts ideologically and culturally grounds
the ensuing dispute: Doris's womb is contested space. Despite their betrayals, the men wish literal confirmation of their virility and potency; symbolically, feminine creativity and dynamism—both in short supply in a world of
wars and random violence—are both demanded and made subject to patriarchal control.

    The novel is self-critical about this paradox. Demby (author? character?)
states:

I too dream. Thieflike, a spiritual spy, I come. Doris, I shout (my lips
move, there is no sound, nor does she see me, nor do I see myself,

though I know I am *there*), Beginning and End are One, are Birth, have
no color, have no face, Memory has turned to ritual and stone: Be not
afraid, my Doris—the Spiral, that is your comfort, your secret, guard
it wisely, eat well, guide the vulgar functions of your body, speak gently, hold your breath, guard that which must leave and that which
must enter: the sacred twin doors. (159)

But provocatively, I would argue, the novel allows Doris to speak too:

William, William, I do not feel generous. I *do* resent being used as a
subject for your novel. I *do* resent being used as an island-place where
Birth takes place. And yet I suppose someone has to be the woman
where Birth takes place. . . . Do you feel more guilty as a writer or as a
man? (185)

Directing this speech toward "William," as opposed to Bill, Doris does pro-
voke the reader. If rebirth—revitalization, salvation, and resurrection—are to
be guaranteed through the manipulation of a feminine principle and female
bodies, Demby recognizes the way in which this is problematic for any comprehensive sense of justice.

All of this takes place in what Demby has called "cubistic time." We are
never sure whether or not Doris's relationship with the count takes place at
a level different from that of the "Bill Demby" addressing the reader. We do
not know whether the Doris who is a character in Bill Demby's book is somehow different from the Doris who has a relationship with Bill Demby. Nor,
for that matter, do we know how, as readers, to differentiate between William Demby (the name on our text which indicates authorship) and Bill
Demby, who seems to exist as a character in a book who is trying to write a
book. The complicated structure of a novel being written within a novel allows for interesting kinds of reflexivity. Describing an informal meeting of
writers discussing their work in progress, Demby relates: "One novelist even
began to criticize the novel as though it had already been written, which is
perfectly in harmony with the theory of cubistic time I am so recklessly fool-
ing around with" (39–40). This is also a moral issue, the book asserts:

Everything and everybody, real or invented, characters in books or in
newspapers, the "news" itself, stones and broken bottles *do* matter, *are*
important, if only they are looked at, if only they are observed, just because they are composed of matter. Because everything and everybody,
real or invented, characters in books, even the books themselves, even
the book jacket and the colored ink on the cover design, is composed
of matter and for this reason matters, must therefore breathe in harmony with a single governing law, respond according to its aliveness,
its *alertness,* to the degree that it is awake or awakened, to the shifting
humors of the wind-tormented involucre of our physical environment,
which through Penelope's law of tapestry, Penelope's law of changeless
change, can, as so often it does, become transmuted into climate and

weather, weather peaceful or calm, these wild pregnant storm signals
that flash ignored through our minds. (209)

Demby takes James Baldwin's social philosophy of presence and demands
for a moral universe and radicalizes it epistemologically and ontologically.
Like Wilson Harris, Demby suggests that we cannot take refuge in a straightforward realism that depends upon "egocentric histories." Demby more actively forces the reader to experience or confront this moral universe.

The copious use of references to real, yet sometimes obscure, events
makes this book difficult. As readers, we are constantly faced with what we
don't know. Demby's rapid-fire and random litany of current events over-
whelms us even as these events provide the resonances that charge literary
texts. The vision is not so much intensely personal as it is exhaustive and
global. An extended example of Demby's narrative is necessary to illustrate
the experience:

> Today is Tuesday, April 17. At the RAI-TV studios, three blocks from
> my home, we filmed the opening sequence to the show with Louis
> Armstrong. Before I left home, I telephoned Alice. She was well, she
> said. She sounded well and rested. She asked me if I had any news of P.
> Louis Armstrong shook my hand and said that I was a good actor, that
> I should make acting my career. Truman Young, the trombone player,
> said that I was going to make a lot of money as a writer. Photographers
> took pictures of Louis Armstrong and me shaking hands. I read in the
> evening papers that a shepherd was killed and run over three times on
> the twenty-third kilometer of the Via Pontina, which is not far from
> our vineyard. Today is Thursday, April 19. The responsible press is in-
> dignant because the Fascist agitators who attacked members of the
> Congress for the Libertà per il Popolo Spagnolo while they were leaving
> Palazzo Brancaccio at the end of the session the day I read a statement
> on behalf of the American writers, received only light fines. In this
> morning's edition of *Il Giorno*, I read that P., who has been accused of
> trying to "hold up a gas station in Latina, has offered to" take "truth
> serum" and undergo questioning by all those journalists of the ex-
> treme right who have been so mercilessly, and unjustly, attacking him.
> In this morning's *Il Messaggero* I read that an "iguana," a miniature di-
> nosaur, was found walking around in Piazza San Silvestro. Says the
> news story: "But in spite of its repelling aspect, the iguana is a docile
> and unoffensive reptile, easily domesticated. What is surprising is that
> a signora enjoys keeping around her such a monstrous animal.... "The
> "signora" is a South American woman wearing an expensive fur who
> was riding around in an automobile with diplomatic license plates. All
> week the newspapers have been full of animals, flowers, poisons,
> strange and violent deaths. Truly we are in a Gothic age: the Year of the
> Plague is here.... (37–38)

The novel presents itself as neither stream of consciousness nor traditional realism. The author is clearly influenced by modernist technique, yet does not so much violate a pattern of reference as overload it.

Within the midst of this bombardment, the "writer" asserts: "I am beginning to have the strangest feeling that we are all nothing more than shadows, spirits, breathed into life and manipulated by Pirandello's fertile mind." The novel's importance (and seriousness, the reader might add) is not, however, negated by this. The book creates its own narrative unity, logic, and ultimate comprehensibility. The reader is introduced not only to Doris's crisis, but also to Bill Demby's writer's crisis, and a whole series of global confrontations and events. We hear not only of Algeria, but also of Cuba, the assassination of Kennedy, the distribution of oral contraceptives, Karl Barth on the cover of *Time*, Vatican II (the Concilio devoted a great deal of time to race relations), Baldwin's *The Fire Next Time*, and a damaged communications satellite, which, it was feared, would come crashing down into some heavily populated area. The didactic component of the novel is heightened by the insertion of recurring discussion of the early fights of Cassius Clay—which not only had to do with images of black masculinity but, eventually, with Clay's *conversion* to the Nation of Islam, became a religious battleground as well—and allows Demby to inject some straightforward commentary on race politics.

The intersection of the novel's tone and its narrative structure constitutes its conception and interaction with history. Demby often invokes the image of the "spiral." This has been suggested by one commentator as evidence for the influence of Teilhard de Chardin. It might also suggest, however, the influence of Giambattista Vico; most importantly, of course, it demonstrates Demby's familiarity with the high modernist canon, especially the spirals and gyres of James Joyce and William Butler Yeats. Reminiscent too of Paule Marshall's circling plane delivering Saul and crew to the Bourne Island—and of Romare Bearden's artistic collective, to be discussed in chapter 6—it is an apt conception of history to which African-American antimodernists seem to gravitate. History is never simply past. It literally circles back to find us, to demand that we take its lessons seriously. For Demby's readers this ironically means that it is imperative that the novel's attitude to the future be examined. As mentioned above, some commentators have attempted to use the locale of the Catacombs as evidence of a redemptive structure. (Historically it is important to note that the Catacombs not only represents a space in which Christians surreptitiously practiced the Eucharist, but also one to which rebellious slaves were condemned.) Demby's assertions about cubistic time make any teleological scheme unlikely if not impossible. Instead Demby's text constantly asserts *something is going to happen*. It also asserts that it has probably already happened. Like Paule Marshall, Demby makes significant use of the Christian calendar. And like Marshall, this calendar's significance is less its specific symbolic and historic content than the designation of a "special time."

Demby's manipulation of perspective and character means that the reader must be concerned with personal history too—encouraged to raise questions about the autobiographical character of the text. As Bill Demby confesses his difficulties in writing—his distractions, wrong choices, problems in plot—we must wonder if this is not the omniscient author William Demby speaking to us more directly. And art is never an uncomplicated refuge; we are constantly reminded of how the writing of the book is interrupted because of the necessity of translating another American B movie into Italian. Our introduction to the character Bill Demby's frailties are an invitation to see the actual novel as an admittedly flawed intervention. Given the increasing tendency within the decade toward unassailable monologue, this is an admirable, if initially confusing, gesture on the part of the novelist.

Demby's discussion of the virtues and limitations of the novel form takes place in both inter- and extra-linear fashion. Within the text of the book itself Demby suggests:

> The novel must be like a plum cake: while baking a plum cake or after it is baked one does not remove a raisin or nut just because one doesn't approve of the way it has occupied a choice site or moved too close to another raisin or nut. Novels, in theory, anyway, are supposed to be slices of life, slices of plum cake. So once the cook has created and stirred up the mixture he has no moral right or obligation to censor, or select: all the cook-writer can do is taste and smell and say "yum-yum" or "This stinks!" (93–94)

Despite the playfulness of this passage, we are not led to believe that such disorder or randomness is without a recognizable pattern of meaning. Instead, Demby is more interested in preserving the unfolding order of reality from the ideological and aesthetic whims of the novelist. The novel acts as mirror, if only, perhaps, of the carnival variety. The act of writing the novel—of revealing order and disorder—is traumatic and becomes a kind of dialogic rite of passage:

> This is a dark depressing time for the novel, a strangely critical time of my life. It is a Janus-time of looking back and forward, looking forward toward Birth, looking backwards towards Death. . . . I am moving over a landscape of time and reality totally unlike the dream world I had been living in up to now. These trees and mountains, these rivers and strange fish, these utensils and flowers, these streets and noises are unfamiliar to me. I am here and there. . . and now, saying this, I am no longer afraid, nor do I feel divided. (135)

The novel is less a statement of optimism than a confrontation with the logic of contemporary existence. As Demby himself suggests, the experience of contemporary life can be aptly described as a sense of "living in a novel." William Demby is not so much out of step with the stream of African-American writing in the mid-sixties that seeks to celebrate "blackness" and violate the hegemony of the American literary mainstream, as he is, rather, expansive of that location. Demby not only internationalizes the conversation; he develops a critique of the culture of violence, and challenges simplistic aesthetic philosophies of social change:

> I don't think that there is anything that is really American that will get better or worse. That's because of the dynamics of our society. . . . Will they get better? But what would that mean? We will always have tensions—in this country—between groups. . . . I suppose the total effort now must be to save the country, to get it together somehow, to make it a viable social, historical unit, because there is nothing in the books that says that America has to be eternal.[58]

The novel "ends" with two dialogues. In the first, Bill Demby tells Doris about the above diagnosed sickness of America; in the second, the count tells Doris that he is leaving her. We are left with an image of loss: "She is not there. Doris has vanished. . . . The number of separate graves in the Catacombs has been estimated at two million and more, of all races and colors. . . . ("Doris! . . . Doris! . . . Where are you, Doris. . . . . . Where have you gone?" [244].) We never find out what happens (or has happened) to Doris's child.

PAULE MARSHALL AND WILLIAM DEMBY AS ANTIMODERNISTS: A FANONIAN RESOLUTION

> The colonial world is a Manichean world. . . .
> FRANZ FANON, *The Wretched of the Earth* (1961)[59]

> Fanon explains to you his brothers and shows them the mechanism by which we are estranged from ourselves. . . . This book had not the slightest need of a preface, all the less because it is not addressed to us. Yet I have written one, in order to bring the argument to its conclusion; for we in Europe too are being decolonized: that is to say that the settler which is in every one of us is being savagely rooted out. . . .
> JEAN PAUL SARTRE, preface (1961) to *The Wretched of the Earth*[60]

Thematically or programmatically, we might summarize the relationship between Paule Marshall's *The Chosen Place, The Timeless People* and William Demby's *The Catacombs* by highlighting their shared commitment to critical "internationalism," or a transnationalist conception of America; their informed or hopeful pessimism; and their shared conviction of the necessity of ritual violence and historical memory. The most striking repetition in the texts of Marshall and Demby is the image of the not-yet-born child. Both are instances of the preservation of female control and feminine creativity, a potential hopefulness, yet disruptive of all instrumental rationalities. Nothing is given. Similar too, however, is the critical silence surrounding both texts as historical expressions in the sixties and after. It is especially interesting, given the currency of "theory," that the charge or complaint of complexity and difficulty has been directed at each text. The very "thickness"—both literally and in the Geertzian sense—of their accounts of contemporary culture makes them suggestive counterstatements. As a point of critical difference, we should highlight their divergent attitudes as to the usefulness and effectiveness of "realism." Despite such a difference, the two texts may be more powerfully entangled and explained by briefly revisiting the work of Franz Fanon.[61]

Marshall identifies Fanon as a primary shaping force upon her work and her consciousness in the sixties. In the case of Demby, there is but a trace but an important one—his fascination with the Algerian conflict as a paradigmatic event in the definition of contemporary culture. Even without any direct connection, there is a shared set of interests and a shared sensibility. The intricacy and snarl of colonial and imperial relations, the ethics of violence, and the redefinition of national self-definition were central to Fanon and appear in concentrated fashion in both Demby and Marshall. Most radically, Fanon recognized that the "risk of death" is a necessary component of the decolonization process. A Manichean world can only likely be broken through violence.[62]

Fanon is also helpful in explaining and exploring the unique approach to writing an American novel which does not include an American setting. Patrick Taylor writes that there is an important distinction to be made in Fanon's work between national consciousness and nationalism:

> Nationalism is compatible with internal domination within the society and Manichean opposition in relation to other groups or societies. The task of the national movement is to "create a prospect that is human because conscious and sovereign men dwell therein." National consciousness goes beyond individual and group narcissism to a recognition of other individuals and national groups; it is accompanied "by the discovery and encouragement of universalizing values."[63]

The possibility generated here is that—as suggested at the opening of this chapter—the great American novel may indeed be deconstructive of its political locale. As exceptionalism is criticized, a new concord or national self-definition may be discovered within a new consciousness. The work of Demby and Marshall is suggestive of the possibilities of a comprehensive cultural criticism on foreign terrain.

However, Fanon not only contributes to our understanding of the construction of the ideological and philosophical basis of the novels. His work also elucidates and clarifies our responsibilities as readers. Fanon's emphasis on participation within history suggests a unique relationship that we must have with the text. Nicely reminiscent of Emerson's emphasis upon the "active soul," it suggests that the most radical challenge that each novel makes to the reader—and one definitive of African-American antimodernism—is a demand that the reader participate actively and self-consciously in the process of making meaning. Nathan Scott has suggested of Demby that:

> like Faulkner's *The Sound and the Fury* and Malraux's *The Walnut Trees of Altenberg* and Bellow's *Mr. Sammler's Planet* and Toni Morrison's *Beloved*, it wants . . . to bid us to "change your life."[64]

If American fiction of the sixties is aptly characterized for Warner Berthoff by its "qualityless-ness," then Marshall and Demby must be read as hopelessly out of step. They place responsibility upon the reader to act as a partner in a very strict interrogation of the very idea of quality itself.

Finally, we might say that Fanon also offers insight into the critical silence surrounding Marshall's and Demby's accomplishment. Again, his particular psychoanalytic framework raises the question of repression or resistance, as the model of decolonization raises the specter of neocolonialism. In Fanon's framework, championing "national consciousness" over "nationalism" involves questioning the motives and interests of the "national bourgeoisie." Do the questions raised by Marshall and Demby's texts strike too close to our professionalist hearts?[65] Who wants to read a text too carefully which seems to raise questions about our faith in unmediated democratic conversations about literature? Who wants to know too much about the responsibilities of reading? Who wants to know about the ways in which contemporary America demands a new definition of teaching?

There is, perhaps, some difficulty on the horizon. Is the distinction between nationalism and national consciousness difficult to maintain in the face of, say, an unrelenting racism? There is here some suggestion of potential difficulty to come. Does the utilization of tropes of family and kinship begin to invoke a conservatism that will in turn begin to lose sight of its prior critical ambitions? Certainly some readers have found in later Marshall novels, for instance, the beginnings of a mystification of kinship somewhat distant from her strategic challenge to the West in the sixties. And while historical memory is clearly a crucial weapon against false optimism, it can also begin inadvertently to slide toward nostalgia, especially if the dominant culture refuses to acknowledge black subjectivity. Myth as hyperbole or exaggeration as opposed to myth as truth can begin to get the upper hand. Most problematic of all, as we saw with Robert Hayden, there is little evidence as to whether their counterstatements can ever be formulated programmatically. Can this resistance have anything to do with social policy?

Even given this cautionary tale, however, these "sixties novels" offer solutions to a number of dilemmas of "modern" doubt. Even as they displace naive optimism they work to provide careful readers with solutions to cross-cultural anxiety (interracial, international, and so on) as they sympathize with our plight within a radically pluralistic world. They do not provide new certainties. At their best they offer imaginative and moral journeys which provide respites from a sense of cultural or intellectual paralysis, De Beauvoir's "numbness." Of course, to follow the spiral of communication means to acknowledge that one may find oneself back where one began. The problem with an "eruption of funk" is that it is rarely predictable. The evaporation of traditional structures of meaning (political, national, ideological) does not necessarily mean "homelessness"; it may be the beginning of some kind of return, a "re-placement" as opposed to a displacement. This is surely a privilege, and the best that we can hope for in a "postmodern" world.

CHAPTER FOUR

MEDITATIONS

JOHN COLTRANE AND FREEDOM

We live in a time of massive social breakdown, and this breakdown is related in the breakdown of the forms of art. European art forms have afforded the black artist useful media of expression, and all European forms, creative and performing, have been mastered to the point of excellence by at least a few black artists. However, all of the writings of Ellison, Jones, Baldwin, et al., all of the paintings of Lawrence, do not weigh as much as one John Coltrane solo in terms of the force of its thrust, the honesty of its statement, and in the originality of its form.

A. B. SPELLMAN, "Not Just Whistling Dixie" (1968)[1]

I've found you've got to look back at the old things and see them in a new light. I'm not finished with these studies because I haven't assimilated everything into my playing. . . . I want to progress, but I don't want to go so far out that I can't see what others are doing.

JOHN COLTRANE (1960)[2]

In May 1957, John Coltrane's life changed. His career had progressed steadily but—it was whispered—his abuse of drugs and alcohol was making him a risk. While Miles Davis knew that Coltrane could be the sideman to provide him with a lifetime's worth of musical challenges, he was increasingly concerned that Coltrane simply did not embarrass him on the bandstand by nodding off to sleep. In some ways it was fundamentally perplexing. This was—everyone agreed—a young man who was going places. Moreover, he was positively driven toward mastery of his instrument and jazz tradition. Why get caught up in the madness of heroin? There are no adequate answers, really. Some have speculated that he had begun using it to get relief from physical pain, perhaps dental pain, the product of both excessive practicing and an out-of-control sweet tooth. As satisfying an answer, however, may be that heroin was just around and had become, however irrationally, part of the jazz scene. As "work," playing jazz meant nightlife which meant alcohol and which sometimes meant other stimulants and escapes. There is certainly no evidence that Coltrane was ever caught up in what Nat Hentoff called "emulation-by-needle":[3] If Charlie Parker did it, the thinking went, well, it must be worth a try. Some critics and cultural historians have argued that the conformity of postwar American culture led practitioners of a music that was increasingly emphasizing its discomfort with middle class life to seek a means of radically enforcing distance. This *is* an interesting and worthy cultural explanation, but there is no ready connection to Coltrane's difficulty.

Ultimately, though, the "why" of Coltrane's addiction is unimportant. Coltrane made the decision to quit—cold turkey—and was successful. With the support of family, friends, and fellow musicians, John Coltrane turned his life around in the spring of 1957. Good changes came of this good change. By early summer he had joined Thelonius Monk for a now legendary gig at New York's Five Spot, an important collaboration, to say the least, for the future of American music. This commitment and historical moment was of the utmost seriousness to Coltrane and was not only significant for its impact on his body. Increasingly, he imparted great spiritual importance to this turning point. The idea that one could begin again and start over was a crucial insight and became not only an ethic but a crucial part of his aesthetic too. That much of the event's significance is constructed in hindsight is also meaningful. Like Frederick Douglass, Walt Whitman, and a host of others within American tradition, Coltrane recognized that, in terms of American artistry, more often than not, one's most important act is the act of self-invention. Indeed, as the sixties began, there were others committed to a equally demanding form of musical inquiry—Ornette Coleman, Cecil Taylor, and Charles Mingus, for example—and yet none of them was half as successful as Coltrane in the innovation of such a compelling subjectivity.

The new conception of self—and more obsessive practicing and timely collaboration—seemed to expand Coltrane's vision and musical practice. And again similar to the classic Americanists, Coltrane's art progressed by perceiving that the "new" was somehow intimately connected with one's attitude toward the past. If in the 1950s, Coltrane stumbled a bit, struggled to find his way or voice, intimidated, some suggest, by the influence and accomplishment of some of the other great tenor saxophonists of the day, Sonny Rollins and Sonny Stitt in particular, he entered the American sixties never overwhelmed by the past. Instead, he seemed to find in the past a great deal of inspiration and comfort. What was this new conception of self? It was largely that of the questing shaman/artist. Increasingly, he seemed convinced that there was no significant distance between an individual's aesthetic and ethic. His artistic exploration quickly became a quest for the ecstatic, a search that would rarely be confined to accepted or conventional musical practice. The "path" would never be obviously sectarian, however, and was dramatically cross-cultural. As evidence of the great genius of this personal reorientation, many individuals eventually came to Coltrane as "followers" and sought in his music—and more often than not found—something spiritually satisfying, something which spoke to some absence in American life.

Not everyone was able to follow Coltrane through the totality of his journey. If an artist sets out to articulate the ways in which the previous vocabulary is no longer adequate, it is almost by necessity that some portion of his audience will be alienated by the new commitments. But strikingly, almost everyone did seem to understand the directness of his cultural criticism. At its center was the recognizable injunction to "love." As counterstatement this is both extraordinarily accessible and dangerously open to sentimentalization. Uncompromising musical investigation and challenge, however, in combination with an extended hand to other forms of cultural and political reflection, could make of this mandate and song an emblem of significant intellectual inquiry and substantive cultural resistance.

THE DISCOURSE OF BLACK MUSIC

Of all the antimodern figures that this book has considered, none has attracted so much hyperbole and devotion as the jazz saxophonist and composer John Coltrane. His death in July 1967 heightened the commitment of his followers rather than lessening his impact on the decade. He projected a powerful if insouciant spirituality and was (and is) very much a bridge figure between liberals and radicals, whites and blacks, Americans and Europeans, and musicians and other artists. Coltrane's speeches and writings, however, are very few in number, as are, surprisingly, detailed, descriptive accounts of his performances that are accessible to the layperson. Musicological analysis alone is unlikely to lead to the kind of explanation this phenomenon would seem to demand. Similar difficulties await the cultural historian who would only rely upon Coltrane's own words. The fullest interpretation of his meaning for the sixties will need to rely on a somewhat expanded reading strategy. One critical difference here—certainly different from, say, the experience of Robert Hayden—is that John Coltrane became an object of veneration. A Coltrane profile needs to struggle with both his subjectivity—his substantive intellect and will—and his broad cultural impact. Furthermore, that veneration and impact can best be explained by noting a significant change in American cultural discourse. "Coltrane" can be productively seen as the base statement in an emergent discourse of black music (itself consequentially and demonstrably "antimodern" in character). Coltrane's "notable no" to some aspects of American culture is most fully sustained and explained with some attention to the ways in which an interesting range of artists and intellectuals began to think and write about African derived musical practices in America.

Within the discourse and practice of African-American music in the sixties[4] various contradictory elements were preserved. The integrationist poetics and economics of Motown Records existed concurrently with the introduction of "Black music" charts by *Billboard* magazine and a thriving Stax

Records too, cross-cultural in management, performance, and product. Each claimed to be about, and was about, for that matter, *soul*. In similar fashion, and for various periods of time during the decade, groups like the Association for the Advancement of Creative Music in Chicago and the Black Artists Group in St. Louis were thriving, and simultaneously represented Black cultural nationalism and very Western avant-garde tendencies. James Brown could campaign for Richard Nixon, as Jimi Hendrix revised national symbols at Woodstock, at the same time Duke Ellington and Mary Lou Williams could turn their attention to a remarkably ambitious religious music.

Despite this active and exciting difference, the sign "Black music" was increasingly seen to possess identifiable and pragmatic meaning. The emergence of a critical tradition, initiated in some sense by LeRoi Jones's *Blues People*, which looked to "Black music" as a definitive force within African-American culture, needs always to be contextualized by a consideration of such musical heteroglossia. How are such "contradictory omens," to use Edward Kamau Brathwaite's apt phrase, to be understood? Is the discourse schizophrenic, and ultimately an illusion? Or is there a logic to such contradictions? These contradictions provide theorists of American culture with new means to examine the invention of American race and ethnicity while also revealing the *strategic value* of such cultural interventions. The discourse of "Black music" is a prime reservoir of antimodern and anti-Western longing. "Black music" is understood as specifically counter to Western literary values, a challenge to Euro-American aesthetics, a foundation for African-American literature, and potentially a revolutionary encounter with the American social order.

The specific historical emergence of the phrase "black music" is difficult to ascertain. Ornette Coleman's recording *Free Jazz* (1957) was disruptive enough that it seemed to set off a whole wave of attempts to clarify, revise, and establish the nomenclature of African-American popular music. The list of sixties categories is actually quite impressive: anti-jazz, the "new thing," soul, rhythm and blues, funk, blues ("classic" and "country"), rock and roll, fusion, gospel, and so on. It seems unlikely that, given such diversity (and, theoretically, such polyphony), any viable unification might be established. But with the publication of LeRoi Jones's *Blues People* (1963), and in subsequent texts by Jones and others, there emerged a kind of talk about the function and significance of the various styles of music which trace their roots to Africa. "New thing" jazz collective The Art Ensemble of Chicago's late sixties performances of "Great Black Music: Past to Present" were especially suggestive of the growth of this musical ecumenism, and a noteworthy (and successful) attempt to put such unity and diversity to culture-critical ends.

The historical analysis of the roots of African-American musics was basically sound, if not precise. It could be suggested with a certain amount of confidence that jazz, rock & roll, rhythm & blues, etc., shared formal characteristics. Ethnomusicological research tended to reinforce this viewpoint, as did less formal observance of performance styles, the recurrence of a blues paradigm, and, in particular, the response of audiences to the music. Less attention was paid to the syncretic character of much of American culture—the tendency to exchange practices, beliefs, and styles, making all "New World" expression immediately and radically "American"—although it would also be a mistake to assert that there was some kind of conspiracy to eliminate European roots. More often than not, the concern of musical commentators in identifying this African lineage was to confront theories or histories that saw such an inheritance as either pathological or of little value. The anthropologist Melville Herskovits and the philosopher Alain Locke had provided the intellectual groundwork many decades previously, and white jazz critics like Marshall Stearns were just as likely to tell a version of this story as black critics and historians.

At some point, however, early in the sixties, the character of this historical reconstruction changed. Perhaps as a result of thinking about why there were so few African-American music critics, "Black music" was posited as a formidable oppositional discourse and practice. The survival of a vital African-American culture was seen as intimately related to the potency of African-American musical practice. Black music had led and was to continue to lead the cultural revolution, especially as the civil rights revolution began to lose momentum in the urban north. Weighty claims were made for Black music's contemporary importance in a new, more aggressive (cultural) struggle for racial justice. John Coltrane, Albert Ayler, James Brown, Ray Charles, Aretha Franklin, Otis Redding, Sam Cooke, Archie Shepp, Sun Ra, and even Mahalia Jackson were not only (or primarily) accomplished artists, but were new revolutionaries on the front lines of the movement. Increasingly, some African-American intellectuals shaped the discourse of "Black music" to frame the struggle to achieve justice in the United States in terms of the decadence of Western culture and its ultimate decay and destruction. LeRoi Jones's *Blues People* led the way in this regard, and Jones (soon to be Amiri Baraka) became the decade's foremost theorist of African-American musical accomplishment, and, not secondarily, the most proficient arbiter of black music's culture-critical potential.

Blues People remains an important document as the first extended work of jazz criticism by an African-American. Its analysis is sound even when shrill and its conclusions insightful even if occasionally, but not always, surpassed by more scholarly research.[5] It is arguably a "classic" of sixties American culture; its value to us is not purely a product of the historical reconstruction it undertook. The poet Sterling Brown and the anthologist and composer James Weldon Johnson had made limited efforts to place African-American musical history and practice at the center of African-American culture many years prior to the appearance of *Blues People*, but Jones was the first to expand a set of instincts and hunches into a full-blown theory. Little credit has been given to Jones, in American Studies circles or elsewhere, for pioneering in the study of American popular culture and giving such work an important credibility. Yet no one has duplicated the systematic character of Jones's work, that comprehensiveness that makes *Blues People* appear as a summa of African-American culture, although he can be seen as the initiator of broad-ranging works on African-American music *and* those works of Sixties and Sixties-influenced African-American culture theory which centered "Black music" as paradigm or paradigmatic practice.[6]

Jones had written liner notes for a number of jazz record labels throughout the late fifties and early sixties, especially while he worked for the traditional jazz journal *Record Changer*, and had, more recently, begun contributing to *Downbeat*, but he had little experience in writing critical prose, and definitely nothing of this scope or length. He was, perhaps, the *only* African-American who could claim to be a professional jazz critic or writer. *Blues People* has significant biographical importance too. As a statement of self, it seems an important part of the journey that took LeRoi Jones from the "Beat Period" and Greenwich Village (and a white wife)—discussing art and literature in a circle that often included Charles Olson, Allen Ginsberg, Jack Kerouac, and others—to the politically engaged Amiri Baraka of Harlem and eventually Newark. Jones's opening sentence signaled that *Blues People* was going to cover ground different from that of a jejune and callow Beat rebelliousness: "I am trying in this book, by means of analogy and some attention to historical example, to establish certain general conclusions about a particular segment of American society" (ix). More dramatically and comprehensively, he asserted:

> I am saying that if the music of the Negro in America, in all its permutations, is subjected to an anthropological as well as musical scrutiny, something about the essential nature of the Negro's existence in this country ought to be revealed, as well as something about the essential nature of this country, i.e., society as a whole. (x)

This was not to speak to some truism about "jazz" or "blues" being America's music. Neither was it to be a simplistic celebration of an oppositional "style." Theories of African-American and American culture had become commonplace, but Jones was breaking new ground.

The crisis that Jones means to identify is associated with the history of American slavery. While he has no lack of invective for racism, greed, imperialism, etc., he identifies the great tragedy of the middle passage as the forced movement of peoples into a world altogether alien. Utilizing Herskovits's work on the unity of a West African cultural cosmology, Jones details the ways in which this world view was totally "other" to the emergent Western humanist world view. If you are West African, he argues:

> and believe in the supernatural, and are issued from an ecological determinant that does not permit of such a psychological extreme as American Puritanism (which, said William Carlos Williams, is a "thing, strange, inhuman, powerful, like a relic of some died out tribe whose practices were revolting"), the circumstance of finding yourself in a cul-

ture of white humanist pseudo-Puritanical storekeepers must be re-
volting. And if you are the slave of such a culture, your sorrow must be
indeterminable. (10)

"Blues," then, is an aesthetic, philosophic, and religious response to the
shock treatment of modernity. Historically, Jones argues, the viable legacy of
Africa in America was in the area of religion and the arts. Luckily, it was just
these elements that proved most useful in preserving some trace of the previous world view and allowed some small sense of self.

Jones proceeds to effectively outline a history of early African-American
music, a genealogy of blues and jazz through the worksongs, shouts, and
spirituals. He provides a broad and useful survey of early scholarship (and
misconceptions), and forcefully begins to construct the argument that the
African-American musical tradition is the most effective tradition of opposition within the context of the United States. If modernity is a product of
Enlightenment consciousness:

> The discarding of the religious attitude for the "enlightened" concepts
> of the Renaissance also created the schism between what was art and
> what was life. It was, and is, inconceivable in the African culture to
> make a separation between music, dancing, song, the artifact, and a
> man's life or his worship of his gods. *Expression* issued from life and *was*
> beauty. But in the West, the "triumph of the economic mind over the
> imaginative," as Brooks Adams said, made possible this dreadful split
> between life and art. Hence, a music that is an "art" music as distin-
> guished from something someone would whistle while tilling a field.
> (29)

This viable countertradition is especially suited, then, to living with "eco-
nomic-mindedness." Thinking about, listening to, and practicing Black
music provides one with the intellectual armor and armament to resist the
rationalization and compartmentalization of modern industrial society.

The troubling shift—for most readers—that Jones begins to make is his
identification of middle-class status with a desire to be "mainstream," to surrender marginality for the false dream of acquisition. Following E. Franklin
Frazier, Jones argues that the black middle class, in particular, is *compelled* to
act "economically," and thus dismiss blackness's critique of Enlightenment.[7]
"The black middle class, from its inception . . . has formed almost exclusively
around the proposition that it is better not to be black in a country where
being black is a liability" (123–24). More generally, he argues:

> When the supernatural goal of the society . . . yielded to the more prac-
> tical, positivistic ideals of industrialized twentieth-century America,
> salvation belonged to those who realized that the worth of man was his
> ability to make money. The black middle-class responded to this call,
> as it would to any call that would assure it respectability and prestige
> and their concomitant privilege. But religious or positivist, the adjust-

ment necessary for the black man to enter completely into a "white" American society was a complete disavowal that he or *his part of the culture* had ever been anything else but American. (The cruel penalty for this kind of situation is the socio-cultural temperament of America today, where the very things that have served to erect a distinctive culture on this continent are most feared and misunderstood by the majority of Americans!) But the fact was that by the time of the move north (and precipitated in part because of it), the oppression the Negro knew America capable of—his indestructible bond with this country—and the space and light he saw it capable of producing sat dictating the narrow path most negroes could travel on their way toward *citizenship*. (126–27)

How can "America" be anything more than an economic imperative? Jones's perspective is troubling because it does not seem to allow for any social space in which someone can be "comfortable," or, following the antimodernism considered by Jackson Lears, not "nervous." The kind of opposition that Jones has in mind—in some sense, that represented by a West African cosmology—centers on accident and unpredictability, mystery and tragedy. Comfort, especially as understood in the phrase "material comforts" may, indeed, not be possible. This begins to explain the central role that Black music plays in the development of oppositional groupings and countercultures, like the Beats or youth culture generally. Black music identifies structures of meaning that do not reduce individuality to earning potential. In the best of jazz, the most interracial and intercultural of Black musics, argues Jones, "the freedman-citizen conflict is most nearly resolved, because it makes use of that middle ground, the space that exists as the result of any cleavage, where both emotional penchants can exist as *ideas* of perhaps undetermined validity, and not necessarily as 'ways of life'" (140). Black music, then, works to preserve difference and celebrate pluralism. The ultimate *middle class* music, for Jones, is Swing. Quoting Hsio Wen Shih: "There is a terrifying record, an anthology called *The Great Swing Bands*, on which most [of the best known] bands are represented. If they are played without consulting notes or labels, *it is impossible to distinguish one from the other*."[8]

In order to reduce the homogenizing effects of the economic imperative of American society, black music has been most effective when it was most firmly grounded in local contexts and its distribution decentralized:

Jazz demonstrated how the blues impulse, and thus Afro-American musical tradition, could be retained in a broader musical expression. Big-band jazz showed that this music could exist as a peculiarly American expression (and also that there was a commercial use for it), which included, of course, the broadened social perspective of the post-Depression, urban Negro. But as a true expression of an America which could be celebrated, as Whitman said, "in a spirit kindred to itself," jazz could not be understood by a nation which had finally *lost* the Civil

War by "placing private property above other values"—the result being such denials of human dignity as the legislation of inhumanity and oppression all over the South. As a folk expression of a traditionally oppressed people, the most meaningful of Negro music was usually "secret," and as separate as that people themselves were forced to be. (176)

The economic imperative, or Weber's capitalist spirit, requires that potential resisters be willing to "head for the forest." This is, of course, an ongoing process. And, as Jones and others tell the story of jazz or black music, its numerous "changes" are an expression of a consistent desire to start anew, to recreate the "New world" space.[9]

In summary, then, "Black music" destabilizes the hegemony of "enlightenment" values. In speaking of the emergence of free jazz, and the lamentations of some that it was, in practice, anti-jazz, Jones concluded:

I cannot think that the music itself is a more radical, or an any more illogical, extension of the kinetic philosophy that has informed Negro music since its inception in America. Negro music is *always* radical in the context of formal American culture. What has happened is that there are many more Negroes, jazz musicians and otherwise, who have moved successfully into the featureless syndrome of that culture, who can no longer realize the basic social and emotional philosophy that has *traditionally* informed Afro-American music. . . . But perhaps the proportion is being significantly adjusted as even more young Negroes begin to consciously flee the stale purity of the missionaries' legacy. It is a curious balance, though one, as the West finds itself continuously redefining its position in the world and in need of radical reassessment of its relationships to the rest of the world, that will prove of the utmost importance. . . . What is it that [young African-Americans] are being asked to save? It is a good question and America had better come up with an answer. (235–36)

The hostility that each major new movement in black music generates is a result of the questioning that is instigated of the "idea" of America. Bebop, rock & roll, free jazz, and rap each reveal the ways in which the meaning of "America" is not wholly agreed upon. Black music becomes a social space for the ritual negotiation of our central cultural values.

Ralph Ellison offered the most extended (and in some ways hostile) response to the accomplishment of *Blues People*. Ellison's essay, which originally appeared in the February 6, 1964, issue of the *New York Review*, and was subsequently included in *Shadow and Act*, articulates no single objection, except, perhaps, that Jones places on the music "the tremendous burden of sociology." "*Blues People*," Ellison argues, "like much that is written by Negro Americans at the present moment, takes on an inevitable resonance from the Freedom Movement, but it is in itself characterized by a straining for a note of militancy which is, to say the least, distracting."[10] If Jones is sometimes guilty of overzealousness in the sweeping character of his analysis, Ellison does not so much displace with specificity as he disrupts with his own capaciousness. For Ellison, culture, a "concord of sensibilities," always allows for infinite variety; he holds fast, in particular, to the unpredictability of the American social order, to the myths and realities of class mobility.

Ellison is, not surprisingly, at his strongest when pointing out the diversity in the unities perceived by Jones. In response to Jones's assertions about modern jazz as oppositional culture, Ellison cleverly and accurately responds:

> Today nothing succeeds like rebellion (which Jones as a "beat" poet should know) and while a few boppers went to Europe to escape, or became Muslims, others took the usual tours for the State Department. Whether this makes *them* "middle class" in Jones's eyes I can't say, but his assertions—which are fine as personal statement—are not in keeping with the facts; his theory flounders before that complex of human motives which makes human history, and which is so characteristic of the American Negro. (253)

Ellison is correct to direct our attention to the demands of technique within the context of a single musical tradition; it is surely true that Charlie Parker responded to the accomplishment of Coleman Hawkins as much as he attempted to craft a response to American society. Jones's emphasis on Black music as counterstatement can frustratingly overlook the accomplishments of African-American artistry in tradition, what Ellison calls the "will towards expression." Ellison's retort, however, especially if it is rooted in an emergent cynicism—that *all* conscious rebellion is but a *stance*—is surely more dangerous than Jones's narrative hyperbole.

Moreover, to magnify Ellison's objections may obfuscate what is a crucial unanimity—a concord—between the two thinkers. Ellison himself points to this when he states:

> Perhaps more than any other people, Americans have been locked in a deadly struggle with time, with history. We've fled the past and trained ourselves to suppress, if not forget, troublesome details of the national memory, and a great part of our optimism, like our progress, has been bought at the cost of ignoring the processes through which we've arrived at any given moment in our national existence. We've fought continuously with one another over who and what we are, and, with the exception of the Negro, over who and what is American. (250)

Ellison too can articulate this general discomfort or need for counterstatement. He too consistently gravitates toward a critique of optimism through an obsession with history and complicates (if unwittingly) our understanding of citizenship. While Ellison notes that this is a major point of agreement, he chooses not to explore its implications. This becomes more important when he suggests, as his own strategy for approaching Black music, that:

> The blues speak to us simultaneously of the tragic and the comic aspects of the human condition and they express a profound sense of life shared by many Negro Americans precisely because their lives have combined these modes. This has been the heritage of a people who for hundreds of years could not celebrate birth or dignify death and whose need to live despite the dehumanizing pressures of slavery developed an endless capacity for laughing at their painful experiences. This is a group experience shared by many Negroes, and any effective study of the blues would treat them first as poetry and as ritual. . . . Bessie Smith might have been a "blues queen" to the society at large, but within the tighter Negro community where the blues were part of a total way of life, and a major expression of an attitude toward life, she was a priestess, a celebrant who affirmed the values of the group and man's ability to deal with chaos. (256–57).

Whatever the differences between Ellison's and Jones's positions, the similarities between the two of them are of great significance, and represent an important covenant. They both see a culture of great value and even greater complexity, which has contributed much to the shape of American culture. Suggestive of the ways that antimodernism might be a useful paradigm to bring to the interpretation of African-American culture and the American sixties, they both highlight the religious goals of a resistant African-American culture, although, as Jones highlights the sacred West African cosmology, Ellison chooses to focus upon the ritual, and thus transformative, function of black musical practice. This concord is of immense consequence and reiterates the need for a cultural history of the sixties which takes as seriously such points of intersection as it does obvious differences in style and tone.

Part of Ellison's discomfort can be explained by noting his description of *Blues People* as the "record of an earnest *young* man's attempt to come to grips with his predicament as Negro American during a most turbulent period of our history" [my emphasis].[11] Ellison was perceptive in seeing that the nation was undergoing rapid and vital change; new modes of thinking and *speaking* were being considered. And Ellison, only ten years after coming to his great success, was in danger of being surpassed by a generation of spokesmen and artists more attuned to the mode and expression of the day. Only a year after defending himself in public battle with Irving Howe, a white leftist critic of *his* generation, Ellison found himself faced with the reality of a younger generation of *black* critics, not so willing to declare an affinity for, or attachment to, the kind of humanistic inquiry within which he had achieved success and fame.

———————————

To reiterate, the key to where the black people have to go is in the music. Our music has always been the most dominant manifestation of what we are and feel, literature was just an afterthought, the step taken by the Negro bourgeoisie who desired acceptance on the white man's terms. And that is precisely why the literature has failed. It was the case of one elite addressing another elite. . . . But our music is something else. The best of it has always operated at the core of our lives, forcing itself upon us as in a ritual. It has always, somehow, represented the collective psyche.

LARRY NEAL, "And Shine Swam On" (1968)[12]

The success of Jones's work resulted in a number of imitators, who wrote with varying degrees of insight and success.[13] Jones had defined a coherent field within which the authority to speak had not clearly been determined. This cultural field—"black music"—had a intellectual lineage (folklore scholarship, anthropology and sociology, musicology), but, more importantly, spoke to the centrality of youth cultures and disruptions. Later in the decade, Paul Goodman, the white poet and social theorist, stated:

We now have the abnormal situation that, in the face of the extraordinary novelties and complexities of modern times, there is no persuasive program for social reconstruction, thought up by many minds, corrected by endless criticism, made practical by much political activity. . . . The young are honorable and see the problems, but they don't know anything because we have not taught them anything.[14]

But younger intellectuals were willing to ignore the scoffing of an Ellison, or the despondency and skepticism of a Goodman, and proceed with their own social theorizing, upon a ground that was important and familiar to them. And what they produced was impressive.

Charles Keil (in his *Urban Blues* [1966]) was especially successful in combining an analysis of black music with social concerns.[15] Keil had the advantage of focusing on a relatively small locale (Chicago Blues) and first-hand knowledge of a broad range of traditions, some of which, like gospel, Jones had failed to acknowledge; he demonstrated a more complete knowledge of American social theory, and this work was published by the more academic University of Chicago Press, thus taking the conversation to different locations. A. B. Spellman offered up a biographical study upon some of the same ground. His *Four Lives in the BeBop Business* (1966), a collective biography of the musicians Ornette Coleman, Cecil Taylor, Herbie Nichols, and Jackie McLean, each of whom was somewhat identified with the musical avant-garde, chronicles the discomfort with which America approached the newest direction in jazz in the early sixties. Opposition and black music are here conceived in terms of the "outsidership" of the avant-garde jazz musician, operating without institutional support or audience consensus, not so much a romanticization of the bohemian life as a critique of the banality of the mainstream and blindness of the American audience. Although Larry Neal was never able to write a book-length study, he consistently and effectively articulated the possibilities of this new discourse for the development of a viable cultural nationalism. In "The Ethos of the Blues," Neal offers a more pronounced, if not more precise, class analysis:

> The blues are the ideology of the field slave—the ideology of a new "proletariat" searching for a means of judging the world. Therefore, even though the blues are cast in highly personal terms, they stand for the collective sensibility of a people at particular stages of cultural, social and political development. The blues singer is not an alienated artist attempting to impose his view of the world on others. His ideas are the reflection of an unstated general point of view. Even though he is part of the secular community, his message is often ritualistic and spiritual. Therefore, it is his ritual role in the community which links him to the traditional priests and poets of Africa.[16]

In some ways—the ways in which ritual and ideology are not necessarily separate concerns—Neal was the bridge between Ellison and Jones.[17]

The subtitle of Ben Sidran's *Black Talk* (1971)—How the Music of Black America Created a Radical Alternative to the Values of Western Literary Tradition—identified, in a single phrase, what the thrust of this whole black music discourse was to be. Sidran was not as accomplished a prose stylist as Jones, Spellman, or Neal, but he was perceptive as to new possibilities for research. Sidran was especially interested in black music as wholly unique language and "perceptual framework." The oral orientation of the black music tradition was uniquely qualified, argued Sidran, to negotiate the vicissitudes of modern life. Perhaps hoping for a bit too much, Sidran claims:

> the revolutionary nature of the music itself—its influence in the raw, perceptual sphere—is perhaps more important than its overt social function. It is a way of seeing things and a manner of projecting that vision. When the musician plays, he is objectifying his experience, and, further, playing it for others makes everybody feel better because there is great solace in the experience of community. Music is thus a great force for unity and peace today.[18]

The conscious establishment of the discourse of black music is, after all, a rhetorical gesture within an ongoing cultural argument about the canonicity of various art forms themselves, as well as individual works and artists.[19]

Other critics and commentators seemingly worked the same ground but often their interpretations and synthesis either attempted to repress dissonance and multivocality or else were motivated to ultimately undermine the rebelliousness being unearthed.[20] Frank Kofsky, for instance, firmly located on the revolutionary left, captured and exuded the tenor and substance of the discourse, but had a tendency toward programmatic statement and analysis. While there are interesting moments of cross-disciplinary insight in his work—and real courage to ask direct questions of musicians who were rarely taken seriously as thinkers—it is hard to make claims for his role in *clarifying* anything.[21] His *Black Nationalism and the Revolution in Music* makes the argument that the new black music—by which he mostly means avant-garde jazz—is the most productive cultural space for black nationalistic sentiment, and, by extension, nurtures "radicalism" generally. In some ways, Kofsky's enthusiasms point toward (while being ideologically hostile toward) the discovery of black music subcultures by (white) academic social scientists.[22] Given what Albert Murray has referred to as the power of "social science fictions"—especially in his own contribution to this discourse, *Stomping the Blues* (1974)—it is imperative to consider the significance of this interesting historical moment. For the purposes of this discussion, it is enough to note that the central paradigm under which black musical practice was discussed was that of "deviance." Clearly certain representatives of the academic community saw this discourse as counter to shared norms and conventions, although such violations could largely only be seen in a threatening and pathological manner.

Like all cultural discourse—especially those constructed around race—the discourse of black music spent a great deal of energy on questions of authenticity.[23] For some, black music was an ecumenical expression, encompassing Motown pop, Atlantic Records rhythm and blues, Dixieland revivalist, avant-garde experimentalism, and perhaps even the Ray Charles who released a country and western album in 1961. For others, black music was a particular social attitude, and had less to do with musical style than with the temperament, outlook, or stance of the particular performer: for these listeners, James Brown's version of rhythm and blues was revolutionary, and Rufus Thomas's regressive. Still, what may be most important, in advancing an argument about the decade as a whole, is that the conversation took place at all. African-Americans (and many white Americans) turned to conversations about their diverse and resilient musical traditions to work out questions of central cultural importance. The most important question at this point might be: What were they looking for?

Black music appears, like black poetic identity, to be a performed discourse; despite its openness, it retains and locates meaning insofar as it can effectively define itself in opposition to a particular set of values and cultural issues. It may lack musicological (and sociological) precision, but it still possesses great rhetorical power within ongoing cultural debates about the value of African-American culture, especially as it relies upon "secrecy" and "initiation" to relocate cultural authority upon the margins. America's *attraction* to African-American musical styles creates a unique opening for African-American intellectuals to assume the lectern and speak (within an admitted diversity) about the most central questions of the day. For LeRoi Jones, and other purveyors of the discourse of black music, the most significant figure in African-American music in the sixties was John Coltrane.[24]

JOHN COLTRANE AND THE "NEW THING"

> Every individual's relationship to Trane's music is personal—it's
> sort of like a Protestant religious connection in which one commu-
> nicates with God unmediated by intercession of a priest. But the re-
> lationship is also formal. We refer to him by his surname, Coltrane,
> rarely by his given name John or his spiritual name Ohnedaruth.
> Part of this is the mystery of Coltrane.
>
> KALAMU YA SALAAM, "The Man Who Walked in Balance"[25]

Coltrane's biography, that is to say the story of his life before 1957, is highly
pertinent to unraveling his emergence as an emblem of cultural resistance.[26]
John William Coltrane was born in the South, in Hamlet, North Carolina, on
September 23, 1926, and raised nearby in the town of High Point. Coltrane
had a substantial religious heritage through his grandfather, the Reverend
Walter Blair, who was pastor of St. Stephen's A.M.E. Zion church. The
Coltrane family home had a good library, and Coltrane apparently took
good advantage of it. But music was the central aspect of his early life. His father, J. R. Coltrane, a tailor, played violin and ukulele, and his mother played
piano. His formal musical education began in the community when he took
up the clarinet in the town band. It was not until he was a senior in the
William Penn High School Band, however, that he began to informally take
up the alto saxophone. His most important early influence—as he was for
many—was Johnny Hodges of the Duke Ellington Orchestra, known for his
lyrical and elegant playing. Upon graduation, Coltrane embarked on the
pragmatic *and* mythic journey of South to North, and headed to Philadelphia with some local friends, where he found work in a sugar refinery. He
soon decided to pursue music again—and very seriously—and was accepted
at a local conservatory, the Ornstein School of Music, to study saxophone. In
1945, he was called into active service with the Navy, and was assigned to the
Navy band—clarinet again. He remained with the band, which was stationed
most of the time in Hawaii, until his discharge in June 1946.

Upon his return to Philadelphia, he began to find regular work with
rhythm and blues singers like King Kolax, Joe Webb, Shirley Scott, and Big
Maybelle. In 1947, he toured with Eddie ("Cleanhead") Vinson, and, since
Vinson played alto, Coltrane took up the tenor saxophone, the instrument
with which he would achieve the greatest fame. He continued to tour—
which took him to every part of the United States—until the middle of 1948,
when he felt ready to pursue gigs in the jazz community. As a tenor player
influenced by Charlie Parker and Coleman Hawkins, he played with the
Heath brothers and Howard McGhee, before joining Dizzy Gillespie and his
seminal bebop orchestra. In the course of three years, Coltrane had gone
from playing military marches to rhythm and blues standards to finding a
place with the definitive modern jazz orchestra. These career moves need not
be seen as part of a Whiggish history, but they do represent an encounter

with a variety of styles and sensibilities. In this third "setting," besides getting a chance to observe Gillespie's excellent business sense, management skills, and virtuoso performance and composition, Coltrane met the musician Yusef Lateef, who encouraged his emerging interest in Eastern religions, and regularly provided him with reading material.

Unhappy with his progress as a musician—despite performing admirably in the most critically acclaimed band of the day—Coltrane left Gillespie in early 1951. He returned to Philadelphia and the Granoff School of Music, where he became a student of well-known teachers, Dennis Sandole and Matthew Rastelli. Here he was immersed in the European art music tradition, and especially the late romantics and moderns—Debussy, Ravel, Bartok, and Stravinsky. He returned to the jazz life in 1952, first with Earl Bostic, and then with his hero Johnny Hodges. In 1955, he married Juanita Grubbs, who was soon to become a Muslim, and began important working relationships with Miles Davis and Sonny Rollins. At some point in his famous tenure with the Miles Davis group, he picked up the nickname "Trane," which, like "Bird," Charlie Parker's mythic designation, would, in the years to follow, become a kind of mantra for his followers.

While it should not displace the story above, and the obvious commitment to learning and craft, Coltrane experiences—like Hayden and Romare Bearden—a major breakdown during the decade of the fifties, brought about by the entanglement of drugs and alcohol described at the beginning of this chapter. This can be, at some level, fundamentally uninteresting. Tales of such decline and recovery were common enough in the entertainment industry for them to be mostly banal. As a turning point, its valence is mostly to be measured by the ways in which this historical moment would be revisited at later dates as evidence of sanctification. Whatever the truth about his conversion—and all such tales tend, of course, toward the mythic—Coltrane begins around 1957 to shape (or have shaped for him) his identity as a "seeker."

After 1957, and especially after his experience working with Thelonius Monk, it became increasingly clear to most observers that Coltrane was likely to become one of the major innovators in jazz, eventually to join the pantheon that included Louis Armstrong, Duke Ellington, and Charlie Parker. His 1960 album *Giant Steps* demonstrated his dramatic "technique of arpeggiation in which he broke chords into their constituent notes and piled them and their variants into voluminous runs of unprecedented height and depth [which] opened the instrument's range."[27] For the listener, this meant an extremely dense music, sometimes characterized as "sheets of sound," which was not to everyone's taste. Miles Davis, however, argued that: "I don't understand this talk of Coltrane being difficult to understand. What he does, for example, is to play five notes of a chord and then keep changing it around, trying to see how many different ways it can sound. It's like explaining something five different ways."[28] To elucidate "five different ways" can be and should be construed as a kind of pluralism. It is, perhaps, indicative of the ways in which this music of transformation and transition was both pragmatically and allegorically a kind of open-ended inquiry.

Another component of the interesting intellectual substance of this liminal stage of Coltrane's musical life can be highlighted by pointing to his rejoining Miles Davis, in 1959, to record *Kind of Blue*. Martin Williams notes one aspect of the album's historical significance:

> *Kind of Blue* seems to me key evidence of one of the most remarkable events in Western music in this century. Why should a comparable modality suddenly appear—coincidentally and almost simultaneously—in the music of Ornette Coleman, of Miles Davis and John Coltrane, of the Detroit rock and roll groups, of the British rock groups, of the American "folk" ensembles, and even crop up in the music of the more traditional Chicago-based blues bands?[29]

"Modal" based music, that is medieval subscales anchored to one note with varied intervals—and, not incidentally, associated with early Christian music in the West—tends to be less complex harmonically, yet not necessarily a less profound aesthetic experience. Interestingly, Bill Evans, pianist on *Kind of Blue*, describes the accomplishment of this "modal jazz" in terms of Japanese painting:

> There is a Japanese visual art in which the artist is forced to be spontaneous. He must paint on a thin stretched parchment with a special brush and black water paint in such a way that an unnatural or interrupted stroke will destroy the line or break through the parchment. Erasures or changes are impossible. These artists must practice a particular discipline, that of allowing the idea to express itself in communication with their hands in such a direct way that deliberation cannot interfere.... The resulting pictures lack the complex composition and textures of ordinary painting, but it is said that those who see well find something that escapes explanation.... Group improvisation is a further challenge. Aside from the weighty technical problem of collective coherent thinking, there is the very human, even social need for sympathy from all members to bend for the common result.[30]

Although everyone, including musicians, was skeptical about how long such modal playing would keep the interest of listeners, Coltrane continued to profitably visit this musical reservoir for some time.

One of the most striking "visits" was *My Favorite Things*, which was recorded in October of 1960 and released within the next few months. It sold over 50,000 copies during the first year, which was unheard of for a jazz album. The title song, written by Richard Rodgers, from the then popular musical *The Sound of Music*, clearly was influential in its success. Martin Williams's commentary here is useful. "My Favorite Things," Williams suggests:

could serve his purposes in almost the same way that "How High the Moon" had served Parker's and Gillespie's. Here was a popular song that had, built-in so to speak, the same sort of things that he had been working on: very little chordal motion, folk-like simplicity, a quasi-Eastern mystery, and incantation. Simple but at the same time sophisticated, the piece could contain Coltrane's prodigiousness as an improviser. In no sense was "My Favorite Things" a compromise—and it should not be a surprise that his first recording of it was a best seller.[31]

The album and song also marked Coltrane's reintroduction of the soprano saxophone which was, in many ways, a tribute to the jazz pioneer Sidney Bechet. The title song also contained a clever piece of "signifying": the melody line was based upon the folk tune "Freré Jacques," whose chorus in English translation is most often sung with the line, "Are you sleeping? Are you sleeping? Brother John. Brother John." While some critics and musicians continued to feel that the music was too trite and too popular to serve Coltrane in the long term, the success of *My Favorite Things* led to a lucrative deal with Impulse Records, and an association with a sympathetic producer, Bob Thiele, that provided Coltrane with the financial security to be able to pursue experimental projects.

With Impulse, his audience and his interests continued to grow in depth and breadth. *Olé* (1961) was Coltrane's version of Miles Davis's *Sketches of Spain* and, like that recording, featured folk sources. *Africa/Brass* (1961) was indicative of his interest in non-Western musics, both African and Indian (Coltrane would name one of his children after Ravi Shankar), and, like other black musicians, in the new independence of African nations. However one chooses to interpret (or feel about) his success with a Broadway show tune, there can be little doubt about his historical consciousness. Recordings from the years 1960 to 1962 include "Blues to Bechet," "Liberia," "Songs of the Underground Railroad," "Dahomey Dance," and "Africa." Whatever foundation this may have provided for interpreting or contextualizing his music, it did not satisfy the (mostly white) critics. The "anti-jazz" fervor was becoming so deafening that Coltrane (along with his regular collaborator Eric Dolphy) agreed to answer his critics in print. The April 12, 1962, issue of *Downbeat* included their attempts to explain what they were trying to do. Neither Dolphy's highly technical explanation or Coltrane's insistence that music "was another way of saying this is a big beautiful universe we live in," likely did much to lessen the criticism.[32] One interesting response to the objections of the critics was initiated by Thiele. He encouraged Coltrane to pursue—if only, on the side—a number of more traditional projects. Some of Coltrane's most interesting work, and revisionary and revitalizing in its own way, was in his collaborations with Duke Ellington (1962) and the ballad singer Johnny Hartman (1963).[33] The success of these associations was both critical and popular, and there is plenty of evidence to suggest that Coltrane approached them with the utmost seriousness. The importance of these projects for describing the emergence of African-American antimodern sentiment was the credibility he gave these "past-oriented" recordings. Revealingly, in the liner notes to *John Coltrane & Johnny Hartman*, A. B. Spellman writes of the significance of this collaboration:

> Where are they now? That jazz singing, especially among male singers, has declined since the fadeout of the bebop band is one of the least controversial topics in jazz. Replacing the masculinity of the crooner with the effeteness of the lark is only another kind of the premature destruction of artists by factors which have nothing to do with their art, which destruction we are the passive witnesses of in these times.[34]

From the perspective of the sociology of art, Spellman's observation is not wholly incorrect, but his striking remarks about gender recall earlier emphases within American culture on revitalizing masculinity and are suggestive of the ways in which attempts to actively reclaim the African-American past would (and do) get entangled with a limited gender politics.

Coltrane had the chance to travel to Europe twice during this period, and this, along with his reading, combined to continue to expand his horizons and his ambition. J. C. Thomas describes Coltrane's reading habits:

> He didn't hang around bookstores, but he'd been influenced through the years by many articulate people who had persuaded him to join several book clubs and make some careful selections. He was particularly fond of books about religion and philosophy. Sonny Rollins had suggested *Autobiography of a Yogi*; Bill Evans had recommended Krishnamurti's *Commentaries of Living*. Edgar Cayce, Kahlil Gibran, Egyptology, Scientology, Plato, Aristotle; hundreds of books were stacked on the shelves, scattered around the rooms, and strewn across the bed where his tenor and soprano often rested, for he was also fond of playing as well as reading before bedtime, as if serenading his wife to sleep.[35]

While this is a somewhat populist library of "spirituality," it clearly identifies Coltrane as a thinker, an aspiring intellectual, and also suggests an odd interplay between "Eastern" and "Western" perspectives. As engagement with the world—and in particular an attempt to discover a spiritual realm that might clarify the racial—there is an interesting resonance with the great African-American modernist writer Jean Toomer.

In summary of Coltrane's work from 1957 through 1963, there are two points in particular worth accenting. The first is the importance and propriety of installing him as an intellectual, so that his mysticism to come will be seen as substantive and not crassly escapist or a substitute for engagement with the world. Coltrane's investigation of a plural "attack" on the saxophone and his cooperative scrutiny of the possibility of musical modes has quite interesting cultural valence and is pursued with *intent*. The second element to accentuate, intimately related to the first, is that there are two emerging dialectics within his career: popular appeal and worldliness work with and against an increasingly monastic or ascetic approach to the "profession," and consciousness about black history and culture functions cooperatively with and in contradistinction to an "eastward gaze." In terms of the first dialectic, "woodshedding" is, of course, a central component of the jazz tradition, but in Coltrane it convincingly becomes a search for something more than cultural power or professional mastery. Coltrane resists self-involvement even as his performance practice increasingly comes to rely upon radically extended solos. Ideally, the significant "outward content" of his music and its revealed context hold off the charge of a destructive narcissism, ostensibly the very target of his critique of American culture. With regards to the second dynamic, like Robert Hayden, William Demby, and Romare Bearden, an immersion in African-American cultural forms, stories, and practices does not banish the need to look outside the familial and familiar. The complexity of these two dialectical processes is sustained so scrupulously that it should make obvious the rectitude of Coltrane as intellectual.

But insisting upon that intellectual substance of Coltrane's approach to the world is not to deny the fragility of each dialectic. They are open to misapplication and distortion by others, and exaggeration or unthoughtful repetition on the part of the artist. To proceed without either Coltrane's great Whitman-like self-invention or, more importantly, his significant personal investment in maintaining a tension that is creative and productive is to potentially select at will and replace that which is fundamentally out of step with American culture with something much more easily maintained by the consumer capitalist ethos. Like the emergent discourse of black music itself, even a revolutionary artistic practice (or talk about that practice) can become stagnant if applied without continued attentiveness to what was originally at stake. Coltrane's sixties masterpiece *A Love Supreme* is a prime example of his ability to get the most out of this double dialectic, and hold off both *despair* and frivolity. It is recognizable and disruptive, a work of significant aesthetic and cultural power, and yet there are still hints of real difficulty on the horizon.

"EVERYBODY GET TOGETHER": THE LOVE ETHIC AND COLTRANE JAZZ

> My goal is to live the truly religious life and express it through my music. . . .
>
> JOHN COLTRANE (1964)[36]

The themes which monastic discipline assigned to friars for meditation were designed to turn them away from the world and its affairs. The thoughts which we are developing here originate from similar considerations. At a moment when the politicians in whom the opponents of Fascism had placed their hopes are prostrate and confirm their defeat by betraying their own cause, these observations are intended to disentangle the political worldings from the snares in which the traitors have entrapped them. Our consideration proceeds from the insight that the politicians' stubborn faith in progress, their confidence in their "mass basis," and, finally, their servile integration in an uncontrollable apparatus have been three aspects of the same thing. It seeks to convey an idea of the high price our accustomed thinking will have to pay for a conception of history that avoids any complicity with the thinking to which these politicians continue to adhere.

WALTER BENJAMIN, *Illuminations*[37]

Coltrane's music of the sixties, like his religious interests, is of significant range and complexity.[38] Larry Neal notes that Coltrane's music "indicate[s] devices, procedures, functions, attitudes, and concerns, that are not vividly indicated in Euro-American culture. They indicate a synthesis and a rejection of Western musical theory at the same time."[39] Comfortable with the "classic Coltrane quartet" (Elvin Jones on drums, Jimmy Garrison on bass, McCoy Tyner on piano), Coltrane could depend upon his regular sidemen to be supportive—musically and fraternally—of his musical quests. Usually his musical expansiveness is described as taking place in two directions. He developed a number of different methods to make the saxophone (and the jazz saxophone repertoire) sound "different";[40] this may be the technological equivalent of Davis's comment about his improvisations being an attempt to explain something in as many ways as possible. At any rate it should be most definitely seen as consistent with the tendency within jazz (and other African-American musical traditions) of celebrating voice or specific marks of identity in sound and style. Secondly, and in some ways more of interest to the casual listener, he expanded the *shape* of jazz—its thematic content, instrumentation, base structures, and performance practice.[41]

Not enough work has been done in linking musicological concerns to cultural movements, although this chapter certainly means to encourage thinking in that direction.[42] Martin Williams's not-so-hypothetical question about the reemergence of modes (the musical grounding of church plainsong and chant), for instance, deserves (still) further reflection.[43] Again, Frank Kofsky attempted to be most forceful in this manner with respect to the specific form and content of Coltrane's work, but as John Gennari points out, he "is so anxious to have Coltrane assent to the view that his music is vitally and irreducibly connected to Malcolm X's political messages that he doesn't seem to be able to hear what Coltrane is saying."[44] At certain points in Coltrane's sixties career, the work invites and demands a willingness to engage the social text. In particular, this is true of his recording, from November of 1963, "Alabama," in response to the Birmingham church bombings. It is, on the one hand, clearly a dirge, and one of Coltrane's most striking works in an elegiac mode. In terms of its "feel," Martin Williams writes that it "begins as if with solemn meditation, moves to prayer, to hope, to affirmation, and ends again in prayer."[45] In his liner notes to *Live at Birdland*, LeRoi Jones notes, however, that its accomplishment may be of a whole other order. "I didn't realize until now," he writes, "what a beautiful *word* Alabama is." Jones extends his reflection to make what is now, perhaps, a common observation, but for 1964 to be talking of black musicianship in jazz in such terms was somewhat unusual. Of Coltrane's accomplishment in "Alabama," he writes, "That is one function of art, to reveal beauty, common or uncommon, uncommonly."[46] "Alabama" is both representation and revelation. Jones quotes Coltrane speaking directly to the historical moment and his aesthetic response. It represents, suggests Coltrane, "musically, something that I saw down there translated into music from inside me." While music itself is always somewhat of an indirect response—and while Coltrane kept close to the vest his own political opinions—careful attention to "history" can be suggestive of the ways in which Coltrane attempted to fuse a specific response to the world. "Alabama" is a striking moment of antimodern cohesion. It is transforming, critical, regretful, and hopeful. Most importantly, it seems as if it was a necessary step toward a musical accomplishment even more historically and aesthetically rich.

It is generally acknowledged, even by those who do not favor his music, that Coltrane's masterpiece was *A Love Supreme* (1964). A musical suite of four sections—Acknowledgment, Resolution, Pursuance, and Psalm—it was incredibly well received. By 1970, Lewis Porter reports, the album recording released in 1964 had sold over 500,000 copies, especially striking when one considers that a typical Coltrane album had to that point sold about 30,000 copies. The thrust of the recording, which is slightly over half an hour long, was partially captured by the cover photograph of Coltrane printed on both the back and front. (See figure 1.) Eschewing more conventional representations which would focus upon the man and his instrument, this profile shot drew the viewer's attention to Coltrane's eyes. The musician/artist was captured looking intently into the distance. It is a richly meditative photograph and pose that reinforced the album's commitment to a general religiosity and spirituality. In addition to the photo and the section titles, Coltrane also included a prayer poem and a letter to the listener which powerfully recounted his conversion some seven years previous. No listener/reader could avoid the religious mood, sentiment, and content.

The intersection of jazz and religion was not wholly without precedent. Since the early 1950s periodic appeals to "youth" by both Protestant and Catholic churches had resulted in "jazz masses" and other hybrid and populist liturgies. Duke Ellington, Mary Lou Williams, and Lalo Schifrin each experimented with longer works with religious themes (distinctly austere and noble in tone), works that were meant to have specific religious resonance, and works specifically liturgical in character. Despite this minirenaissance, there was some obvious tension. Even while acknowledging its

Figure 1. Album cover, John Coltrane, A Love Supreme, *ca. 1964 (MCA Records).*

roots in West African cultural tradition, it is necessary to note that the de-velopment of jazz in the United States has largely been in profoundly secular contexts.[47] Granted that Coltrane was in the process of shaping himself as a "seeker," and, perhaps, that "Alabama" is funereal, it is still a risky venture on Coltrane's part to enter into the fray in such a sweeping manner. On the one hand, the religious experiments by Ellington, Williams, Coltrane, and, soon to come, Albert Ayler, are suggestive of a general discomfort with the shape and direction of American jazz and culture, and yet, on the other hand, the music remained closely connected with components of that culture suppos-edly distant from that religious sensibility: the nightclub and consumer cap-italism, the buying and selling of records.

More often than not, commentators have focused on the amorphous character of Coltrane's religiosity, especially in *A Love Supreme*. Despite the overwhelming number of religious signals, he never declares himself to be a follower of any particular religion. For some critics, and even more celebrants, this is crucial. Kalamu Ya Salaam argues that:

> Trane's non-sectarian religiosity is a major aspect of his revolutionary thrust. Trane was neither Christian nor Muslim. Describing himself, Trane said "I believe in all religions." His outlook was larger than any single orthodoxy and this enabled him to creatively use religious material to maximum effect because he could discern and draw on the spiritual truths of all of them. This spiritual and musical ecumenicalism was a completely different track from that taken by most people who became deeply spiritual.[48]

Such a leveled religiosity can, of course, also appear bland and without real intellectual content. Close attention to contextual clues and textual artistry might, however, suggest something a little different. In his note to "Dear Listener," for instance, Coltrane writes:

> ALL PRAISE BE TO GOD TO WHOM ALL PRAISE IS DUE. Let us pursue him in the righteous path. Yes it is true; "seek and ye shall find." Only through Him can we know the most wondrous bestowal. During the year 1957, I experienced, by the grace of God, a spiritual awakening which was to lead me to a richer, fuller, more productive life. At the same time, in gratitude, I humbly asked to be given the means and privilege to make others happy through music. I feel this has been granted through His grace. ALL PRAISE TO GOD.[49]

It can be established that Coltrane's religiosity in the packaging of *A Love Supreme* is significantly invested in a patriarchal supreme being to whom the subject must give thanks for both "grace" and worldly abilities. While it is true that the rhythms of this presentation are not obviously Christian, in some ways the rhetoric here seems to suggest the influence of any number of musician friends who converted to Islam in the late 1940s and 1950s. The direct address and praise of the divine would place his investigation and encounter most comfortably within the purview of Islam and Christianity. It is reasonable to suggest that Coltrane has not entirely left his black Methodist (A.M.E. Zion) heritage behind, as Robert Hayden could not wholly divest himself of his Baptist inheritance, even if that past is inflected with the rhetoric and piety of the peculiar jazz-Islam intersection. (Neither is it thoroughly inappropriate to note that such testimony is reminiscent of Puritan conversion narrative. While Coltrane is not what LeRoi Jones called a "Puritan shopkeeper," he has seemingly inherited an obsession with public austerity and moral perfection.) A special concern for the individual's flawed nature is also evident. While the tone of his letter is triumphant, he does make clear that as "time and events moved on, a period of irresolution did prevail." At some level, Coltrane's grand theme—here and elsewhere—is sin. "I entered into a phase which was contradictory to the pledge and away from the esteemed path; but thankfully, now and again through the unerring and merciful hand of God, I do perceive and have been duly re-informed of his OMNIPOTENCE, and of our need for and dependence on Him." This kind of testimony would not be unfamiliar in the A.M.E. Zion churches of North Carolina. The insistence that Coltrane is "universal" may again—as we saw in the case of Robert Hayden—have more to do with the desires of listener/readers than it does with the content of his religiosity. His cultural criticism is not necessarily well served by insisting upon a global, nonsectarian consciousness. Coltrane's cosmopolitanism cannot be questioned, but that should not inhibit the careful evaluation of specific components of his religiosity. In speaking the language of human limitation—of personal and cultural ruins—Coltrane does participate in a fairly focused challenge to myths of progress and the denial of death. *A Love Supreme* can be experienced as a substantive and even unrelenting jeremiad. He reminds the reader/listener that he has been to the precipice and come back. The musician/seeker opts for reenchantment in his encounter with the dialectic of Enlightenment.

The acknowledgment of backsliding is surely part of what makes Coltrane an attractive human being and typical of the great humility that so many individuals ascribed to him. But it is somewhat surprising, given the way Coltrane grew to be such a celebrated countercultural figure, that the context for the music would seem to be so heavily invested in "submission." Furthermore, the language of submission, especially in the context of recalling his battle with drugs and alcohol, is also reminiscent of 12-step programs like Alcoholics Anonymous. While Coltrane certainly nods in the direction of his readings in traditional and derivative Eastern religions, in other ways his epistle is firmly rooted in mid-century Protestant angst and American civil religion. Most commentators have opted for "mystery" to explain its appeal, but the popularity of *A Love Supreme* may have much less to do with its rebelliousness or its opposition than it does with its recognizability.

Close attention to Coltrane's prayer poem allows for some expansion of this reading. On the one hand, it is immediately noticeable for its repetition of a particular theme: the goodness, necessity, oneness, expansiveness, and incomparability of God. Indeed, the poem is interesting for the way in which it—unlike "Dear Listener"—holds off both narrative and lyric sensibilities. Still, it is varied enough that it is clearly not "chant."

Help us to resolve our fears and weaknesses.
Thank you God.
In you all things are possible.
We know. God made us so.
Keep your eyes on God.
God is. He always was. He always will be.
No matter what . . . it is God.
He is gracious and merciful.
It is most important that I know Thee.

Words, sounds, speech, men, memory, thoughts,
  fears and emotions — time — all related . . . all
  made from one . . . all make in one.
Blessed be his name. (lines 8–20)

There is a nice tension between the repetition of its theme and its formal wandering that forestalls somewhat the poem's urgency and earnestness. Ironically, such meandering may clarify the totality of the faith statement. It is certainly unlikely that the poem's variation is due to Coltrane being relatively unlettered. As it is presented on the album's inner sleeve, the poem is divided into two parts, each a numerologically rich 33 lines. Most importantly, as Lewis Porter has effectively documented, the poem is "recited" during the saxophone improvisation in "Psalm." In the "Dear Listener" section, Coltrane describes "Psalm" as "a musical narration of the theme 'A Love Supreme' which is written in the context . . ." The literary text, his theme, and musical practice become — as is his theme — one.

The abstractness of "written in the context" is, of course, usefully illustrative of the abstractness with which spiritual content is supposedly communicated. The question of how the composition's "spiritual" concerns are musically present is not straightforwardly resolved. Samuel Floyd, for instance, suggests that when individuals ascribe "mystery" to Coltrane they are really articulating something about the difficulty of his work.[50] Indeed, one thing that is striking about *A Love Supreme* is just how distant the music is from jazz's popular musical roots. Certainly listeners were increasingly expectant of such challenges — again, Charles Mingus and Ornette Coleman were making this a matter of course, and Duke Ellington always had similar aspirations — but with Coltrane's *Love* there is a kind of dramatic and final break. No doubt such disorientation can place the listener in a kind of quasi-ritual or sacred context. Lewis Porter, pursuing a different strategy, highlights what he calls the connection between the structural plan and the spiritual message. Musical patterns are put to special theological ends. Noting, for example, the appearance of the "Love Supreme" chant toward the *end* of the solo in "Acknowledgment," Porter connects Coltrane's "reverse development" and "revelation." "He's telling us that God is everywhere — in every register, in every key — and he's showing us that you have to discover religious belief."[51] A good example of a more general description is John Litweiler's:

A Love Supreme is a suite of reflections . . . and the subject of the suite's program is his 1957 spiritual awakening. Yearning — for transcendence? — underlies the suite and in fact is specific through most of the music. The line of triplets in the opening "Acknowledgment" has little relief; without succumbing to compulsion, this solo at least presents the characteristics of obsession. The "Resolution" of the second movement's theme begins in temporary resignation that is penetrated by a yearning blue note in measure 4, but acceptance arrives in the consonant conclusion of the next phrase. Tyner plays big 3/4 chords on the

4/4 rhythm to mount grand tension for Coltrane's improvisation, and now, for one of the few times in a long modal solo, the tenorist's phrasing is varied so that the patterns are not compulsive but distributed; the powerful movement of "Resolution" is of the full heart and mind. "Pursuance" begins in extroversion that is quickly cast away: Suddenly yearning becomes overwhelming with shrieks and lurching, while in "Psalm" Coltrane's spiritual odyssey becomes disheartened.[52]

The language here obscures as much as it reveals and thus what is arguably the central difficulty in ascribing to Coltrane "opposition" is identified. How do we resolve our ephemeral experience of the music to a desire to have the religious context "mean" something specific? In other words, given the social context of the sixties, how can *A Love Supreme* "answer questions" about destiny, providence, or whatever? (Of course, Litweiler does intuit a great deal as he goes on to identify "failure" and "limitation" as central to the "epiphany" that the suite provides.) If the music is "abstract" and ultimately lacking in social coherence, how do we explain the fervor of his followers? Technically, as Porter demonstrates, Coltrane attempts to deal with the paradox by rhythmically binding the language of the prayer to the playing of individual notes. But this too seems potentially the articulation of a language so personal as to be counter to the production of an effective conversation about the strengths and weaknesses of the culture out of which it emerges, to be counter to communicating a message. Porter points out, for instance, that the musicians in Coltrane's band were unaware that Coltrane was "playing the poem" during the Psalm solo.

These questions are not so much meant to install a permanent skepticism around the question of musical critique, or to disavow the specific culture-critical potential of the discourse of black music; far from it. There is, however, good reason to resist the urgent tendency to politicize Coltrane. Indeed, much of the music's resistance to cultural denotation makes this necessary, as does Coltrane's own reticence about speaking directly to the political situation of the day. Most straightforwardly, it may be worth restating the variability of the discourse of black music, perhaps, to get some real sense of the multivalent possibility of someone like Coltrane, or at least to serve as reminder that it is a sense of vigorous inquiry toward the world that may be most representative of the antimodern attitude. Coltrane's most accomplished criticism may have to do with his unwillingness to accept that which is "natural," the world as it is.

One complication worth following through, however, is to note the ways in which the lack of ideological precision leaves open the possibility of distortion or worse. Similar to the ways in which Hayden's work is claimed as nonracial, the expansiveness of Coltrane's "love ethic" is potentially swallowed up by the tendency of consumer culture to sentimentalize love or to seek to define it only in the terms of the popular romance. Todd Gitlin has nicely described "everybody get together" as one of the great, if limited, themes of sixties pop musical sensibility. With the arrival of the Beatles (also c. 1964), and a slide toward the Haight-Ashbury vortex, *everyone* was singing the praises of *a love supreme*.[53] In the same way that Coltrane's celebration of the authority of the divine can be complexly immersed within American civil religion—become, in Sacvan Bercovitch's formulation, a "ritual of consensus"—so too can the critical potential of a love sermon be quickly swallowed up by a culture easily enraptured by sentimentality. This may be doubly the case when that love is surrounded by the aura of mysticism or astral irrationality. Gitlin writes:

> Thus the looming popularity of astrology, the I Ching, and other founts of mystical wisdom and explanation. The stars (or the Book of Changes, or the chakras, or the more esoteric systems of yoga, Sufism, etc. to which the real cognoscenti graduated) were all at once a relief, a link to a mysterious past, a connection to the ultimate, a guarantee of personal meaning, a grid of "rationality," and an alibi. (204)

To be interested in any or all of these does not necessitate a kind of cultural quietism, but from Gitlin's perspective—as the battle-scarred activist—that is certainly how these enthusiasms felt. In some ways, they emerged directly counter to the concrete political interventions of the civil rights and free speech movements.

Still, Coltrane had been pursuing these interests for at least a decade and a half prior to their faddishness. Coltrane's *love supreme* is not necessarily corrupt. There is evidence that he had access to and was influenced by thinking on the subject outside of this degrading minimization. Martin Luther King Jr.'s exacting efforts throughout the early to mid-sixties to distinguish between "eros" and "agape" are extremely pertinent here. Increasingly under attack from those impatient about the pace of change and suspicious that nonviolent resistance was not resistance at all, King worked hard to articulate the specificity of the love that he had in mind. Arguing for what he called "the most durable power," as early as 1957, King noted that:

> *Agape* means nothing sentimental or basically affectionate; it means understanding, returning good will for all men, an overflowing love which seeks nothing in return. It is the love of God working in the lives of men. When we love on the *agape* level we love men not because we like them, not because their attitudes and ways appeal to us, but because God loves them. Here we rise to the position of loving the person who does the evil deed while hating the deed he does.[54]

Distancing himself from popular conceptions of love rooted in *romance*, King attempts over the course of the decade to emphasize love as action, force, and power. Responding to Kenneth B. Clark's question about the usefulness of love in the face of Birmingham, King asserts that "I don't think of love, as in this context, as emotional bosh. I don't think of it as a weak force, but I think of love as something strong and that organizes itself into powerful direct action."[55] (It is worth noting that at least part of the elegiac tone of *A Love Supreme* may have been related to the force of *eros*. Perhaps distracted by what Denis de Rougemont called the "passion myth," Coltrane experienced the deterioration and break-up of his marriage in the early sixties, partially driven by an extended relationship he pursued outside of the marriage—possibly his period of "irresolution.")[56] There is little question about the influence of King, and the drama of the civil rights movement more generally, on Coltrane. He may also have known about the work of the black mystic Howard Thurman. In Thurman's *Disciplines of the Spirit* (1963)[57] (a book whose organization is strikingly similar to Coltrane's suite: "Commitment, Growing in Wisdom, Suffering, Prayer, Reconciliation") he sketches out another possible resisting mode of love:

> There is a steady anxiety that surrounds man's experience of love. It may stab the spirit by calling forth a bitter, scathing self-judgment. The heights to which it calls may seem so high that all incentive is lost and the individual is stricken with utter hopelessness and despair. It may throw in relief old and forgotten weaknesses to which one has made the adjustment of acceptance—but which now stir in their place to offer themselves as testimony of one's unworthiness and to challenge the love with their embarrassing reality. (123)

This nicely recalls Coltrane's relentless self-evaluation. But Thurman insists —as does Coltrane—that this is not cause for *permanent* angst. A critical love, he insists, has "no traffic in sentimentality.... Instead, there is robust vitality that quickens the roots of personality, creating an unfolding of the self that redefines, reshapes, and makes all things new" (123). Coltrane has access to—indeed should be seen as part of—an African-American tradition of articulating the possibilities of love as a revitalizing force within American culture. His cosmopolitanism—potentially problematic here as a shallow intellectual tourism—is balanced by more local rootedness. The discourse and *practice* of the civil rights movement, in addition to his commitments to African-American history and culture, provide for *A Love Supreme*, and, to a certain extent, more challenging experiments to come, a moral center not easily dislodged by a trifling escapism.

Regardless of how one feels about the rightness of the mainstream civil rights movement's strategy of nonviolent resistance, *A Love Supreme* can still feel oddly like a kind of negative prophecy. The album is recorded in December 1964, the same month that Coltrane would do a benefit concert for *Freedomways* magazine, and is released in early 1965, a crucial watershed year for the civil rights movement.[58] The Selma to Montgomery march in March is, perhaps, the pinnacle, but there are severe (and shocking) difficulties to come. In August of 1965 was the conflagration in the Watts section of Los Angeles, and, arguably, there was an immediate shift in tone to the movement. The orientation of the SNCC leadership changed that fall from the consensus integrationist, nonviolent perspective to something more nationalist and confrontational. The war in Vietnam would begin to escalate and, in general, for most individuals actively involved in concretely challenging the state, a universal ethic of love was increasingly irrelevant.

This sense of historical slow-footedness is potentially reinforced by a latent class politics. In the liner notes to *Meditations* (1966), in some ways the most important *spiritual* follow-up to *A Love Supreme*, Nat Hentoff reports Coltrane as saying:

> Once you become aware of this force for unity in life . . . you can't ever forget it. It becomes part of everything you do. . . . My goal in meditating on this through music, however, remains the same. And that is to uplift people, as much as I can. To inspire them to realize more and more of their capacities for living meaningful lives. Because there certainly is meaning to life.[59]

"Uplift" is a striking word choice here. It is consistent with the imagery of transcendence in Coltrane's work (especially *Ascension*), and, for that matter, consistent with a whole body of African-American folk material on "rising" and "flying." However, in other ways it is even more reminiscent of a (black) middle-class ideology of mobility and change.[60] Through moral perfection, entrepreneurial aptitude, and "leadership," the race can be raised up. The "civil rights" paradigm itself, of course, was heavily invested in demanding of the American nation that they put into practice the totality of America's standing (if sometimes inactive) tradition of political liberty and respect for human achievement, and for many folks—by no means all—such a challenge meant getting on with the business of bourgeois acquisition. One corollary, then, to Gitlin's critique of escape in the search for the ecstatic, is to note the (potentially) comfortable complacency of this religiosity with middle-class existence.

So while critics and celebrants have largely endorsed *A Love Supreme*'s spirituality without question, there is that sense that the recording and composition is just slightly behind the social relevance curve. None of this should deflect attention away from the unquestionably significant aesthetic accomplishment on its own terms. Without question, part of *A Love Supreme*'s appeal and accomplishment is the superb musicianship of Coltrane, Garrison, Tyner, and Jones. It is compelling listening even without the spiritual packaging. As a composition, there is carefully managed tension and drama. Time and expectation are manipulated so that a feeling reminiscent of William Demby's injunction that "something is about to happen" is constantly at hand. Again, however, neither is this hesitation meant to permanently forestall an appreciation of *A Love Supreme* as an important work of American cultural criticism. It is to insist that that criticism is not transparent and is entangled in complicated ways with that which it may mean to challenge. If *A Love Supreme* is caught in the past it may be so productively. Like Paule Marshall's distracting commitment to a dense realism, the anachronistic character of this composition and recording may be part of its message and enduring legacy.

COLTRANE AND FREEDOM

Coltrane's experiments after *A Love Supreme—Downbeat*'s album of the year for 1965—were increasingly controversial. It is striking that Coltrane's next benefit concert was for the Black Arts Repertory Theater and School in March of 1965, an indication, perhaps, that he was choosing to cast his lot with the avant-gardism of the youngest black musicians, especially Archie Shepp, Pharoah Sanders, and Albert Ayler. Even the members of his group became increasingly skeptical: McCoy Tyner and Elvin Jones both had left Coltrane—while still fully supporting his need to search—by early 1966. He was committed to adding extra players (beyond the quartet that had been so successful) and compounding the complexity of his compositions by opening up patterns of improvisation. (Ironically, some of the best of this music is reminiscent of the raucous collective improvisation of New Orleans or Dixieland jazz.) Solos now extended beyond the stamina *and* comprehension of many audience members, including many of those who had been most enthusiastic about *A Love Supreme*. Recording engineers had to resort to "fading out" his performances, for they did not fit any standard time format. Of this period one critic wrote:

> By the time of his death [1967], I think Coltrane himself realized that he had reached a place he did not know how to get out of. There is nothing left to strip out of his music, nothing forbidden he could try, no freedom left. Only the universal rumble and buzz which is random, which is utterly liberated, which is noise.[61]

Meditations (1965), for example, is the obvious follow-up to *A Love Supreme* and there is significant repetition in the titling of particular pieces: "The Father and the Son and the Holy Ghost," "Compassion," "Love," "Consequences," "Serenity." In some respects, Coltrane's (and African-American culture's) Christian heritage is straightforwardly on display, as is his more broadly transcendental side. The most significant change is in instrumentation, with the addition of a second tenor (Pharoah Sanders) and second drummer (Rashied Ali) that alters somewhat the tension at the center of Coltrane's oeuvre, between control and multiplicity, and shifts it toward the radically plural. Nat Hentoff describes the new interplay between the horns as similar to the "gift of tongues." It is the insistence upon the necessity of a special language to accomplish transformation. Coltrane's late work is more likely to insist upon extraordinary and portentous articulation over everyday musical speech. A distinction between varieties of American poetic modernism may be somewhat helpful here: *A Love Supreme* may be profitably compared to Ezra Pound's strategic remembering, whereas the later Coltrane might be seen to be working more along the lines of Charles Olson's "projective" verse. Coltrane is willing to work the totality of the musical page, disregarding "margins," and both narrative and lyric expectation. The limitation of this analogy is that what is retained is an absolute commitment to the sacred, or, more accurately, a reunification of sacred and secular, as found in West African worldviews. This critical difference makes of Coltrane, even as he pushed beyond a straightforward commitment to memory as central to aesthetic practice, an antimodernist (and, as Lorraine Hansberry prophesied, quasi-romantic), rather than situating him at the cusp of debates about the boundary between the modern and postmodern.

As with most artistic modernisms, the danger here is that the artist's vocabulary becomes so personal, so distinct from cultural heritage or contemporary history, that the freedom of creation on the part of the artist, and the freedom of interpretation on the part of the audience both become meaningless. And yet the charge that is often made—that *Ascension*, *Kulu Se Mama*, and *Om* (all 1965), for example, are "unlistenable"—is overstatement and simplification, not especially distant from and ideologically consistent with the anti-jazz fervor of the early part of the decade. If one examines the titles of recordings from this late period—1965 to 1967—there is indeed a decline of titles obviously rooted in African-American history and culture; on the other hand, new patterns begin to emerge, patterns rooted in the language of "space": astrology, astronomy, interstellar travel, and the calendrical. (See, for instance, "Sun Ship," "Stellar Regions," "Sun Star," "Seraphic Light," "Mars," "Venus," all 1965–1967.) Coltrane *begins* to work out a new cohesive myth for the post-Watts universe. (Notably, it's a myth simultaneously explored by Sun Ra and Samuel Delany.) While some may charge that Coltrane's (and others') biggest crime is to dismiss or devalue central rituals of African-American musical culture—i.e., you can't dance to this music—pop-funkster George Clinton will appear on the scene within a half dozen years and reveal that the new myths, at least, had plenty of possibility for conventional mythic exploration.

Perhaps most disappointing about the charge of "unlistenability" is that it downplays significant musical diversity. Coltrane's first album after *A Love Supreme* was *The John Coltrane Quartet Plays* (1965) and included striking versions of the show-tune "Chim Chim Cheree" and the Nat Cole nugget "Nature Boy." *Meditations* (1965) and *Ascension* (1965) do rely upon an energetic cacophony (although hardly unstructured) and make room for looser individual and collective improvisation; *Kulu Se Mama* (1965) is one of Coltrane's most striking recordings, largely because of the contribution of vocalist and percussionist Juno Lewis and its comfortable synthesis of post-bop jazz with a more obviously West African approach to rhythm and ensemble play. (It is perhaps indicative of where Coltrane may have headed had there been more time to pursue his interest in African music.) *Om* (1965) is the least intellectually satisfying of all of the post-*Love* recordings. It is the only occasion in

Coltrane's substantial body of recorded work where the cross-cultural urge feels more like tourism than a successful effort at syncretic transformation. (If the rumors of Coltrane's extensive use of LSD are true, then, yes, *Om* may indeed be an outright embarrassment, but on those terms no more embarrassing than 75 percent of American pop, which was also drug-inflected by that point in the decade.) Most impressively, Coltrane's 1966 tour of Japan—chronicled on *Coltrane Live in Japan*—was compelling and beautiful evidence of his ability and willingness to shift back and forth between musical approaches and commitments. Coltrane was obviously honest in his insistence that this was a real quest on his part to discover the breadth of possibility in human musical activity. This is not to say that there is not real unease at the middle of this multiple practice. Ravi Shankar's response that there seemed to be a great deal of "turmoil" at the center of this music is prescient. Some have speculated that the musical restlessness was perhaps related to a perception on Coltrane's part that, indeed, his time was short.

Alice Coltrane recalls:

> When he became avant garde, as they termed it, he lost many people, many followers. They didn't like it, they didn't approve of it, they didn't appreciate it. And there was no way he could go back, there was no road to return on. It was his commitment, it was his decision.[62]

As John Coltrane put it, "There was nothing else to do but go ahead."[63] Regardless of how one feels about these new musical experiments, it is admirable that Coltrane would be willing to risk audience loyalty (and significant financial reward) in his pursuit of a musical truth. Perhaps most importantly, much of the late work seems to anticipate many of the very complications suggested here by *A Love Supreme*'s openness to assimilation and sentimentalization. If nothing else, Coltrane's questing towards the end of his life demands new work on the part of his audience, an extension again, perhaps, of a kind of Puritan ethic applied to interpretation. Listeners have to abandon preconceptions of how music is to be organized and presented, even how individual instruments should sound. They need to consider new intellectual and religious frames of reference. They need to challenge themselves—once again—to move beyond provincial perspectives and the monotony of convention.

Martin Williams offers up the most famous hesitation toward Coltrane's rapid and challenging quest:

> I know that Coltrane's audiences were usually enthralled. I know the sincerity, the powerful and authentic emotion, and the frequent skill involved . . . and yet—to be entirely subjective about Coltrane's music at this period—I was, and am, repeatedly disengaged. . . . One man's incantation is another man's monotony. . . . The changes in his work may, of course, have been signs of growth, and if they were, few impor-

tant jazz improvisers have grown and developed as much as Coltrane
did in so short a time. But on the other hand, the changes may have
been naive. Or they may have been signs of personal indecision or frustration. . . . The deeper purpose of the incantory sections in his music
has to be—as with any incantation—to evoke the gods and the demons
whose ways are timeless and yet always contemporary. Perhaps, if his
music does not quite reach me and satisfy me as it has reached some
others, the answer is that the gods he sought to invoke are not my
gods.[64]

Williams points in the direction of the historicist suspicion of modernism in
a way not unlike Georg Lukás's critique of modernist fiction. Distrustful of
subjectivism, it is ultimately convinced that a lack of faith in history is destructive. While Williams suggests that this is ultimately a question of taste
and faith, the real (if implied) invective here is against narcissistic repetition
and an engagement with irrationalism. This is not an unreasonable fear but
by not pursuing it Williams does not ask the important question: What does
this music do? Of course, it cannot comfortably be asked insofar as it can be
straightforwardly turned around: What does your music do? In one respect,
Williams' "to be entirely subjective" indirectly endorses Coltrane's search,
and yet, to misrepresent the whole of Coltrane's oeuvre as "incantation"
(non-history) ultimately enables the possibility of marginalizing the musical
search. *The Smithsonian Collection of Classic Jazz*, under Williams's direction, includes a single selection from Coltrane's work, "Alabama."

Insofar as African-American antimodernism effectively insists upon a
tragic component to history, it is appropriate to note the necessity of disrupting Whiggish histories of either jazz or Coltrane in which, as Scott Deveaux points out in "Constructing the Jazz Traditions" all artistic production is seen as inevitably leading toward more effective democratic
expression or conversations. John Litweiler asserts that:

The quest for freedom . . . appears at the very beginning of jazz and
reappears at every growing point in the music's history. The earliest
jazz musicians asserted their independence of melody, structure,
rhythm, and expression from turn-of-the-century musics that surrounded them; Louis Armstrong symbolized the liberation of the late
twenties jazz soloist; the Count Basie band offered liberation of jazz
rhythm; and Parker and Gillespie offered yet more new freedoms to
jazz.[65]

This is mostly true—and suggestive of how intertwined this vernacular
American art form was with any number of Western modernisms (yet never
reducible to it)—but such an imperative is too easily translated into in-
evitability. The crucial question may be "What *kind* of freedom?" LeRoi
Jones's question from *Blues People* is here pertinent: "What is it that [young
African-Americans] are being asked to save?" In the specific context of the

sixties, the real irony associated with this search for freedom is that as its practitioners (and supporters invested in the discourse of black music) continue to push at the boundaries they come face to face with the European avant-garde. We might describe the interesting overlap between the work of an Anthony Braxton and a Karl Stockhausen as the "postmodern problem." If the discourse of black music was, as many of its instigators insisted, counter-Enlightenment, anti-Western, etc., how was it that the twentieth-century extension of the Western art music tradition looked suspiciously in 1965 like "African" activity? There is significant room here to talk about shared disaffection (the role of Jewish musicians, for instance, in advancing particular kinds of changes) and, perhaps, about the entanglement of African and European perspectives in the earliest modernisms. What is clear, however, is that the question of resistance with regard to black musical practices within American culture was (and still is) somewhat undertheorized. The compelling dialectic in Coltrane's career between popular acceptance (and revision of popular forms) and avant garde marginalization is cause for further thinking and a distinct and compelling caution.

Liver cancer would not permit Coltrane to complete his artistic journey. His death was slow and painful; he suffered dramatic fluctuations in weight, making it necessary for him to have two sets of clothes. Despite the triumph of his tour of Japan, the years 1966 and 1967 were traumatic. His "new life" ultimately came too late. He died on July 17, 1967; his funeral was at St. Peter's Lutheran Church in New York, whose pastor, John Gensel, was well known for his ministry to musicians, and was attended by individuals who came from all parts of the world. J. C. Thomas writes:

> Tenor saxophonist Albert Ayler was one of several musicians performing at the service. His band was playing in the balcony, overlooking the dashiki-draped body of John Coltrane. . . . During his portion of the music, Ayler stopped, twice, and screamed; not with his horn but with his voice, the first scream like a cry of pain and the other like a shout of joy that Coltrane, though dead, would live forever.[66]

It is clear that at the point of Coltrane's death his work was incomplete. Given the limitations of his abstract musical practice in performing the kinds of cultural work that he had in mind in shaping his artistic identity, the fullest extension of his cultural critique would be made by followers. Individuals who understood the thrust of his antimodernism—and who recognized the value of the discourse of black music—would come forward to relocate Coltrane in history. Given the breadth of his goals, it would require individuals of a great diversity of talents and skills to make this possible. The calculated indeterminacy of the sign "Coltrane," like that of "Black music," provides for a multiplicity of oppositional stances and strategies.

COLTRANE CULTURE

> When you begin to see the possibilities of music, you desire to do
> something good for people, to help humanity free itself from its
> hangups. I think music can make the world better, and if I'm
> qualified, I want to do it. I'd like to point out to people the divine in
> a musical language that transcends worlds. I want to speak to their
> souls.
>
> JOHN COLTRANE (c.1965)[67]

> He captivated everybody's imagination. . . .
>
> ELVIN JONES[68]

> John Coltrane's dead & some
> of you
> have yet to hear him play
> How long how long has that Trane been gone.
>
> JAYNE CORTEZ,
> "How Long Has Trane Been Gone"[69]

Coltrane culture is the body of myths, rituals, and representations that utilize Coltrane or his work as a point of focus. They constitute a "culture" in
that they attempt to communicate something fundamental about the crisis
in American society in the sixties and beyond.[70] Real collectivities that may
have emerged as a result of Coltrane's legacy or influence are somewhat rare,
although, to be sure, one of the most interesting phenomena associated with
Coltrane culture would be the appearance of the "One Mind Evolutionary
Transitional Church of Christ" in San Francisco, which dedicated a shrine to
Coltrane, and centered his music in their liturgy. The variety of Coltrane cultural artifacts is diverse and impressive: New York sculptor Bradford Graves's
sculpture called "Trane" that was installed in the Carpathian mountains of
Czechoslovakia in 1968; a dance performed by the Alvin Ailey company, *Cry*;
invocations in introductions, letters to the editor, obituaries, etc., by critics,
musicians, and others, as a "guru."[71] And Coltrane became the inspiration
for new art and music.[72] Obviously, even within days of his death, the idea
celebrated is no longer the historical John Coltrane, and more often something in process of being defined. It seems unlikely that all of these artists (or
artworks) can be construed as endorsing Coltrane's "centering moment," his
reconstruction and reinterpretation of his life around about 1957. Like the
creator/instigators of the discourse of black music, these post-sixties
thinkers engaged with Coltrane seem in search of some emblem of wholeness, some way back to the not now.

The most interesting element of Coltrane culture may be what the critic
Kimberly Benston has called the "Coltrane poem." There are examples of this
kind of work from as diverse a group as Amiri Baraka, A. B. Spellman,
Michael Harper, Sonia Sanchez, Edward Kamau Brathwaite, Don L. Lee, and

Jayne Cortez, among many others.[73] This is a *serious* group of artists; any commitment on their part to be associated with the artistry of Coltrane must be taken as significant. Coltrane's ability to provide a sustainable common ground for individuals of such diverse ideological and aesthetic commitment deserves attention too. Benston identifies the Coltrane poem as "that genre of modern black poetry in which the topos of performed blackness is felt most resonantly."[74] His construction of this subtradition, and his consideration of its significance, is worth quoting at length:

> To the Afro-American elegist, the death of Coltrane is not experienced as an event; it is a recession of Coltrane from the minds of the living. It is an enforced deprivation, a radical discontinuity, the chill of absence—and hence, it is both an instigator of Afro-American alienation and a provoker of the black poet's crisis of expression. . . . The mourner's questioning of vacancy and death becomes, inevitably, the poet's meditation on chaos and silence, the antitheses of language. How, each asks, can the paralyzing pain of loss be transformed into collective progress and productive speech? For the mourner the task is to find celebratory praise where only lamentation seems possible; for the poet, the quest is for expression that dispels the silence, for a restorative *poesis* that reestablishes culture as a possibility.[75]

It is important to take seriously the caution of Stephen Henderson "against universalizing or particularizing the 'Coltrane poem' as a type, not only because it does not encompass the range of such poems, but also because it shares features with many poems on the death of other musicians like Eric Dolphy and Charlie Parker."[76] Cheryl Wall also asks the important question of how accepting the Coltrane poem (or Coltrane culture) as a paradigm for the sixties or the performance of blackness genders interpretations, and, through the back door, reinscribes a kind of heroic masculinity that much African-American feminist criticism of the past twenty years has tried to undo.

In general, this body of creative work figured Coltrane as creative principle—as a call to creativity, to which one must offer a response; as model of improvisation; as historical allusion (or key to a whole set of allusions); or, most profoundly, as incarnation of a history of the sixties in which the issues of violence, masculinity, and the cultural appreciation of African-American creativity are central. The Coltrane poem thus established, and Coltrane culture represents, the pragmatism of the elegiac mode as response to the particular character of American modernity, especially as it is shaped in the American sixties. The death of John Coltrane, and the birth of this loose oppositional movement, are first linked to a philosophy of history in which "providence" is understood as the principle of mortality, and then to a way of living. If African-American antimodernism is elegiac, the death of John Coltrane is the most dramatic emblem of its necessity. Kimberly Benston suggests:

> Remembering becomes re-collection: the recovery of a lost being de-
> pends upon a figural resanctification of history and family, of the
> being himself. What we witness is the metamorphosis of Coltrane into
> "Trane," of man into archetype. The death of Coltrane becomes in
> modern black poetry, a central topos of renewal and is accepted ulti-
> mately as beginning—as a question: How long how long has that
> Trane been gone? (177)

Ironically, then, as Coltrane pursued the path of "total freedom," other
artists came along to relocate him in history, ostensibly qualifying that romantic quest. His ability to locate meaning outside of the self, outside traditional understandings of success, was (and is) worth preserving, even as he
felt compelled to explore the implications of "anti-structure." In some sense,
Coltrane the poet was on the right track, even though occasionally betrayed
by the imprecision (if sometimes unbearable beauty) of his musical art. Of
course, it is important to remind ourselves that Coltrane died at forty-one
years of age, and may have known exactly what he was doing and exactly
where he was going. Indeed, his interest, late in his lifetime, in African music
(prefiguring the current vogue for world music) was indicative, perhaps, of
the next great change to come, the insistence again on self-invention. Just
prior to his death, he was beginning to plan a trip to Nigeria, so that he could
study with the masters of Yoruban tone music. Whether Coltrane was beginning to locate himself within an even more demanding pluralism, or
whether this was a romantic mistake, we will never know. More than any
other antimodern figure, however, Coltrane seems to reach out to the 1990s,
to be argued about all over again.

So Coltrane remains indeed a "bridge" figure,[77] although arguably not
necessarily the one seen by either Hart Crane or Sonny Rollins. On a guitar
or violin, the bridge supports the strings, and transmits their vibrations to
the belly of the instrument. We can also talk of a "bridge passage," a short
musical passage that marks a transition from one section to the next, linking
musical themes and ideas. Coltrane identified a nascent American desire—to
rediscover the transcendent at the apex of consumer culture—and his legacy
is, no doubt, his willingness to explore to its fullest the implications of that
desire. (And, of course, it is crucial that we remember, once again, Wilson
Harris's cautionary tale about such rainbow bridges.) Ultimately, while the
hope invested in Coltrane may prove naive or misplaced his diagnosis can remain "sound."

CHAPTER FIVE

THE PREVALENCE OF RITUAL IN AN AGE OF CHANGE

ROMARE BEARDEN

Such devices . . . as distortion of scale and proportion, and abstract coloration, are the very means through which I try to achieve a more personal expression. . . . It is not my aim to paint about the Negro in America in terms of propaganda. It is precisely my awareness of the distortions required of the polemicist that has caused me to paint the life of my people as I know it—as passionately and dispassionately as Brueghel painted the life of the Flemish people of his day.

ROMARE BEARDEN, "Rectangular Structure in
My Montage Paintings" *(1969)*[1]

One suspects that as an artist possessing a marked gift for pedagogy, [Bearden] has sought here to reveal a world long hidden by the clichés of sociology and rendered cloudy by the distortions of newsprint and the false continuity imposed upon our conception of Negro life by television and much documentary photography. Therefore, as he delights us with the magic of design and teaches us the ambiguity of vision, Bearden insists that we *see* and that we see in depth and by the fresh light of the creative vision. Bearden knows that the true complexity of the slum dweller and the tenant farmer requires a release from the prison of our media-dulled perception and a reassembling in forms which would convey something of the depth and wonder of the Negro American's stubborn humanity.

RALPH ELLISON, "The Art of Romare Bearden" *(1970)*[2]

One could ask for no more compelling example of the paradox of continuity and change in American culture than that presented by the career of Romare Bearden.[3] His "Two Women in a Landscape" (1941; see figure 2) is regarded by most art historians as a work derivative of the end of American social realist and regionalist painting, of an artist not yet aware of the

Figure 2. Romare Bearden, "Two Women in a Landscape," 1941. © Romare Bearden Foundation/Licensed by VAGA, New York, NY.

dramatic changes coming to American art and society during and after World War II. Like a swing trumpeter not yet aware of the musical changes being wrought by Dizzy Gillespie or Charlie Parker at Minton's, the mythic home of modernist jazz, one might see Bearden as backward, unable to commit to either the social program of the realists or the disruptions of the avant-garde. His "Blue Lady" (1955; see figure 3) might extend the tale. Despite the emerging dominance of a Jackson Pollock–Mark Rothko axis in the world of American art, this misguided artist flirts with narrative, the barely visible shape of the woman on the canvas further evidence of an artist unable to dispense with an outmoded humanism. Finally, the story of the living anachronism might culminate with a discussion of "The Prevalence of Ritual: Conjur Woman" (1964; see figure 4). Now the ascendancy of "pop art," its worship of the "image," a "media-ocrity," displaces the "figurative" dimension of this constructed, pieced-together art and artist.

Of course, another story is also possible. These three artworks can also be seen as nodes within an alternate history suggested by the hermeneutic "African-American antimodernism." This surrogate story can be told either to counter constructions of monolithic opposition or to counter a reductive and crassly assimilative "mainstream." In either case, what is striking is the artist's commitment to the human activity, lived life, a determination to continue to center the struggle of the everyday. Bearden's life and aesthetic practice dramatically bring together all elements of African-American antimodernism: the moment of crisis, the reordering of the artistic and intellectual

Figure 3. Romare Bearden, "Blue Lady," 1955. © Romare Bearden Foundation/ Licensed by VAGA, New York, NY.

life, a comprehensive critique of American culture, and a distinctly elegiac mode. In the above three paintings we can observe the emergence of a sophisticated discomfort both related to and separate from the dominant and countercultural aesthetic practices of the time. Even as the painter experiments with the most radical (and conservative) techniques of his day, he cannot repress the human element, even as he redefines the nature of African-American and American identity consistent with contemporary skepticism about the existence of a unified subject. Romare Bearden was afraid neither of change nor of a return to the familiar. For Bearden, memory is, paradoxically, the catalyst to change and the centering mechanism in a world of seem-

Figure 4. Romare Bearden, "The Prevalence of Ritual: Conjur Woman," 1964.
© *Romare Bearden Foundation/Licensed by VAGA, New York, NY.*

ingly boundless fluctuation and variance. His "no" to American culture is always a partial "yes."

Like previous figures in this study, Bearden had a dramatic international experience and emerged from that experience thoroughly changed. Furthermore, Bearden—like Hayden, Marshall, Demby, and Coltrane—is a "convert." The experience of exile, interior and exterior, has left him with a sense of alienation from the world, or, perhaps more correctly, from a variety of

worlds, aesthetic, political, and racial. Like the other figures, Bearden paradoxically, but without equivocation, condemns the excesses and sickness of
Western and American culture:

> I suggest that Western society, and particularly that of America, is
> gravely ill and a major symptom is the American treatment of the
> Negro. The artistic expression of this culture concentrates on themes
> of "absurdity" and "anti-art" which provide further evidence of its ill
> health. It is the right of everyone now to re-examine history to see if
> Western culture offers the only solutions to man's purpose on this
> earth.[4]

What makes Bearden's experience and accomplishment so profound is that,
of all these figures, he is the most successful in discovering, developing, and
perfecting a method and form able to contain this new life and fierce culture-
critical focus. The set of artistic practices (mode of reflection and mechanical
procedures to make visual images) he perfects in the early sixties allows him
to display his commitment to African-American community, capture the
character of contemporary American life, and develop a unique artistic vocabulary that has remarkable cross-disciplinary and cross-cultural resonance.

These three artworks propose a specific heritage—the content of the "looking backwards"—and are suggestive of the complexity of the path towards
his sixties artistic practice. "Two Women in a Landscape," while folk representations, also remind the knowledgeable viewer of Byzantine frescoes. The
emphasis upon simple gesture, religion and religious allusion, and, most
profoundly, human subjects who seem to *demand a presence*, make clear that
even Bearden's earliest work is particularly well suited to exploring questions
of modernity, resistance, and art. The painting negotiates historical and cultural distance and expands the viewer's horizon of expectation. The audience's reading is frustrated, however, by the enigmatic placement of the
women's hands in the painting. The specific key to the meaning of these
poses remains obscure. Often forgotten, however, is the attempt on the part
of the figures to communicate with the viewer. This is in and of itself of great
repercussion. There is an attempt—as was particularly the case with the novels of Demby and Marshall—to initiate a kind of dialogue with the audience.
The reality of the body and its strange resistance to obvious elucidation and
account reintroduce, in an age of technocratic authority, the simple mystery
of human statement and touch.

Another kind of dialogue is inititated by the second painting: "Blue Lady"
alludes to a period of modern painting, even as it resonates with a primary
African-American cultural form. The relationship of "Blue Lady" to a "Blues
Woman" may, like the image of the figure itself, be but a trace, yet it continues to frame the character of our reception of the painting and Bearden's
artistic message. Similarly, "Conjur Woman," a more obviously African-
American figure, a manipulator of the materials of the world (so as to manipulate good and evil), introduces a whole alternative cosmology. Yet, it also

invokes a Western tradition of representing seated women and, in its distortion, claims an affinity with the diverse body of modernist transformations of reality. (It also parodies with the utmost seriousness the inventedness or constructedness of such figures.) Heritage, then, is simultaneously the collective history of the West and the more particular history of African-Americans. And while it will become increasingly clear that Bearden found some advantage in foregrounding that African-American tale, he would insist that the appeal of that cultural inheritance—and especially its simple humanity—be read within, if sometimes in struggle with, the history of Western artistic practices more generally.

It would be imprudent, however, even when one is relying upon paradox, to place Bearden amidst practices of remembering and proposing both European and black allusions without acknowledging the concrete and discrete racisms of twentieth-century art. Bearden's accomplishment is connected to that of Picasso, for instance, not only by their varying degrees of rejection of the language of verisimilitude. Bearden's strategic reclamation of the language of African masks is neither accidental nor of obvious explanation, yet it is certainly politically charged.[5] William Demby negotiated the terrain of exclusionary social practices and artistic histories with a version of "cubism" that insisted upon a familial history, the reminder of "black modernisms." In a similar manner, Romare Bearden survives the twentieth century's vexed race history by insisting upon a method both original and derivative.[6] Part of the anxiety of the mid-century black intellectual is certainly agonistic. Betwixt and between in terms of "temporal expression," cultural connectedness and the concrete politics of race, Bearden has to become an incredibly talented improviser.

Mary Schmidt Campbell has clearly identified the cost associated with such an enigmatic performance: "History has had a difficult time with the art of Romare Bearden."[7] She continues:

> In spite of all the accolades, in spite of the critical praise and his success in the marketplace, art historians have consistently overlooked his achievement. Major texts on post–World War II American art mention him only peripherally or omit him altogether. Museum exhibitions surveying American art of the 1960's or 1970's, the period when Bearden's collages quite literally burst upon the scene, rarely include him. Critics who abundantly praised his one-man gallery shows and museum retrospectives fail to mention him when speaking of American art in general.[8]

It is clear, she suggests, that Bearden's "world was foreign to most observers." The noted American critic Hilton Kramer writes that "there is never any doubt that [Bearden] does, indeed, *have* a subject and that the subject is not art itself."[9] While admiring the aesthetic accomplishment, mainstream art critics are mostly at a loss as to how to explain the moral commitment or cultural language to which Bearden devotes himself. The question that Mary

Schmidt Campbell finally comes to could also be addressed to the viability of African-American antimodernism as a useful interpretive paradigm:

> Will Romare Bearden appear to be an anachronism in American art, his new forms an aberration, exotic and interesting, but ultimately not part of the central story of the art of this century? Or is his art, with its reliance on memory and history, its storytelling narrative technique, a nostalgic attempt to recreate the Black American past and, therefore, hopelessly old-fashioned and retrogressive? . . . In many ways his repudiation of mainstream art, a concept which implies a monolithic, cultural supremacy, his embrace within his art of cultural pluralism, and, at the same time, his fierce assertion of his own cultural identity and history may, in fact, be a metaphor for what has become of American art in the 1990's. . . . *What makes Bearden's art particularly difficult to grasp . . . is that even as his art points to the future, it also wholeheartedly embraces the past.* [my emphasis][10]

This book will seek to demonstrate that Bearden is arguably one of a series of *related* anachronisms, an invented tradition, able to produce profound cultural work, and is not so much silent as ignored.

THE DEVELOPMENT OF ROMARE BEARDEN

> One must be very careful about the matter of racial identity and evaluating it. The difficulty is when (the artist) denies himself, or assumes other identities. As a Negro, I do not need to go looking for "happenings," the absurd, or the surreal, because I have seen things that neither Dali, Beckett, Ionesco, nor any of the others could have thought possible; and to see these things I did not need to do more than look out of my studio window above the Apollo theater on 125th Street. So you see this experience allows me to represent, in the means of today, another view of the world.
>
> ROMARE BEARDEN (1964)[11]

From the 1930s to the late 1950s Romare Bearden was an accomplished, if somewhat marginal, modernist painter on the New York art scene. Part of the circle of artists attached to Samuel Kootz's gallery, Bearden mastered the most avant-garde techniques of the day. As important and moving as much of this painting is, ultimately his legacy is not to be discovered there. In the sixties his work underwent a dramatic transformation, first working with photostatic enlargements of striking photo montages, and then moving to a full-fledged commitment to multimedia collage. In collaboration with his close friend, the novelist Albert Murray, Bearden described his new art—a diverse and memory-infused representation of the African-American community—in terms of the "prevalence of ritual," their shared shorthand for a premodern dimension in black culture. Bearden's work is crucial for understanding African-American antimodern sentiment and particularly useful to facilitate discussion of the relationship within American culture of discourses of the margin to those of the center. His career generates difficult questions that are suggestive of the relationship of African-American antimodernism to American culture. Why, since Bearden's art has been consistently celebrated, is he inadequately considered in histories of contemporary American art? If Bearden's art was genuinely an attempt to challenge the mainstream, is there cause for alarm in the way that his work has, in recent years, come to adorn any cultural product having to do with blackness? Is there a fatal flaw in Bearden's effort to balance past and future perspectives?

"I paint out of the tradition of the blues," writes Bearden, "of call and recall. You start a theme and you call and recall."[12] An understanding of Bearden's dramatic sixties transformation requires an introduction to his past, some sense of the historical workings of this call and recall. A crucial starting point is to recognize that part of the diversity of Bearden's art can be attributed to the geographic diversity and "black cosmopolitanism" he experienced growing up. Born in Charlotte, North Carolina, in 1912, Bearden moved to Harlem not long after his birth, likely because of the dangers the family faced as a result of a marriage between an extremely light-skinned woman and a dark-skinned man. His parents were very active in the emerging black metropolis. His mother Bessye, in particular, turned the home into a cultural center of sorts; as the New York editor of the *Chicago Defender*, she had the opportunity to bring the most important black intellectuals and artists into the presence of young Romare. W.E.B. Du Bois, Langston Hughes, Paul Robeson, Aaron Douglas, Duke Ellington, and Fats Waller all spent time in the Bearden household. Of equal importance, however, Bearden returned— religiously—to North Carolina to spend his summers with his grandparents. This dual experience became a rich, if complex, patrimony for the artist. Whatever the pace and tone of his unusual northern experience, it was always balanced with a reminder of southern rhythms and rituals. This inheritance and history was complicated once more when he was sent to spend his high school years with his maternal grandmother, who ran a boardinghouse in Pittsburgh. In this more working-class city, and away from the authority of his mother, Bearden discovered a somewhat broader black cultural canvas. In contemporary parlance, Bearden discovered an urban black vernacular.

Despite having some college education, Romare's father, Howard, often had difficulty in securing employment. It seems likely that much of the moving around that Bearden experienced was due to that financial insecurity. However, given his mother's political organizing, it may also have been true that she was especially interested in Romare recognizing and understanding his diverse roots. Whatever the case may be, Bearden had a most varied childhood: he lived in the South with its unique cosmology and social conditions; he lived within a dynamic black working-class culture in an industrial city; and he lived in the nation's first black metropolis and experienced its nascent cultural and political ambitions. It is at least a triple class and cultural inheritance: agrarian, urban working, and emergent bourgoisie.

His earliest exposure to "art" took place during the Pittsburgh days; his close friend Eugene Bailey drew elaborate (and often lewd) pictures of individuals in their neighborhood, and most especially those individuals associated with the local house of prostitution. Bearden had an interest in drawing himself, but claimed to be intimidated by Eugene Bailey's talent. He was most certainly traumatized by Bailey's early death at thirteen years of age. He lost a friend, an accomplished artist, and, implicitly, his Virgil to the world of art. This informal education would be followed by a solid, if less emotionally rich, formal education. It was not until his days at New York University (after transferring from Boston University, and after a brief semi-pro baseball career[13]), where he would take a degree in mathematics in 1935, and a meeting with E. Simms Campbell, the famed *Esquire* and *New Yorker* cartoonist, that Bearden once again took the "art world" seriously.

Bearden gained experience in cartooning in a number of different locations. He contributed on a regular basis from 1931 to 1935 to the *Baltimore Afro-American*, although he occasionally sold work to *Colliers*, the *Saturday Evening Post*, and an NYU magazine, *Medley*. In some ways this early experience as a cartoonist, and especially as an "editorial" cartoonist, is important to understanding his later work. Bearden would always insist on a "message" (although distant, in his mind, from propaganda) and his work was always seemingly a pedagogical device. By the mid-1930s, although not entirely sold on the idea of art as career, Bearden had become aware of a community of African-American artists. Art programs associated with the Works Project Administration, on the one hand, and, more interestingly, on the other hand, the "306" group of black artists and intellectuals who met in painter Charles Alston's loft at 306 West 141st St., provided Bearden with an informal but comprehensive education in debates within African-American culture, especially in the immediate, if fading, shadow of the Harlem Renaissance.[14]

His more formal training took place at the Art Students League, and most intensely with George Grosz, the German Dadaist and political artist. Grosz's vibrant political art—in both conventional cartoons and wickedly funny photomontages—no doubt impacted the apprentice cartoonist and painter. Through Grosz in particular, and his experience at the League more generally, he gained an introduction to the breadth and depth of the modern European avant-garde. Grosz also led Bearden "to study composition, through the analysis of Brueghel and the great Dutch Masters and . . . in the process of refining . . . draftsmanship initiated [him] into the magic world of Ingres, Dürer, Holbein and Poussin."[15] This training is the single most important experience in the specific shaping of the self as artist. Difficult questions were, however, still to be answered: What kind of artist would he be?

His training with Grosz—and the atmosphere of the day—would suggest that he would become a "political" painter. Bearden was suspicious of the social-realist project, and especially the ways in which African-American artists in particular were being encouraged to take it up as a method. Of lasting import, his exposure to the "306" group and conversations with his neighbor Claude McKay and his friend Ralph Ellison made it unlikely that he would ever be provincial in outlook. The Harlem of the 1930s provided a vital intellectual community within which to develop both an ethic and aesthetic. While the heyday of the Harlem Renaissance was past, "306" still attracted a diverse array of artists, writers, and musicians to its doors. He also demonstrated a great deal of initiative in pursuing questions of African-American artistry and intellectual life on his own. In a justly famous 1934 article written for *Opportunity*, he opined:

> Let us look back into the beginnings of modern art. It is really nothing new, merely an expression projected through new forms, more akin to the spirit of the times. Fundamentally the artist is influenced by the age in which he lives. Then for the artist to express an age that is characterized by machinery, skyscrapers, radios, and the generally quickened cadences of modern life, it follows naturally that he will break from many of the outmoded academic practices of the past.[16]

Bearden here stakes a claim to the discourse and crisis of modernity as his artistic subject. The use of modern forms is commendable, Bearden suggests, for they "substituted for mere photographic realism, a search for inner truths." As will become typical of his work and commentary, his intervention is a double task. If mostly personal manifesto, he also means to speak to the situation of the African-American artist and the viability of black intellectual tradition. He scoffs at the complaints of "Negro artists" who believe that it is impossible for them to develop a unique modern art. "One can imagine," Bearden wrote, "what men like Daumier, Grosz, and Cruikshank might have done with a locale like Harlem." Reminiscent of Hayden's "Counterpoise" statements, Bearden criticized those artists who rely upon a racial chauvinism without any real sense of craft; Bearden's ideal artist sounds much like Hayden's ideal poet:

> He must not be content with merely recording a scene as a machine. He must enter wholeheartedly into the situation which he wishes to convey. The artist must be the medium through which humanity expresses itself. In this sense the greatest artists have faced the realities of life, and have been profoundly social. . . . An intense, eager devotion to present day life, to study it, to help relieve it, this is the calling of the Negro artist.[17]

Bearden's conception of "blackness" has to do with an evaluation of those elements of existence that place the self within a culture; it has very little, Bearden seems to suggest, to do with excluding one's self from the most challenging conversations of the day.

His earliest shows, of which "Two Women" is typical, demonstrate a commitment to an art shaped by religious allusion, even as it works within (and certainly modifies) the motifs of American social realism. Sharon Patton notes that:

> Bearden's interest in spiritual symbols is evident in "Two Women in a Landscape," and other paintings of similar style from the same period. In one, the biblical meeting of Mary and Anne is represented as an encounter between two southern Black women. There is an element of religiosity in "Two Women in a Landscape" that suggests the Annunciation, the hand positions and Christian iconic gestures recalling Byzantine and fourteenth-century Italian panel paintings and frescoes.[18]

As he continued to show throughout the 1940s, even as his commitment to an art "clearly" portraying "black figures" waned, he maintained an attachment to such a religious worldview, supplementing his system of allusion with elements of modern literature. While his work now began to look like a synthesis of cubism and medieval stained glass, the titles of shows and individual works were clearly centered around a religio/literary axis: "The Passion of Christ," works based on García Lorca's "Lament for Ignacio Sanchez Meijias," works based on Rabelais' *Gargantua and Pantagruel*, works based on the *Iliad*, and works influenced by André Malraux and Ernest Hemingway.[19] This axis is suggestive of how even at such an early point in his career he gravitates toward the mythic. The religious and literary texts provide a kind of dynamic rootedness in standing intellectual traditions and concerns such that his artwork is always the elaboration or extension of a highly charged conversation.

These works gained him the attention of the New York modernist art establishment and by the mid-1940s he was exhibiting in Samuel Kootz's gallery, the same gallery that featured Robert Motherwell, William Baziotes, Adolph Gottlieb, and David Hare. Bearden's success did not result in the end of his search. Patton writes:

> Bearden read widely on art, including the letters of Camille Pissarro, Vincent Van Gogh, and Jean-Auguste Ingres; the *Journal* of Eugene Delacroix; and the writings of Albrecht Dürer, Piet Mondrian, Henri Matisse, Wang Wei, and Katsushika Hokusai.[20]

Perhaps as a direct response to this reading, he began to keep richly detailed journals himself. There he speculated on questions of art and heritage, the mathematical basis of all art, and general questions of religion, art, and metaphysics. Like Coltrane, Bearden proved to be obsessive about art *and* life, and was determined to make the most of himself as a human being and artist. Around this time, he also began a practice that he was to continue for many years — copying "masterpieces":

> I made reasonably free copies of each work, substituting my own choice of colors for those of these artists, except for those of Manet and

Matisse when I was guided by color reproductions. The Rembrandt I chose, "Pilate Washing His Hands," gave me the most difficulty. While studying this masterpiece, I found so many subtle rhythms and carefully planned relationships that I finally surrendered the work, having learned that there are hidden, mysterious relationships which defy analysis.[21]

By the late 1940s Romare Bearden was an incredibly well-read and sophisticated painter. He had achieved critical acclaim for his shows of the 1940s and major American museums had purchased his paintings. Given the relative paucity of general knowledge about the African-American visual arts tradition, this should have guaranteed his place within history, and, moreover, through the self as exception, established for him a comfortable lifestyle. Bearden could continue, if he so chose, to draft visual interpretations of modern literature and religious scenes and reasonably expect financial support and thoughtful criticism. He chose, or had chosen for him, something significantly different.

TRANSFORMING ROMARE BEARDEN

I felt that the Negro was becoming too much of an abstraction, rather than the reality that art can give a subject. What I've attempted to do is establish a world through art in which the validity of my Negro experience could live and make its own logic. . . .

ROMARE BEARDEN (1964)[22]

When studying the life of Romare Bearden one is struck by the striking silence of the 1950s.[23] It is compelling not so much for being out of step with the times—in chapter one I have discussed the significant chill of cold war conformity upon black artistry—but more so for the way it was personally unlikely, given the great momentum he seemed to have established throught the mid- to late 1940s. The blame for this absence might be placed squarely at the feet of a somewhat unpredictable New York art establishment. By 1948 Samuel Kootz had closed his gallery, and when he reopened he did so to promote a new school of American painting, the radical abstractionists, and most especially Jackson Pollock. Modernism of Bearden's variety or just about any variety, was quickly passé. The general "falling-out" that African-Americans were having—once again—with American culture is also pertinent. The wartime promise of "Double V"—victory abroad and victory at home—with which African-Americans once again motivated themselves to participate in the war effort, was, as after World War I, largely betrayed. Bearden himself had experienced this betrayal when he was selected for Officer Training School and sent to the deep South, where he experienced segregated training facilities. More generally, the Harlem that was so important to Bearden never fully recovered from the 1943 uprising and the slow economic downturn that blighted black urban enclaves. With the disappearance of the WPA and the various intellectual and artistic groups that were rooted in that patronage, Bearden was somewhat adrift. (Mary Schmidt Campbell also notes that his "mother's death in 1943 was yet another loss, breaking apart the tight cocoon of community he had enjoyed as a young adult."[24]) In some ways, the elegiac tone of his *Passion of Christ* (1945) and *Lament for Ignacio Sanchez Mejias* (1946) foreshadowed a sense of mourning and loss with which he would come to perpetually struggle. Like many others intellectually inclined, Bearden responded to this dislocation by taking advantage of the G.I. Bill and leaving for Europe.

In 1950, Bearden headed for Paris, to study philosophy at the Sorbonne. This would, of course, also be an opportunity for him to carry on with his intensive self-education in the arts. Bearden took full advantage of what Paris had to offer and was able to interact with both the African-American expatriate community and the cultures of the art world and the Left Bank. He thereby became good friends with James Baldwin and Albert Murray, in particular.[25] While in Paris, he did little if any painting. Bearden cryptically suggests that he was so busy he had no time to paint, but it seems more likely that he was slowly moving toward a deep depression that would become artistic paralysis. Despite this new Paris community, Bearden describes himself as "not well." The artistic crisis generated by the triumph of abstract expressionism and the devaluation of order and structure precipitated a personal crisis. Mary Schmidt Campbell says that staying "away from painting, Bearden became increasingly nervous."[26] He never, however, ceased with his education: he studied philosophy with Gaston Bachelard and Etienne Sauriot, visited galleries and museums, met with artists (especially the sculptor Constantin Brancusi), and travelled to Italy. His letters to the artist Carl Holty give ample evidence of the intensity of his thinking and his emotional struggle.[27] Increasingly, absence from painting became a burden, and there was the real question of whether he could rediscover his voice, technique, and commitment. Could he put to canvas everything he had learned and experienced? Could he productively utilize that overwhelming sense of dread and loss?

Back in New York in late 1951, Bearden was to discover just how far he had "fallen." Kootz had redefined the American avant-garde and Bearden was not part of it. "Kootz felt that these artists' [Bearden and other "subjectivists"] lingering dependency upon Cubist structure was incompatible with what he . . . saw emerging (and desired to promulgate) in American art, a tendency away from nature as source and one turning inward instead."[28] No doubt, Bearden was also struck by Harlem's continued decline and the McCarthyist scourge. (Paul Robeson had long been a good friend of the Bearden family; there is some evidence to suggest that Bearden was impacted by Robeson's dramatic difficulties with blacklisting and the U.S. government throughout the late 1940s and 1950s. As Mary Schmidt Campbell put it, "The perfect model of Black achievment in the arts became a warning of its consequences."[29]) So, completely unsure of his artistic future and direction, Bearden turned for a short time to writing popular songs, having one great success with "Seabreeze," recorded by Billy Eckstine and others. This, however, was not the life for which he had studied. His neighbors—the philosophers Hannah Arendt and Heinrich Bluecher—encouraged him to continue, however, and he did continue his "studies." The vocational and spiritual crisis did, however, begin to result in physiological symptoms. For a long time he was convinced he was dying, often telling family and friends that he must have cancer. Everything culminated in 1954 when "Bearden collapsed on the street and woke up in the psychiatric ward at Bellevue Hospital. When he asked what had happened to him, a doctor explained, 'You blew a fuse.'"[30]

That Bearden's mid-1950s experience is very similar to those of Robert Hayden and John Coltrane (and, to a lesser extent, those of Paule Marshall and William Demby) is very significant.[31] Psychologically, historically, and theologically, such "break-downs," developmental structures which point to mental chaos, foreshadow or are a necessary prelude to a new synthesis. The values of the mid-1950s art world—and mid-1950s America—were not affirming of Bearden's artistic or racial identity. (There were no group exhibitions of African-American artwork in the 1950s as there had been in the 1940s and would be numerously in the 1960s.) Similar to the experience of other African-American antimodernists, two factors point to Bearden's slow reconstruction of self. Most straightforwardly—and few commentators give this the attention it deserves—Bearden married, in September of 1954, Nanette Rohan, whose family was from the French Caribbean.[32] Also a significant part of Bearden's change—and again, like that of the other figures discussed in this book—were important cross-cultural experiences. Bearden began to study carefully Chinese painting with the assistance of a Mr. Wu, a Chinese calligrapher that Bearden met by chance in a bookstore.[33] This tradition of "abstract landscape" painting allowed Bearden to reshape and rethink questions of form. It is also worth highlighting, however, that Bearden was paying the bills at this time by doing social work for the New York Department of Social Services, where he was assigned to assist with the "Gypsies." Myron Schwartzman asserts that:

> No matter how bizarre, poignant, or conniving the way of life Bearden found among the Gypsies, he saw their unique culture threatened on every side by the encroachment of modern technology and the resultant homogenization of life. . . . There is a distinct parallel between Bearden's feeling for the eradication of the Gypsies' unique identity and his feeling about the South in which he spent his earliest years.[34]

As the Gypsies' plight brought home to him his mission, and Chinese painting provided him with a new way to order his materials and his experience—and as his wife provided the necessary stability to guarantee continuous work—Bearden moved closer to the form (and content) which would mark his entry into the American sixties.[35]

It is appropriate here to point to the not so mundane fact of Bearden's *survival* as crucial to the designation of him as antimodernist. His skepticism toward the ethos of the dominant movement in American art—whose distancing of social subjects has been seen by some as a product of, and not as resistance to, a cold war mentality—is certainly part and parcel of his reintegration to come. Despite the shock of the rapid devaluation of his art and artistic practice, Bearden continued to search for the artistic voice and stance most appropriate for continuing his "teaching." Bearden refused to compromise either the expansive social capacity of African-American art or what he came to call his "classical" language and orientation. By beginning to actively mourn his personal losses and the collective loss of the community, he slowly pieced together an artwork of extraordinary power.

BEARDEN, SPIRAL, AND AFRICAN-AMERICAN ARTISTIC COMMUNITY

> Why the frequent, seemingly imperative suspension of expected patterning? In the British West Indies patchwork dress keeps the *jumbie*, a spirit, away from a resting place. In Haiti a man procures from a ritual expert, when necessary, a special shirt made of strips of red, white, and blue to break up the power of the evil eye. Nelly Bragg, an old black woman of Warrensville Heights, Ohio, was asked "Why one red sock and one white sock worn deliberately mismatched?" to which she replied, "To keep spirits away.". . . Those pilgrims of the Mande concept of *fadenya* (individuality, with all its attendant dangers) . . . continue to venture into disordered regions . . . The double play of Mande influences, *individuality and self-protection*—suggested by the rhythmized, pattern-breaking textile modes, and the *group affiliation* mediated by communal rounds of cone-on-cylinder houses—completes a history of resistance to the closures of the Western technocratic way.
>
> ROBERT FARRIS THOMPSON, *Flash of the Spirit* [36]

The stories which surround Bearden's eventual arrival at collage are often vague. Some historians have even been inclined to represent it as an occurrence "out of the blue," so to speak, without philosophic or aesthetic precedents. Sharon Patton's rubric for considering Bearden's art even leaves a clear two-year gap; she moves from considering works in the period 1955–1962 to the period 1964–1965. In some sense, this is a response similar to the same critical crisis described in relation to the work of John Coltrane. How seriously should we take questions of the social basis of either Bearden's or Coltrane's art when both were so closely associated with the avant-garde? Or when both artists responded with some reticence about that social ground? And, moreover, does saying that the artistic practice of each is a result of social turmoil really say anything at all?

A more useful starting point for reconstruction of this transformation might be initiated if we consider the absence of satisfying community in Bearden's life, which was not "fixed" by his late 1950s "changes." If Bearden's life had been made anew by his time in Paris, his encounter with Chinese painting, and by the support and inspiration of his wife (also an artist and a dancer), he had not yet been able to recreate the intellectual exchange that he experienced at "306." The most important sixties change, then, is Bearden's instrumental leadership in the formation of the artists group Spiral, which met at Bearden's Canal Street studio. Spiral was thirteen men and one woman: Charles Alston, Romare Bearden, Felrath Hines, Norman Lewis, Alvin Hollingsworth, Merton Simpson, Earl Miller, William Majors, Reggie Gammon, Hale Woodruff, Perry Ferguson, Calvin Douglass, James Yeargans and Emma Amos.[37] Jeanne Siegel reported that they were a "dynamic and totally divergent group ranging in age from 28 to 65, that includes a court clerk, art dealer, floorwaxer, Ph.D. candidate and restorer of old masters."[38] Floyd Coleman argues that "not since the opening of the Harlem Community Arts Center in 1937 had so many highly educated, technically prepared and professionally committed, seasoned, and emerging artists of African descent formed a group in a northern city to explore social artistic, intellectual, and political and ideological issues" (149). The group's name "represented the mathematical symbol of its aesthetic and human philosophy. The Archimedean spiral was chosen "because, from a starting point, it moves outward embracing all directions, yet constantly upward" (figure 5).[39] Richard Mayhew suggests that "the name 'spiral' embodied [an] extended concept of evolving and unifying, bonding and constructively supportive relationships with one another, which was an art of Afro-American sensibility."[40]

Spiral's existence in and of itself is important for understanding one component of African-American artistic sentiment in the American sixties. Like the origins of Bearden's commitment to collage, its specific roots are still a little vague. Certainly connected to the energy generated by the March on Washington in the summer of 1963, some have suggested that it came about at A. Phillip Randolph's insistence that black artists become involved more actively in the struggle. At the first meeting in Bearden's studio,

> One of those present, the distinguished painter Hale Woodruff, asked the question "Why are we here?" He suggested, in answering his own question, that we, as Negroes, could not fail to be touched by the outrage of segregation, or fail to relate to the self-reliance, hope, and courage of those persons who were marching in the interest of man's dignity. . . . If possible, in these times, we hoped with our art to justify life.[41]

The issue, suggested fellow Spiral member Richard Mayhew, was *honesty*. How could one pursue "art"—especially within the "mainstream"—given the intensity and pragmatism of the Freedom movement? On the other hand, as

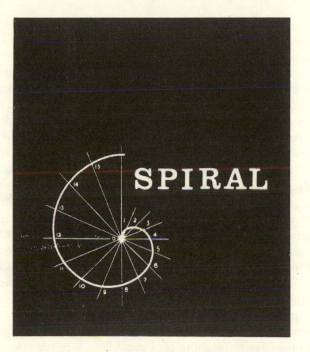

Figure 5. "Spiral," ca. 1965. Courtesy of Richard Mayhew.

a group, there was significant discomfort with defining their purpose as solely based upon race. Mary Schmidt Campbell argues that two "distinct poles" began to emerge. Norman Lewis, in particular, was adamant about the centrality of "aesthetic ideas." In agreeing with Norman Lewis, Woodruff stated "I am not interested in some 'gimmick' that will pander to an interest in things Negroid."[42] James Yeargans suggested, however, that "We should look to our past for a distinct identity. The Negro artist should take something out of the present upheaval as part of his expression. The Negro has a deep cultural heritage to be explored."[43] The unpleasant truth was, however, that as African-American artists they were often outside of the important social and institutional circles neccessary to make a name for oneself in the "art world." Spiral spoke to their unusual and uncomfortable position as African-American artists; regardless of the particular urgency of the march on Washington, this gathering together was necessary to promote, encourage, and sustain their commitment to their art.[44] Whatever anxieties were active and present in the group owing to different conceptions of art and its relationship to society, they actively threw themselves into the task of collective education. They studied African art and culture and the most challenging ideas about "blackness" then circulating. They also organized a collective show. When the possible theme "Mississippi 1964" was rejected as too political,

Bearden, ever the mediator, suggested the compromise "Black and White"—not only obvious social commentary, but also a decision to limit, for the show, their collective palette.

At best, we are left to make only general assessments of the nature of Bearden's change and the ultimate extent of his leadership and participation. Sharon Patton suggests that these "discussions obviously caused Bearden to reassess his style of painting and artistic responsibilities."[45] But Myron Schwartzman notes that Bearden's first signed collage was dated 1961, and there is reasonable evidence to suggest that Bearden had been toying with collage and assemblage for some time. (As a technique it had fairly deep modernist roots.) How should we evaluate his "transition"? The most widely circulated "genesis" story associated with Bearden's transition to multimedia collage is that at one of the first meetings of Spiral, Bearden emptied out a bag of fragments—magazine clippings, pieces of photographs, etc.—and suggested that the group put together a collaborative piece. All accounts of the event note that there was little enthusiasm for the idea. Conversations about the role of the African-American artist largely continued as before. Most ironically then, Bearden pursued, paradoxically and suggestively, the "collaborative" project on his own.

So a moment of real epiphany seems unlikely and is mostly unnecessary. The story of collage as teaching tool provides a nice framework for constructing the story of Bearden's new work as a teaching device, a cultural heuristic. The public was made aware of Bearden's stylistic improvisation when, almost accidentally, his work caught the eye of the gallery owner Arne Ekstrom, who organized the first "Projections" show. It is just as important to our understanding of African-American antimodernism that there is recognition of Bearden's willingness to circulate the Spiral story—notoriously short on details—in a search for some decisive social moment at which he makes the decision to become a collagist. (Conversions, like racial identities, are often performed.) Bearden fully becomes an antimodernist by recognizing the necessity for an art of *disintegration* that teaches audiences about the necessary work to be done and possible social and aesthetic structures within which such work might be accomplished. While Bearden would be uncomfortable about the ways in which his new art would, at least initially, be relentlessly interpreted in terms of contemporary race politics, it is nearly impossible to perceive the accomplishment of the collages simply in terms of formal innovation. Bearden perceived in the sixties a call to reevaluate—mourn and elegize—African-American and American community, and he chose to manipulate the experience of his past toward a recognition of available structures and available beauty.

PROJECTIONS

"Projections" opened in October 1964 at the Cordier & Ekstrom Gallery in New York.[46] Ekstrom wrote:

> Romare Bearden has done a series of twenty-one collages which have been photographed in quite large format, some 2 × 3 and some larger. I am showing these as an edition of six, each signed and numbered, mounted on board and put on strainers and framed by Kulicke Frames in narrow silver frames. They are really extraordinary and constitute a sort of re-living and re-telling of his memories as a Negro. The subjects range from burials and cotton fields to jam sessions, Harlem streets, Conjur women, etc. In these days of civil rights strife they are, on the sociological side, a unique statement of pride in tradition, dramatic in many instances but never a form of protest or agitation. Artistically they are most remarkable. . . . I think they will receive a lot of attention.[47]

The mixture of economic and aesthetic discourses is very interesting here, but Ekstrom's perceptions were basically accurate. The enlarged photostatic reproductions of Bearden's photomontages—really a distortion of a distortion—were an interesting and quite startling escape from the dead-end of radical modernism and his own previous literary derivations. Bearden had found a way to reintroduce his past and transform the present; he had found a way to celebrate tradition without reverting to a simplistic chauvinism. Most profoundly, he had found a way to represent a complex resistance to the status quo, whether that condition is understood as the world of contemporary American art, or simply contemporary America.[48] Of course, he would not be able to quit his job as a social worker until 1966, the first year he was able to support himself wholly from the proceeds of his art.

The twenty-one photomontages were broadly representative of African-American culture, rituals, and crises. They included scenes of the urban north and rural south, representations of black cultural rituals, scenes of musical performance, and, perhaps most notably, representations of women as figures of significant power. Most immediately, one is struck by the great magnitude of this cultural vision. It certainly problematizes any generalization about the nature and character of African-American culture. On the one hand, there is the sense that past and present environments are wholly different. The rural south seems distinctly premodern in orientation. Lifeways seem intimately connected to an African (and early Christian) past. Emphasis in representation is often upon the presence of the natural world: landscape and wildlife and the community's interaction with each. Yet, modernity, or "white civilization," is never far off. The repetition of themes, objects, and actions in urban and northern settings discourages viewers from making too neat a distinction.

They established a personal vocabulary of great potential. Mary Schmitt

Figure 6. Romare Bearden, "The Dove," 1965. © Romare Bearden Foundation/ Licensed by VAGA, New York, NY.

Campbell suggests that what is most striking is the "conceptual unity . . . coherence and inner logic" of the "Projections." Bearden carefully chooses or commits to the elaboration of a set of cultural narratives, figures, and symbols: the Conjur woman, birds, trains, musicians, biblical tales, religious rituals, and domestic scenes. This vocabulary (which is at once ancient and modern, western and nonwestern) is richly connected to the development of African-American cultural tradition and yet allows for extended and often pointed commentary upon traditions of representation within Euro-American and European art. More specifically, how did the photomontages create meaning? Matthew Teitelbaum suggests this general guideline:

> The compositional device of dramatic foregrounding provokes the viewer to rethink the relations between objects, to re-establish a hierarchy of correspondences. In this sense, among others, montage practice is about radical realignments of power. In escaping the "limits" of the straight photograph by dramatically repositioning various figures and objects, montage suggests new paradigms of authority and influence.[49]

In "The Dove" (1965; see figure 6), perhaps Bearden's most striking "urban representation" from the series, through the manipulation of scale Bearden creates the illusion of movement, the sense that this environment is active, alive. The flattened space is utilized to its fullest potential by slight distortions in the size and shape of faces. For instance, if one moves from the cen-

Figure 7. Romare Bearden, "The Prevalence of Ritual: Baptism," 1964. © Romare Bearden Foundation/Licensed by VAGA, New York, NY.

ter of the image to the right (mirroring the left to right of reading a page) the slight increase in the size of each head creates the sense of an image moving slightly towards you. The eyes of each figure represented face toward a relatively open space in the center foreground, a space of possibility, in which the figure of the dove hovers slightly overhead. It is very difficult for viewers to escape the gaze of the eyes, and, if one attempts to do so, one is often caught up by the vaguely threatening presence of enlarged, displaced hands. The presence of the dove in the increasingly contested urban space is, at one level, a straightforward enough assertion of a desire for the restoration of public meaning. But the technique of distortion and alteration also limits (although it does not dismiss) such a literalist meaning. Finally, what one cannot escape is the complexity of subjectivity proclaimed and illustrated; its particular sensibility, in this case, is largely lyric. In "The Prevalence of Ritual: Baptism" (1964; see figure 7), however, Bearden displays the depth of emotion and cultural resonance possible by recalling (syncretic) cultural narratives. The extended use of fragments of African masks to illustrate a baptism by immersion in a southern setting necessitates on the part of viewers the creation of a complex cultural intersection. The setting and masks recall a particular cultural survival—West African river rites—while not attempting to hide its Christian incarnation, and, at the same time, recalling modern art's own revitalization through engagement with African motifs.

Choosing photomontage to facilitate this change also invokes in interesting ways his apprenticeship under George Grosz. There can really be no question that Bearden was at some level recalling Grosz's tutelage. While the origins of photomontage are contested, it seems likely the case that Grosz was somewhere near its center. Grosz wrote:

> In 1916, when Johnny Heartfield and I invented photomontage in my studio at the south end of town at five o'clock one May morning, we had no idea of the immense possibilities, or of the thorny but successful career, that awaited the new invention. On a piece of cardboard we pasted a mishmash of advertisements for hernia belts, student song books and dog food, labels from schnapps and wine bottles, and photographs from picture papers, cut up at will in such a way as to say, in pictures, what would have been banned by the censors if we had said it in words. In this way we made postcards supposed to have been sent home from the Front, or from home to the Front. This led some of our friends, Tretyakov among them, to create the legend that photomontage was an invention of the "anonymous masses."[50]

The tension here between the specificity of the Grosz/Heartfield innovation and the "invention of the 'anonymous masses'" nicely foretells the ways in which Bearden attempts to utilize photomontage as a collective vehicle only to have the community project turned back to him. Most importantly, Bearden may be recalling the relationship between the birth of the artistic technique and *the moment of historical crisis* and the technique's ability to speak around the censors. Bearden's work was not really Dada, of course, although the irrational as principle was a good counter to bureaucratic conceptions of subjectivity. Bearden was definitely no anarchist. He was obsessive about formal structure and could cast no lot with Dada's insistence upon chance and chaos as disruptive of the modern state. The "piecing together" was important for Bearden in its critique of monolithic subjectivity and realism. Bearden came to adore the "artificiality" of art, and thus its implicit resistance to the quantifiable—the sociologists' approach to the "negro problem"—but also insisted upon its ordering function, human creativity as a distinct counterweight to modernity's faith in the machine. Bearden discovered how the irrational could serve the community. At some level, this is to say he recovered the religious element at the core of black cultural production, and ironically, it is a return or a remembering of his European Dadaist teacher that facilitates this impressive remembering.

To celebrate the irrational—and this is now a common refrain in this book—is not to downplay craft, agency, or intent. Indeed, Bearden insisted on what he called the classicism of his language and technique. The photomontage technique was at least partially a product of his return to painting by copying the masters. When finally convinced to return to painting, he began that journey of return by enlarging paintings by the photostatic method so that he could discern compositional techniques and the "narrative" relationship among objects. Like Coltrane's late work, the immediate appearance of disorder and cacophony has much more to do with the viewer's expectations than with any real commitment, if such a thing is possible, to chaos. Over and against increasingly *political* demands for the formation of new kinds of black community or black power, Bearden insists upon this romantic, counter-Enlightenment vision. And he does so with amazing self-confidence. There is some irony (and perhaps, in this emergent political context, it is intended) in the title "Projections." While this certainly captures, at some level, the specific mechanics at work, its intersection with psychoanalytic jargon suggests the possibility of something more dangerous. Is there risk in such desired artificiality? At what point does the imagined community become something no longer resistant to modernity's destruction of the self and more of an ac-complice? (Indeed, at what point does it become a vision of romantic nation-alism, the very statist fascism that Grosz was intent on disrupting?) It may also point to a second crucial irony. Bearden relies at this particular historical moment upon the exemplary modern technology of photography to articu-late a largely premodern vision of black culture. In some sense the "enlarge-ments" were meant to critique "reductions." Still, Bearden complained—reminscent of Robert Hayden—that individuals placed too much emphasis upon the sociological in the interpretation of the "Projections." He was suspi-cious that the photomontage technique, in particular (and its oblique critique of photojournalism), was encouraging such a reading. After this initial show-ing, he was never to return to photomontage again. The vocabulary and or-ganizing myths remained largely the same, but the remainder of his sixties work moved wholeheartedly toward multimedia collage in color.

THE SIXTIES IN COLOR

> In most instances in creating a picture, I use many disparate ele-ments to form either a figure, or part of a background. I build my faces, for example, from parts of African masks, animal eyes, mar-bles, mossy vegetation. . . . I then have the small original works en-larged so the mosaiclike joinings will not be so apparent, after which I finish the larger painting. I have found when some detail, such as a hand or eye, is taken out of its original context and is frac-tured and integrated into a different space and form configuration it acquires a plastic quality it did not have in the photograph.
>
> ROMARE BEARDEN (1975)[51]

> In regard to the question as to what "a Bearden" really *is*, Albert Murray's answer cannot be improved upon: it is, he says . . . "a de-sign or ornament or decoration for a wall, where it may hang not primarily as a record but as an emblem or badge or shield or flag or banner or pennant. . . . A Bearden . . . works on the beholder not only as a work of art but as something even deeper: a totemistic device and talisman for keeping the blues at bay."
>
> NATHAN SCOTT, "Romare Bearden"[52]

If anything clearly distinguishes Bearden's artistic universe it is its moral center.[53] Its subject matter often has to do with the manipulation of good and evil, rituals of purification, the commemoration of the everyday, or the frequency of quest or journey motifs. Figures like the "Conjur Woman" (1964; see figure 4) or "She-Ba" have power over the "materials" of the world. There is a long tradition of women in the African-American community who "worked roots." She is "also a conduit for the spiritual powers and knowledge of Africa," writes Sharon Patton. "She is an herbalist, a diviner, a priestess. . . . Her mysterious persona and penetrating gaze denote her traditional stature and power in society."[54] "Conjur Woman" (1964) also initiated the series *The Prevalence of Ritual*, developed in consultation with Albert Murray, a phrase Bearden would come back to over and over again in framing his art. Bearden's art world begins to suggest (or reveal) a way of organizing human experience. If "Conjur Woman" is a "seated woman"—and thus in dialogue with Western art history—she also sits in judgment on the white and black community. For Bearden this means, in the obvious sense, the community he is re-calling, but also everyone is thus called to wonder what it is that may need judging. Despite his diverse geographic heritage and cosmopolitanism, he returns, in the midst of the sixties, to Mecklenburg County, North Carolina. There he must reconsider the inhabitants, their way of life, and the meaning of their existence for himself—and others.

We also note in "Conjur Woman" the repetition of familiar hand gestures; this woman like other Bearden women is trying to tell us something. She holds in one hand a leaf, the only plant life in what seems to be an inner confined space. Now "pieced together," the figure of the woman is a conglomeration of photographs of people, reproductions of African masks (a very clever reclamation of the tradition of modernism), framed with various found objects—reproductions of part of a wooden window, door frames and so on. Somewhat of a distraction in the lower left corner sits some kind of utensil; it might be a knife and bread, or an artist's trowel and clay. As a knife it could either dispense nourishment or be a tool in a rite of initiation. Most striking, and typical of Bearden's art, is that despite the radical constructedness of the picture, the way in which it calls our attention to its artificiality, the seated figure clearly *has* the power of the conjure woman. The woman—perhaps as a function of the eyes, literally from the outside, if not more than one place—demands that we take her and her world seriously.

A second example also points to the conjunction of the local and universal, the past and the present, and the ritual reinscription of the landscape and history of the South. The central motif of "Watching the Good Trains Go By" (1964; see figure 8) is repeated often (and Bearden's attachment to repetition—of themes, within frames, and over time—is reminiscent of Coltrane); "Sunset Limited"(1978), "Southern Limited"(1976), "Evening Train to Memphis"(1976), "Daybreak Express"(1978), and "The Afternoon Northbound"(1978) all represent the passage of a train through the southern landscape. Such a motif has both personal and historic resonance; Bear-

Figure 8. Romare Bearden, "Watching the Good Trains Go By," 1964. © Romare Bearden Foundation/Licensed by VAGA, New York, NY.

den grew up in Charlotte, which was a major stop on north/south and east/west routes, and he remembered both the sight and sound of the train punctuating the countryside. The train is also, as Houston Baker points out, the point of focus for onomatopoeic representations by blues performers. As symbol of geographic freedom, it represents the possibility of the better life. And, for Bearden:

> I use the train as a symbol of the other civilization—the white civiliza-
> tion and its encroachment upon the lives of blacks. The train was al-
> ways something that could take you away and could also bring you
> back to where you were. And in the little towns it's the black people
> who live near trains.[55]

Bearden paintings are, however, never one-dimensional. No matter how powerful the theme or great its possibility of resonance, Bearden's collages are active, and take a great deal of work on the part of the viewer to be fully appreciated. Again, despite the mythic consonance of the train story, the viewer is first made aware of the centrality of a figure holding a guitar (which resonates with the title of Albert Murray's novel *Trainwhistle Guitar*). The blues figure gathers the community around him, even as he is associated with the two trains heading in opposite directions, inevitably forming a crossroads, the place of the trickster. The constructedness of the painting is emphasized by the multiple patterns of clothing, and the multiple textures they suggest. The community is also challenged or confronted with the figure of the rooster, whose comb attracts the reader's eyes to a single male character with his back to the viewer. Again, the viewer is compelled to ask the question, "What is going on here?" or "What has happened here?" Such narrative and dialogic engagement distinguishes Bearden from the dominant ethos of the American art establishment.[56]

"Conjur Woman" and "Watching the Good Trains Go By" demonstrate that:

> The underlying concept of Bearden's collages is the penetration of black life through ritual, the everyday customs and ceremonies that bind friends and family together. His people are posing formally as they bathe, eat, make music, attend funerals, hoe corn, play cards, listen to sermons and catch trains. This ceremonial dimension saves Bearden's art from undue sentimentality; the stylization leads the viewer away from emotionalism. . . . The Benin-like heads and the insertion of sophisticated references to Gauguin, Matisse, and Ingres render the drama more sonorous and serenely impersonal than one would predict.[57]

If Bearden's emphasis is to be on the everyday, it is the everyday transformed into something aesthetically charged. The ceremonial aspect of such mundane tasks points to a kind of cultural resistance which does not need to be part of a grand rhetorical gesture. Bearden inscribes African-American antimodernism through his insistence (and efforts to reveal) the beauty inherent in such human determination. Of course, the danger associated with the conjure woman, or the negative cultural experiences associated with the train, remind viewers that "ceremony" is required to designate sacred space because of the tragic character of history.

Other Bearden re-presentations in the sixties suggest a different kind of multivalence. At one level "Black Madonna and Child" (1969; see figure 9) is representative of Bearden's willingness, even after the move to collage, to demonstrate directly his indebtedness to the Western European art tradition, in this case to both the long tradition of "Madonna and Child" paintings and the techniques of Henri Matisse, certain effects of whose paintings Bearden was trying to duplicate in this piece.[58] The reinterpretation of the figures as black may not be as straightforward as first thought; to be sure, there were churches emerging in the sixties, most notably Albert Cleage's in Detroit, that were making a conscious effort to substitute black figures for those traditionally represented as white. In discussing a much later series of collages Bearden writes that:

> A Japanese student asked me why all the people in the series were black, because it's Homer's *Odyssey*. I said, well, everyone says that this

Figure 9. Romare Bearden, "Black Madonna and Child," 1969. © Romare Bearden Foundation/Licensed by VAGA, New York, NY.

is a universal statement. It has to do with a search for a father. It has to do with adventure. . . . So if a child in Benin or Louisiana . . . sees my paintings of Odysseus, he can understand the myth better.[59]

Bearden turns the motivation for "Africanizing" on its head; it is no longer a project of territoriality, but now an attempt to preserve universality. Analysis of this painting is further complicated by attempting to place it in the context of Bearden's long-standing practice of representing black women in iconic poses. (Bearden executes a "Madonna and Child" in 1945 and a "Black Mother and Child" in 1970—where there is repetition of the stylized hand gestures seen in figure 2.) Any consideration of the possible meanings of "Black Madonna and Child" must recognize that the power of its reversal

Figure 10. Romare Bearden, "Patchwork Quilt," 1969. © Romare Bearden Foundation/Licensed by VAGA, New York, NY.

may not necessarily be related to "black is beautiful" sloganeering. A reading based on a knowledge of African-American antimodernism would also require that we not reject out of hand the Western history of the Madonna—as artistic subject or mythic personage. The organizational principle of African-American antimodernism has shown the ways in which certain meanings of the sixties can only be discerned by taking seriously the manipulation (or representation) of the feminine. These would include understanding the feminine as dynamic creative force or as sacrificial victim; both reflect the resistance of modernity and the critique of the banality of contemporary life. In Bearden's work—as in the work of other male antimodernists—this feminine principle (which is seen sometimes as a temptress) is countered by strong representations or assertions of maleness; the rooster performs this function in the painter's vocabulary, as warrior posturing might in the work of Baraka. It is important not to generalize here; Bearden is to be congratulated (or understood as a protofeminist) for the varieties of black female identity he is able to imagine. In any series of Bearden collages, he has always guaranteed that a multiplicity of roles and identities are provided.

The significance of the feminine within a particular narrative context is illustrated by a fourth example. "Patchwork Quilt" (1969; see figure 10)[60] is one of Bearden's most famous and most frequently reproduced works, and suggests the diversity of Bearden's female representations. The motif of a viewer observing a nude woman bathing in a rural scene recurs often in Bearden's work. The presence of the quilt in the center of the collage acts as a synecdochal device; the painting itself is a patchwork quilt. In a similar fashion, the window as predominant feature in the painting reinforces the notion of voyeurism. The right side of the painting is dominated by a (or pieces of a) photograph of the inside of a cabin and a male figure with hidden face. The viewer is forced to ask the question, "What is happening here?"

No one has adequately decoded Bearden's color symbolism; the blue line across the top of the painting is, however, certainly a central trope.[61] It defines space by ironically directing the viewer's attention to the somewhat two-dimensional perspective. Bearden displays in the construction of his collages an interesting willingness to have the viewer discover that Bearden's arrangement is fabrication. In fact, Bearden's moral universe is here implied by the inability of the viewer to answer questions about what has taken place or is taking place within the narrative context of this painting, or, to put it another way, to struggle with the painting's two dimensions. The figures are back to back; any sensuality implied by the woman's nudity is, in some sense, undone by the man's disinterest as also by the dreariness of the work clothes photographically represented. This moral universe, along with our attempts to interpret it, is also effective at displacing efforts to designate the African-American experience as negative. Clearly, Bearden's work asks the viewer to participate in a process more theological and philosophical than sociological.

This is particularly so when it is brought to the viewer's attention that Bearden was especially attracted to the biblical story of Susanna and the Elders. The image of the women at her bath became for him a central trope of cleansing and ritual purification. As Bearden himself noted, the simple act of bathing could be invoked to raise in the viewer's mind not only a whole history of Judeo-Christian notions of redemptive action, but also a West African cosmology which centered such acts. The juncture of the two is the meaning of Bearden's accomplishment and might be described as the universal in the local. Of course, it may also be true that Bearden was significantly inattentive to the objectifying function of the male gaze in the tale. To highlight this incomplete reading is to suggest the complexity of artistic overturning. The gesture that alters the relationship of blacks to the Western art tradition can also rationalize maintaining the gender status quo.

Hilton Kramer found the metaphor of the patchwork quilt to be of central importance in understanding Bearden's work:

> The patchwork quilt is, after all, a kind of primitive Cubism in itself, and its use allows the artist both a free play on personal memory and the discipline necessary for art. It evokes a certain vein of experience and association, and at the same time provides—because of its affinities with Cubist origins of collage—a structure for the expression of that experience.[62]

It should also be pointed out that the quilt and quilting are central meta-phors in the recovery of an African-American women's literary tradition, and, as Robert Farris Thompson suggests, are also very suggestive of an ongoing and practical resistance against the sterilizing effects of rational Western cul-ture. They keep the god(s) alive. While perhaps obvious at this point, the cen-trality of women in Bearden's artistic universe should be highlighted. As Mary Schmidt Campbell has argued:

> No one could doubt the reality of the women in Romare Bearden's art. Women, as he perceives them, are the heart of his community, the Black community, and his concept of women is particularly well-suited to the sensuousness of his collage technique; he has penetrated their reality and found something profound, basic.[63]

I am not sure that the verb "penetrate" is unproblematic; still, Bearden does provide, perhaps, the most complex range of representations of black female identity made by a male artist in the context of the American sixties.

Campbell has also made the clearest statement of the relationship be-tween Bearden's new art and the social context of the sixties:

> The summer he worked on his first collage pieces was the summer that Harlem, his childhood community, erupted like communities all over the country into civil insurrection. The distortions, energy and vivid images of Bearden's first collages, black and white photographic blow-ups, were the seismographic readings of the turbulence within the inner cities. For Bearden the cynical detachment of Pop Art, the un-emotional cool of minimalism, simply were not an option for him.[64]

In some ways this reads like descriptions of Coltrane's art and interaction with the world. One way to read Bearden's art, to confront this associational problem, is to see the collages as chapters or scenes of an ongoing autobiog-raphy. Collages are the story of his life not only in the ways in which they re-call the past of the rural south, Pittsburgh, or Harlem, but in the ways they replay his artistic investigations as well. Ultimately Bearden escapes neither the structured life of his early southern past, nor the later practices of Cu-bism. Each is part of the African-American artist who inherits the legacy of Euro-modernism *and* the blues.

How do we reconcile Campbell's description of social context with Bear-den's commentary?

> From far off some people that I have seen and remembered have come into the landscape. I let this happen. Sometimes the mind relives things very clearly for us. Often you have no choice in dealing with this kind of sensation, things are just there. Really, all sorts of people want to live and, if you let them, they will help you. There are roads out of the secret places within us along which we all must move as we go to touch others.[65]

At this point Bearden sounds like Paule Marshall imagining/recalling Merle marching over the face of the earth—and, at this juncture, they sound together as if they understand Du Bois's assertion that "there is no deed but memory." This call and recall points to the centrality of "re-collection" as the only viable means of surviving the past and imagining the future; the African-American antimodernist artist creates new worlds as he reinterprets past failures.

So Arne Ekstrom was right: this work did get people's attention, and kept it for the next twenty-four years, up until Bearden's death in 1988 (and likely beyond, I suppose). He had a major retrospective at the Metropolitan Museum of Art; received honorary degrees and awards; became a respected art historian;[66] and was awarded the National Medal for Art in 1987. He never stopped refining his vision. The collages of the 1970s were more elaborate still, in construction, scope, and ambition. In the 1980s he began to visit regularly the Caribbean, and now had a completely different world of landscapes and religious, literary, and cultural systems from which to draw. In particular, this led to a dramatic collaboration with the poet Derek Walcott. Most powerfully, perhaps, he expanded his system of allusion to include the world and mythologies of jazz and blues. This development was extremely appropriate as:

> Collage is almost by definition an improvisational medium, in that it allows the artist to combine found objects from the everyday world— pieces of wood, fragments of photographs from old catalogues, fabrics—and literally "play with" them until they form a coherent composition. Bearden had known long before he made his first collage that painting was play: not child's play, he observed in a 1947 journal entry, "but a kind of divine play."[67]

THE NEW INSTITUTIONAL CONTEXT

> When I was a little boy, I was in a theater. The lights went on, the show was stopped, and the manager came out. He had everyone rise and played "The Star-Spangled Banner" because Lindbergh has just flown the Atlantic and had landed in France. When we came out, people were shouting, walking on their hands; it was like Armistice day, people were going wild. And I remember George M. Cohan's "Lucky Lindy, the Eagle of the USA." Everybody was playing that song. But the greatest poem written on that flight was done at the Savoy: the Lindy hop—the dancers throwing the girls, their skirts billowing—you realize that everything it did in that way was the essence of flight. So sometimes we tend to look in the book store or the museum for our history, while neglecting other aspects of it.
>
> ROMARE BEARDEN (1983)[68]

Figure 11. Jeff Donaldson, William Wlader and others, "Wall of Respect," ca. 1967, Photograph by Robert Sengstacke.

The completion in 1967 of the Wall of Respect (figure 11) presents an interesting challenge to African-American antimodernism as represented by Bearden. The Wall was produced at the encouragement of AfriCobra—the African Coalition of Bad Relevant Artists—in a south Chicago neighborhood. In Chicago Black Arts lore, it is a paradigmatic event, celebrated as galvanizing the community to cooperate to complete the project, and becoming a dynamic symbol of community pride. It is, in many ways, typical of community center art; not distinguished in style or in command of subject matter and generally emphasizing the representation of black heroes and heroines. Does Bearden's sophisticated defense of craft exclude the possibility of such "texts" doing effective cultural work? What is his place in a rapidly changing "arts context"?[69]

Bearden's place in this political context is not straightforward. His participation in "art worlds" was not at all hostile to forms of cultural nationalism. Bearden started no less than three galleries, including The Storefront Museum, and The Studio Museum in Harlem, dedicated to the promotion and distribution of art by minority artists. The Cinque Gallery (1969), the most famous of these ventures, celebrated the leader of the Amistad Rebellion (also documented by Robert Hayden), and has proved to be a resilient presence.[70] These pioneering institutions became models for institutions "which supported not only Black American art but all kinds of cultural expressions the mainstream museums for one reason or another would not ac-

Figure 12. "Africobra" symbol. Courtesy of Jeff Donaldson.

commodate."[71] He also organized the exhibitions "Contemporary Art of the American Negro" (1966) and "The Evolution of Afro-American Artists: 1800–1950" (1967). It is also interesting—as a response to Mary Campbell's question about history's treatment of Bearden, and as a response to questions about his connections to the masses—to note that "Bearden was not a mainstream artist, as evidenced by the paucity of his works in major museum collections. . . . Instead Bearden is better represented in the permanent collections of universities . . . small museums . . . corporations and in numerous private collections. Although his art is essential for the history of contemporary art, his acclaim rests not in the mainstream art world, but among ordinary people."[72]

This by no means exhausts the possibilities. The group AfriCobra proved themselves to be powerful satirists (not unlike the Romare Bearden who worked for the *Baltimore Afro-American*)—their group symbol (figure 12) an African Gelede mask with sunglasses—and they were interested not in "bad" art, but in a credible and enduring political art. The key here, I think, is not to see Bearden and AfriCobra as polar opposites or combatants. The Wall of Respect, after all, was meant to be a place of worship, a concept that Bearden understood perfectly well.

Collage brings to the work . . . elements that continually proclaim
their foreignness to context of presentation. These elements—like a
newspaper clipping or a feather—are marked as real, as collected
rather than invented by the artist-writer. The procedures of (a) cutting out and (b) assemblage are of course basic to any semiotic message; here they are the message. The cuts and sutures of the research
process are left visible; there is no smoothing over or blending of the
work's raw data into a homogenous representation. To write ethnog-
raphies on the model of collage would be to avoid the portrayal of
cultures as organic wholes or as unified, realistic worlds subject to
a continuous explanatory discourse. . . . The ethnography as collage
would leave manifest the constructivist procedures of ethnographic
knowledge; it would be an assemblage containing voices other than
the ethnographer's, as well as "found" evidence, data not fully integrated within the work's governing interpretation. Finally it would
not explain away those elements in the foreign culture that render
the investigator's own culture newly incomprehensible.

JAMES CLIFFORD, "On Ethnographic Surrealism"[73]

Structure is the anatomy of space, but it also represents the total investment of the artist; the vehicle of his means, and the filter of his
inspiration and imagination. In the end, in a completely realized
work, space and structure have become one.

ROMARE BEARDEN AND CARL HOLTY,
The Painter's Mind (1969)[74]

This chapter concludes by noting Bearden's literal transformation of Ellison's famous formulation from *Invisible Man* and its subsequent reconcep-
tualization, described by Sharon Patton as illuminating the connections between metaphor and memory. In a broad sense, Bearden's chief contribution
is the restoration of the ceremonial character of African aesthetic practice
in contemporary African-American life. If the exigencies of the middle passage and the "tracking" of hegemonic educational practice made "black art"
into "craft" and thoroughly secularized its creation and reception, Romare
Bearden radically reorients the visual arts tradition, and especially so in the
sixties.

We do not, however, have very many answers about the changes Bearden
made; clearly, I believe, his shaping of his artistic identity is related to similar
efforts by Robert Hayden, Mary Lou Williams, and John Coltrane, in particular. Bearden is perhaps more sophisticated in the ways in which he makes
himself an iconoclast or culture critic. From his earliest investigations as
artist or commentator he worked in an editorial fashion. We need to know
more about his mid-1950s breakdown. His transitions were neither smooth

nor a matter of being a modernist one day and an abstractionist the next. Of course, this kind of slipperiness as to identity has proven to be very useful in the (re)construction of African-American antimodernism. These questions may help us to understand the historical questions that Mary Campbell raised about Bearden's reputation. Bearden's relationship to the institution of American art resembles Ellison's to American literature. The critic celebrates the accomplishment, perhaps even the "affirmation," but cannot endorse this idiosyncratic response as an appropriate direction for American creativity.

August Wilson has discussed the influence of Bearden on his work. His grand project to write a play about every decade of African-American experience in the twentieth century is based on his understanding of Bearden's efforts to remake the concept of history, so that it is once again useful to the artist. Wilson's plays *The Piano Lesson* and *Joe Turner's Done Come and Gone* are based upon Bearden paintings. He writes: "In 1977, I made . . . a discovery that changed my life. I discovered the art of Romare Bearden. I was then a thirty-two-year-old poet who had taken his aesthetic from the blues but was unsure of how to turn it into a narrative that would encompass all the elements of culture and tradition. . . . What I saw [in Bearden] was black life presented on its own terms, on a grand and epic scale, with all its richness and fullness in a language that was vibrant and which, made attendant to everyday life, ennobled it, affirmed its value, and exalted its presence."[75] In some sense, I too had the same experience with Bearden. Given what I had learned from James Clifford—and what I have tried to apply in this book—I was not moved to realize, on the scholar's page, such a "constructive" project. But my discovery was also similar to that of Wilson: in Bearden, we find "the art of a large and generous spirit that defined not only the character of black American life, but also its conscience."[76] It is, generally speaking, "conscience" that the hermeneutic "antimodernism" can reveal.

On the cover of *Time*, November 1, 1968, only days before the election of Richard Nixon and near the end of the great decade of change, appeared a Romare Bearden collage. The cover story was "New York: The Breakdown of a City." "*Time*'s cover artists," suggests the editor's note, "often find themselves spending long hours, even days, designing a plan of attack, a theme that will give them some added insight to their work." Somewhat proudly, *Time* asserts that "Romare Bearden, 54, had no such problem." Perhaps ingenuously, perhaps sarcastically, Bearden's response to the question of the importance of his racial identity is presented: "As a Negro, Bearden insists that there is no particular significance in the fact that so many of his subjects have been Negroes." Bearden himself suggests, "My subject is people. They just happen to turn out to be Negro." The cover collage shows a somewhat confused Mayor Lindsay, beneath the eyes of New York children, while beneath him the city skyline rises up to devour him. We are told that after discussing his first (and last) cover assignment with *Time*'s editors on the 25th floor of the Time & Life Building in Manhattan, Bearden happened to look out of the window just before he left for his studio. His worries about New York added an artistic distortion to what he saw. 'The buildings were full of lights. . . . I saw them toppling about the mayor.'" Ironically, this Bearden work had no title. Whether this was a cryptic comment about magazines produced on the 25th floor of a "life" building, or just someone's oversight, cannot be determined.

CHAPTER SIX

W.E.B. Du Bois and Dedication to the Dead

The temptation among us is to split hope and history. As a result, we hold to a religious hope that is detached from the realities of the historical process. Or we participate in a history which ends in despair because the process itself delivers no lasting victories for the participant. The problem is that, even though hope yields victories, history precludes enduring triumphs.

WALTER BRUEGGEMAN, *Hope within History*[1]

If the condemned of the earth do not understand their pasts and know the responsibilities that lie upon them in the future, all on earth will be condemned. That is the kind of world we live in.

C.L.R. JAMES, "On the Origins"[2]

What might it mean to understand the past? Certainly the cliché about not repeating mistakes has relevance, although as a comprehensive ethic or political strategy in the face of entrenched racism it may be dangerously trite. More compelling may be the assertion that through the past one achieves, often at some significant cost, a kind of moral illumination. In this context, the present has meaning (or perhaps has meaning imposed upon it) through the recognition of past suffering, the creation of a kind of ancestral solidarity. Yet this too may melt into thin air. Such a confidence may be shown to be mostly narcissistic projection, indeed even neurosis. If both the instrumental and mythic pursuits of the past prove faulty, if not ephemeral, why does C.L.R. James's assertion remain so compelling, and seem to direct so much sixties—and more recent—African-American cultural practice? A central argument of this book has been that a striking component of post–World War II African-American intellectual and cultural life has been the increasing, if not obsessive, attention to this problem of the cultural significance of historical memory. Black anxiousness about the promise of modernity has been articulated most forcefully through an extended evaluation of the possibilities of "past-ness." A further suggestion of this book has been that the struggle or chase is fundamentally heroic, if equally, and tragically, flawed. This simultaneity is characteristic of and intimately related to the very dialectical energy with which we began: Enlightenment's simultaneous expression of barbarism and civilization. This survey of antimodern exemplars has tried to be suggestive of the scope of both possibility and limitation, an endorsement of the increasing attention paid to black creativity in mainstream American intellectual life, and a call for a reexamination of—to follow the suggestion of Walter Brueggemann in the epigraph—an enthusiasm that sometimes seems to confuse hope and history.

One obvious complication to any attempt to identify or consolidate historical memory as an important "enthusiasm" is the multiple ways in which the historical gaze is framed by exemplars of the antimodern attitude. For Robert Hayden, for instance, the past functioned as both social and aesthetic terrain. Often opening himself up to the charge of bourgeois aestheticism, Hayden nonetheless insisted upon the ethical character of his artistic practice and insisted that interpretive activity, more generally, was fundamentally redemptive. Diverging somewhat from this tack, Paule Marshall seemed to perceive her task as the re-creation—however fleeting—of moments of collective solidarity, moments out of which present action might concretely emerge. For William Demby, memory is the means par excellence by which we are reminded of the tenuousness of the present order. The "looking backwards" is the rational stratagem by which we discover the irrationality and incommensurability of modern existence. John Coltrane utilized reflection upon a past personal moment of crisis as an ordering device. The construction of a vivid personal historical canvas is the space upon which something vitally "new" can be built up. In Romare Bearden's life and work there is, arguably (and provocatively), the attempt to entangle each of these modes. The act of creation is simultaneously an act of mourning and of new possibility, and meant to signal both communal interconnectedness and an intensely personal vision. Needless to say, there is much ideological diversity here, too, and perhaps so much so that the breadth of this survey is somewhat counter to the formation of a pragmatic interpretive paradigm.

At the same time, these exemplars are closely interconnected through a substantial, if slippery, cultural "romanticism" (especially in the sense offered up by Lorraine Hansberry). Over and against the state's bureaucratic regulation of life, including racial regimentation, these exemplars cultivated and celebrated the (individual) imagination's ability to redeem and reconstruct, most provocatively through the restoration of the past in the present. Importantly, however, this romanticism is also marked by the recognition that this investment in the past is a Faustian bargain. The cost of discovery or recovery is a full accounting of the temporal and imperfect reality of the lived life; perhaps inevitably, the jeremiad becomes a central trope and cultural performance, as each thinker insists, with varying degrees of potential nostalgia, that "things ain't what they used to be." The centrality of a "mourning discourse" to the work of each exemplar, and indeed its centrality to an understanding of African-American culture and the American sixties—the insistence that a viable resistance to those aspects of modernity's promised liberation that ring false can only be grounded in an acknowledgment of death—is indicative of a mature sense of the tragic.

But is this sense of the tragic enough to hold off what has become in the twentieth century a dangerous inevitability to this kind of historicist thought, the logic or singular truth of blood, the demand for authenticity, not solidarity but xenophobia? Is this sense of human frailty enough to hold off that sense of the past that leads to intolerance, that makes of imagined historical narratives the guidebook to new horrors? Is a developed sense of irony toward the rarity of some true and authentic transcendence enough to hold off the temptation of despair? These questions are large, perhaps too large, but the ambition of this book has been to foreground such inquiry, to insist on the possibility of understanding the cultural and political dilemmas of the postwar United States through texts, traditions, and thinkers generally shuffled to the cultural margins. A look at one final exemplar, a historian-thinker who was uniquely positioned to examine the intersection of memory, modernity, and resistance—and, most importantly, whose utterances and associations became concretely problematic for the state—may be helpful to sort out and make more manageable these difficult questions.

W.E.B. DU BOIS AND THE AMERICAN SIXTIES

It might be said that, like a specter, W.E.B. Du Bois (and his legacy) haunted the American sixties. Such a bedeviling may have begun on August 28, 1963, at the great civil rights march on Washington. Roy Wilkins, the NAACP executive secretary, made the announcement of Du Bois's death: "Regardless of the fact that in his later years Dr. Du Bois chose another path it is incontrovertible that at the dawn of the twentieth century his was the voice calling you to gather here today in this cause."[3] The announcement came in the midst of much backstage wrangling that had taken place to ensure that, while the government and the nation would be chided and challenged, nothing embarrassing to the Kennedy administration would be spoken. Most particularly, in the draft of a speech by John Lewis, leader of the Student Non-Violent Coordinating Committee, the language of revolution had to go. Du Bois's posthumous appearance and Wilkins's mention of an alternate path was, then, ironic indeed. In the context of the cold war, Du Bois's decision to live out his last days in Ghana was betrayal enough, but, by writing to Gus Hall and declaring his intent to become a member of the Communist Party U.S.A. (CPUSA), Du Bois makes the most complete break any American could make away from what might be called the consensus citizenship contract of the moment.

The decision to formally join the Party and to leave the United States were, in many ways, the completion of a process that began for Du Bois sometime in the late 1940s. After his final break with the NAACP in 1948, he actively gravitated toward an explicitly left wing activism at odds with both mainstream African-American leadership and U.S. foreign policy. His participation in the Peace Information Center—and, in particular, the Center's refusal to address itself to the Foreign Agents Registration Act—led to his indictment in 1951. While those charges were eventually dismissed, Du Bois's relationship with the U.S. government was highly contentious, and was marked, most notably, by the revocation of his passport later in the decade. It is difficult to assess whether state restrictions on speech and movement or the betrayal of friends, colleagues, and chroniclers of African-American achievement, who felt it necessary to distance themselves from Du Bois and his accomplishments and commitments, was the greater blow. He deals forthrightly (if not always unselfishly) with these disappointments in *In Battle for Peace* (1952) and it would not be inaccurate to describe the Du Bois of the 1950s and 1960s as increasingly bitter, isolated, and disillusioned.[4]

His letter to Gus Hall on October 1, 1961, has the feel, then, of an attempt to claim the last word, a retaliatory and even vengeful action.[5] While he speaks eloquently of the "long and slow coming to this conclusion," it is also true that the letter is not so much indicative of a wholly new stage in Du Bois's political thought as it is a reorganization or renaming of previous commitments. Like many other "conversions" of postwar antimodernists, there is plenty of evidence to suggest that there is a great deal of self-aware public performance taking place. Du Bois seemingly chooses to become what the government energetically insisted that he was implicitly and covertly. Most of the letter speaks to Du Bois's perception as to the absence of Marx within communities of learning and seems anxious to address itself to the McCarthyist culture of conformity. His gravitation toward "socialism" is presented in terms of a series of false starts (doctrinal positions he could not support—"the Socialists . . . trying to segregate Southern Negro members"; "the Communists' . . . advocacy of a Negro state"—or accounts of the progress gained by the Soviet republics—"contradictory news from Russia") that is positively completed only by his personal witnessing within "Communist lands." His assertion that "capitalism is doomed to self-destruction" —a belief he shared, it might be added, with agrarian conservatives like Allen Tate—was coupled with his "definition" of communism as "the effort to give all men what they need and to ask of each the best they can contribute." There is little evidence of engagement with Marxism either as a system or as a tradition of thought (although he had no doubt done that reading) and he instead chooses to emphasize an intuitive socialism whose central ethic would not be wholly out of place in his beloved small-town and turn-of-the-century New England. (Strikingly, he does not mention whether any of the previous fears or concerns that provoked his hesitations have been allayed. He makes no assertion as to whether or not the CPUSA now has a more complete or mature approach to the race question or whether or not news from Russia was any less "contradicting.")

As was often the case, there could be some confusing overlap between the political agendas of organizations that Du Bois belonged to and that of Du Bois himself. In the central part of the letter, he wrote:

> The path of the American Communist Party is clear: It will provide the United States with a real Third Party and thus restore democracy to this land. It will call for:
>   1. Public ownership of natural resources and of all capital
>   2. Public control of transportation and communications
>   3. Abolition of poverty and limitation of personal income
>   4. No exploitation of labor
>   5. Social medicine, with hospitalization and care of the old
>   6. Free education for all
>   7. Training for jobs and jobs for all
>   8. Discipline for growth and reform
>   9. Freedom under law
>   10. No dogmatic religion

(It's noteworthy that this list—perhaps with the exception of the dangerously vague "discipline for growth and reform"—is blandly and ambitiously related to the platforms of any number of parties of the postwar democratic left.) While Du Bois no doubt understood and anticipated the uses to which his letter would be put, it is still unusual that in a letter "applying for admission" to an organization one would state what that organization would "call for." The letter concludes: "These aims are not crimes. They are practiced increasingly over the world. No nation can call itself free which does not allow its citizens to work for these ends." Despite his impressive cosmopolitanism and internationalism and Pan-Africanism, there is a strategic provincialism at work here too. Reminiscent of both David Walker and Frederick Douglass, Du Bois signifies upon both the American jeremiad tradition and an Enlightenment-rooted discourse of rights. Despite functioning as the first indication of his forthcoming decision to leave the United States, the tone of his "application" is reminiscent of that archetypal (and vaguely apocalyptic) American call to get one's house in order. Du Bois's socialism or communism is significantly (if obtusely) invested, then, in American nationalism. It is a pragmatic (in every sense of the word) evaluation of capitalism's prospects, and—as always—a personal witness (and even embodiment) of an alternative strategy or outlook.

Part of the historical irony in this late gesture was Du Bois's own stunning lifetime of achievement: institution builder, pioneering sociologist and historian, novelist, editor, and "race man." In many ways, his Alger-like rise might have been used as evidence of the goodness and rationality of the very social order he came to reject. A more subtle strategy to deal with Du Bois's apostasy might have been to reward him with the accolades and attention he craved and deserved. (Perhaps such a strategy was being posthumously invoked by Roy Wilkins in Washington, D.C., in the summer of 1963. Inadvertently, it is called into play by "black history month" type invocations of his legacy, celebrations that carefully ignore any discussion of his last twenty years.) It is interesting to speculate how Du Bois would have responded to such a strategy given his famous ego. Instead, the seeming desperation of the state to limit African-American intellectuals' ability to speak to questions of racism on the international stage provided for Du Bois a timely martyrdom. Instead of having his last years marked primarily by intracultural conflict—his disappointment with what he saw as the bourgeois individualism of the mainstream civil rights leadership or simply having to contend with the emergence of a new generation of race leaders—the twilight of his life would be marked by a much more compelling David and Goliath story: W.E.B. Du Bois versus the government of the United States of America.

Du Bois's grave dissatisfaction with American economic injustice does not qualify him in itself for inclusion among my antimodern exemplars. I mean to suggest that his articulation of a now hopefully familiar mode of mourning, suspicion of mass culture, cultivation of a dynamic historical consciousness, and fear of "despiritualization" will be evidence of a more complete kinship. And yet, in some respects, Du Bois is potentially an immediate *threat* to the cultural consolidation of antimodern sentiment; this is to say that amongst this book's dramatis personae, Du Bois stands somewhat apart. Here might be the combination of learning, scholarly temperament, and investment in a diagnosis of culture more fully at ease with the Enlightenment legacy, such that the future of African American community might be framed in distinctly "modern" terms. Insofar as Du Bois was gravitating towards the "science of socialism," he seemed to be crafting a diagnosis of American racial and economic equality that provided, through its structured political activism and teleology, a means of coping too. As the sixties unfolded, it is unlikely that any other individual was better prepared to articulate a critique of the status quo without knee-jerk recourse to national, religious, masculinist, or cultural mystification. Yet in Du Bois such an informed modernity is not pursued without significant qualification. As is argued above, even Du Bois's scientific socialism seems significantly invested in a vaguely nostalgic—and explicitly exceptionalist—treatment of American possibility. In the sixties, Du Bois's sense of the prospect of new social structures and organizations is always inflected by a narrative of betrayal and failure. Most strikingly, this betrayal lies in the broken promise of the American Revolution and its founding documents. (One suspects, however, that the betrayal is sometimes personal too: a strong—and not always inaccurate—feeling that he has been disrespected, or, more horrific, ignored. Certainly one of the most compelling issues to emerge in Du Bois criticism and historiography is how to resolve the potential contradiction of his substantial ego and his social commitments. The instinct of his biographers has been to make of this question mostly a matter of "personality." There may be, however, good reason to pursue this as emblematic of a deeper and more resonant ambivalence.) Regardless of whether or not one can discern "intent," it is true that this sense of outrage is edifying. A compelling and believable narrative of betrayal and failure certainly guards against the confusion of hope and history.

The predominant (and primarily literary) strain of Du Bois criticism has enthusiastically embraced this contradictoriness—Europe/Africa, collectivist/individualist, modern/antimodern—although mainly with regard to his early career, and especially the now ritualistic treatment of "double consciousness" in *The Souls of Black Folk* (1903). Adolph Reed's recent *W.E.B. Du Bois and American Political Thought* is right to resist this tendency to mystify Du Bois and his political commitments. To reduce the totality of Du Bois's career to a few pithy cultural aphorisms ("double consciousness" or, say, "problem of the color line")—and ignore his systematic evaluation of the organization and prospects of African-American communities and his concrete investigation of various political formations and their utility and justness for all Americans—is certainly a distortion of his legacy. And yet that tendency to distortion (or enthusiasms for a quasi-mystical and, frankly, conservative Du Bois) does not seem to be wholly the product of regressive bourgeois sensibility on the part of literary critics. Du Bois does at least foreground (if not encourage) the possibility of continued misreadings (or partial readings) through his own return, again and again, to compelling statements of mystery, the ineffable, and the transcendent. For instance, even as Du Bois comes to steer clear of organized religion—no mean feat for the Victorian New Englander of a somewhat Brahmin sensitivity—he often resorts to quasi-religious formations to explain the extraordinary character of his life. The combination of a radical philosophic idealism and a hyperbolic rhetorical style often leads to an overheated sense of historical possibility. Du Bois substitutes for the traditional mystic's commitment to union with the divine his own fervent (often allegorical) counterstatement. The attractiveness of this modus operandi to contemporary critics can be its tendency to dehistoricize: he becomes a malleable figure, whose lack of precision can be (and is) used, in particular, to support the mainstream liberal consensus. The latent aestheticism of Du Bois's discourse explains, in part, its appeal to literary critics, and should be cause for some prudent hesitation. Aestheticism per se is not problematic, of course; instead, it is the selectivity with which it is usually engaged or invoked. "Double consciousness," for example, can only be accurately described with reference to Du Bois's concrete political aims—how and where black political allegiance is to be situated and distributed—and should not be casually summoned up as a therapeutic talisman.

Given the disproportionate tendency of Du Bois's readers to psychologize his accomplishments at the expense of his investment in the scientific documentation of racism in the United States, the important critical task is to discover the strategic importance of this distinctly antimodern mode and its possibilities and limitations. Why is Du Bois's faith in reason and the modern organization and regulation of knowledge consistently undermined or qualified by his recourse to fundamentally ahistorical constructions and speculations? (And we should certainly not dismiss the obvious: the transformative possibilities of the beautiful; the impact of European Calvinist and black folk traditions of preaching; an understanding of the possibilities of rhetoric *and* poetics.) In W.E.B. Du Bois, and especially the Du Bois of the sixties, then, there is an opportunity to consider "antimodern" sentiment as a kind of necessity. Given his extraordinary social-scientific skill and political acumen, why resort to the psychologizing of experience or the sacralization of the passage of time? This certainly sets up the possibility of a broader historical inquiry: What is there about the formation and evolution of African-American culture (or its political relation to the mainstream) that makes the "looking backward" so compelling? A second component of such a substantial critical evaluation of the late Du Bois should be an investigation of continuities in his critical outlook and in his relationship to American thought broadly conceived.

It's especially crucial to note, of course, the extraordinary length of Du Bois's career as an important public intellectual. The great span of Du Bois's career—say, from his 1890 commencement speech on Jefferson Davis through his ghostly presence at the 1963 march on Washington, close to seventy-five years—allows for some consideration of the relationship between various movements of cultural revitalization. This book began, for instance, with a rationale for the pirating of the descriptive language of "antimodernism" from Jackson Lears's account of a largely WASPish group of late nineteenth-century resisters to the consolidation of American modernity. Readers may recall that Lears revealed and interrelated late nineteenth-century and early twentieth-century obsessions with artisanship and craftwork, martial idealism supportive of American imperialism and "muscular Christianity," the recovery of (imagined) medieval modes of thought and manners. They had in common a faith in authentic experience. This nexus of cultural practices existed in conscious counterstatement to an increasingly despiritualized, bureaucratized modernity, argues Lears. That this configuration of resistance is revealed to be supportive of the maintenance of a racist, masculinist, and classist status quo should not disqualify it as potentially illuminating of post–World War II African-American cultural resistance. It was a vital and often instructive (if irrevocably flawed) critique of the development and consolidation of American modernity. Its failures (narcissism, racism, its inability to reconcile rational and counterrational modes of inquiry, and its cultural, political, and biological nostalgia) may be revealing of the structural conditions of American protest, the ways in which the voicing of the negative is inevitably inflected in American thought and action. (To inquire about such affinities should not necessitate suggesting that there is an equivalence to the positions of social power held by the speakers nor, for that matter, should we assume that there is any equivalence in justification for speaking. On the other hand, neither should we assume the sanctification of either group.)

It is the instinct of this book that the increasing centrality of "memory" (among other aspects of this revitalization movement) in post–World War II African-American cultural practice resonates in interesting ways with this past mode of resistance. In the most extreme forms (and the plural is important here) of sixties black nationalism one can find powerful repetition of both the positive (challenge to despiritualization; critique of the devaluation of the [black] body; desire to revitalize historical inquiry) and the negative (misogyny; glorification of violence; absence of any fully transcendent vision) aspects of that critique. But even in more mainstream sixties African-American cultural life one can find invocations of ancestral legacy, the protective and redemptive power of memory, and a relentless search for the meaning of black authenticity. Why should this repetition be of concern? Nineteenth-century antimodernism proved to be no match for capitalism's commitment to desacralization or its reduction of human agency in exchange for consumer "choice." Neither could it effectively hold off the enforced amnesia necessary for the celebration of "progress." Most damning of all, according to Lears, antimodern resistance of significant social breadth was too easily transformed into narcissistic projection and paved the way for the triumph of the therapeutic ethos. As such it seems necessary to reflect on the long-term efficacy of these cultural practices, and to ask whether or not there is any relationship between these failures and current pessimism in progressive thinking about race and race relations.[6]

Insofar as contemporary African-American thought and cultural practice has been especially challenged—and certainly revitalized once again—by the question of Africa, it may be worthwhile to consider briefly Du Bois's own struggle with that fact and idea and its relationship to turn-of-the-century anxiety. Du Bois's quite willful construction of "African-ness" is one of the most compelling points of intersection with this past. It seems to share with turn-of-the-century dissent a desire for simplicity, and, as such, detailing Du Bois's encounter with Africa and its potentially primitivist longing may be helpful. The utopianism of this encounter (and, of course, its basic inaccuracy and incompleteness) at least partially envelops and informs his approach to the question of modernity and, it can be argued, his approach to communism too. Eric Sundquist argues that as early as *Dusk of Dawn* (1940), Du Bois began to articulate the "view that the 'primitive' communal organization of African villages offered an antidote to capitalized, industrialized models of Western life."[7] What makes the analysis of this component of Du Bois's thought so complex is that he did display an instinct for the "deconstruction" of his own faith and of his tendency toward political invention. In "The Realities in Africa" (1943), for instance, Du Bois writes, "For convenience we refer to 'Africa' in a word. But we should remember that there is no one 'Africa.' There is in the continent of Africa no unity of physical characteristics, of cultural development, of historical experience, or of racial identity."[8] This startlingly prophetic essay—its critique of colonialism and insistence on an eventual cost to Western prosperity is mature and concise—does not make clear whether or not one should continue to utilize such a convenience. "The cultural possibilities of the African native are undeniable," writes Du Bois only one page later, willfully repressing the question of "native-ness." Du Bois is torn between assuming the role of the philosopher and that of magician. On the one hand, he must insist on a non-negotiable truthtelling. He writes, "It is necessary to renounce the assumption that there are a few large groups of mankind called races, with hereditary differences shown by color, hair, and measurements of the bony skeleton which fix forever their relations to each other and indicate the possibilities of their individual members" (663). On the other hand, Du Bois is hard pressed to resist the temptation of political conjure. The only efficacious means at hand to defeat continued European attempts at subjection, even in the context of decolonization, is the creation of continental solidarity, reinforced by the cultivation and invention of international black concord and rapport.

His address "The Future of Africa" (1958) was addressed to "fellow Africans" and began with a complaint that "the books which we studied in the public school had almost no information about Africa, save of Egypt, which we were told was not Negroid."[9] This excellent essay—a collage of styles and commitments—was prepared for the All-African People's Conference in Accra and was read by his wife, Shirley Graham Du Bois, as he was unable to leave the United States. In one of his typical impressive rhetorical flourishes, Du Bois commanded:

> Africa, ancient Africa, has been called by the world and has lifted up her hands! Africa has no choice between private capitalism and socialism. The whole world, including capitalist countries, is moving toward socialism, inevitably, inexorably. You can choose between blocs of military alliance, you can choose between groups of political union; you cannot choose between socialism and private capitalism because private capitalism is doomed! (665)

The messianism of this passage—and its teleology—is justified by Du Bois by noting that "the African tribe, whence all of you sprung, was communistic in its very beginnings. No tribesman was free. All were servants of the tribe of whom the chief was father and voice." "Communism" is the natural state of African life, he asserts, oddly mimicking the simplifications of those early-twentieth-century European artists who saw in Africa respite from the dullness and despair of the modern West. His thinking is extended (and certainly complicated) when he adds:

> Great Goethe sang, *"Entbehren sollst du, sollst entbehren"*–"Thou shalt forego, shalt do without." If Africa unites, it will be because each part, each nation, each tribe gives up a part of its heritage for the good of the whole. That is what union means; that is what Pan-Africa means: When the child is born into the tribe the price of his growing up is giving a part of his freedom to the tribe. This he soon learns or dies. When the tribe becomes a union of tribes, the individual tribe surrenders some part of its freedom to the paramount tribe. (667)

These impressive rhetorical assaults are strong indications of the ambivalence associated with much black antimodernism. There is, of course, an important pragmatism here—Du Bois also asserts, not necessarily popularly, the importance of the surrender of individual African languages—but perhaps an even stronger irony. The commandeering of Goethe, as he had sixty years previous in *Souls*, and the implication of the very German romantic nationalism that led to the carving up of Africa in the first place, is suggestive of a strange and frustrating circularity. (Similarly, in this essay and elsewhere, Du Bois hints at an admiration for Zionism too: "The African movement means to us what the Zionist movement must mean to the Jews, *the centralization of race effort and the recognition of a racial fount*.[10] [my italics]) If it produces confusion, it is most striking that it seems to be done deliberately rather than as an unanticipated component of a more marginal assertion. Even at the height of his scientific socialist stage, these statements of Pan-Africanist possibility are clearly meant to be the emotional centerpiece of his argument.

If these late-career writings are indicative of a fascinating but potentially paralyzing contradiction, a final essay, "Whites in Africa after Negro Autonomy" (1962), is suggestive of the potential gain through a retreat to an essential, unfragmented Africa. In this piece, in some sense a conclusion to Du Bois's career as a public intellectual, he relentlessly connects the destruction of Africa and the decadence of the West. In reflecting upon the possible use of nuclear arms in regional and/or internal conflicts in the developing world, for instance, Du Bois asserts: "God forbid that this awful catastrophe should ever threaten; but if it does, the best people of Europe and America, living and carousing on the degradation of Africa, will bear the blame."[11] Such apocalyptic is merely a sensational setup for his dramatic peroration:

> There was a day when the world rightly called Americans honest, even if crude—earning their living by hard work, telling the truth no matter whom it hurt, and going to war only for what they believed in, a just cause, after nothing but force seemed possible. Today millions of us are lying, stealing, and killing. We call all this by finer names: Advertising, Free Enterprise, and National Defense. But names in the end deceive no one; today we use science to help us deceive our fellows; we take wealth that we never earned; and we are devoting our vast energy to prepare ourselves to kill, maim, and drive insane—men, women, and children who dare to refuse to do what we want done. Some profess to know why we fail. They say we haven't taught our children mathematics and physics. No, it is because we have not taught our children to read and write or to behave like human beings and not like hoodlums. Every child on the street is whooping it up with toy guns, and the big boys with real pistols. When Elvis Presley goes through his suggestive motions on a public stage, it takes the city police force to hold back teen-age children from the hysteria. The story of the rigged TV quizzes completes the picture of our spiritual decadence. (674)

Was there a day when the world rightly called Americans honest? If so, when was it? Slavery? Reconstruction? Jim Crow? How can Du Bois seemingly allude without irony to the just cause of American warfare after the imperialism of late-nineteenth and early-twentieth-century American military action or of the debacle of his own First World War experience? This passage recalls the title of the great Mercer Ellington tune "Things Ain't What They Used to Be" and what was always assumed to be its implicit rejoinder: "And you know, they never was." Why would Du Bois utilize such an odd trope given that in some ways it contradicts his arguments about the corruption at the heart of capitalism? Certainly a partial explanation is to be found in the moral energy associated with the passage's own irrationality. It communicates a strong sense of outrage. Furthermore, the imagined past functions as a kind of Platonic ideal. By positing or inventing a moment of unambiguous goodness, the very real list of ills can be distinguished from any kind of natural order. By saying, for example, the poor have not always been with you, one might direct attention to their current presence and plight. Neither does the passage wholly abandon the strategy of truth-telling or unmasking. Du Bois's demand for the elimination of double-talk introduces into the nostalgic mix a mode more consistent with his scholarly commitments. The potential elitism of this strategic collaboration—magical rewriting with supreme self-confidence combined with the call to properly name concepts and ideas—is hinted at in the suspicion and summary dismissal of mass culture, here (and later) embodied by Elvis Presley. (Du Bois's oft commented upon discomfort with the black masses is ironically alluded to in his disgust with Presley's minstrel projection of black working class style.) As a lamentation, it is especially impressive because its target is not only (or even specifically) a lack of prosperity or structural inequality, but, rather, "spiritual decadence." Even at this late stage in Du Bois's political development, there is the sense that a call for fundamental structural change—which is, of course, always an explicit demand for the surrender of territory, property, privilege, or wealth—must be packaged in otherworldly form such that there is potentially an immediate and perhaps irreparable erosion of that call.

What are the structural conditions of American protest that produce such a gaze? Does such rhetorical ambivalence or contradiction resist or make inevitable the triumph of the status quo? Sacvan Bercovitch refers to American "rituals of consensus" in his discussion of the jeremiad tradition and of post-Puritan revisions too.[12] The commitment to the restoration of the past seems to make *history* of John Winthrop's prophecy of a "city on a hill"—to dangerously merge prophecy and recollection. One unfortunate result is, of course, that one reinscribes over and over a version of American exceptionalism. From this perspective, Du Bois's meditations lock Africa and America into a vaguely Biblical dialectic in which one can never quite determine which is (or is not) the promised land. Du Bois's extreme apostasy becomes a kind of regenerative linguistic violence, oddly reproducing the conditions from which the protest emerges. And, again, it is important to insist that this is not mere accident, but is willed. The necessary and strategic effort to speak a language that is recognizable becomes an intimate part of any number of social and cultural rituals of reconciliation, while at the same time ensuring that the reconciliation is marked by ambivalence and absence. The never-ending call is never only for forgiveness or unity or wholeness, but is always about redistribution and rethinking and, ironically, distancing too.

On the other hand, and definitely less negatively, Du Bois seems to share with Walter Benjamin a commitment to the necessity of anamnesis as a means of confronting the depletion of "experience" in modern life, itself intimately related to the very degradation of language that Du Bois deplores. (Also like Benjamin, Du Bois wavered between a quasi-mystical longing for authentic community and a rigorous evaluation of modernity's prospects; this duality is captured in interesting ways in the dictionary definition of anamnesis, referring on the one hand to "recollection" and "reminiscence," but also, in the context of the study of Christian liturgy, that part of the Eucharist in which the sacrifice of Christ is 'recalled.'[13]) Memory provides a landscape of hopeful possibilities against the administration of modern life. From the Du Boisian-Benjaminian perspective, authenticity is not the narrow conscription of identity, but rather the *possibility* of identity over and against modernity's tendency to erode our ability to place the self in any permanently meaningful context. Such a recovery allows for individual mourning, passage to a new preparedness, and, at the same time, working to foreground communal conditions of action. And indeed, despite the extremes of his personality that might preclude the cultivation of a productive collective consciousness, Du Bois's success in midwifing twentieth-century Pan-Africanism is testimony to the possibilities of this memory-work.

Du Bois's last effort at self-revelation and his last major work—*The Autobiography of W.E.B. Du Bois*—is an extraordinary document for the ways in which it structures the muddle of his contrariness. If W.E.B. Du Bois, the faithful scholar of Enlightenment reason, is "troubled" by the recurring nightmare of the suspension of liberty, this final engagement with the public is suggestive of the ways in which African-American antimodernism may provide balance. Disenchantment (or the unveiling and nullification of power) is by neccessity combined with a gesture towards re-enchantment, or perhaps, more accurately, respiritualization. The unique combination of commitment to historical documentation or placement and the poetic transformation or invention of life in autobiography as genre make it an ideal text to conclude this study of the antimodern tendency. Most importantly, if the dominant perception of the American sixties insists upon unfettered boundary breaking then the *Autobiography* points to a countertendency of stocktaking, lamentation, and the search for order. *The Autobiography of W.E.B. Du Bois* allows for a sustained reading of the tension between testimony and unfettered optimism, and foregrounds prudence in our attempts to accurately and productively tell stories about the meaning of the sixties.

THE STATUS AND RECEPTION OF *THE AUTOBIOGRAPHY* OF *W.E.B. DU BOIS*

The Autobiography of W.E.B. Du Bois: A Soliloquy on Viewing My Life from the Last Decade of Its First Century[14] was written in 1958 and 1959, appeared in abridged form in the Soviet Union and East Germany in the early 1960s, and was finally published in its entirety in 1968, five years after Du Bois's death. The convoluted introduction of the text to the United States is both ironic and appropriate. As a final presentation of his life, its posthumous appearance parallels the complicated relationship of Du Bois's presence to American and African-American intellectual history. At the same time, this sense of return, "after the fact," highlights Du Bois as a *peculiar* historical consciousness haunting the American sixties.[15] The *Autobiography* reveals a mind capable of retrospective vision and systematic exegesis in almost medieval fashion. Part Augustinian confession, part *Summa*, and written in his ninetieth year, Du Bois's final autobiography presents the self as a special kind of cultural irritant. Having lived longer than expected (or respected), he comments, in his opening "soliloquy," on the necessity of memory for social understanding. The life that it documents had come to hold an old Left position at the moment that the New Left was coming of age. Many of the social disruptions of the decade—changes in dress, in popular culture, in the expansion of the hegemony of television, in attitudes toward sexuality—would certainly have been distasteful to Du Bois. Indeed, a significant portion of the *Autobiography* does decry the omens of that change. In other ways, however, its appearance in the annus mirabilis 1968 is timely, even poetic in character. Its publication by International Publishers in New York, in June of that year, in the midst of the Columbia University uprising—modernism in the streets, as Lionel Trilling called it—reintroduced to the American scene a consciousness which was fundamentally shaped by the last years of the previous century. If one of the sins of sixties progressivism was its insistence on its own originality, Du Bois gives testimony to prior covert and overt traditions of resistance. Like Paule Marshall's *The Chosen Place, The Timeless People,* Romare Bearden's collages, and Robert Hayden's symbolist technique, the *Autobiography* is committed to a mode of inquiry and representation somewhat out of step, and is vaguely suspicious of the unqualified value of the new.[16]

The *Autobiography*—or perhaps more generally the late Du Bois—is often dismissed as duped by the Soviets and Chinese. It (and he) is a *failure*. For Eric Sundquist, for instance, arguably the most eloquent advocate for Du Bois's place in the American canon, Du Bois's later efforts are a distinct embarassment. It is, he suggests, "a case study in conversion from democratic faith to faith in tyranny—to faith, ironically enough, in slavery." Keith Byerman, also an eloquent interpreter of Du Bois's cultural legacy, provides a fine close reading of the text, but describes the book as "the deepest threat to his speaking the truth." Adolph Reed's admirable recent study of the continuity of Du Bois's political thought, mentioned above, which takes to task literary and cultural critics who have made a regressive icon of the late 19th century Du Bois and "double consciousness," is conspicuously silent on the *Autobiography*.[17] There is no question that issues of ideology cannot and should not be ignored. The stakes are certainly high and whatever the political commitment of the reader, he or she would be remiss in not noting Du Bois's willingness to overlook Stalin's "excesses." At the same time, performing a kind of critical acrobatics to make canonical the early Du Bois through condemnation of the later pro-Soviet Du Bois displays a lack of insight into the *Autobiography*'s *cultural* dynamics. The *Autobiography* was never to be successful as agit-prop; given his greatly eroded status by 1960, Du Bois clearly knew this. In parts of the text, Du Bois no doubt furthers his own banishment by pointedly lamenting the commitment to bourgeois individualism among the African-American intellectual class, the talented tenth he had once championed. It is hardly conceivable that Du Bois is attempting any kind of seduction, or, less perjoratively, attempting to convince African-Americans of the necessity of their joining the Communist Party U.S.A. The *Autobiography* could be successful, however, as an audacious act of memory, the Benjaminian restoration of the past in the present. (And as such, it becomes oddly appropriate that the text is published posthumously.) In the aftermath of cold war blacklisting—and amidst new efforts by the F.B.I. to surveil black activists—a period when, as Du Bois put it, "the colored children ceased to know my name," the *Autobiography* heroically pursues a vision restorative of community however contested.

There is certainly *some* failure to be documented and described. Du Bois too often relies upon a quasi-ethnographic or touristic account of the Communist West and China to develop his argument. This was obviously counter to his own rigorous historiographic and social-scientific method. The Du Bois who painstakingly pursued a block-by-block survey of turn-of-the-century black Philadelphia to construct an accurate picture of African-American urban culture—and refute the rapidly coalescing pathology model—is too willing here to engage in an unconvincing anecdotalism. As there is little articulation of any new methodological commitment, his "imaginativeness" (or willful silence) as regards the state of civil liberties in the USSR and China is less in a distinctively antimodern mode and more about anger and disgust. (Although it might be argued that this *is* a real tendency of such memorializing and mourning.) Once again, regardless of one's political orientation, it is worth noting that we do lose something here. A historian and sociologist of Du Bois's stature and experience could indeed have left to posterity important insights into the accomplishments and failures of the noncapitalist world in the post-War period. A less threatened and disappointed Du Bois might have articulated more fully the obvious failures of twentieth-century state communism, although this is certainly risky speculation. It is inappropriate, however, to excoriate Du Bois as if all questions about the practice of the cold war were settled—or without at least acknowledging, as Eric Lott puts it, "the plain fact that the Communist Party U.S.A. was one of the few institutional spaces of racially integrated left activism at mid-century."[18] Perhaps, needless to say, there remains more than a little truth to Du Bois's critique of American culture. When he does err most distastefully, such representation should at least *partially* be read with the knowledge of his systematic harassment at the hands of the United States government in the 1950s. Is Du Bois vindictive? No doubt, and yet Du Bois must have recognized that any positive reception the book might receive would less likely have to do with his converting readers to the CPUSA and—as always—much more to do with his long, varied, thoughtful, and accomplished life.

Given recent conversations about the legacy of the late Du Bois, it is somewhat suprising that reviews contemporary to the book's release were not so ready to dismiss the book nor his final historical judgements.[19] Reviews in media designed to reach a broad reading public, for instance, were strikingly nonchalant about Du Bois's apostasy. The *New Yorker* suggested that readers "should not be put off by the first fifty-odd pages, in which Du Bois tours the world in 1958 and 1959 and finds only progress and happiness in the Communist countries." Alden Whitman in the *New York Times* could assure readers that the book was "reflective, moving, and gracefully written" and was most taken by the concluding "prayer for biracial democracy" which was "a testament to the largeness of Dr. Du Bois's spirit." Gilbert Osofsky suggested that the *Autobiography* "contains not the least hint of crabbiness or senility" and described as a "fresh contribution" the book's "synthesis of Du Bois's activities and thought since the Great Depression" (42). This component of the public discourse surrounding Du Bois's book was respectful and appreciative of his contributions to American life and culture. While this approval did not necessarily represent political neutrality, there was some sense that Du Bois's lifestory should or could transcend ideological critique. To the broadest American public, then, the *Autobiography* was presented as important, if for no other reason than that it had come from the hand of a cultural icon.

In more scholarly settings, there exists more nervous maneuvering. In the *American Historical Review*, Louis Filler describes the book as "an event in American historiography," and goes on to assert, reasonably, that "Du Bois's judgements . . . from his approval of John Brown to his approval of Hungarian Communism, are controversial and should be argued with established historical means" (316). Filler works hard to maintain the commemorative tone of the reviews by Osofsky and Whitman, while at the same time allowing—almost with a wink—that perhaps not all is well. W. M. Brewer, in the *Journal of Negro History*, heads in a distinctly different direction and, somewhat in imitation of Du Boisian hyperbole, describes the *Autobiography* as a "definitive analytical autobiography of the greatest Negro Leader that has appeared in the Western world!" (72). Despite this adoration, Brewer is clearly more anxious than Filler about Du Bois's communism. On the one hand, he rightly notes the impact of McCarthyism and the indignities that

Du Bois must have suffered under arrest. On the other, largely choosing to ignore much direct testimony in the book at hand, Brewer writes:

> This reviewer offers no brief beyond the evidence contained in this autobiography that does not seem to warrant conviction on the charges although they have been relentlessly emphasized by several reputable historians who have branded Du Bois a "confirmed Communist." (74)

Brewer's sensitivity and anxiety is to prevent the total rejection of Du Bois's social and historical insights by those who would use the most recent political turn to be dismissive of the whole of his career, and, it should be added, be dismissive of African-American protest as a whole. Unrealistically, Brewer —arguably somewhat in despair—insists that "this reviewer shares the opinions of thousands that Du Bois allowed his interest in the theories of Communism and socialism as historian, scholar, and writer to be misunderstood! The evidence shows, however, that he was merely pleading with America to save its soul by practicing its principles of Christianity and democracy!"(74). This is oddly moving, but, of course, just plain wrong. While they differ in their overall presentation, Du Bois's *Autobiography* has generated in Filler and Brewer anxiousness as to how to preserve black resistance and celebrate black accomplishment in the context of cold war parameters for speech and political association.

Three reviews are striking for the way they break away from the purely commemorative or implicitly apologetic. Richard Kostelanetz's review in *Commonweal*, for instance, was the most noteworthy exception to the unconditional extension of goodwill.[20] It is not that Kostelanetz is without respect—he describes Du Bois as a "brilliant, honest, idealistic and persevering intellectual"—but that respect is offered up largely to establish the narrative of the fall. The post-1945 Du Bois, and indeed the *Autobiography*, is "riddled with contradictions, which this book expresses, rather than understands" (162). Du Bois and the *Autobiography* are guilty of "toeing the line" and ultimately of "parochialism." Part of the context here is certainly Kostelanetz's own allegiance to Ralph Ellison and the implicit (and imprudent) celebration of the novelist as an anticommunist icon. In this context, anything other than anticommunist struggle is parochial. Sometimes dripping with hostile irony—Kostelanetz describes Du Bois in Ghana as a "carpetbagging eminence" and writes of "the book's sponsorship by International Publishers, also noted for its editions of Marx, Lenin, and Herbert Aptheker"—he lays claim to a populist democratic centrism that confidently condemns the frustrated and marginalized Du Bois, and, implictly, all "Negro thinking." The ultimate sin, from Kostelanetz's perspective, is Du Bois's unwillingness to recognize his essential American-ness. "*The Autobiography* . . . is an important book," he writes nonetheless, "informed, like Malcolm X's memoir, by the American theme of possibility and disciplined accomplishment in spite of racial prejudice and social disadvantage" (162).

Where Kostelanetz sees confusion and parochialism, Truman Nelson's re-

view in the *Nation* chooses instead to focus on Du Bois's struggles of conscience. In direct contradistinction to Kostelanetz, Nelson describes the
book's tone as "collective." Where Kostelanetz sees a lack of critical precision,
Nelson—certainly overstating the case—describes the *Autobiography* as "the
forged ore of his life, honed to a cutting edge." If Kostelanetz is suspicious of
self-justification and Communist propaganda, Nelson feels confident about
the book's success as inquiry:

> It was in his years of exile in his own country, suspected of being a for-
> eign agent, shut off from contact with the world in which he had a life
> of conspicuous achievement . . . that he wrote this great soliloquy and
> finally understood what had happened to him. (574)

Nelson argues that the book is remarkable if, for nothing else, "writing . . .
unbelievably strong and young, without self-pity and vibrant with righteous
anger" (575). More than anything else, it is crucial, Nelson seems to argue, to
recognize the integrity and vitality of last decades of Du Bois's life, so that we
will maintain the vision and imagination to articulate and rearticulate the
revolutionary commitments of that life.

Peter Shaw, in *The American Scholar*, takes a somewhat different tack, attempting to steer clear of the obviously treacherous cold war terrain. Alter-
natively, he highlights the book's predictable mix of history and memoir,
and, in the end, is most struck by the unlikelihood of Du Bois's continued
commitment to education and reason. Pointing to Du Bois's enthusiastic
proposal to the Soviet Academy of Sciences for a comprehensive Pan-African
institute, Shaw writes that "a scholar to the end, Du Bois had retained his
Enlightenment faith that Truth was the strongest weapon of change" (51).
Noting the flawed and incomplete character of most great autobiographies—
and suggesting, as will Albert Stone later, a very productive comparison to
The Education of Henry Adams—Shaw insightfully comments that Du Bois's
last effort is noteworthy for its continued attempts at teaching. Indeed, Shaw
argues, what makes this text aesthetically satisfying is the significant effort
necessary to resolve the contradiction between the book's purported revolutionary commitment and its author, "the very opposite of a revolutionary in
manner and spirit" (51). If Du Bois's *Autobiography* aspires to be an apologia,
to explain his political transformation, Shaw insists—contradicting both
Kostelanetz and Nelson— that "one is left not with the author's polemical
message but with wonder at the capacity of society to dash the dreams of its
best spirits, and even greater wonder at the repeated renewal of hope in
America" (53). At the same time, Shaw is perplexed by the *Autobiography*'s
style, which he finds "flat and matter of fact." Du Bois's hopeful spirit, he
suggests, is somewhat out of step with the "preponderant pull from the historical pole of autobiography" (54).

The breadth of responses to the *Autobiography* seems to have less to do
with the literary or historiographical merits of the book and more to do with
anticipation of the disputes to come as regards Du Bois's legacy. Regardless

of his political perspective, each reviewer seems especially concerned to preserve for Du Bois a vital and distinguished place within American culture. Kostelanetz and Nelson, in particular, have some inkling of the political difficulties facing Du Bois's readers. Other reviewers are simply amazed at the grand course of his life, and, with varying degrees of anxiousness, are happy to replay and list the most significant highlights. It is most striking, however, that *no* writer spends any time addressing Du Bois's critique of contemporary American culture or his explanation of his personal transformation. This anticipates both the extracanonical situation of the *Autobiography* and, more pointedly, the special challenge that the complex combination of Du Bois's socialism, Enlightenment faith, and embrace of the antimodern presents. While it remains to be seen whether or not there is something uniquely discerning about this fusion of political method and cultural sentiment, it is clear that it is difficult to frame any reaction that will simultaneously guard one's own ideological investment and also do justice to the specificity of his critique. This critical silence is at least partially connected to the adhesive work that Du Bois—and the other antimodern exemplars too—requires of "memory." (As such, autobiography as genre—or mode—may have special status in any historical reconstruction of post–World War II African-American cultural and intellectual life.) If memory is to become central to a real politics, it potentially invokes a frustrating (and circular) disputation. What is the historical status of testimony or witness? Whose memory is most reliable? This is not to offer a defeatist postmodern shrug in Du Bois's direction. There is still substantial critical work that can be performed. But it is true that the trappings of the sacred, if not institutional, religious discipline can create a hesitation in readers of the antimodern, and especially, perhaps, readers of this last grand literary gesture on Du Bois's part. Even those readers most likely to find the 1950s martyrdom of Du Bois ideologically distasteful seem hesitant to make any frontal attack and thus erode his iconic status.

This contestation is slightly reformulated in a brief exchange about the veracity of the *Autobiography* and the true character and shape of the manuscript. In a subsequent letter to the *Nation,* editors at International Publishers reacted angrily to Truman Nelson's concerns about Herbert Aptheker's billing as editor. Nelson had reported that he had seen a different version of the manuscript in Shirley Du Bois's possession in Accra, a version which did not include his account of his last travels or his account of his conversion to Communism. (Richard Kostelanetz had also hinted on a couple of occasions—with a certain amount of implicit delight—at the possible "assistance" of Shirley Du Bois herself.) In reply, perhaps a little disingenuously, Nelson drew attention to the overall approving tone of the review and suggested that he was mainly implying a literary preference for a version of the life that began more simply: "I was born by a golden river . . ." (see *Autobiography,* 61). Nelson's remarks are disingenuous insofar as he must have understood that the suggestion of editorial manipulation would potentially be received as implying distortion and exploitation. In 1968, the external shaping or reshaping of the words of W.E.B. Du Bois by any predominantly white institution—whether it be International Publishers, the CPUSA, Harvard University, or the Elks Club—would hardly be received in many quarters as a declaration of mere "taste." (The obvious parallel in 1968 would be the controversy surrounding William Styron's *The Confessions of Nat Turner*.) Du Bois's return to American politics in the sixties participates in the worrying of hard-to-coalesce cultural boundaries. International Publishers' sensitivity to the charge of tampering with the manuscript certainly has roots in cold war anxieties about communist conspiracy, but also in an atmosphere in which the white mediation and exploitation of black culture heroes was receiving close scrutiny. What is most noteworthy, however, is the way in which the "reading" of black cultural expression in and of the American sixties remains oddly external and surface. The content of Du Bois's narrative remains distant such that as larger ("secondary") narratives about the shape of sixties discourse begin to emerge they are oftentimes obsessed with social dramas at the expense of history and purpose.

Of course, in the vaguely cloak-and-dagger environment of American far-left politics in the sixties, the manipulation of a legacy as valuable as Du Bois's is not hard to imagine. But textual veracity—W.E.B. Du Bois as shaping, authorial consciousness—is largely confirmed by stylistic components of the clearly new parts of the text. The unique hyperbole and allegorization of the postlude, which is distinctly unscientific in character, would have been unlikely to survive editorial scrutiny if the primary purpose of "review" or "assistance" was to assure ideological purity. Neither does the forthrightness of the chapter "My Character" lend itself to an exercise in Communist hagiography. There is certainly room to argue that Aptheker's role (or that of Shirley Du Bois) is more extensive than suggested by the editor's preface. Du Bois was after all writing in his late 80s and early 90s and it would be hard to begrudge him the occasional use of an amanuenesis. And like many autobiographical texts within the African-American literary tradition—the *Autobiography of Malcolm X*, Harriet Jacobs's *Incidents in the Life of a Slave Girl*, or, say, *All God's Dangers: The Life of Nate Shaw*—there is a great deal of room for revealing (and often enhancing) scholarly investigation of editorial mediation. It would not be so completely disruptive of this book's argument if it were to be shown that what is finally on the page is an external representation of Du Bois as "memorialist."

Indeed a few commentators also pointed out that the *Autobiography* included substantial sections of his previous books, and, one commentator suggested, diaries too. This decision in shaping (and inventing) creates once again an interesting continuity between African-American protest of the 1960s and turn-of-the-century anxieties. It places misgivings about the promises of modernity squarely in the midst of the discourse of civil rights and black power. Given the limitations of the racial romanticism, obsession with authenticity, and patriarchalism of that earlier generation of resisters, the *Autobiography* (as, it might be said, a book with a "history") becomes crucial to a consideration of the possibilities and limits of ethnically or racially centered culture criticism. Straightforwardly, the *Autobiography* is an interesting place to begin a consideration of the accomplishments of multiculturalism and more aggressive nationalisms and separatisms. Perhaps just as straightforwardly, however, this parasitic revisiting of earlier writings has made some scholars nervous and no doubt eroded the status of the book and marked it as a curious "reprint." Once again, just as recent scholarship on "borrowing" in the writing and speaking of Martin Luther King, Jr. has suggested important cultural contexts for that practice, this need not be the end of the story. There is no conclusive evidence that the *Autobiography* is not the product of Du Bois's substantial and careful literary consciousness. Indeed Du Bois's cut-and-paste—reminiscent of Romare Bearden's own liberatory practice if not that of William Burroughs—may be the most prescient selection of artistic tactic by any of the antimodern exemplars.

However one sorts out the politics of the closing years of Du Bois's life (and they are likely to remain controversial for some time), the *Autobiography* should be recognized as an important sixties text and as a fixture within African-American and American literary canons. In many ways, it feels much less dated or more continuously relevant than some texts often thought of as central to the intersection of black culture and the American sixties. (Eldridge Cleaver's *Soul on Ice* certainly comes to mind here.) Its assertion of the importance of memory to the maintenance of a viable black counterstatement is prophetic of contemporary developments in Afrocentric thought, while at the same time it reiterates once again Du Bois's grand theme, that the health of American democracy is directly related to its ability to cope with the color line. Perhaps important to a renewed interest in the book is a close look at its attachment to a diasporic or at least internationalist consciousness; in addition to anticipating American difficulties in Vietnam, it forms the backbone of what might be called a contemporary canon of African-American postcoloniality, a canon that might include Richard Wright's *White Man Listen!*, John A. Williams's *The Man Who Cried I Am*, and Marshall's *The Chosen Place, The Timeless People*. Neither residual questions about textual probity nor unease with Du Bois's political choices should get in the way of a substantial (re)reading of its accomplishment.

The next section of this chapter will attempt to describe and evaluate the *Autobiography*'s "logic." The heart of Du Bois's purposeful ordering is a challenging dialectic. The irrationality of the book's "dedication" (broadly conceived) and the sentimental invocation of communal solidarity is meant to work—that is confront, challenge, contradict, and qualify—against and with a dramatic historical repetition or "testimony." The contested narrative voice of the book *attempts* to valorize the gaze of the scholar, but it is self-consciously and sophisticatedly undermined by its recognition of desire and dream. Its grand conclusion, one of the great perorations in American literature, presents Du Bois's final improvisation within American intellectual history. And it suggests, once again, the possibilities and limitations of African-American antimodernism.

THE *AUTOBIOGRAPHY*: BETWEEN ALLEGORY AND HISTORY

The text of the *Autobiography* as published in 1968 has four distinct sections, even if they are not always clearly identified as such. The first is a "dedicatory," which establishes the ceremonial or unscientific character of the text. It is, however, not necessarily limited to the formal "statement of dedication" which appears on the copyright page, but also includes other introductory material including an explanation of the book's origin. The second section ("Interlude") is primarily an ideological disruption and mainly includes the story of his conversion to Communism. The third and largest section of the book—and mostly ritual in nature—is the "history" of his life, implictly a claim (or reclaiming) of cultural and intellectual authority. Finally, this reclamation sets up his "postlude" or closing meditation, a striking and memorable valedictory to his life and commitments. (In some sense, the decision here to make sense of these "parts" is a dismissal of Truman Nelson's nostalgic preference for a much simpler accounting of Du Bois's life.) The complex interplay of these parts is evidence of the coherence of the text and, perhaps, an attempt to work out a productive working amalgam of Enlightenment commitment and antimodern skepticism. In his last representation of self, Du Bois captures a fundamental dilemma of postwar African-American life and plays it for all it's worth. The urgent desire to move ahead, progress, advance, is perhaps permanently entangled with the Siren's song, the call to look back, to immerse oneself in and perhaps even *return* to an always ill-defined past.

"Dedication" is an appropriate opening figure for the book. The copyright page includes the statement:

> *Dedicated to*
> My Great Grandfather: James Du Bois
> My Grandfather: Alexander Du Bois
> My Parents: Alfred Du Bois and Mary Burghardt
> My Children: Burghardt Gomer Du Bois
>   Yolande Du Bois
>   David Graham Du Bois
> My Granddaughter: Du Bois McFarlane

Reminiscent of Etheridge Knight's great poem "The Idea of Ancestry" (1968), this "introduction" emphasizes unbroken (if patriarchal) lineage, an answer of sorts to the pathologization of black family life.[21] The repetition of "Du Bois" and "Burghardt" is indicative of a kind of familial nationalism, perhaps a further repetition of W.E.B. Du Bois's counter-Enlightenment construction of collective mentalities and affiliations. In terms of scope and content, however, the dedication can be seen to extend significantly beyond the mention of multiple generations of the Du Bois family, although this certainly remains its conceptual and moral center. Truman Nelson reported that one distinct change he recalled in the version of the manuscript he saw in Accra was that this opening statement was titled "Dedication to the Dead" and included among those "dead" listed above "My First Wife, Nina Gomer Du Bois." (A sad deletion, if Nelson's memory is correct, and speculation about Shirley Du Bois's editorial assistance is accurate.) "Dedication to the Dead" is dramatically descriptive of the text's sympathies, and functions too, however, as a compelling emblem of the ways in which African-American antimodernists attempted in the postwar era to achieve (with varying degrees of self-consciousness) a kind of ancestral solidarity. "Dedication to the Dead" is especially multivalent (and organically appropriate once we read closely his closing benediction) if some consideration is given to more than the commonplace interpretation that the book is thus somehow "for" the persons subsequently named. "Dedication" is suggestive of not only memorialization, but also sacralization, the sacrifice of egoistic interest, and singleness of purpose too. To be dedicated to the dead can be seen as a kind of provocative political and cultural conjure and the means by which the past might have "present presence."

For such dedication to be successful, however, more will need to be done than just ritually invoke the names of the dead. If the text is to bring about that sense of sacralization and sacrifice, some means will have to be established to account for autobiography's obvious investment in self-justification. Part of the dedication, then, must be Du Bois's compelling meditation on the character of autobiography itself. After briefly accounting his difficulties with the State Department as prologue to the first chapter, "My 15th Trip Abroad," he writes:

> I mention this trip in some detail because it was one of the most important trips that I had ever taken, and had wide influence on my thought. To explain this influence my Soliloquy becomes an autobiography. Autobiographies do not form indisputable authorities. They are always incomplete, and often unreliable. Eager as I am to put down the truth, there are difficulties; memory fails especially in small details, so that it becomes finally but a theory of my life, with much forgotten and misconceived, with valuable testimony but often less than absolutely true, despite my intention to be frank and fair. (12)

This is not a simple rhetorical trick. Du Bois pushes harder to ensure that readers are forced to engage what he calls his "twisted life." The relationship between truth and autobiography, he insists, is not one of simple correspondence. "What I think of myself, now and in the past, furnishes no certain document proving what I really am," he writes (12). Most importantly, he reflects that "my life today is a mass of memories with vast omissions, matters which are forgotten accidentally or by deep design" (12). Such "design," of course, raises questions about representations not only of the past but of the present too, including his often uncritical representations of the Communist world that make up the bulk of this dedication. Finally, and quite movingly, he writes:

> One must then see these varying views as contradictions to truth, and not as final and complete authority. This book is the Soliloquy of an old man on what he dreams his life has been as he sees it slowly drifting away; and what he would like others to believe. (13)

One implication that Du Bois perceives is that "life seldom goes by logical completeness," perhaps necessitating the need "to speak with a certain sense of unity" (13).

This meditation ends by noting the energy associated with his last twenty years:

> In my own family old folk found a home with relatives; but in the surrounding community the first worry of the average citizen was for provision for his old age. Personally this problem never bothered me until suddenly at 75 I was retired from work with practically no savings, and no pension in view sufficient to support me. Failure to give attention to this part of my future was due to no laziness or neglect. I was eager to work and work continuously. (13)

While this is slightly distinct from his encounter with the character of autobiography, there is an important continuity in the effort to reconcile the "facts" of his living with cultural, political, and social ideals. It foreshadows both his commitment to the establishment of a comprehensive social safety net through Communism in the pages to come, but also looks backward longingly to the intimate (and purportedly authentic) community life of Great Barrington. It seems odd considering Du Bois's long and accomplished life, but the writer appears fearful that he might be perceived as somehow slacking. Despite his commitment to a revolutionary future, the sense of self that the autobiography sets out to explain seems as fully invested in the New England Puritan past, a godly work ethic, and a concern for salvation.

In these reflections, then, Du Bois nicely highlights the utopian character of the autobiographical act, and adds significant qualification to the implicit religiosity, solemnity, and earnestness even of "dedication." (It's certainly worth noting the ways in which this qualification is dramatically out of step with, say, the witness of a figure like James Baldwin that relies upon the urgency of "I was there.") Given Du Bois's real wounds and already fractured authority, it is a statement of real courage and distinguishes itself from the self-righteousness of much sixties posturing of both the political right and left. The oddest "qualification," highly ironic given the great length and accomplishment of Du Bois's life, is the presence of Herbert Aptheker's preface in the 1968 International Publishers' edition of the text, dramatically recalling the long tradition of white interlocutors, editors, promoters, etc., which inevitably foregrounded questions of authenticity and truthfulness. This is typical, as Albert Stone rightly notes, of the book's complex mix of "novelty and tradition." The placement of the Aptheker preface makes it inevitably (if not necessarily of Du Bois's design) part of the dedication and both troubles the waters and clarifies intent and function. Part of the preface's accomplishment is simply documentary. Aptheker tells of the manuscript's journey to Ghana and its eventual rescue from Accra; he distinguishes this book from the previous autobiographical volumes by mentioning the "significantly altered outlook of its author" (5). On the one hand, and to his credit, Aptheker himself chooses to point to and highlight the subjectivity of Du Bois's narrative. He writes that Du Bois "reminds the reader . . . of the intense subjectivity that inevitably permeates autobiography; hence he writes, he offers this account of his life as he understood it and as he 'would like others to believe' it had been" (6). Given the inevitable questions that were to arise about the book's propagandistic intent, this is, once again, helpful and ethical. More generally, Aptheker would seem to share in Du Bois's project of challenging absolute authority on any subject matter. On the other hand, and perhaps somewhat in contradiction, it does reasonably create discomfort among even Du Bois's most sympathetic readers. Aptheker writes: "It is published as Dr. Du Bois wrote it; changes have been few and only of a technical nature—correcting a date, completing a name, and the like." While meant to reassure readers, in recalling the mediation of slave narration, through a necessary attention to authenticity and veracity, it inadvertently tends to alarm and worry. There is real dissonance here. Why should one of the intellectual giants of the twentieth century require such a mediator?

This extended acknowledgement of autobiography's utopianism (and its particular inflection in the African-American tradition) qualifies and lends a hermeneutic of suspicion to the ideological disruption that makes up the second structural component of the book that Du Bois refers to as "Interlude." This is obviously not to suggest that one might comfortably pursue the same reading strategy as did W. M. Brewer and attempt to create out of thin air one's own subject of the autobiography, a subject "cured," one might say, of distasteful commitments and characteristics. Du Bois's account of his conversion to Communism should be taken with the utmost seriousness and as a real measure of his discontent. As Du Bois himself suggests, the autobiography becomes "soliloquy" by necessity. This final performance arises at least partially out of American democracy's failure to protect free inquiry and the subsequent devaluation of personal affirmation. What is most striking about this statement of conversion is its brevity, distinction, and careful erudition. It is a mere two pages and yet clearly demarked as a separate section of the book, dramatic in intent and execution. If autobiography is ultimately utopian and an invention, and Du Bois invested in a "dreamlike" investigation, the conversion is described with recourse to rationality and reason. He begins by noting that "I have *studied* socialism and communism long and carefully" [my italics] and makes his statement of belief "after earnest observation" (57). Reminiscent of his letter to Gus Hall, he writes,

> I mean by communism a planned way of life in the production of wealth and work designed for building a state whose object is the highest welfare of its people and not merely the profit of a part. I believe that all men should be employed according to their ability and that wealth and services should be distributed according to need. (57)

He notes that communism will "call for *progressive* change in human nature and a better type of *manhood*" (58, my italics). Du Bois the distinguished and accomplished scholar is in command here. He writes with the confidence and faith of the student, the teacher, and the early race leader. If he will resort to emotional appeals, mythic constructions of community, even claims made by reputation and stature alone, it is important that at this moment that his style is restrained and reasonable. If he must articulate discontent with the Enlightenment project's treatment of race—and of the Negro people in particular—Du Bois is still willing to articulate its possibilities. Perhaps at this moment it is Enlightenment itself that is being memorialized?

The transition to the next section of the book is pursued quite deliberately and self-consciously:

> Who now am I to have come to these conclusion? And of what if any significance are my deductions? What has been my life and work and of what meaning to mankind? The final answer to these questions, time and posterity must make. But perhaps it is my duty to contribute whatever *enlightenment* I can. This is the excuse for this writing which I call a Soliloquy. (58, my italics)

"Enlightenment" and "soliloquy" exist here in a nice tension. The commitment to enlightenment is suggestively public and provoking, obviously referring to a kind of revelation and edification, but, perhaps, slyly admitting intellectual context too. Soliloquy, however, indicates more private speech uttered to and for the self, except, of course, insofar as we think and use soliloquy in the context of a literary drama. Indeed, his use of "interlude" as the broadest designation for this section (and "postlude" for his conclusion) itself recalls and reemphasizes the dramatic context. William Cain thinks that while soliloquy "connotes . . . a theatricalized or dramatic posture and pose, a vividly prosecuted, intellectually dense and complex form of speech that highlights self-reflection and risks unanticipated self-exposure . . . [the] *Autobiography* does not really take such a cast or tone." For Cain, the book is "less a soliloquy than an elaborate lecture or . . . the prolonged testimony of an unyielding conscience that accosts America with truths that this nation . . . was too imprisoned in Cold War defensiveness and guilt to discern itself."[22] It is not clear, however, that these are necessarily mutually exclusive modes, and Du Bois's real accomplishment may be the ways in which he was able to productively mix them such that neither fully achieves the *absolute au-*

thority to which it aspires. The autobiographer is by necessity betwixt and between the annalist and the poet; Du Bois seems less engaged by this as problem than as possibility. His audience, especially in the context of the cold war, would be disinclined to believe or paralyzed to respond to the straightforward recounting of betrayals and failures. "Soliloquy," however, can make of this mendacious knot a philosophic rather than a political problem. Du Bois the allegorist begins to come to the fore. As distasteful as the conversion may have been to many readers, Du Bois manages to transform it from the realm of the traitorous to something implicitly theological. Conversion itself is now partially a readerly concern. The audience is engaged not only with — and I suspect that for many readers only secondarily with — the process by which the American scholar becomes Communist, but in some substantive way with the transformation from autobiography to soliloquy. If autobiography is, as Du Bois suggests, a shaky epistemological proposition, we should be surprised — even shocked — by the totality of his commitment to this documentation that is transformation. A broad social and cultural analogy might be the name changes undertaken by many African-Americans during the sixties. Simultaneously this is a gesture of dismissal and commitment. If such urgent personal reshaping of the self is indicative of the failure of Enlightenment, America, or democracy, there is evidence of "reforming" too. This starting over, by turning to an African past, is suggestive of the ways in which African-American antimodernism may be a process of sifting good from bad, where the disturbing irony may be that salvation is itself caught up with the devil's work.

In similar fashion, the hermeneutic of suspicion must come to bear on the third section of the book, which is both personal and communal history. The long accounting of his childhood, education, scholarship, editorship of *The Crisis*, his tenure at Atlanta University, Pan-Africanist leadership, and subsequent difficulties with the United States government in the 1950s is unlikely, in any straightforward way, to become reasonably explanatory of his heresy. Having been reminded of the autobiography's subjectivity, of Du Bois's sense of anger and betrayal, and the unreliability of his memory, readers will demand more as an acceptable apologia. In its totality, however — rather than in its logical elaboration — history does become its own authority, both the warrant to speak and the obligation to witness. Du Bois's longevity and accomplishments do make him all but unique among autobiographers. Readers are inevitably in a position (and this was borne out by contemporary reviews) of deference to Du Bois's experience and knowledge.

General deductions about this component of the text can and should be made by attending to the amount of space that Du Bois gives to certain subjects or stages of his life. Birth, boyhood, and education, for instance, make up perhaps the largest component of the book. This is noteworthy insofar as there seems to be some relationship between the order of Great Barrington's mostly preindustrial roots and existence and the shaping of his contemporary belief in communism. Somewhat surprisingly, the middle period of his life, roughly from his role in the Niagara movement through to his 1940s tenure at Atlanta University, that component of his life upon which his stature relies, makes up the smallest section of the book. Mostly consistent with the book's attempt at ideological disruption, he dedicates much more energy and space to the elucidation of his struggles with the Departments of Justice and State than to the recounting of major life successes. All of this, however, deserves to be examined in light of the emergence of a distinctly antimodern mode.

For instance, it is not so obviously consistent with a crude ideological mission to begin with a compelling utopian (and eventually exceptionalist) mode. "I was born by a golden river," begins Du Bois, "and in the shadow of two great hills, five years after the Emancipation Proclamation, which began the freeing of American Negro slaves" (61). Continuing his description, he notes: "The town of Great Barrington, which lay between these mountains in Berkshire County, Western Massachusetts, had a broad Main Street, lined with maples and elms, with white picket fences before the homes. The climate was to our thought quite perfect." This idyllic setting is combined with a strong sense of historic gravity: Du Bois's birth is connected to that of George Washington and black enfranchisement, "an extraordinary experiment in democracy" (61). His reflection just a couple of pages later on the house that he grew up in ("I planned eventually to make it my country home.") is strangely more suggestive of Du Bois as gentleman farmer than it is of Communist revolutionary. Great Barrington is shaped as an ideal (if compact) political organization. "Gradually," Du Bois writes, "I began to see [the Town Meeting] as the essence of democracy: listening to the other man's opinion and then voting your own, honestly and gently" (92).

Of course, this is not to last—race must impinge itself on the narrative and qualify this story—but it remains a vivid and respectable ideal in Du Bois's recollection. Eventually, Du Bois notes, a "new loyalty replaced my Americanism: henceforth I was a Negro." As a result of his studies at Fisk and Harvard and his travels through the South this new loyalty eventually becomes a vocation. What emerges is a complex and fragile tension between his utopian instincts and his personal experience of race, a tension that complicates our perception of the autobiography's ultimate commitment and meaning. Du Bois most enthusiastically recalls his training as a "scientist" and the emergence of his faith in reason to better the lot of Negro people. William James is his guide to "clear thinking" (143) and turns Du Bois "back from the lovely but sterile land of philosophic speculation, to the social sciences as the field for gathering and interpreting that body of fact which would apply to my program for the Negro" (148). While Du Bois confidently came to see "sociology as the science of human action" (148), at some point in this narrative, however, this too is tested. "I regarded it as axiomatic," Du Bois insists, "that the world wanted to learn the truth and if the truth were sought with even approximate accuracy and painstaking devotion, the world would gladly support the effort" (222). With the difficulties he began to face in locating support for his research, he concedes his "young man's idealism" (222). Eventually even the momentous Atlanta University Studies seem inadequate:

> My faith in [the Studies'] success was based on the firm belief that race prejudice was based on widespread ignorance. My long-term remedy was Truth: carefully gathered scientific proof that neither color nor race determined the limits of a man's capacity or desert. I was not at the time sufficiently Freudian to understand how little human action is based on reason; nor did I know Karl Marx well enough to appreciate the economic foundations of human history. (228)

That this moment occurs prior to the extensive popularization of Freud's ideas on the American scene is certainly a clue to the ways in which this hindsight represents a slightly unfair self-critique on the part of Du Bois. Still Du Bois vividly paints for us the attractiveness of the Enlightenment ideal (in terms of both politics and learning) and the drama of his gravitation to the most significant critiques of its achievements and limitations. What makes Du Bois provocatively antimodernist (as opposed to making him a nascent modern), however, is his sustained, longing, and sometimes fundamentally illogical return to the past.

It is also crucial that Du Bois continues to qualify the trustworthiness and capability of the narrative. The movement toward a critique of Enlightenment is hardly a matter of simple substitution. The question of reliability is raised in especially interesting ways by the introduction of the wholly new chapter "My Character" into this section. As so much of the book is recycled, and some parts straightforwardly predictable, the appearance of this "new" commitment is striking. This is even more true given Du Bois's traditional reticence to reveal much about the private self and as the opportunity that certainly existed to make a claim for Communist sainthood. It has significance, of course, beyond the "tearing down." It is unquestionably a gesture familiar to American autobiography, and makes of Du Bois a compatriot to Benjamin Franklin. Indeed, Du Bois's insistence upon discussing "character" is itself strikingly pre- (if not anti-) modern. "It is typical of our time," he writes, "that insistence on character today in the country has almost ceased." Interestingly, he rejects the very critique of Enlightenment that he had previously identified as marking his incomplete vision. "Freud and others," he interjects, "have stressed the unconscious factors of our personality so that today we do not advise youth about the developement of character; we watch and count their actions with almost helpless disassociation from thought of advice" (277).

Predictably by now, and again echoing his New England roots, Du Bois recounts his honesty and frugality. Despite this "typicality," he suggests — meaning mainly here the use of alcohol — that black "men imitated an American culture which I did not share" (279). As part of this delineation of character, he also includes letters of testimony which cheerlead for his liter-

ary and academic skill, letters which seem somewhat calculated to relieve or
redirect the "frank" examination (and potential diminishment) of his character. Indeed, why shouldn't he? Less predictably, perhaps, and certainly admirably, he notes his failures as a father and husband. Most unexpectedly, he
details the development (and frustration) of his sexuality. Of his time in Europe, he writes, "I went through a desperately recurring fight to keep the sex
instinct in control" (280). Perhaps his greatest hesitation, however, comes as
he talks about his aloofness and suspicion of close friendship. "I was not
what Americans called a 'good fellow'" (283). One does get a sense of how
difficult such self-revelation is for Du Bois. Even as he articulates a defense
of "character" and "virtue" (largely consistent with the anti-modernist role
that this chapter would ascribe to him), there is also a strong sense that he
is not being wholly honest. It is certainly confusing, for instance, that the recent Communist convert has no confession to make of class crimes. Indeed,
one effect of this chapter is to cause readers to examine more closely those
aspects of his character that are not put forth here for evaluation. In speaking, for instance, of his return from Europe in 1894:

> What happens when 350 people of the lower classes are for nine days
> thrown together with very little outside government? The answer to
> this can be seen on this voyage and is most interesting. . . . The better
> classes here, the better and more orderly elements though scarcely
> greater in numbers, have been distinctly more influential. . . . The sev-
> eral classes here developed differences in no great degree different from
> the classes elsewhere in the world—it is the same old strife of finer
> souls against brutality. (181)

This does not wholly discredit Du Bois, but does sustain and extend the critique of "modern selfhood" in ways he may not have predicted nor intended.
(And is also suggestive of the ways in which Du Bois may have been as consistently invested in a notion of class stability as he was in class warfare.) On
the other hand, if there is concern about editorial intervention such that previous accounts of events are somehow laundered to be more consonant with
the CPUSA "line," such an intervention is fascinatingly incomplete. One of
the most interesting results of the cut-and-paste that makes up the book is
a productively confused narrative voice. It is immensely difficult to ascertain
the temporal location of the author's organizing utterance. In ways that
would be otherwise impossible to articulate in writing, Du Bois's commitment to the past and utopian desires for the future are provocatively inter-
mingled.

In total, then, the "history book," or third structural component of the autobiography, manages an interesting dialectic of reliability and unreliability
that itself is structured around (or invested in) other binaries: public and private, faith and reason, past and future, communism and capitalism, Europe
and non-Europe, civilization and barbarism. Instead of dissolving into a
morass of ambiguity, however, it somehow communicates to readers a sense

of wholeness and continuity. Part of this "wholeness" is a result of a blurring of the authority of each and every ideological competitor for the readers' allegiance. Democracy, Communism, Enlightenment: each is flawed, so that what really captures our attention is the "looking backward" itself. Furthermore, the structural integrity of the book (and the meaning-making capability of the above binaries) is reinforced by the introduction and repetition of certain thematic material. Before considering Du Bois's dramatic peroration, it is worthwhile to briefly consider and highlight two recurrent emphases that allow for the consolidation of the antimodern voice and simultaneously forestall its claims to total authority.

Albert Stone argued that one of the most striking components of the book is its reliance on metaphors of travel. From entitling his first chapter "My 15th Trip Abroad," through his peripatetic life in the United States (Great Barrington, Nashville, Cambridge, Wilberforce, Philadelphia, Atlanta, and New York), Du Bois is "made" en route. Anticipating Paul Gilroy's meditations on "black Atlantic" identity, Stone writes that:

> Knowing, in fact, a wider world than most previous American memoirists . . . Du Bois anticipates by a generation or more the Third World consciousness of Richard Wright and Malcolm X. Thus his double legacy to twentieth-century Americans—helping to revolutionize American black attitudes toward caste and almost single-handedly creating conditions for a black intelligentsia—is symbolically and literally represented in *The Autobiography* by the ceaseless train trips and steamer crossings which punctuated his life for over seventy years.[23]

Speaking of his sense of outsidership after having completed a challenging undergraduate education, Du Bois himself wrote that it "was as though moving on a rushing express, my main thought was as to my relations with the other passengers on the express, and not to its rate of speed and its destination" (156). To describe a particular troubling moment in his early career, he writes: "I meant still to be captain of my soul, but I realized that even captains are not omnipotent in uncharted and angry seas" (193). In the future, Du Bois would come to the conclusion that his "attitude toward current problems arose from [his] habit of keeping in touch with world affairs by repeated trips to Europe and other parts of the world" (286). In this context, it is symbolically appropriate that the core of his struggle in the 1950s was over his passport and right to travel. Du Bois emerges as a fundamentally migratory figure—"internationally minded," as he put it—whose intellectual stature and accomplishment are at least partially a result of his witnessing multiple ways of organizing the world. There is also, however, some erosion of the writer's ability to convincingly valorize any single component of his identity, whether racial, national, or ideological. While he might insist otherwise, in some real fashion he is permanently a pluralist. This never really becomes, and Du Bois would be loathe to endorse, what Paul Gilroy and many others call hybridity, and yet there is a sense that the communal and ancestral solidarity that Du Bois pursues with increasing devotion must always be invention.

Closely related, then, the second important thematic emphasis — on the struggle to reconcile or account for the problem of a singular and absolute "Truth" — is felt and articulated most clearly in his discussion of religion and faith. On the one hand, Du Bois now has a stated commitment to materialism coupled with the modern's commitment to the disenchantment and demythologization of religious faiths and institutions. (As many commentators have noted, however, the *Autobiography* is much less impressive than say, *The African Slave Trade* or *Black Reconstruction* in extended attention to the relationship between economics and culture.) This takes many forms: his valorization of the deinstitutionalization of Soviet religious life and freedom from "dogma"; his celebration of Chinese attacks on Tibetan "divine slavery"; and, most notably, his sense of the inadequacy of New England Christianity as it was presented to him in Sunday school. Du Bois notes that "in Germany I turned still further from religious dogma and began to grasp the idea of a world of human beings whose actions, like those of the physical world, were subject to law" (205). But elsewhere, of course, Du Bois has also begun to articulate some skepticism about the permanence of such a straightforward Enlightenment commitment. In "My Character," he decides to describe his "religious development." It is "slow and uncertain," and yet still something of a presence. (285) (It is important, I think, that this meditation comes immediately after recounting the death of his first son.) This is consistent with the language of character and virtue to which he would cling, but sometimes suggests an interesting friction with his Marxist conversion. His acknowledgment that religion both "helped and hindered my artistic sense" is revealing. In some real way the recovery project that is his commitment to African-American culture is best served by the prodding of his (and perhaps that of African-American culture's) "artistic sense." After all, while Du Bois's historiography and social science work is incontrovertibly "major," as an intellectual he just as often — and arguably more often — opted for the "aesthetic" and seemingly aimed for the transcendent. In the very existence of his fiction writing, his interest in debates about the representation of black characters in American literature, his extensive autobiographical meditations, and the allegorical method of many of his finest essays, there is substantial counterstatement to his own account of his gravitation away from the religious. And indeed Du Bois seems to want to hedge his bets in the *Autobiography* by focusing almost exclusively upon the corruption of the clergy and institutional religion more generally. While he articulates, for instance, that part of the necessity of escaping Wilberforce is its repressive institutional religion, he suggests that to stay would have meant "spiritual death" (193).

This inconsistency on matters of faith is further crucial insofar as he continues to gravitate toward a specifically moral and spiritual condemnation of American culture. Even as he works hard to mark change in his stance, there is simultaneously a reiteration of past possibility if not of the past itself. Condemning the "Negro intelligentsia" for its decision to follow "Western aquisitive society" he writes:

> I have long noted and fought this all too evident tendency, and built my faith in its ultimate change on an inner Negro cultural ideal. I thought this ideal would be built on ancient African communism, supported and developed by memory of slavery and experience of caste, which would drive the Negro group into a spiritual unity precluding the development of economic classes and inner class struggle. This was once possible, but it is now improbable. (392)

This is a striking passage for the way in which it once again wields the term "faith" and its confused (once again) sense of past and present. While the last sentence of the above quote suggests the triumph of his new Marxism, he can only settle upon improbability as opposed to impossibility. In the final reordering of his life there is still the sense that some transcendent "cultural wholeness" has an important role to play. Despite a conversion to materialism, Du Bois is able to muster as conclusion to the section of the book dedicated to the recounting of his accomplishment this ode to memory:

> Above all the American Negro needs to be taught to read and to support a school of art and literature which will preserve his history and culture and add to the great treasure of human accomplishment; rather than let the unique and marvelous life and experience of the black race in America be distorted or even lost to memory as it threatens to be today. (339)

Sometimes it seems, even against his best intentions, that Du Bois cannot help but continue to articulate the necessity of a vital collective memory in the maintenance of some kind of "spiritual race health." In "advising" Kwame Nkrumah, and ostensibly to take Nkrumah to task for not fully understanding the dynamic of the cold war, Du Bois writes:

> Seek to save the great cultural past of the Ashanti and Fanti peoples, not by inner division but by outer cultural and economic expansion toward the outmost bounds of the great African peoples, so that they may be free to live, grow, and expand; and to teach mankind what Non-Violence and Courtesy, Literature and Art, Music and Dancing can do for this greedy, selfish, and war-stricken world. (400–401)

Du Bois does not just gravitate toward a reenchanted modernity, sometimes he tumbles headfirst.

The thematic, that is the treatment of travel and "spirit," reinforces formal or structural effects by pushing readers toward a necessary (if malleable) relationship between past and present. Nostalgia is entangled with reformation and revolution. Novelty and tradition interact to form something between a productive dialectic and simple contradiction. But given the harsh political context in which it was written, this is a book that speaks well—regardless of the reader's political orientation—to the occasion of its writing. One of the great accomplishments of the *Autobiography* is the way in which Du Bois shifts attention from questions of identity to questions of method. (And by method here I mean strategies of both intellectual and political engagement.) While identity struggles are not permanently banished, *The Autobiography of W.E.B. Du Bois* does work hard to suggest that to solve the problems of modernity is not primarily to clarify one's sense of self. Reminiscent of Walt Whitman's ironic question "Do I contradict myself?", Du Bois has placed in front of the reader a perhaps unsolvable paradox as regards Enlightenment. (Reminscent too of Audre Lorde's primal question: "Can the master's tools be used to dismantle the master's house?") *Liberty* is the collective birthright of all moderns and yet we must continue to unravel its investment in its opposite. Du Bois wrote that "my career as a scientist was to be swallowed up in my role as a master of propaganda. This was not entirely to my liking" (253). This sense of loss or sense of what might have been is a central part of the *Autobiography*'s own investment in the elegiac. It might be referred to as a knowing nostalgia, a permanent sense of mourning, in which the only ethical practice is a commitment to proceeding in such a way that we do not hide these fissures in history.

"IT IS THE FINALITY WE MUST NOT FALSIFY": POSTLUDE AND VALEDICTORY

What is left, to discuss, then, is Du Bois's compelling conclusion to this final representation of his life. In his "Postlude" Du Bois *becomes* the African-American antimodernist par excellence. Part of its accomplishment is Du Bois's ability to proceed without selfish rancor after retelling—to say nothing of having experienced—the events recalled in the last chapters. Indeed, it is striking that his modus operandi becomes more and more outward. "It is the tragedy of the day that the democracy of which we prate so glibly is being murdered in the house of its friends, and in everyday life far more than in broad governmental decisions" (337). The events that lead to his becoming an "indicted criminal" are, however, desperate enough that Du Bois feels he must give the most severe of warnings:

> We must not make the error of the German Jews. They assumed that if the German nation received some of them as intellectual and social equals, the whole group would be safe. It only took a psychopathic criminal like Hitler to show them their tragic mistake. American Negroes may yet face a similar tragedy. They should prepare for such an eventuality. (392–93)

But he is to begin his Postlude in cool and meditative fashion. It appropriately opens on a ship with the somewhat overdetermined name *Liberté*. On arriving back in the United States, he notes that "all went well. . . . Our passports were not seized, and the chief inspector of Customs passed our bags quickly and welcomed us home. Our relatives and friends swarmed to greet us" (409). Familial reunion is artistically appropriate and points the reader back to his original "dedication." But, of course, kinship is only part of the dedication's message.

"I am a little puzzled now," says Du Bois, "about the ordering of my life. Several times in the past I find that I have prepared for death and death has not come" (409). If so much of the energy which drove the first four hundred pages of this book was rooted in uncertainty, in the space between science and culture, faith and reason, and encouraged by Du Bois's testimony about autobiography's unreliability, he shifts now to a mode not so much about uncertainty as about inescapability. Zeroing in on modernity's denial of death, Du Bois systematically recalls his previous attempts (in every autobiographical narrative he wrote) to come to terms with this fact and condition. "From then until now the wraith of Death has followed me, slept with me and awakened me and accompanied my day. Only now it is more commonplace and reasonable. It is the end and without ends there can be no beginnings. It is the finality we must not falsify" (412). From this certainty, he begins to weave the multiple faiths and commitments of his life together. Starkly, he again dismisses religious dogma for its role in redirecting our attention from this truth and certitude and for its becoming a handmaiden to the consumerist fantasy of escaping aging. But rather than write an ode to fate and determinism, Du Bois marvelously alters course. "I have seen miracles in my life," he teases, and further notes, "I was brought up in the shadow of modern science where all that happens had a cause and there were many things unlikely to happen" (413). Relieving his readers of gloom and dejection, he recalls the dramatic changes he has experienced, and, perhaps not surprisingly at this point, is especially enthusiastic about changes in transportation. Climaxing with the Soviet's success with Sputnik, Du Bois's ode to scientific reason almost makes us forget his cautionary tale about "finality." But a celebration of modernity is not his stopping place.

Shifting into one of the most stunning jeremiads in American literature, Du Bois comments that his long life is "distasteful" to the nation. Novelty demands that the elderly forget their experience and disavow their knowledge. "This is because in the face of human experience the United States has discovered that Youth knows more than Age. . . . If living does not give value, wisdom, and meaning to life, then there is no sense in living at all" (414). The result is more than just troubling: "I see a land which is degenerating and faces decadence unless it has sense enough to turn about and start back." The topics of the succeeding litany of complaints are, for readers of this book, I hope, old and familiar: advertising, modern technologized warfare, youth culture, and reductionist religion. Du Bois laments:

Perhaps the most extraordinary characteristic of current America is the attempt to reduce life to buying and selling. Life is not love unless love is sex and bought and sold. Life is not knowledge save knowledge of technique, of science for destruction. Life is not beauty except beauty for sale. Life is not art unless its price is high and it is sold for profit. All life is production for profit, and for what is profit but for buying and selling again? (418)

After having celebrated modern science and "technique" for "advancements," he turns, and with little sense of contradiction, finds it invested in capitalist decadence. What this decadence proscribes—and the dialectic of Enlightenment makes difficult—is criticism:

America must never be criticized even by honest and sincere men. America must always be praised and extravagantly praised. . . . Criticism is treason. . . . (417)

Of course even Du Bois's construction of antimodernism is "ambivalent." In revolutionary socialism Du Bois believes he has found "progress." One suspects, however, that the apologetics for a particular ideology is primarily an attempt to *negate* congratulatory American boosterism in the context of the cold war. It seems difficult to imagine any bureaucratic Marxists who would end an account of their life as follows:

Reveal, Ancient of Days, the Present in the Past and prophesy the End in the Beginning. For this is a beautiful world; this is a wonderful America, which the founding fathers dreamed until their sons drowned it in the blood of slavery and devoured it in greed. Our children must rebuild it. Let then the Dreams of the Dead rebuke the Blind who think that what is will be forever and teach them that what was worth living for must live again and that which merited death must stay dead. Teach us, Forever Dead, there is no Dream but Deed, there is no Deed but Memory. (422–23)

Du Bois's "unscientific postscript" and high allegory thus introduces and concludes "African-American antimodernism and the American sixties." It suggests that antimodern sentiment is linked to knowledge of human limits against the transcendence and hubris of technological culture. This sentiment might be further identified as a lament for those things—personal and social—still undone. (Benjamin's famous aphorism, "Allegories are in the realm of thoughts what ruins are in the realm of things," is turned by Du Bois in this peroration toward his own "ruination.") At the end of an unimaginably full life, Du Bois's attention is directed toward the inefficacy of his own intervention. The unqualified "progress" of Enlightenment is transformed into the bittersweet mixing of dream, deed, and memory.

Du Bois's final summary dramatically returns to "Dedication to the Dead":

I whisper to the great Majority: To the Almighty Dead, into whose pale approaching faces, I stand and stare; you whose thoughts, deeds and dreams have made men wise with all wisdom and stupid with utter evil. In every name of God, bend out and down, you who are the infinite majority of all mankind and with your thoughts, deeds, dreams and memories, overwhelm, outvote, and coerce this remnant of human life which lingers on, imagining themselves wisest of all who have lived just because they survive. Whither with wide revelation will they go with their stinking pride and empty boasting, whose ever recurring lies only you the Dead have known all too well? Teach living man to jeer at this last civilization which seeks to build heaven on Want and Ill of most men and vainly builds on color and hair rather than on decency of hand and heart. Let your memories teach these wilful fools all which you have forgotten and ruined and done to death. (422)

Why a turn toward the ineffable? It may be imprudently speculative to suggest that it is a romantic referral to the legacy of slavery. The life that begins only a few years after emancipation and concludes in exile after imprisonment is suggestive of a dangerous modern continuity. One must always contend with the possibility of being ripped from all that grounds one to a particular social order. Alienation, the distrust of comfort, the belief that in the end all that can be trusted is belief, are what remains for the conscious man. Du Bois's allegorical wanderings, his dedication to the dead, can be seen as an extension, perhaps, of the anthropological and historical meditation on just what would have survived the middle passage. Faced with even the unpreservability of language itself, memory must become sacred territory.

This is of course a poetic conclusion and ignores many of the more pragmatic inquiries I tried to foreground at the beginning of this chapter. The necessity of antimodern sentiment appears amidst the above reflections as something vaguely therapeutic. Ostensibly antimodernism is about holding the line against the transformation of the political into narcissistic agendas. Is Du Bois able to generate a productive amalgam of antimodern sentiment and rational diagnosis? It may seem that in the political and ideological context in which he found himself that to risk humiliation through the valorization of the "not-America" is perverse at best. Still compared with some current Afrocentric fantasy work — and I do not mean that as pejoratively as it sounds — Du Bois's attempt is (or remains) heroic insofar as it is cosmopolitan, self-critical, and pursued with a real sense of limits. Elegy, to be sure, is not prophecy, but it is rarely outright equivocation. Benjamin wrote that "only that historian will have the gift of fanning the spark of hope in the past who is firmly convinced that *even the dead* will not be safe from the enemy if he wins."[24] After the middle passage, after Auschwitz, after Rwanda, to be dedicated to the dead is to restore meaning to the idea of the tragic.

WHAT'S GOING ON (?)

"THE MOST TRULY MODERN OF ALL PEOPLES"

The Blacks of the Americas now face a historic choice. To survive, they must abandon their search for a past, must indeed recognize that they lack all claims to a distinctive cultural heritage, and that the path ahead lies not in myth making and in historical reconstruction, which are always doomed to failure, but in accepting the epic challenge of their reality. Black Americans can be the first group in the history of mankind who transcend the confines and grip of a cultural heritage, and in so doing, they can become the most truly modern of all peoples—a people who feel no need for a nation, a past, or a particularistic culture, but whose style of life will be a rational and continually changing adaptation to the exigencies of survival, at the highest possible level of existence.

ORLANDO PATTERSON (1972)[1]

On theoretical as well as empirical grounds, the dialectical concept pronounces its own hopelessness. The human reality is its history and, in it, contradictions do not explode by themselves. The conflict between streamlined, rewarding domination on the one hand, and its achievements that make for self-determination and pacification on the other, may become blatant beyond any possible denial, but it may well continue to be a manageable and even productive conflict, for with the growth in the technological conquest of nature grows the conquest of man by man. And this conquest reduces the freedom which is the necessary *a priori* of liberation. This is freedom of thought in the only sense in which thought can be free in the administered world—as the consciousness of its repressive productivity, and as the absolute need for breaking out of this whole. But precisely this absolute need does not prevail where it could become the driving force of a historical practice, the effective cause of qualitative change. Without this material force, even the most acute consciousness remains powerless.

HERBERT MARCUSE, *One-Dimensional Man* (1964)[2]

Patterson's statement is, perhaps, the clearest statement to be found that is distinctly counter to the historic and cultural tendency described in this book. *To become the most truly modern of all peoples*, suggests Patterson, is to deny ethnic, racial, national, and religious ties. Needless to say, this call has been largely ignored. Some critics and cultural practitioners have certainly refined its aims. They have approached its demand for change via the perspective of *theory*. That is to say that they have approached the categories of race and nation mainly to subject them to extensive deconstruction. Oddly enough, although one can easily imagine the political and insitutional necessity, African-American tradition or culture always seems to emerge unscathed from such rereadings. Others have pursued unapologetic cultural and socioeconomic nationalisms, amassing evidence of the success of any number of ethnic immigrant communities, asserting that this is indeed the modern way. Patterson's call is, then, certainly much more prophetic desire than it is good sociology, and, in a post-Yugoslavia, post-Rwanda world, it is not difficult to read that call as no less fantastic than the identity tangle from which he insists we must escape. On the other hand, while the concrete experience of racism is explanatory of most pragmatic and emotional resistance to this admirable future, it does not fully explain the enthusiasm with which a broad spectrum of critics, readers, and consumers—both black and nonblack—have determined that the *question* of African-American culture is fundamentally one of memory. From Toni Morrison's subtle "re-memory" to the glorious Africa of (some varieties of) Afrocentrism to the more generalized and often benign recoveries of the broad discourse of multiculturalism, the *reaching back* has become a staple of American culture's strategy for confronting racism. (Is it a coincidence that as the most effective program for addressing race-based inequality, affirmative action, is being dismantled, there is an enthusiasm for a national apology for slavery?)

Why was Patterson's post-civil rights, post-black power call ignored? Cynically, one would note that to ignore what he calls "the epic challenge" allows one to perpetually put off the difficult questions of the present and to encourage bickering about the character of the past. But the experience, patience, and endurance of the antimodern exemplars I have considered suggests that there was at least the possibility of some other result. Memory is, perhaps, the most effective means by which one can restore self-consciousness to Enlightenment. By never forgetting the ways by which (as a concrete political project) Enlightenment was, from the beginning, compromised by its fraternization with slavery, there remains the possibility that one can reimagine its principles such that they can have real meaning. There is within this complex act, a ritual recovery pursued by individuals and communities, the hint of a productive "Africanist" countermodernity. After all, the belief that the past has meaning, literally has continual presence, is *engaged* to and with West African beliefs about the simultaneity of past and present worlds.

One interesting figure who bridges the gap between the mostly high cultural actors whom I have considered and more popular culture is Marvin Gaye. In February of 1971 his masterpiece *What's Going On* was released to critical acclaim and not a little shock. There was little preparation for the socially engaged, radically Christian, artistically eclectic intervention, and little precedent—save Curtis Mayfield—in rhythm and blues or soul music. Representing neither the pretentiousness of the ideology of art rock nor the aggressive intellectualism of much "out jazz," *What's Going On* grew out of Gaye's increasing discomfort with the decline of urban community, and, more specifically, the horrors of the Vietnam war as reported to him by his brother. At its center is a moving faithfulness, a confidence that with the right commitments, energy, and vision, things can be turned around. While purportedly asking a question—What's going on?—it was, of course, making a statement: "Rockets, moon shots / Spend it on the have-nots / Money, we make it / 'Fore we see it, you take it / Oh, make you wanna holler / The way they do my life[3] . . . And yet a memorable—and for me, by now, well expected—refrain, too: "Mercy, mercy me / Things ain't what they used to be."[4] Aesthetically, the looking backward was more readily apparent in the album's creative embrace of a multitude of black musical styles. Gospel, blues, jazz, soul, and even straight-ahead pop were entangled such that not only was the old now new, but the very notion of what might be accomplished in a popular genre was transformed. *What's Going On* was a great closing to the sixties and was suggestive of the ways in which "dedication to the dead" could really mean the elaboration of the living.

And yet as deeply as I hear Marvin Gaye's griot song, I hear quite clearly Marcuse's warning in the second epigraph too. What material force would or could emerge to envelop this higher consciousness? In practice—indeed, in looking backward—the answer would seem to be none at all.

————————

STEPHEN CARTER ARGUES in a provocative essay that the legacy of the 1960s is a negative investigation and correlation of race and citizenship.[5] Speaking of E. J. Dionne's *Why Americans Hate Politics*,[6] Carter suggests that:

> what the Republicans understand and the Democrats do not is that most Americans despise the sixties. The high-blown rhetoric, the topsy-turvy values, the rejection of tradition, the lurch toward egalitarianism, all of which continue to be cherished by many liberal intellectuals, are anathema to most voters. It is less that they liked things the way they were before than that they think they have had enough radical change for a while, and in any case, they are tired of being blamed for everything that is wrong and are tired of learning that the solution to every problem is to strike down another traditional value.[7]

Even if one does not direct attention to who "they" are in his restatement of Dionne's lament, or what might have constituted "radical" change, we need

to pay close attention to the confidence with which the "meaning" of the sixties is considered self-evident or transparent. Carter and others assume that
the ground is in some sense uncontested and uncluttered. The transition in
which the sixties moves from being "experience" to "history" is not problematized.

This book set out to document the expansive social capacity of African-
American art in the American sixties. The story I have tried to tell—hopefully
with significant humility and all necessary tentativeness—is that of a period
structured by conversations in tension, interdependent, and radically plural.
The notion of the sixties having a single or clear victor is largely a rhetorical
product of today's race politics. Carter, inadvertently perhaps, may indeed
have found the central issue or nexus of issues which best describes the cultural, political, and social conditions negotiated within the decade: what
does it mean to be an American, or, less chauvinistically I would suggest,
what does it mean to be a citizen? Judith Shklar argues that American citizenship has historically been a process of distinguishing oneself from the enslaved.[8] (Du Bois's renouncement of his citizenship and subsequent move to
Ghana would seem to be one direct example of this paradox and how it really
played out during the sixties.) If Shklar is right (and I think she is) about our
individual and national self-definition being related to our ability to distinguish ourselves from the "enslaved," than it is of the utmost importance that
we pay careful attention to the efforts, sometimes inchoate, sometimes structured, of those formerly enslaved to redefine the boundaries and character of
our community. My engagement with a series of African-American figures—
whom I have all too confidently referred to as "antimodern exemplars"—is an
attempt to re(per)form current debates about the sixties, citizenship, and
modernity. Most importantly, I wanted to disrupt the confidence with which
we might identify the period as a whole, or individual persons or events, as
"radical," "liberal," or "conservative." Within the landscape of the sixties such
political and cultural descriptors are—and perhaps not obviously—rela-
tional, that is to say they are ultimately in flux. What defines and "relates" the
contributions of my figures and their discourses under the rubric of antimodernism is, I believe, a commitment to the revision of structures and not
the dismissal of structure itself. Sometimes these revisions were subtle,
sometimes more dramatic. "Liberal" social goals, for instance, like a commitment to and celebration and protection of diversity (as a "good" thing),
are articulated and demanded within conversations often understood as
"conservative": serious consideration of ritual and religion, commitment to
a moral universe, acceptance of human frailty, imperfection, and sinfulness,
an insistence that dialogue be grounded in complexity.

I have worked hard—increasingly, I think, in vain—to prevent this work
from becoming autobiography. But at this point I hope readers will indulge
me a few sentences. This is, I suspect, a very unusual "first book." It is as
much provocation as measured set of close readings. Part of its struggle has

been to resolve two contradictory urges or ethics. On the one hand, a pragmatic, socially engaged, democratic leftist self, while on the other, a self strongly attracted to the prophetic, the visionary, and perpetually *nervous* about our prospects. In the rich diversity of African-American responses to modernity and the legacy of slavery, what I have found is that these contradictory urges—omens, Kamau Brathwaite might call them—are not so contradictory after all.

NOTES

CHAPTER 1

1. Collected in Pete Seeger and Bob Reiser, eds., *Everybody Says Freedom: A History of the Civil Rights Movement in Songs and Pictures.* (New York: Norton, 1989), 117–18.

2. Damon Stetson, "President Notes Racial Progress," *New York Times*, September 16, 1963.

3. See John Sekora, *Until Justice Rolls Down: The Birmingham Church Bombing Case* (Tuscaloosa: University of Alabama Press, 1991).

4. The recent reopening of the case (and attendant publicity) is suggestive of how this event still has powerful resonance. See, for instance, David J. Garrow, "Back to Birmingham," *Newsweek*, July 21, 1997, 37.

5. Harold Cruse, *The Crisis of the Negro Intellectual* (New York: Morrow, 1967), 456–57.

6. "The Black Arts Movement," in *Visions of a Liberated Future: Black Arts Movement Writings* (New York: Thunder's Mouth Press, 1989), 64.

7. "The Fire Next Time," *The Price of the Ticket: Collected Non-Fiction, 1948–1985* (New York: St. Martin's, 1985), 371–73.

8. "The Novel as a Function of American Democracy," in *Going to the Territory* (New York: Vintage, 1986), 318–19.

9. "Black Studies: Bringing Back the Person," in *Civil Wars* (Boston: Beacon Press, 1981), 48–49.

10. Paul Gilroy, *The Black Atlantic: Modernity and Double Consciousness* (Cambridge, Mass.: Harvard University Press, 1993), 46.

11. Jackson Lears, *No Place of Grace: Antimodernism and the Transformation of American Culture, 1880–1920* (New York: Pantheon, 1981).

12. See David Howard-Pitney, *The Afro-American Jeremiad* (Philadelphia: Temple University Press, 1990). Howard-Pitney writes: "The ebb and flow of optimism about American promise and progress is a pervasive motif in this analysis, affording much inner drama behind these figures' public words. Douglass, Du Bois, and King in particular vacillated with regard to America's perfectibility. Their rhetoric reveals that the intractability of white racism could plunge them into profound crises of faith and that they struggled often at cost of great personal turmoil, to sustain a vision of America's democratic promise" (16). My project is to reveal some of this "inner drama" at a particular historic moment. My shared interest with Howard-Pitney might be traced to the influence of Sacvan Bercovitch's *The American Jeremiad* (Madison: University of Wisconsin Press, 1978), especially chapter 5, "Rituals of Consensus."

13. Houston Baker, *Modernism and the Harlem Renaissance* (Chicago: University of Chicago Press, 1987).

14. It is usually assented to in a general way, but the impact of the founding of Black Studies programs on the contemporary discourse of multiculturalism (and its associated curricular reform projects) deserves careful study. While these programs were certainly concerned with the diversification of university faculty and an attempt to gain real power within institutions of higher learning, in other ways they

were the pragmatic vehicle for the consideration of the transformative power of cultural memory.

15. See Lezlek Kolakowski, *Modernity on Endless Trial* (Chicago: University of Chicago Press, 1990).

16. Victor Turner, *The Ritual Process: Structure and Anti-Structure* (Ithaca, N.Y.: Cornell University Press, 1969), 95.

17. Harold Cruse, *Rebellion or Revolution* (New York: Morrow, 1968), 12.

18. George Lamming, *The Pleasures of Exile* (Ann Arbor: University of Michigan Press, 1992).

19. William James, *The Varieties of Religious Experience* (New York, Penguin, 1982), 189.

20. Michel Fabre, *The Unfinished Quest of Richard Wright*, 2nd ed. (Urbana: University of Illinois Press, 1993), 316.

21. This almost wholly male list certainly makes one wonder whether or not expatriation was a peculiarly male rite of passage. A few women musicians made the journey (Billie Holiday, Mary Lou Williams, Sarah Vaughan, Hazel Scott—Josephine Baker's exile was permanent), but other than Elizabeth Catlett's move to Mexico, African-American women were more likely to stay on the home front in the immediate postwar period. Michel Fabre has documented the slightly later moves of Sarah Webster Fabio, Barbara Chase Riboud, Faith Berry, Carlene Polite, Angela Davis and others in his seminal *From Harlem to Paris: Black American Writers in France, 1840–1980* (Urbana: University of Illinois Press, 1991). See also Tyler Stovall, *Paris Noir: African-Americans in the City of Light* (Boston: Houghton Mifflin, 1996), and James Campbell, *Exiled in Paris: Richard Wright, James Baldwin, Samuel Beckett, and Others on the Left Bank* (New York: Scribner's, 1995).

22. In "The New Lost Generation (1961)," collected in *The Price of the Ticket* (New York: St. Martin's, 1985), 313.

23. See Richard J. Powell, "Pride, Assimilation, Dreams," in his *Black Art and Culture in the 20th Century* (London: Thames and Hudson, 1997). Powell appropriately complicates this picture even further by noting the practice of artists like Jacob Lawrence, Elizabeth Catlett, and Charles White, who worked a more highly politicized middle ground. Less interested in either the pole of "abstraction" or that of "folk," they produced an artwork that communicated in a direct way the inequalities of American life. Lloyd Brown's novel *Iron City* ([1952] Boston: Northeastern University Press, 1993) might be the most interesting literary parallel; while it contains elements of both, it is not primarily concerned with being formally either a proletarian or modernist novel.

24. Despite the monumental impact of Ellison's novel, the African-American novelistic tradition is arguably the most stable of all African-American artistic traditions in the fifteen years after the end of the Second World War. Certainly Gwendolyn Brooks's *Maud Martha* is some kind of *interruption* but generally the status quo holds firm. William Demby, William Gardner Smith, John Killens, Willard Motley, Ann Petry, Paule Marshall, and, despite his Jamesian pretensions, even James Baldwin, all largely stay the realist/naturalist course.

25. See Eric Lott, "Double V, Double Time: Bebop's Politics of Style," *Callaloo* 11.3 (1988): 597–605.

26. Bernard Gendron has convincingly argued that jazz critics of the period inherited a vocabulary and rhetoric from the battles associated with a variety of modernisms. See " 'Moldy Figs' and Modernists: Jazz at War (1942–1946)," in Krin Gabbard, ed., *Jazz among the Discourses* (Durham, N.C.: Duke University Press, 1995), 31–56.

27. Henry Louis Gates, Jr., and Nellie McKay, eds., *The Norton Anthology of African American Literature* (New York: Norton, 1997). Periodization in this exciting and monumental anthology is wonderfully messy and illustrates the need for some of the rethinking I am trying to instigate here. Robert Hayden lands in the section "Realism, Naturalism, Modernism: 1940–1960," including his 1960s poems. Following this comes "The Black Arts Movement: 1960–1970," although no text is included that was written before 1963; Paule Marshall is placed in something called "Literature Since 1970," although most of the selections included were written in the 1960s. There are similar displacements in the cases of Langston Hughes, James Baldwin, and Albert Murray, among many others. All of this is, of course, at least partially a result of the difficult task of organizing a history, but also represents something more like desire. At some levels, occasionally the pedagogical and political, it makes sense, but really should not get in the way of making clear the entanglements of writers from different periods and traditions.

28. See Nat Brandt, *Harlem at War: The Black Experience in WWII* (Syracuse, N.Y.: Syracuse University Press, 1996) and the aforementioned essay by Eric Lott.

29. Robert Bone, *The Negro Novel in America*, rev. ed. (New Haven, Conn.: Yale University Press, 1965), 161.

30. The question of African-American interpretations of and responses to the Holocaust is an interesting one. Increased knowledge and understanding of the Holocaust likely created unease in the minds of many African-Americans as to the ability of the modern bureaucratic state to bring about destruction upon any component of the nation deemed expendable. It is, however, striking that there was no immediate wave of artistic representations or interpretations of the Holocaust; this is one of the reasons that Gardner Smith's novel stands out.

31. Bernard Bell, *The Afro-American Novel and Its Tradition* (Amherst: University of Massachusetts Press, 1987).

32. It is appropriate, in the context of this discussion, that Bell takes his title from Richard Chase's *The American Novel and Its Tradition*, given that text's role in the solidification of a national canon in the midst of the cold war.

33. There has been much excellent writing on the relationship between the institutionalization of the New Criticism and the exigencies of cold war culture. See Alan Nadel, *Containment Culture: American Narratives, Postmodernism, and the Atomic Age* (Durham, N.C.: Duke University Press, 1996); Donald Pease, ed., *National Identities and Post-Americanist Identities* (Durham, N.C.: Duke University Press, 1994); Thomas Schaub, *American Fiction in the Cold War* (Madison: University of Wisconsin Press, 1991); William Spanos, *The Errant Art of Moby Dick: The Canon, the Cold War, and the Struggle for American Studies* (Durham, N.C.: Duke University Press, 1996); and Mark Walhout, "The New Criticism and the Crisis of American Liberalism: The Poetics of the Cold War," *College English* (1985).

34. Stephen J. Whitfield, *The Culture of the Cold War* (Baltimore, Md.: Johns Hopkins University Press, 1991), 21.

35. See Mary Dudziak, "Josephine Baker, Racial Protest, and the Cold War," *Journal of American History* 99 (1994): 543–70; Gerald Horne, *Black and Red: W.E.B. Du Bois and the Afro-American Response to the Cold War* (Albany, N.Y.: SUNY Press, 1986); Brenda Gayle Plummer, *Rising Wind: Black Americans and U.S. Foreign Affairs, 1935–1960* (Chapel Hill: University of North Carolina Press, 1996); and Penny Von Eschen, *Race Against Empire: Black Americans and Anticolonialism, 1937–1957* (Ithaca, N.Y.: Cornell University Press, 1997).

36. See Christopher Lasch, *The Agony of the American Left* (New York: Knopf, 1969).

37. See, for example, Clenora Hudson-Weems, *Emmett Till: The Sacrificial Lamb in the Modern Civil Rights Movement* (Troy, Mich.: Bedford Books, 1994).

38. J. P. Sartre, "Orphée Noir," originally published as preface to *Anthologie de la Nouvelle Poésie Nègre et Malgache de langue français*, ed. by Leopold Sédar-Senghor. (Paris: Presses Universitaires de France, 1948). A good challenge to the film's "universalism" is to be found in Robert Stam's "Samba, Candomblé, Quilombo: Black Performance and Brazilian Cinema," *Journal of Ethnic Studies* 13.3 (1985): 55–84.

39. *New York Herald-Tribune*, October 27, 1963.

40. In addition to "Moldy Figs," mentioned in a previous note, see "A Short Stay in the Sun: The Reception of Bebop (1944–1950)," *Library Chronicle of the University of Texas at Austin* 24.1–2 (1994): 137–59.

41. Anthony Giddens, *The Consequences of Modernity* (Stanford, Calif.: Stanford University Press, 1990). Giddens's description of the "modern" world has been extremely useful to me. His attempt to demonstrate the ways in which the world we live in is *not* postmodern or postindustrial is also very pertinent to my study.

42. Patricia Williams's *The Alchemy of Race and Rights* (Cambridge, Mass.: Harvard University Press, 1991) is suggestive along these lines.

43. On what they missed, see James A. Snead, "On Repetition in Black Culture," *Black American Literature Forum* 15.4 (1981): 146–54.

44. Nathaniel Mackey, *Discrepant Engagement* (New York: Cambridge University Press, 1993).

45. There is no question in my mind that the most frustrating blind spot within sixties-bashing is its ignorance of the dynamic conservatism at the center of many of the most active social reform movements. A good call is made by Paul Lyons in his *New Left, New Right, and the Legacy of the Sixties* (Philadelphia, Pa.: Temple University Press, 1996), although his concern (and that of others) is more with documenting the activities of self-identified conservatives.

46. Theodor Adorno and Max Horkheimer, *Dialectic of Enlightenment* (New York: Continuum, 1972), 216.

47. Larry Neal, *Hoodoo Hollerin Bebop Ghosts* (Washington, D.C.: Howard University Press, 1974), 81.

48. See Peter Sacks, *The English Elegy* (Baltimore, Md.: Johns Hopkins University Press, 1985) and Jahan Ramazani, *Poetry of Mourning: The Modern Elegy From Hardy to Heaney* (Chicago: University of Chicago Press, 1994). Ramazani's extension of Sacks's psychoanalytic framework is quite compelling. Utilizing Freud's commentary on melancholia, he establishes a productive hermeneutic for getting at the "recalcitrance" of modern mourning. In his treatment of African-American elegies, however, I think he marginalizes the more declarative function—really lamentation in the strongest sense—of Hayden, Brooks, Hughes, and others. Also useful to me were Susan Letzler Cole, *The Absent One: Mourning, Ritual, Tragedy, and the Performance of Ambivalence* (University Park: Penn State University Press, 1985) and Alan Friedman, *Fictional Death and the Modernist Enterprise* (New York: Cambridge University Press, 1995).

49. I am indebted here to Eric Sundquist's introduction to his *To Wake the Nations* (Cambridge, Mass.: Harvard University Press, 1992).

50. For Archie Shepp, see Aldon Nielsen's *Black Chant: Languages of African American Postmodernism* (New York: Cambridge University Press, 1997). The book edited by Dudley Randall and Margaret Burroughs is *For Malcolm: Poems on the Life and the Death of Malcolm X* (Detroit: Broadside Press, 1967). It is a fascinating collection that includes contributions from central African-American literary figures

(or soon to be such) like Jay Wright, Clarence Major, Gwendolyn Brooks, Mari Evans, and others. Strikingly, however, it also includes contributions from less well known poets—and individuals who seemed to decide to become poets strictly to mark Malcolm X's passing. While this lends to the book a distinct amateurishness, it also contributes to its becoming a distinctly moving document.

51. On African-American funerary practices see Hosea L. Perry, "Mourning and Funeral Customs of African-Americans," in Donald Irish, et al., eds., *Ethnic Variations in Dying, Death, and Grief: Diversity in Universality* (Washington, D.C.: Taylor and Francis, 1993).

52. A. B. Spellman, *The Beautiful Days* (New York: The Poet's Press, 1965). On Spellman's disappearance from, and continued presence within, the cultural scene, see Nielsen, *Black Chant*.

53. But neither purely aesthetic either: see Ronald Radano, *New Musical Figurations: Anthony Braxton's Cultural Critique* (Chicago: University of Chicago Press, 1994).

54. A number of books have been indispensable in shaping my understanding of the sixties: Todd Gitlin, *The Sixties: Years of Hope, Days of Rage* (New York: Bantam, 1987); Allen J. Matusow, *The Unraveling of America: A History of Liberalism in the 1960's* (New York: Harper and Row, 1984); and Taylor Branch, *Parting the Waters: America in the King Years, 1954–63* (New York: Simon and Schuster, 1988) have been especially helpful. David Chalmers's bibliographic essay in his *And the Crooked Places Made Straight* (Baltimore, Md.: Johns Hopkins University Press, 1991) is a good survey of available scholarship.

55. Frederic Jameson, "Periodizing the 60's," in Sohnya Sayres et al., eds., *The Sixties Without Apology* (Minneapolis: University of Minnesota Press, 1984).

56. Furthermore, this negotiation is "ideological." It has become almost a cultural-critical convention to take to task Daniel Bell for his assertion that as the 1960s approached America would witness the "end of ideology." Bell has adequately defended his analysis of mid-century American political culture, yet one suspects that he does so with the benefit of hindsight. It seems unlikely that anyone could have adequately predicted the *moral* consequences of the civil rights, free speech, and antiwar movements. While Bell's assertions about the organization of American political culture might be defensible, anyone who connects a nonideological political climate with a blind defense of American progress is misled. Indeed, some individuals or groups (in celebration of "objectivity") try to proceed in a nonideological manner, but that hardly addresses the intellectual currency of "particularist dialogues." See Daniel Bell, "Afterword, 1988: The End of Ideology Revisited," in *The End of Ideology: On the Exhaustion of Political Ideas in the Fifties* (Cambridge, Mass.: Harvard University Press, 1988), 409–47. Indeed, Bell has never come to terms with African-American culture or intellectual history. C. Wright Mills responded: "The end-of-ideology is very largely a mechanical reaction—not a creative response—to the ideology of Stalinism. As such it takes from its opponent something of its inner quality. What does it mean? That these people have become aware of the uselessness of Vulgar Marxism, but not yet aware of the uselessness of liberal rhetoric." See "The New Left" in *The Collected Essays of C. Wright Mills* (New York: Ballantine, 1963), 247–59.

57. Richard Bernstein, *Philosophical Profiles* (Philadelphia: University of Pennsylvania Press, 1986), 1. My thinking on these questions has also been strongly affected by my reading of the work of Wilhelm Dilthey. He has been largely ignored in the making of contemporary cultural studies, despite his pioneering attempts to negotiate a synthesis between the social sciences and the humanities, which he

called "human studies." Most importantly, he locates in the practices of biography
and autobiography the emergence of a consciousness appropriate for the
understanding of modernity. Because it is not "scientific," biography cannot be the
only historical tool—hermeneutics, in particular, must be brought to the fore—but
it is ideal for introducing the concepts of understanding and meaning. See Wilhelm
Dilthey, *Pattern and Meaning in History: Thoughts on History and Society* (New York:
Harper and Row, 1961), H. P. Rickman, *Dilthey Today: A Critical Appraisal of the
Contemporary Relevance of His Work* (Westport, Conn.: Greenwood Press, 1988) and
Theodore Plantinga, *Historical Understanding in the Thought of Wilhelm Dilthey*
(Toronto: University of Toronto Press, 1980). Also helpful to me in developing a
"biographical theory" have been Warren Susman, "'Personality' and the Making of
Twentieth Century Culture," in John Higham, ed., *New Directions in American
Intellectual History* (Baltimore, Md.: Johns Hopkins University Press, 1979), 212–16,
and Edward Sapir, "The Emergence of the Concept of Personality in a Study of
Cultures," *Journal of Social Psychology* 5(1934): 412.

58. I am certainly well aware and respectful of the accomplishments of the Black
Panther Party. While the Cuban revolution and Marxist-Leninist ideology certainly
impacted the Party's approach to neighborhood organizing (and especially their
commitment to consciousness raising among the lumpen), I am not convinced it
was a significant part of their impact upon the popular consciousness. At any rate,
there is certainly a need for more work in this area. See Van Gosse, *Where the Boys
Are: Cuba, Cold War America, and The Making of a "New Left"* (New York: Verso, 1993)
and Hugh Pearson, *The Shadow of the Panther: Huey Newton and the Price of Black Power
in America* (New York: Addison-Wesley, 1994).

59. See Michele Wallace, *Black Macho and the Myth of the Superwoman* (New York:
Verso, 1990).

60. Of course, this is not to give in to an absence. Rather, it acknowledges a
certain limitation of resources. The effectiveness of the "culture industry" in giving
only minimal space to women's voices and concerns has clearly complicated my
project. Ultimately, oral history and archival materials will be needed to "thicken"
my descriptions. See, for instance, the dilemma of Paula Giddings in her *When and
Where I Enter* (New York: Morrow, 1984). Compelling rereadings of civil rights
history have recently appeared: Wini Breines, "Sixties Stories' Silences: White
Feminism, Black Feminism, Black Power," *NWSA Journal* 8.3 (1996): 101–21, and
Joan C. Browning, "Invisible Revolutionaries: White Women in Civil Rights
Historiography," *Journal of Women's History* 8.3 (1996): 186–204. Other pertinent
texts would be Sara Evans, *Personal Politics: The Roots of Women's Liberation in the Civil
Rights Movement and the New Left* (New York: Knopf, 1980); Gloria Hull, et al, eds., *All
the Women Are White, All the Blacks Are Men, But Some of Us Are Brave: Black Women's
Studies* (New York: Feminist Press, 1982); and Barbara Smith, ed., *Home Girls: A Black
Feminist Anthology* (New York: Kitchen Table—Women of Color Press, 1983).

61. One might reasonably interpret turn-of-the-century antimodernism as an
exploration and reading of whiteness. The association of a vigorous racism with
turn-of-the-century antimodernism suggests that a certain portion of the
"protection" of traditional cultural hegemony was the discovery of the difference (or
lack of it) signified by "white-ness."

62. This book, I hope, is to be the first volley in a long rereading of sixties
America. I intend to follow it up with an extended reading of the jazz pianist and
composer Mary Lou Williams who, following her conversion to Roman Catholicism
in 1957, spend much of the 1960s writing some spectacular religious music.
Finally, I mean to complete the trilogy with a study of the development of a

variety of cultural institutions and their relationship to class formation and consciousness.

63. See for instance, George Hutchinson, *The Harlem Renaissance in Black And White* (Cambridge, Mass.: Harvard University Press, 1995).

64. With the noteworthy exceptions of Charles Valentine and John Szwed.

65. This is less true within social, political, and intellectual history. See David Chalmers, *And the Crooked Places Made Straight: The Struggle for Social Change in the 1960's* (Baltimore, Md.: Johns Hopkins University Press, 1991); Aldon Morris, *The Origins of the Civil Rights Movement: Black Communities Organizing for Change* (New York: Free Press, 1984); Doug McAdam, *Political Process and the Development of Black Insurgency, 1930–1970* (Chicago: University of Chicago Press, 1983); Juan Williams, *Eyes on the Prize* (New York: Viking Press, 1987); Robert Weisbrot, *Freedom Bound: A History of America's Civil Rights Movement* (New York: Norton, 1990); August Meier and Elliot Rudwick, *CORE: A Study in the Civil Rights Movement, 1942–1968* (New York: Oxford University Press, 1973); Clayborne Carson, *In Struggle: SNCC and the Black Awakening of the 1960's* (Cambridge, Mass.: Harvard University Press, 1981); Kenneth O'Reilly, *Racial Matters: The FBI's Secret File on Black America, 1960–1972* (New York: Free Press, 1989); Steven F. Lawson, *In Pursuit of Power: Southern Blacks and Electoral Politics, 1965–1982* (New York: Columbia University Press, 1983); and many others. Oral history, biography, and autobiography are especially strong. See for instance Howell Raines, *My Soul is Rested: Movement Days in the Deep South Remembered* (New York: Putnam, 1977); David J. Garrow, *Bearing the Cross: Martin Luther King, Jr. and the Southern Leadership Conference, 1955–1968* (New York: Morrow, 1986); Taylor Branch, *Parting the Waters: America in the King Years, 1954–63* (New York: Simon and Schuster, 1988) and *Pillar of Fire: America in the King Years, 1963–1965* (New York: Simon and Schuster, 1998); and James Farmer, *Lay Bare the Heart: An Autobiography of the Civil Rights Movement* (New York: Arbor House, 1985), among many others.

66. And in this way I am interested in participating in the conversation nicely outlined by Shelley Fisher Fishkin in "Interrogating 'Whiteness,' Complicating 'Blackness,': Remapping American Culture," *American Quarterly* 47.3 (1995): 428 ff.

67. See the inside front cover of *Black Scholar 18* (1987).

68. "The Black Arts Movement and Its Critics," *American Literary History* 3.1 (1991): 93–110.

69. Useful texts include C.W.E. Bigsby, *The Second Black Renaissance* (Westport, Conn.: Greenwood Press, 1980); Houston Baker, *The Journey Back: Issues in Black Literature and Criticism* (Chicago: University of Chicago Press, 1980) and *Afro-American Poetics* (Madison: University of Wisconsin Press, 1988); Abby Arthur Johnson and Ronald Maberry Johnson, *Propaganda and Aesthetics: The Literary Politics of Afro-American Magazines in the Twentieth Century* (Amherst: University of Massachusetts Press, 1979); Reginald Martin, *Ishmael Reed and the New Black Aesthetic Critics* (New York: St. Martin's, 1988); Carole Parks, *Nommo: A Literary Legacy of Black Chicago: 1967–1987* (Chicago: OBAhouse, 1987); Werner Sollors, *Amiri Baraka/LeRoi Jones: The Quest for a Modernist Populism* (New York: Columbia University Press, 1978); Adolph Reed, Jr., ed., *Race, Politics, and Culture: Critical Essays on the Radicalism of the 1960's* (Westport, Conn.: Greenwood Press, 1986). Personally, I find that two works of African-American literary criticism especially resonate with this project: W. Lawrence Hogue's *Race, Modernity, Postmodernity: A Look at the History and the Literatures of People of Color since the 1960s* (Albany, N.Y.: SUNY Press, 1996) and the vastly underrated *Afro-American Literature in the Twentieth Century: The Achievement of Intimacy* by Michael G. Cooke (New Haven, Conn.: Yale University Press, 1984).

Ronald Radano's *New Musical Configurations* and Aldon Nielsen's *Black Chant* have also been crucial to me. To reiterate: My goal is to go beyond bipolar constructions of African-American culture in the 1960s; to explain the transition from the poetics of integration to the poetics of difference; to disrupt all reductionist and conspiratorial analyses.

70. Gerald Horne, *The Fire This Time: The Watts Uprising and the 1960s* (Charlottesville: University of Virginia Press, 1995). Horne's remarks are worth quoting in full: "By 1965 many blacks were 'cut off' from anti-imperialist and trade union politics; 'cultural questions' filled the vacuum. Writing poems was deemed to be more important than who controlled the means of production. And just as Senghor's praxis was marked by the bacchanalian influence of Baudelaire and Rimbaud, the cultural nationalists in L.A. were marked by a certain libertine abandon that took full advantage of the unfolding "sexual revolution," a revolution that was marred by the rise of gangsters and their particular approach to heterosexual and homosexual relations. Thus sexual abandon, along with year-of-arrival consciousness and nationalism, evolved to fill the vacuum created by the erosion of class consciousness" (20–21). I think Horne gets Senghor wrong—and I need more convincing as to the immanent emergence, in Los Angeles or anywhere else, of a productive black class consciousness—but still think this is a very helpful reformulation of the terms on which questions of race and the 1960s should be approached. He is especially strong in his critique of acquiescence to patriarchy, although here too I diverge from his reading somewhat: "A problem with the brute force of adult masculinity was that it was accompanied too often by an anti-intellectualism. The decline of the left and its post-Enlightenment views paved the way for the increased intellectual hold of a number of regressive religious sects. This had disastrous consequence for a discrete racial minority in need of allies. Confrontation was stressed without its necessary complement, study. Black nationalism in an atmosphere of bi-racial polarity was one thing; but this nationalism in a region where other minorities had legitimate grievances was something else altogether" (186).

71. William Van Deburg, *New Day in Babylon: Black Power and American Culture* (Chicago: University of Chicago Press, 1996). Van Deburg aggressively launches a preemptive strike on "those seeking to make a case for the 'essential Americanness' of the black cultural core by using the melting pot (rather than the salad bowl) as the most appropriate sociocultural metaphor" (x). To my mind, both metaphors are reductions and rely upon rarely sustainable cultural assumptions. I have a great deal of respect for Van Deburg's demonstration of the seriousness of black power as a contemporary social movement. It seems to me just as important, however, to be willing to articulate criticism too. His more recent *Black Camelot: African-American Culture Heroes in Their Times, 1960–1980* (Chicago: University of Chicago Press, 1997) is much more compelling, and I think there is an interesting relationship between his interest in the heroic and my own coming to an interest in the biographic.

72. Selected papers of the conference were collected in the volume *The American Negro Writer and His Roots* (New York: American Society for African Culture, 1960); it is striking that Hansberry's contribution was not included in this volume. It was first printed in *Black Scholar* (March–April 1981); citations are from reprint in Gerald Early, ed., *Speech and Power*, v. 2 (New York: The Ecco Press, 1993), 129–41. The best account of Hansberry's work currently available is Stephen R. Carter, *Hansberry's Drama: Commitment and Complexity* (Urbana: University of Illinois Press, 1991).

CHAPTER 2

1. Stephen Greenblatt, *Renaissance Self-Fashioning: From More to Shakespeare* (Chicago: University of Chicago Press, 1980), 1.

2. James Clifford, "On Ethnographic Self-Fashioning," in *The Predicament of Culture: Twentieth-Century Ethnography, Literature, and Art* (Cambridge, Mass.: Harvard University Press, 1988), 112.

3. See Robert Hayden, *Collected Prose* (Ann Arbor: University of Michigan Press, 1984), 22.

4. Kimberly Benston, "Performing Blackness: Re/Placing Afro-American Poetry," in Houston A. Baker and Patricia Redmond, eds., *Afro-American Literary Study in the 1990's* (Chicago: University of Chicago Press, 1989), 164–85.

5. See C.W.E. Bigsby, "The Black Poet as Cultural Sign," in *The Second Black Renaissance* (Westport, Conn.: Greenwood Press, 1980), 257–301 and June Jordan, "The Difficult Miracle of Black Poetry in America," *Massachusetts Review* 27 (summer 1986): 252–62. Of obvious importance here also is Saunders Redding's *To Make a Poet Black* (Ithaca, N.Y.: Cornell University Press, 1988). There is a dearth of first-rate academic criticism, which, given the agonistic identity drama that I wish to outline, is itself interesting. Helpful are: Stephen Henderson, *Understanding the New Black Poetry* (New York: Morrow, 1973); Donald Gibson, *Modern Black Poets: A Collection of Critical Essays* (New York: Prentice Hall, 1973); Eugene Redmond, *Drumvoices: The Mission of Afro-American Poetry* (New York: Anchor, 1976); Bernard Bell, *The Folk Roots of Afro-American Poetry* (Detroit: Broadside Press, 1974), D. H. Melhem, *Heroism and the New Black Poetry: Introductions and Interviews* (Lexington: University of Kentucky Press, 1990); and Blyden Jackson and Louis Rubin, *Black Poetry in America: Two Essays in Historical Interpretation* (Baton Rouge: Louisiana State University Press, 1974). Philip Richards's "Phillis Wheatley and Literary Americanization," *American Quarterly* 44 (1992): 163–91, Marcellus Blount's "The Preacherly Text: African-American Poetry and Vernacular Performance," *PMLA* 107 (1992): 582–93, and James Sullivan's "Real Cool Pages: The Broadside Press Broadside Series," *Contemporary Literature* 32 (1991): 553–72 were also helpful in the conception of this chapter. Sixties sources (and texts) are discussed below.

6. It is interesting to note that the first two poems of Robert Hayden's last book, *American Journal* (Taunton, Mass.: Effendi Press, 1978)—in retrospect his summing-up of his life and career—were about Wheatley and Dunbar. Hayden seems to understand the role his life has played in an ongoing identity drama within the practice of African-American poetry. It is also interesting that the posthumously published Liveright edition of *American Journal* changed the order of presentation of these two poems, dissolving the vinculum.

7. Henry Louis Gates, Jr., "Literary Theory and the Black Tradition," in *Figures in Black: Words, Signs, and the Racial Self* (New York: Oxford University Press, 1987), 24.

8. See Cornel West, "A Genealogy of Modern Racism," in *Prophesy Deliverance!: An Afro-American Revolutionary Christianity* (Philadelphia, Pa.: Westminster Press, 1982), 47–68.

9. Interestingly, for Jackson Lears in *No Place of Grace: Antimodernism and the Transformation of American Culture, 1880–1920* (New York: Pantheon, 1981), this obsession is what ultimately leads to the "failure" of Anglo-American antimodernism ("Through the prism of antimodern vitalism we can see the hidden affinities between two apparently contradictory strands in recent American cultural history—between the liberationist ideology of avant-garde bohemians and the acquiescent leisure ethic of the mass society they deplored. Both sanctioned a new nonmorality

of self-gratification," [160]) and entangles it, both relating and differentiating it, with African-American antimodernism of the sixties. As we will see, African-American antimodernism will be haunted by its relationship to and inevitable obsession with "the cult of authentic blackness."

10. See, for instance, Scott Lash and Jonathan Friedman, eds., *Modernity and Identity* (Cambridge, Mass.: Blackwell, 1992), an excellent collection which de-centers European privilege in the discussion, and reconceives of modernity as something not at all static.

11. A previous version of this chapter contained a long section, omitted here, on negritude, perhaps the most problematic of discourses of "black-selfhood." While by the sixties it was long past its primary chronological apex in terms of influence, it still had a significant role to play in African-American thought. Interestingly, this was primarily a rejection of its tenets and thrust despite the role that this discourse would play in the "decolonization of African literature" movement. The fullest consideration of this paradox will have to be delayed, hopefully to be part of a project thinking through the "reception" of Africa in the United States since the independence movements. For now, what is important is that African-American artists and critics, nationalists and integrationists alike, were ironically suspicious of its "universal" applicability—which supports, I believe, my argument about the ultimate failure of polar constructions of African-American discourse in this decade. See St. Clair Drake, "The Negro's Stake in Africa: The Meaning of Negritude," *Negro Digest* 13.8 (1964): 33–48, and Lewis Nkosi, "The Literary Impact of Negritude," *Negro Digest* 14.7 (1965): 70–74. The reception of "negritude" can also be examined in the United States by considering the coverage of the First World Festival of Negro Arts in Dakar, meant to be a showcase of negritude, in "First World Festival of Negro Arts," *Negro Digest* 14.10 (1965): 62–69, and "Festival Time in Dakar," *Negro Digest* 15.6 (1966): 56–82. The discomfort with which African-Americans (of both the "militant" and "integrationist" variety) receive the philosophy can be understood as part of the "real differences" discovered between themselves and Africans living and working in the United States. See John A. Williams and Thomas O. Echewa, "A Dialogue: Negro vs. African," *Negro Digest* 14.11 (1965); Bernard Magubane, *Ties That Bind: African-American Consciousness of Africa* (Trenton, N.J.: Africa World Press, 1987); and "African/American Tensions in Black Writing of the 1960's," *Journal of Black Studies* 19.4 (1989). The most complex representation of this disjuncture might be seen on the back cover of *Negro Digest* 14.5 (1965) ("What Is This Thing Called Negritude") in which blackness, as idea and knowledge, is commodified, a tool to sell magazines. The impact of negritude in the United States can also be traced by examining the reception of Sartre's "Black Orpheus" essay, and the work of Franz Fanon. Also important to think through for a full appreciation of this section might be the similarities and differences between Robert Hayden and Wole Soyinka. See Willfried F. Feuser, "Wole Soyinka: The Problem of Authenticity," *Black American Literature Forum* 22.3 (1988): 566–75.

12. A specific definition would be hard to develop. The prime conventions were the establishment of a theme, the gathering of a diverse group of writers, and the forming of various panels. It is significant that *Negro Digest*, put out by Johnson Publications, should often try to recreate the conference format in print. Not only did they regularly report on the proceedings but they often tried to create textual equivalents. Most notable was "The Task of the Negro Writer as Artist: A Symposium," *Negro Digest* 14.6 (1965): 54–82. The editors solicited written responses to the question "What is the task of the Negro writer concerned with creating a work of art in a segregated society and how does his task differ from that of the white writer?" The

most complete textual account of a conference is to be found in Herbert Hill, ed., *Anger and Beyond: The Negro Writer in the United States* (New York: Harper and Row, 1966), which collected the proceedings of the Berkeley conference. (See also the interpretive coverage in *Negro Digest* for September 1964 and *Ebony* for November 1964, and the essay by Kenneth Rexroth, "Panelizing Dissent," in the *Nation*, September 7, 1964.) The historical lineage of the writer's conferences would also include, I think, the Pan-African Conferences (1911, 1921, 1923, 1927, and 1945), with a related contemporary event being the First World Festival of Negro Arts in Dakar (April 1966) and the infamous Town Hall Debate—"The Black Revolution and the White Backlash"—which included LeRoi Jones, John Killens, Paule Marshall, Ruby Dee, and Ossie Davis debating Charles Silberman and other white liberals (June 1964) (It was covered in James Wechsler's columns in the *New York Post*, June 22 and 23.) Most important, from a literary-critical and cultural-historical perspective, is Le Congrès des Ecrivains et Artistes Noirs held in Paris in 1956. See also the extensive coverage of American conferences in Harold Cruse's *The Crisis of the Negro Intellectual* (New York: William Morrow, 1967). It is also worth mentioning as a methodological and argumentative point that Cruse would not be sympathetic to my reading of the "work" of the conferences. For Cruse, the interracial character of the conferences was a betrayal of any possible accomplishment, and the negotiation of identity which took up a great deal of space and time an illusionary obsession and distraction from the creation of sustainable nationalist organizations. I cannot quarrel with Cruse as to the need for such institutions, yet I believe that he makes a crucial mistake in reading the "text" of the conferences—as is often done with African-American literary texts—as transparent and having a direct relationship to "politics."

13. As the decade proceeds, the tone of the meetings changes, becoming increasingly hostile and increasingly chaotic. Compare the description of the first and second Fisk University Black Writers Conferences (1966 and 1967) with the proceedings of the Southern Historical Association Meeting Panel on "The Uses of History in Fiction," documented in *Southern Literary Journal* 1(Spring 1969). See Albert Stone's extended analysis of this event in his *The Return of Nat Turner: History, Literature, and Cultural Politics in Sixties America* (Athens: University of Georgia Press, 1992). Thus the characterization of the aggression as "two-pronged" is a structural simplification, but still useful to an understanding of the case of Robert Hayden.

14. George E. Kent, *A Life of Gwendolyn Brooks* (Lexington: University of Kentucky Press, 1990), 191.

15. *Newsweek*, August 24, 1964.

16. Hoyt Fuller, "The Negro Writer in the U.S.: Assembly at Asilomar," *Negro Digest* 13.11(1964): 42–48.

17. "Harlem Writers' Guild Conference—The New School for Social Research," *Negro Digest* 14.8 (1965): 56. See also Harold Cruse's coverage in *Crisis*, 498–519.

18. Significantly, the most praised gathering at the New School conference was a women's panel which included Paule Marshall, Abbey Lincoln, Alice Childress, and Sarah Wright. The decision of primarily male reporters and editors not to preserve the dialogues of this nascent black feminism is one of the great frustrations for the student of this project. Extensive oral history is necessary, not only for the reconstruction of generalized cultural resistance, but for a more complete understanding of the origins of the African-American feminist renaissance. Paule Marshall's presentation at the New School Conference was entitled "The Negro Woman in American Literature." This text is clearly pioneering as a foreshadowing of the feminist renaissance, yet it is rarely discussed as such. See *Freedomways* 1966 (First Quarter): 8–25.

19. *Negro Digest* 14.8 (1965): 60. Interestingly, Hayden wrote to Hoyt Fuller (July 12, 1965): "I'm awfully glad we had a chance to come to know each other better—about the only thing I am glad for when I think back over *that conference.*" Hayden's response is ironic in that it relates his good feelings about Fuller to the negative atmosphere of the Alabama conference, and doubly so given that a falling-out with Fuller began after the Fisk conference.

20. Page 56 of David Llorens's extended report, "Seeking a New Image: Writers Converge at Fisk University," *Negro Digest* 15.8 (1966): 54–68.

21. Obviously, my work in this chapter is greatly indebted to the work of Victor Turner. See in particular his "Liminal to Liminoid, in Play, Flow and Ritual: An Essay in Comparative Symbology," *Rice University Studies* 60 (1974) and "Social Dramas and Stories about Them," in W.J.T. Mitchell, ed., *On Narrative* (Chicago: University of Chicago Press, 1981) and *The Ritual Process: Structure and Anti-Structure* (Chicago: University of Chicago Press, 1969). The entanglement of my work with that of Sacvan Bercovitch, alluded to in the first chapter, must also be taken up here again as it speaks to the "political" possibilities of antistructural metaphors/events. Turner's conception of the "liminoid" speaks to the characteristics of postindustrial rituals. Contemporary inscriptions of ritual space and their performances tend to be more critical and disruptive of social order. Bercovitch suggests, however, that "In this country, the *unmediated* relation between structure and social ideal has made the very exposure of social flaws part of a ritual of socialization—a sort of liminal interior dialogue that in effect reinforces the mainstream culture," Bercovitch, *The American Jeremiad* (Madison: University of Wisconsin Press, 1978), 204–205. My reservation about Bercovitch's reservation is that the special character of African-American discourse is that it has *attempted* to mediate the distance between reality and dream. While I will make an argument that indeed African-American antimodernism may be destined to "fail," I raise this hesitation given the work that Bercovitch wants "liminality" to perform in the explanation of "classic American texts."

22. Dating the movement is a difficult task, but one that historians might have good cause to take up. We might date it by Leroi Jones's leaving his white wife Hettie Jones; we might date it by the founding of the Black Arts Repertory Theatre School in Harlem. At any rate, the important point is that such a description of a "Black Arts movement" existing in 1966 may in fact be anachronistic, the imposition of a contemporary critical frame.

23. Kent, *Gwendolyn Brooks*, 189.

24. Kent, *Gwendolyn Brooks*, 190.

25. Robert M. Farnsworth, *Melvin B. Tolson, 1898–1966: Plain Talk and Poetic Prophecy* (Columbia: University of Missouri Press, 1984).

26. On scapegoating see René Girard, *Violence and the Sacred* (Baltimore, Md.: Johns Hopkins University Press, 1977). While perhaps invoking a different set of cultural problems than those raised by Turner, I think that Girard's thought offers another interesting possibility for understanding Robert Hayden's experience in the sixties. Girard's notion of "sacrificial substitution" should offer rich possibilities for further exploration into Hayden's life, and, for that matter, into the character of the sixties itself. I'm also tempted by Girard's theorizing because of the ways in which he uses the exploration and elucidation of the "primitive" to explain the modern dilemma. Girard writes: "Modern man flatly rejects the notion that Chance is the reflection of divine will. Primitive man views things differently. For him, Chance embodies all the obvious characteristics of the sacred. Now it deals violently with man, now it showers him with gifts" (314). This could be the source both of a critique of progress, and an inscription of historical indeterminacy. At any rate, in *tone* it seems

to reflect much of what I am trying to communicate about the decade and African-American experience. As Ishmael Reed puts it, "God must be a trickster."

27. I am unable to determine what rumors there might have been in 1966 about Hayden's sexuality. A very few years later he would confess his bisexuality. (See the discussion in Pontheolla Williams, *Robert Hayden: A Critical Analysis of His Poetry* (Urbana: University of Illinois Press, 1987), x.) It is a strong possibility that this would have been a contributing factor in his scapegoating. In some sense, for Hayden, the problem was not lack of power or moral authority, but the *appearance* of that lack.

28. Tolson scholarship is in not much better shape than Hayden scholarship, although it is greatly advanced by the publication of Michael Bérubé's *Marginal Forces/Cultural Centers: Tolson, Pynchon and the Politics of the Canon* (Ithaca, N.Y.: Cornell University Press, 1992). Bérubé treats Tolson with the seriousness he deserves. Bérubé's introduction effectively describes the weaknesses of Joy Flasch's *Melvin Tolson* (Boston: Twayne, 1972) and Robert Farnsworth's *Melvin B. Tolson, 1898–1966*. Other useful essays include Roy Basler, "The Heart of Blackness—M. B. Tolson's Poetry," *New Letters* 39: 63–76; Rita Dove's "Telling It like It I-S *IS* : Narrative Strategies in Melvin Tolson's *Harlem Gallery*," *New England Quarterly* 8: 109–17; William Hansell's "Three Artists in Melvin B. Tolson's *Harlem Gallery*," *Black American Literature Forum* 18.1 (1984): 122–27; Dan McCall, "The Quicksilver Sparrow of M. B. Tolson," *American Quarterly* 18:538–42; Patricia Schroeder, "Point and Counterpoint in *Harlem Gallery*," *College Language Association Journal* 27: 152–68; Gordon Thompson, "Ambiguity in Tolson's *Harlem Gallery*," *Callaloo* 9.1 (1986): 159–70; and Melvin B. Tolson, Jr., "The Poetry of Melvin B. Tolson (1898–1966)," *World Literature Today* 64.3 (1990): 395–400.

29. See Mary Douglas, *Purity and Danger* (London: Routledge and Kegan Paul, 1978).

30. The poet Sarah Webster Fabio nicely summarized Tolson's own cultural dilemma, and, more importantly, was able to direct attention toward the ironic role of cultural power in Tolson's career, the agent that would drive Tolson's accomplishment toward a kind of "black humor": "Melvin Tolson was not a beat poet; he was a part of the neoclassical scene who—although as able as any to attempt the Quixotic feat of reviving a dead horse, albeit a Trojan horse—was denied a rightful place in this theatre of the absurd. Like many Negroes of this period he was told to go back and perfect the art, and then, in the great democratic tradition, he would be accepted into the society of the neo-classicists. He accepted and perfected the art of classical reference as a pillar for an American tradition in literature but became victimized by the cultural lag that is common between the white and Negro worlds. About this time Allen Tate, the Nashville Agrarian poets, and other champions of this movement, gave up this vain pursuit of doing battle with tilting windmills. Therefore, while Tolson busied himself out-pounding Pound, his fellow poets forgot to send him the message that Pound was out." "Who Speaks Negro?" *Negro Digest* 16.2 (1966): 54–58.

31. Gwendolyn Brooks's experience is perhaps the most "dramatic" of the three and further elaborates the notion of the performance of blackness in the American sixties. She was not, however, in the audience that evening in 1966 at Fisk. The third member of that trinity of Renaissance-influenced, African-American modernists, she could not attend the conference.

Brooks did however attend the Second Fisk conference in 1967. Compared to the first conference, the second, called The Black Writer and Human Rights, had a clear Black Power thrust. An antiwar petition in support of Martin Luther King's increasingly radical stand on the war was circulated. John Henrik Clarke argued for the use of the self-descriptive term "Afro-American" as opposed to "Negro"; Lerone Bennett spoke on the need for a literature of "transformation."

For Brooks, arriving from a speaking engagement in the Midwest, the atmosphere and its implications were dramatic. In her autobiography, *Report from Part One* (Detroit: Broadside Press, 1972), she recalls: "Coming from white white white South Dakota State College I arrived in Nashville, Tennessee, to give one more 'reading.' But blood-boiling surprise was in store for me. First, I was aware of a general energy, an electricity, in look, walk, speech, *gesture* of the young blackness I saw all about me. I had been 'loved' at South Dakota State College. Here, I was coldly Respected." (84) Brooks saw this "respect" as an *improvement* over the previous adoration. It spoke to her vocation as poet: "I was in some inscrutable and uncomfortable wonderland. I didn't know what to make of what surrounded me, of what with hot sureness began almost immediately to invade me. *I* had never been, before, in the general presence of such insouciance, such live firmness, such confident vigor, such determination to mold or carve something DEFINITE." (85) Her autobiography shapes the experience of the conference into a clear narrative of conversion.

After Fisk, Brooks returns to Chicago ready to engage actively and with incredible commitment to a dialogue with the Blackstone Rangers, and with up-and-coming poets—Don Lee, Carolyn Rodgers, Johari Amini, Walter Bradford, and others. Her mediation of communal identity will be done "in person" and suggests, perhaps, a feminist counterperformance to the competitiveness of Tolson. Personally, she has come to a new "position," which paradoxically may be multiple; she concludes her meditation on the conference experience by writing:

> I—who have "gone the gamut" from an almost angry rejection of my dark skin by some of my brainwashed brothers and sisters to a surprised queenhood in the new black sun—am qualified to enter at least the kindergarten of new consciousness now. New consciousness and trudge-toward-progress.
>   I have hopes for myself. (86)

32. Hayden scholarship is, not surprisingly, still in its infancy. Indeed, Hayden is the example par excellence of a repression of dissonance. It is difficult to talk about Hayden within the contours of a limited and limiting politics. Useful texts include John Hatcher, *From the Auroral Darkness: The Life and Poetry of Robert Hayden* (Oxford, England: George Ronald, 1984); Pontheolla T. Williams, *Robert Hayden: A Critical Analysis of His Poetry* (Urbana: University of Illinois Press, 1987); and Fred Fetrow, *Robert Hayden* (Boston: Twayne, 1984). Charles Davis's "Robert Hayden's Use of History," in his *Black Is the Color of the Cosmos: Essays on Afro-American Literature 1942–1981* (New York: Garland, 1981), is the best single essay on Hayden's work, although these are also helpful: Fred Fetrow, "Robert Hayden's 'Frederick Douglass': Form and Meaning in a Modern Sonnet," *College Language Association Journal* 17 (1973): 79–84, and "Minority Reporting and Psychic Distancing in the Poetry of Robert Hayden," *College Language Association Journal* 33 (1989): 117–29; Fritz Oehlschlaeger, "Robert Hayden's Meditation on Art: The Final Sequence of *Words in the Mourning Time*," *Black American Literature Forum* 19 (1985): 115–19; Michael S. Harper, "A Symbolist Poet Struggling With Historical Fact," *New York Times Book Review*, February 22, 1976, 34–35; Julius Lester, "For a World Where a Man," *New York Times Book Review*, January 24, 1971, 4–5, 22; Maurice J. O'Sullivan, "The Mask of Illusion in Robert Hayden's 'The Diver,'" *College Language Association Journal* 17.1 (1973): 85–92; and John O'Brien's interview with Hayden in *Interviews With Black Writers* (New York: Liveright, 1973). Hayden's *Collected Poetry* and *Collected Prose* have

been published by the University of Michigan Press (1984). I have also had access to Hayden's collected letters currently being edited by Professor Xavier Nicholas of Tuskegee University and am grateful for his permission to quote from the letters.

33. In 1949, he and a small circle of writers primarily under his tutelage published the manifesto *Counterpoise*. The document was meant to initiate a series of books, edited by Hayden, published in Nashville. It asserted:

> we are unalterably opposed to the chauvinistic, the cultish, to special pleading, to all that seeks to limit and restrict creative expression
>
> . . .
>
> as writers who belong to a so-called minority we are violently opposed to having our work viewed, as the custom is, entirely in the light of sociology and politics
>
> . . .
>
> as poets we naturally believe that it is more profitable for our generation to read good poetry than it is to listen to soap opera, since poetry has humanistic and spiritual values not to be ignored with impunity
>
> we believe in the oneness of mankind and the importance of the arts in the struggle for peace and unity.

See Robert Hayden, *The Collected Prose* (Ann Arbor: University of Michigan Press, 1984), 41–42.

The "we" of this manifesto sounds much like the "we" who were not trying to escape during the conference. Hayden was consciously trying to imagine a community which might celebrate humanistic values. Ironically, Hayden was given little credit for this or any other literary accomplishment. While Hayden's racial politics would continue to disturb cultural nationalists, the document's forthrightness, its refusal to compromise might have made it a useful resource or at least a significant milestone. It is worth noting that he articulates here many of the elements of the social critique I am trying to document in this book: suspicion of mass culture, veneration of the aesthetic realm, and commitment to a general set of "spiritual values."

34. "During the fifties, Hayden's personal life was saddened by the death of his natural parents, and it was made even more insecure by an identity crisis. Having lost both of his adoptive parents . . . with whom he lived until they died, he lost his natural father between 1950 and 1955 . . . and in 1957 suffered his most traumatic loss when his natural mother died. Prior to her demise and free of the Haydens' presence, he enjoyed a closer relationship with her—a relationship in which she irrevocably secured his kinship and artistic ties to her family and to her forebears. She convinced him that the Haydens did not legally adopt him, and she declared that his true name, the name she and his father gave him, was Asa Bundy Sheffey. It was the name he wished to legally adopt" (Williams, *Robert Hayden*, 29–30).

35. As well as William Demby and Julius Lester, Hayden taught and mentored Lonnie Elder, C. Eric Lincoln, Norman Loftis, and Nikki Giovanni, among others.

36. See "Bob's Place: An Oasis of Civility," reprinted in Gerald Early, ed., *Speech and Power* vol. 2 (New York: Ecco Press, 1993), 526–28.

37. See Robert Hayden, *Collected Prose*, 47–54. Originally published in James E. Miller, Jr., Robert Hayden, and Robert O'Neal, eds., *The United States in Literature*, (Glenview, IL: Scott, Foresman, 1973)

38. In the case of Jones/Baraka, for instance, there was certainly evidence that Hayden did not wish to simply condemn. In a letter to Hoyt Fuller, January 26,

1968, Hayden expressed regret at his recent in-print treatment of Jones. "In view of his recent imprisonment and the dubious circumstances surrounding it, I certainly have no desire to add to his pain or attack him for his 'militancy.' I am not so much of the 'Establishment' that I take pleasure in injuring, either by word or deed, fellow artists with whom I disagree."

39. See Robert Hayden, *Collected Prose*, 55–59. Originally published in Robert Hayden, ed., *Kaleidoscope* (New York: Harcourt, Brace, & World, 1967).

40. See Robert Hayden, *Collected Prose*, 60–65. Originally published in *The New Negro*, ed. by Alain Locke (New York: Atheneum, 1968).

41. Gwendolyn Brooks, "Review of Robert Hayden's *Selected Poems*," *Negro Digest*, October 15.12 (1966), 51–52.

42. In a letter to the anthologist Rosey Poole, October 19, 1961, Hayden wrote: "As to "No Words", —this poem was salvaged from a longer piece which was more racial rhetoric than poetry. I found that when the integration riots occurred I was so appalled and so angry that what I wrote was propaganda rather than poetry. The present poem crystallizes better than anything else I was able to write what my inmost, deepest feelings must have been. On the whole I would say that I certainly have no desire to escape the implications of the Negro situation but want always to deal with them as an artist (pretentious me!) rather than a journalist or pleader of a cause." This is extremely revealing and should contribute to a revision of the belief that there is no tension in Hayden's aesthetic. By transforming *and* salvaging his feelings he acknowledges the simultaneity of identities.

43. Robert Hayden, *Collected Prose*, 74–75. Originally published as "The Poetry Scene" to accompany the recording *Today's Poets: Their Poems—Their Voices*, 4 (Scholastic Records FS11004), edited by Stephen Dunning.

44. The Robert Hayden Papers are located at the Baha'i National Archives, Wilmette, Illinois.

45. Letter from Hayden to David Littlejohn, September 2, 1966.

46. Arguably, Hayden only received two negative reviews throughout the 1960s and the 1970s. *Selected Poems* went into a fourth printing. And by the late sixties there was a clear circle of African-American writers who had gravitated toward him, including Jay Wright, James Allen McPherson, Michael Harper, Lucille Clifton, and James Emmanuel. And whatever bad feelings were left were in some ways exorcised by Julius Lester's rightfully famous review of *Words in the Mourning Time* in the *New York Times Book Review*, January 24, 1971, 4–5, 22. Lester wrote: "Now I know that his desire to be regarded as nothing more or less than a poet was not a denial of his blackness, but the only way he knew of saying that blackness was not big enough to contain him. He wanted to live in the universe."

47. Unpublished letter from Hayden to Rosey Poole, October 18, 1967.

48. Pontheolla Williams, *Robert Hayden*, 30.

49. All friends and acquaintances of Hayden's too. It is also worth noting at this point that Hayden and Tolson had a respectful friendship, making their Fisk exchange that much more mysterious.

50. And this use of the "figurative" is parallel to my own, and, I hope, as I alluded to in my preface, a prime example of the ways in which I am trying to take cues from my subject matter.

51. See *Collected Poems*, 27. Other poems could be used here. Perhaps especially pertinent would be "Frederick Douglass," the poem that Hayden wanted read by Michael Harper at his memorial, which suggests how he wanted his crisis to be understood (*Collected Poems*, 62.):

When it is finally ours, this freedom, this liberty, this beautiful
and terrible thing, needful to man as air,
usable as earth; when it belongs at last to all,
when it is truly instinct, brain matter, diastole, systole,
reflex action; when it is finally won; when it is more
than the gaudy mumbo jumbo of politicians:
this man, this Douglass, this former slave, this Negro
beaten to his knees, exiled, visioning a world
where none is lonely, none hunted, alien,
this man, superb in love and logic, this man
shall be remembered. Oh, not with statues' rhetoric,
not with legends and poems and wreaths of bronze alone,
but with the lives grown out of his life, the lives
fleshing his dream of the beautiful, needful thing.

52. Hayden's contact with surrealism occurs through an introduction to the 1940s and 1950s work of Romare Bearden. See Williams, *Robert Hayden*, 58.

53. Robert Hayden, *Words in the Mourning Time* (New York: October House, 1970).

54. The publication of *Ballad of Remembrance* was delayed for some time. After Hayden had won the Grand Prix for Poetry at the Dakar Festival, he was, some months later, still trying to find someone who would confirm the award and present him with his prize money. In his correspondence, Hayden suggests that he had expected *Words* to have appeared a full year earlier.

55. John Hatcher suggests that the soldier is Sinda's brother; Fred Fetrow suggests that the soldier is Sinda's son. I was initially inclined to believe that Sinda was the soldier's grandmother, but am now convinced that Pontheolla Williams is correct not to attempt to "solve" the relationship at all. In some respects, this indeterminacy best supports Hayden's aims for this section of the book.

56. See Williams, *Robert Hayden*, 122–24.

57. No commentator has explored what would have been the ironic historical resonance of the title. The story of the "Soledad Brothers" was front page news in the winter of 1969. George Jackson and two other black men were accused of killing a white prison guard at Soledad prison. An attempt by Jackson's brother, Jonathan, to free them through the taking of hostages in a courtroom resulted in Jonathan's death. The prison writings of George Jackson were published in the fall of 1970 around the same time as *Words in the Mourning Time*.

58. It is true that Baha'i teachings emphasize a terrible upheaval before all individuals can live in peace. And indeed, Hayden does directly point to such teachings. On the other hand, the sophistication of his "private poems" maintains mystery and unsolvability over and against all systems.

59. Edith Hamilton and Huntington Cairns, eds., *Plato: The Collected Dialogues* (Princeton, N.J.: Princeton University Press, 1961), 94.

60. Stephen Henderson, *Understanding the New Black Poetry* (New York: Morrow, 1973), 27.

61. See "Discovering America: Generational Shifts, Afro-American Literary Criticism, and the Study of Expressive Culture," in *Blues, Ideology and Afro-American Literature: A Vernacular Theory* (Chicago: University of Chicago Press, 1984).

62. With our tendency to put a "few" black aesthetic poets (usually male, understood as misdirected) in opposition to a "few" craftsmen ("good" poets, but not REALLY good) we risk letting slip through the cracks (which are becoming canyons)

the multiple varieties of African-American poetic productions in the sixties: the Umbra poets of New York, the Last Poets of Chicago, the Yardbird crowd, early feminist poetry, and so on. Indeed, one convention of African-American culture in the decade might be seen as the poetic manifesto, the statement of aesthetic, political, social, and economic principles upon which the practice of African-American poetry might be based. Despite historical clichés, these were amazingly diverse in concern and focus. See Clarence Major, "A Black Criteria," *Journal of Black Poetry* 1 4:15 (1967); Carolyn Rodgers, "Black Poetry—Where It's At," *Negro Digest*, 18 (September 1969): 7–16; Alvin Aubert, "Black American Poetry: Its Language and Folk Tradition," *Black Academy Review* 2.2 (1971): 71–80; Bernard W. Bell, "New Black Poetry: A Double Edged Sword," *College Language Association Journal* 15 (1971): 37–43; Don L. Lee, "Toward a Black Aesthetic—Black Poetry Which Direction?" *Negro Digest* 17 (October 1968): 27–32; and *Dynamite Voices* (Detroit: Broadside Press, 1971); Richard Barksdale, "Urban Crisis and the Black Poetic Avant-Garde," *Negro American Literature Forum* 3 (1969): 40–44; Arna Bontemps, "American Negro Poetry," *The Crisis* 70 (1963): 509; and Abraham Chapman, "Black Poetry Today," *Arts in Society* 5 (1968): 401–408. And, again, Aldon Nielsen's *Black Chant: Languages of African American Modernism* (New York: Cambridge University Press, 1997) is a superb reconstruction of the diversity of this poetic production.

63. Richard M. Nixon, quoted in Manning Marable, *Race, Reform, and Rebellion: The Second Reconstruction in Black America, 1945–1982* (Jackson: University Press of Mississippi, 1984), 109.

64. From *Where Do We Go From Here: Chaos or Community?* (1967) contained in James M. Washington, ed., *A Testament of Hope: The Essential Writings of Martin Luther King, Jr.* (New York: Harper Collins, 1986), 575.

65. William Rice, "The Example of Robert Hayden," *The New Criterion* 8 (November 1989), 45.

66. Richard Ruland and Malcolm Bradbury, *From Puritanism to Postmodernism: A History of American Literature* (New York: Penguin, 1991), 401.

67. One significant hesitation of this chapter has been to discuss in great depth the psychology of such cultural-identity dramas. American Studies scholars often turn to the work of Erik Erikson (or more cautiously to Freud) for assistance in this regard. Given that African-American psychologists have expressed great reservations about the applicability of Erikson's approach to African-American experience, I have tended to leave this question open for now. For possibilities along these lines see Arnold Rampersad's discussion of the usefulness of psychoanalytic theory for African-American biography ("Biography and Afro-American Culture," in Baker and Redmond, eds., *Afro-American Literary Study*, 194–208) and discussions taking place in the field of African-American psychology: W. E. Cross, Jr., et al, "Stages of Black Identity Development: Nigresence Models," in R. L. Jones, ed., *Black Psychology* (Berkeley, Calif.: Cobb and Henry, 1991), and Charles Valentine, "Deficit, Difference, and Bicultural Models of Afro-American Behavior," *Harvard Educational Review* 41 (1971): 137–57.

68. See Davis, *Black Is the Color of the Cosmos* for a complete discussion of Hayden's "historicity."

CHAPTER 3

1. Leslie Fiedler, *Love and Death in the American Novel*, rev. ed. (New York: Dell, 1966), 27. Despite Fiedler's manipulation of the language of "blackness"—and his status as a kind of sixties enfant terrible of the literary critical world—I have not been able to find any commentary that connects his work to the "Black aesthetic."—

Given that "exceptionalism" and "nationalism" have much in common, this investigation may prove fruitful.

2. Franz Fanon, *Les Damnés de la terre* (1961); *The Wretched of the Earth* (New York: Grove, 1963), 316.

3. There is an interesting sixties literature that examines these connections from a critical perspective. See for instance, Gwendolyn Brooks, *Report from Part I* (Detroit: Broadside Press, 1972). See also chapter 2, note 11.

4. See Van Gosse's excellent *Where the Boys Are: Cuba, Cold War America, and the Making of a New Left* (New York: Verso, 1993), especially "'From One Liberator to Another': Afro-Cuban-American Solidarity," 147–54. Gosse's treatment of the African-American journalist Richard Gibson is especially pertinent.

5. Quoted in Gosse, *Where the Boys Are*, 122.

6. I am indebted to Philip Dine, *Images of the Algerian War: French Fiction and Film, 1954–1992* (Oxford: Clarendon Press, 1994) and David Schalk, *War and the Ivory Tower: Algeria and Vietnam* (New York: Oxford University Press, 1991) for this discussion.

7. Lewis Gordon, *Fanon and the Crisis of European Man* (New York: Routledge, 1995), 6. It is worth mentioning here that if there was perhaps one African-American intellectual suspicious of much of what has been identified here as antimodern, it may have been Richard Wright. See, in particular, his "Tradition and Industrialization," in *White Man, Listen!* (New York: Doubleday, 1957).

8. *Wretched of the Earth*, 316.

9. John Talbott, *The War Without a Name: France in Algeria, 1954–1962* (New York: Knopf, 1980), 93.

10. Bernard Bell identifies both "continuity and change". "As contemporary Afro-American novelists attempt to displace personal ambivalence and social absurdity with a new order of thinking, feeling, and sharing based on self-determination, a sense of community, and a respect for human rights, most . . . continue the tradition of realism . . . some . . . explore poetic realism. Others . . . experiment with modern forms of slave narrative, romance, fable, and satire." *The Afro-American Novel and Its Tradition* (Amherst: University of Massachusetts Press, 1987), 245. While Bell's "anthropological" study is pioneering—the scope of his vision is broad and inclusive, his catalogue of novels helpful and necessary—his cultural analysis seems obvious and surface. He seems to suggest that Afro-American novelists should hold more vigorously to "hope." The danger here, I think, is a restatement of truisms about "protest." This problem is even more apparent in Melissa Walker's *Down From the Mountaintop: Black Women's Novels in the Wake of the Civil Rights Movement, 1966–1989* (New Haven, Conn.: Yale University Press, 1991) which operates with only the most basic of models—"reflection"—for understanding the relationship between history and literature. Walker writes: "When I began this book, I felt that I was venturing into virgin territory by even raising questions about how narratives reflect, grow out of, or examine the complex set of phenomena that make up the struggle for racial justice. Since then others, including Hazel Carby, have completed projects that confront in different and somewhat larger contexts some of the issues considered here. While I acknowledge that issues of gender, class, feminism, canonization, and literary theory are all relevant to a global comprehension of a body of literature, my aim is limited, linear, and concentrated. The big picture, I believe, will not be a panoramic and synthetic view of carefully integrated parts, but a pastiche of bits and pieces periodically held together in the tension of a moment, only to be rearranged under the pressure of changing times" (12). Walker's conquest of "virgin territory" seems to me ultimately more dangerous than Bell's anthropological

sweep. What Walker most wants to avoid in avoiding "relevant" issues is the question of her own authority. Her neat narrative ensures that discomforting questions about the production and distribution of the idea of "civil rights" and its narratives will remain unanswered.

11. For "exhaustion" see John Barth, "The Literature of Exhaustion, "collected in his *The Friday Book* (New York: Putnam, 1984). The exceptions to the alienation from Black Arts may be Greenlee, who clearly projects a kind of crude novelistic black power statement; George Cain, whose *Blueschild Baby* (1971) is one of the most successful attempts at representing and dramatizing the black vernacular, and is perhaps only matched by Melvin Van Peebles's film *Sweet Sweetback's Baaaaad Aass Song* (1971); and those writers who manipulate what Arthur Davis has called a kind of ghetto realism: Louise Meriweather, Sarah Wright, John McCluskey, and John Wideman in some of his aspects. Similarly, as many commentators have pointed out, Ishmael Reed and Clarence Major's novelistic experiments seem to share much with the Anglo-American postmoderns Pynchon, Brautigan, Barth, and Coover, although little effort has been made to point out the specifics of the genealogy. See Robert Eliot Fox, *Conscientious Sorcerers: The Black Postmodernist Fiction of LeRoi Jones/Amiri Baraka, Ishmael Reed, and Samuel R. Delany* (Westport, Conn.: Greenwood Press, 1987). Morris Dickstein's chapters "Black Writing and Black Nationalism" and "Fiction at the Crossroads: Dilemmas of the Experimental Writer," from his *Gates of Eden: American Culture in the Sixties* (New York: Penguin, 1989) are also very useful in thinking through these connections.

12. Pertinent texts are Kristin Hunter, *God Bless the Child* (1964; Washington, D.C.: Howard University Press, 1986); Ronald Fair, *The Hog Butcher* (New York: Harcourt, Brace & World, 1966); Ernest Gaines, *Catherine Carmier* (New York: Dial, 1964) and *Of Love and Dust* (New York: Dial, 1967); Margaret Walker, *Jubilee* (Boston: Houghton Mifflin, 1966); Gordon Parks, *The Learning Tree* (New York: Harper & Row, 1963); and John Killens, *And Then We Heard The Thunder* (New York: Knopf, 1963) and *'Sippi* (New York: Trident, 1967).

13. It is also worth suggesting that the novelist is constrained by the shape of the institution needed to produce a novel. African-American poetry in the sixties changes dramatically because of the swift transfer of texts among producers and consumers. It is not unusual that a poet in Indiana State Prison (Etheridge Knight) might exchange "work" with Gwendolyn Brooks, nor is it improbable that institutional alternatives like Broadside Press would be viable. The economic and critical resources required to produce novels, however, meant that African-American artists would remain reliant upon the "major" publishing concerns. In the later 1970s, the writers Ishmael Reed and Steve Cannon were able to establish a publishing imprint for novels, and one of their most acclaimed texts was William Demby's *Love Story Black* (New York: Reed, Cannon, and Johnson, 1978). This institutional and formal problem is rich with potential, and as a result I have turned away from a writer of short fiction like James Allen McPherson despite the ways in which his work is consistent with African-American antimodernism.

14. See Reginald Martin, *Ishmael Reed and the New Black Aesthetic Critics* (New York: St. Martin's, 1988) for a full consideration of Reed's engagement with the Black Arts writers.

15. Collected in Larry Neal, *Visions of a Liberated Future* (New York: Thunder's Mouth, 1989), 24–61.

16. Arthur Davis, "Novels of the New Black Renaissance (1960–1977): A Thematic Survey," *CLA Journal* 21.4 (1978): 457–90, provides a vast survey but only offers general statements about the "direction" of the black novel. Melvin Wade and

Margaret Wade, "The Black Aesthetic in the Black Novel," *Journal of Black Studies* 2.4 (1972): 391-408, seem to find few examples of "blackness" in more contemporary novels, even as they attempt to extend Stephen Henderson's work to the novel as form. The most important exceptions to this general characterization might be Addison Gayle's *The Way of the New World: The Black Novel in America* (New York: Doubleday, 1975)—following, as it does, his *The Black Aesthetic* (Garden City, N.Y.: Doubleday, 1971)—and some of the sections of Houston Baker's *The Journey Back: Issues in Black Literature and Criticism* (Chicago: University of Chicago Press, 1980). Gayle speaks of the late sixties and early seventies: "At long last, form and structure were recognized as little more than cousins to content, and the black novelist, machine gunner in the cause of mankind, prepared to move forward in the most monumental undertaking of the twentieth century—the task of redefining the definitions, creating new myths, symbols, and images, articulating new values, and recording the progression of a great people from social and political awareness to consciousness of their historical importance as a people and as a nation within a nation—a task which demanded, in the words of poet Don L. Lee, that black people 'walk the way of the New World,'" xx.

17. David Littlejohn, *Black on White: A Critical Survey of Writings by American Negroes* (New York: Grossman, 1966); Edward Margolies, *Native Sons: A Critical Study of Twentieth Century Negro American Authors* (Philadelphia: Lippincott, 1968); and Robert A. Bone, *The Negro Novel in America*, rev. ed. (New Haven, Conn.: Yale University Press, 1965). Typical of the response to the above is Darwin T. Turner's "The Negro Novel in America: In Rebuttal," *CLA Journal* 10 (1966): 122-34. The general "crisis of authority" can be recounted through the previously mentioned Howe-Ellison debate, Stone's *The Return of Nat Turner*, and Richard Gilman's *The Confusion of Realms* (New York: Random House, 1969). The reprints mentioned are Hugh Gloster, *Negro Voices in American Fiction* (1948; New York: Russell and Russell, 1965); Benjamin Brawley, *The Negro in Literature and Art in the United States* (1921; New York: AMS Press, 1971), and Vernon Loggins, *The Negro Author, His Development in America to 1900* (1931; New York: Kennikat, 1964). Other important contributions to the decade include: Richard K. Barksdale, "Alienation and the Anti-Hero in Recent American Fiction," *CLA Journal* 10 (1966): 1-10; Hoyt Fuller, "Contemporary Negro Fiction," *Southwest Review* 50 (1965): 321-35; Blyden Jackson, "The Negro's Negro in Negro Literature," *Michigan Quarterly Review* 4 (1965): 290-95; and Darwin T. Turner, "The Negro Novelist and the South," *Southern Humanities Review* 1 (1967): 21-29.

18. Warner Berthoff, *A Literature Without Qualities: American Writing Since 1945* (Berkeley: University of California Press, 1979).

19. My general thinking about this subject has been shaped by Randolph Bourne, "On Trans-National America," in his *History of a Literary Radical and Other Essays* (New York: Biblo and Tannen, 1969); Franz Fanon, "On National Consciousness," in *The Wretched of the Earth*; and the essays in Homi K. Bhaba, ed., *Nation and Narration* (London: Routledge, 1990).

20. On Paule Marshall the most complete and challenging reading is offered by Hortense Spillers, "Chosen Place, Timeless People: Some Figurations on the New World," in Marjorie Pryse and Hortense J. Spillers, eds., *Conjuring: Black Women, Fiction, and Literary Tradition* (Bloomington: Indiana University Press, 1985), 151-75. See also Barbara Christian, *Black Women Novelists: The Development of a Tradition, 1892-1976* (Westport, Conn.: Greenwood Press, 1980), 80-136; Edward Braithwaite, "Rehabilitation," *Critical Quarterly* 13 (Summer 1971): 175-83 and "West Indian History and Society in the Art of Paule Marshall's Novel," *Journal of Black Studies* 1

(1970): 225-38; Eugenia Collier, "The Closing of the Circle: Movement from Division to Wholeness in Paule Marshall's Fiction," in Mari Evans, ed., *Black Women Writers, 1950-1980* (New York: Doubleday, 1984), 295-313; Leela Kapai, "Dominant Themes and Techniques in Paule Marshall's Fiction," *CLA Journal* 16 (1972): 49-59; Marcia Keiza, "Themes and Style in the Works of Paule Marshall," *Negro American Literature Forum* 9 (Fall 1975): 67-76; John McCluskey, Jr., "And Called Every Generation Blessed: Theme, Setting, and Ritual in the Works of Paule Marshall," in Evans, *Black Women Writers*, 316-34; Peter Nazareth, "Paule Marshall's Timeless People," *New Letters* 40 (Autumn 1973): 116-31; and Winnifred Stoelting, "Time Past and Time Present: The Search for Viable Links in *The Chosen Place, The Timeless People*," *CLA Journal* 16: 60-71. There has been important new work on Marshall from a variety of perspectives over the past few years: See Joyce Pettis, *Toward Wholeness in Paule Marshall's Fiction* (Charlottesville: University Press of Virginia, 1995); Dorothy Hamer Denniston, *The Fiction of Paule Marshall: Reconstructions of History, Culture, and Gender* (Knoxville: University of Tennessee Press, 1995); and Stelamaris Coser, *Bridging the Americas: The Literature of Toni Morrison, Paule Marshall, and Gayl Jones* (Philadelphia, Pa.: Temple University Press, 1994).

21. See Fredric Jameson, *Postmodernism, or the Cultural Logic of Late-Capitalism* (Durham, N.C.: Duke University Press, 1991).

22. Paule Marshall, "The Poets in the Kitchen," in *Reena and Other Stories* (New York: Feminist Press, 1983), 9.

23. Wilson Harris, *The Womb of Space: The Cross-Cultural Imagination* (Westport, Conn.: Greenwood Press, 1983), 57.

24. Barbara Christian, "Paule Marshall," *Dictionary of Literary Biography*, vol. 33 (Detroit: Gale Research, 1986).

25. Biographical information on Marshall can be found in the entry by Barbara Christian in the *Dictionary of Literary Biography*, 161-170; Alexis De Veaux, "Paule Marshall—In Celebration of Our Triumphs," *Essence* 11 (May 1980): 96, 98, 123-24, and "Paule Marshall," in Evans, ed., *Black Women Writers*. See also the crucial Paule Marshall, "Shaping the World of My Art," *New Letters* 40 (Autumn 1973): 97-112.

26. See Harold Cruse, *Crisis of the Negro Intellectual* (New York: Morrow, 1967), 198-201, 207-208. More importantly see Paule Marshall, "The Negro Woman in American Literature," *Freedomways* 6 (Winter 1966): 21-25. In his introduction to *Soul Clap Hands and Sing* (1961; Washington, D.C.: Howard University Press, 1988) Darwin Turner notes that Killens ridiculed Marshall's work in his 1971 novel *The Cotillion*.

27. *Browngirl, Brownstones* (orig. pub., 1959, New York: Feminist Press, 1981)

28. Marshall, "Shaping the World," 108.

29. See Turner's introduction to *Soul Clap Hands and Sing*, xv-xvii.

30. Barbara Christian notes that in regard to Marshall's work on *Our World* magazine: "Even though she was a Phi Beta Kappa, she was also the only woman on the staff of *Our World* and she felt, she later said, as if 'the men were waiting for me to fail.' This conjuncture of the personal and the political is even more dramatically represented in the attempt to write her second book *Soul Clap Hands and Sing*: [the book] was written after Paule Marshall had just had a baby, her only child, Evan-Keith, to whom she dedicates the book. She reveals that despite her husband's objections, she got help to stay with her son and went off to a friend's apartment every day to work on her new book. . . . At least, in the last ten years, essays such as Tillie Olsen's *Silences* and Alice Walker's "In Search of Our Mother's Gardens" propelled into the public forum discussion about the relationship between woman's artistic creativity and the creativity of her womb. But in 1960 such

discussion was hardly occurring, and the individual woman writer had to rely on the strength of her own belief that her need to express herself was as important as the society's demands on mothers" ("Paule Marshall," 163 and 165). It is also worth pointing out Marshall's provocative evaluation in *Soul Clap Hands* of Yeats's "Sailing to Byzantium," and, again as Darwin Turner observes, her seemingly replaying the litany of T. S. Eliot's themes and criticisms.

31. Collected in Paule Marshall, *Reena and Other Stories* (New York: Feminist Press, 1983).

32. Marshall, "Shaping the World," 110–11.

33. For relevant reviews see Robert Bone, *New York Times Book Review*, November 31, 1969, 24; Bell Gale Chevigny, *Village Voice*, October 8, 1970, 6–8; Jean Carey Bond, "Allegorical Novel by Talented Storyteller," *Freedomways* 1 (1970); Judy Michaelson, "Black Before Her Time," *New York Post*, December 6, 1969; Thomas Lask, "Promise and Fulfillment," *New York Times*, November 8, 1969; and Alice Kizer Bennett, *Dallas Morning News*, January 4, 1970.

34. This complicated landscape suggests that it would be worth exploring the complicated disaster of James Baldwin's *Tell Me How Long the Train's Been Gone*, published in 1969, as were all the texts mentioned above. Baldwin, having chosen one difficult model in Henry James, had become interested in the work of John Cheever in particular, even as he desperately wanted to be part of the new Cleaver/Carmichael/Brown discourse.

35. Marshall's implicit critique of the institution of American social science is also suggestive of the presence of the influence of Ralph Ellison. See Ellison's critique of Gunnar Myrdal's *American Dilemma* in *Shadow and Act*.

36. Paule Marshall, *The Chosen Place, The Timeless People* (1969; New York: Vintage, 1984), 5.

37. Paule Marshall, *Reena*, 109.

38. I would also state here that this is a crucial historical intrusion; it furthers Albert Stone's argument about the centrality of the "consciousness" of the slave rebellion to an understanding of the sixties and suggests that there are interesting textual parallels to be drawn here between Marshall, the William Styron controversy, and its "product texts" like David Bradley's *The Chaneysville Incident* and Shirley Ann Williams's *Dessa Rose*.

39. Hortense Spillers, in "Figurations" (172–73), has documented the response of the critic Judith Fetterly who, given Allen's decision and the association of Merle's rumored lesbian lover with imperialist control, has suggested the novel is homophobic. Spillers focuses on the question of Merle and argues that the important point is the inequality between Merle and her London patron, and that sexuality is a peripheral issue. My own reading is that Marshall conceived—pre-Stonewall rebellion, we might add— of this relationship and Allen's identity as difficult sites of nonconformity in their own right that needed to be unpacked on their own terms. Simply put, this makes things more complex. Unfortunately, when not read in tension with other kinds of resistance, contemporary readers might be inclined to see gay identity in the novel as a "negative." Spillers extends this inquiry in her "Black, White, and in Color, or Learning How to Paint: Toward an Intramural Protocol of Reading," in Jeffrey N. Cox and Larry J. Reynolds, eds., *New Historical Literary Study: Essays on Reproducing Texts, Representing History* (Princeton, N.J.: Princeton University Press, 1993), 267–91.

40. "Without taking allegiance with either the traditionalists or the Black Arts writers, Paule Marshall imbibed the exhilarating spirits of both groups and distilled them into a literature that exudes the spirit of the era." Turner, Introduction to *Soul*

Clap Hands, xxx. While Turner is inclined, I think, not to question the purity of his categories, I would argue that this "distillation" is similar to what I have tried to describe as African-American antimodernism, and the spirit, Hegelian in character, of what I am trying to capture in this book.

41. Most striking, Marshall's long and complex novel gets no mention in the works of Henry Louis Gates, Jr., or Houston Baker. More troubling still, *The Chosen Place, The Timeless People* receives little, if any, attention in most collections of feminist criticism. The absence of *The Chosen Place, The Timeless People* might, of course, be "overread." Paule Marshall herself has suggested that she thinks that the text is now "coming into its own" (Personal conversation, January 1992).

42. While at the same time Marshall has said in describing her allegiance to the work of Thomas Mann, Thomas Hardy, Joseph Conrad, and Richard Wright that "I realize that it is fashionable now to dismiss the traditional novel as something of an anachronism, but to me it is still a vital form. Not only does it allow for the kind of full-blown, richly detailed, visual writing that I love (I want the reader to *see* the people and places about which I am writing), but it permits me to operate on many levels and to explore both the inner state of my characters as well as the larger world beyond them" ("Shaping the World," 105).

43. From Henry Louis Gates, Jr., ed., *Black Literature and Literary Theory* (New York: Methuen, 1984), 263–84.

44. I am attempting to be somewhat reflexive here. I am interested in addressing some of the difficulties inherent in theoretical models to which I have been often attracted. I'm thinking especially of M. M. Bakhtin and Victor Turner. I have interpreted Marshall's novel as a call to interrogate the "radical-ness," if you will, of models of heteroglossia, communitas, carnival, all constructions of textual and ritual transformation. Marshall calls us to evaluate the ultimate subversive potential of these models, and, I would argue, the faithfulness they might represent.

45. Harris, *Womb,* 65.

46. Quoted in Margaret Perry, "William Demby," *Dictionary of Literary Biography,* vol. 33 (Detroit: Gale Research, 1986).

47. Biographical information on Demby can be found in the entry by Margaret Perry cited in note 46, on pages 59–64. On *The Catacombs,* Nathan Scott's introduction (ix–xx) to the new Northeastern Press edition of the text is very helpful (Boston: Northeastern University Press, 1991). See also: Robert Bone, "William Demby's Dance of Life," *Triquarterly* 15 (Spring 1969): 127–141; Joseph F. Connelly, "William Demby's Fiction: The Pursuit of the Muse," *Negro American Literature Forum* 10 (Fall 1976): 1001–03; Edward Margolies, "The Expatriate as Novelist: William Demby," in his *Native Sons: A Critical Study of Twentieth-Century Black American Authors* (Philadelphia: Lippincott, 1968), 173–89; the brief discussion in Roger Whitlow, *Black American Literature: A Critical History* (Chicago: Nelson Hall, 1973), 122–25; John O'Brien, ed., *Interviews with Black Writers* (New York: Liveright, 1973), 34–53. Nathan Scott also notes his enthusiasm for Demby's work and his belief that Demby's *Beetlecreek* "represents the most impressive work done by any Negro writer in the decade following the first emergence of Richard Wright," in his essay on "Black Literature," in Daniel Hoffman, ed., *Harvard Guide to Contemporary American Writing* (Cambridge, Mass.: Harvard University Press, 1979), 287–341. See also my afterword to a new edition of *Beetlecreek* (Jackson: University Press of Mississippi, 1998).

48. Demby's use of "Gothic" should not so much remind us of the characteristics of a Gothic novel, as it should point us to the use of the term in opposition to "classic," and especially in the sense that it had as a critical term for the Romantics. For them, the Gothic "suggested whatever was medieval, natural, primitive, wild, free,

authentic." (Holman, *A Handbook to Literature*, 4th ed. [Indianapolis: Bobbs-Merrill, 1980], 204). It is also worth noting Leslie Fiedler's investigation of the American romance as comprising the sentimental—the narrative of love—and the gothic—the narrative of death. I will return to Marshall and Demby as revisionary of this particular Romantic tradition.

49. *Beetlecreek*, suggests Margaret Perry, "derived from 'St. Joey,' a short story written for Robert Hayden's creative writing class at Fisk in 1946." Perry, "William Demby," 60. Hayden traveled and lived in Mexico in 1954–55.

50. Quoted in Perry, "William Demby," 60.

51. One of the interesting dilemmas or paradoxes that emerge fully with an examination of the contributions of Marshall and Demby is the realization that the most profound antimodernism requires the most involved consideration and, in some sense, submission to modernity. The value of Henry Adams's resistance is his recognition of the connections between the Virgin and the dynamo. Marshall, Demby, and other African-American antimodernists are distinguished from other black artists by their struggle to come to terms with notions like alienation and crisis.

52. Interestingly, Demby wrote for the middle-brow tourist magazine *Holiday* in the mid-Fifties and early Sixties. See "A Walk in Tuscany," *Holiday* 22 (December 1957): 140 ff. and "Blueblood Cats of Rome," *Holiday* 27 (April 1960): 203–206.

53. "For a symptom to be admitted as such in psychoanalytical psychotherapy—whether a neurotic symptom or not—Freud insists on the minimum of overdetermination as constituted by a double meaning: it must symbolize a conflict long dead over and above its function in a no less symbolic present conflict." Jacques Lacan, "The Function of Language in Psychoanalysis," in *The Language of the Self* (Baltimore, Md.: Johns Hopkins University Press, 1968), 32.

54. It is important to relate these various misreadings of Demby to Fiedler's official optimism, an attempt to "repress" the antimodern critique, an avoidance of the tragic character of life. See, in particular, Robert Bone, "William Demby's Dance of Life."

55. Invoking cubism also brings to the forefront European modernism and especially its encounter with African art. See the extended discussion of this in chapter 5.

56. William Demby, *The Catacombs* (Boston: Northeastern University Press), 17.

57. Brian McHale, *Postmodernist Fiction* (New York: Methuen, 1987), 10.

58. O'Brien, *Interviews with Black Writers*, 52–53.

59. *Wretched of the Earth*, 41.

60. Preface to Fanon, *Wretched of the Earth*, 24.

61. In particular, I am thinking of the contribution of *Black Skin, White Masks* (New York: Grove Press, 1968) and *The Wretched of the Earth*. I don't mean to go into great analytic detail here; I simply want to suggest a theorist indigenous to the decade, and who had a great deal of influence on African-American intellectuals, as a individual who might expand the discussion significantly. (See John Henry Jones, "On the Influence of Fanon," *Freedomways* 2 [1968]: 209–14.) I am aware of the dangers raised by Henry Louis Gates, Jr. in "Critical Fanonism," *Critical Inquiry* 17 (Spring 1991): 451–470. As I suggested, I think there are some very specific reasons that make it appropriate to raise his name here. On the other hand, ultimately Fanon does not fit into the "African (American) antimodernist" framework; he has too much faith in the rationality of "decolonization" (as political or psychiatric process) and lacks the tragic understanding of history that is definitive of Marshall, Demby, et al.

62. The applicability of the "colonial" paradigm to American culture is, of

course, a matter of historical debate. In some sense, this might partially explain the decision of Demby and Marshall to locate their texts outside the boundaries of the contemporary United States. At any rate, Demby and Marshall are not so interested in any kind of provincial politics anywise. A sophisticated Pan-Africanism (or maybe even internationalism), like that of DuBois or Baraka, could always translate metaphysics into politics anywise.

63. Patrick Taylor, *The Narrative of Liberation: Perspectives on Afro-Caribbean Literature, Popular Culture and Politics* (Ithaca, N.Y.: Cornell University Press, 1989), 94.

64. Scott, "Introduction to *The Catacombs*," xx.

65. "In an underdeveloped country an authentic national middle class ought to consider as its bounden duty to betray the calling fate has marked out for it, and put itself to school with the people: in other words to put at the people's disposal the intellectual and technical capital that it has snatched when going through colonial universities. But unhappily we shall see that very often the national middle class does not follow this heroic, positive, fruitful, and just path; rather, it disappears with its soul set at peace into the shocking ways—shocking because anti-national—of traditional bourgeoisie, of a bourgeoisie which is stupidly, contemptibly, cynically bourgeois." Fanon, *Wretched of the Earth*, 150.

CHAPTER FOUR

1. A. B. Spellman, "Not Just Whistling Dixie," collected in LeRoi Jones and Larry Neal, eds., *Black Fire* (New York: William Morrow, 1968), 159–68.

2. Quoted in *Downbeat*, September 29, 1960.

3. See Nat Hentoff's pioneering essay "Junk," in his *The Jazz Life* (1962; New York: Da Capo, 1985).

4. Other than those texts that are listed below, works that have shaped my understanding of African-American music and the sixties include: John Litweiler, *The Freedom Principle: Jazz after 1958* (New York: Morrow, 1984); Michael J. Budds, *Jazz in the Sixties: The Expansion of Musical Resources and Techniques* (Iowa City: University of Iowa Press, 1978); Nelson George, *Where Did Our Love Go?: The Motown Story* (New York: St. Martin's, 1985); Peter Guralnick, *Sweet Soul Music: Rhythm and Blues and the Southern Dream of Freedom* (New York: Harper and Row, 1986); Greil Marcus, *Mystery Train: Images of America in Rock and Roll Music* (New York: Dutton, 1976); Samuel A. Floyd, Jr., *The Power of Black Music: Interpreting Its History from Africa to the United States* (New York: Oxford University Press, 1995); Ekkehard Jost, *Free Jazz* (1974; New York: Da Capo, 1994); and David Such, *Avant Garde Jazz Musicians: Performing "Out There"* (Iowa City: University of Iowa Press, 1993). There are two wonderful essays by Lorenzo Thomas: "Ascension: Music and the Black Arts Movement," in Krin Gabbard, ed., *Jazz among the Discourses* (Durham, N.C.: Duke University Press, 1995) and "'Classical Jazz' and the Black Arts Movement," *African American Review* 29.2 (1995): 237–40. Most important is Ronald Radano's seminal *New Musical Figurations: Anthony Braxton's Cultural Critique* (Chicago: University of Chicago Press, 1993), which has dramatically opened up the study of African-American musics.

5. LeRoi Jones, *Blues People* (New York: Quill, 1963).

6. Jones's specific imitators will be listed and discussed below. It is worth mentioning at this point, however, the ways in which this seminal sixties text laid the groundwork for a great deal of contemporary African-American literary criticism. This is especially true of Stephen Henderson's *Understanding the New Black Poetry* (New York: Morrow, 1973), Eugene Redmond's *Drumvoices* (New York: Anchor, 1974); Houston Baker's *Long Black Song* (Charlottesville: University Press of Virginia, 1989) and *Blues, Ideology and Afro-American Literature*—if not of Henry Louis Gates, Jr.,

The Signifying Monkey: A Theory of African-American Literature (New York: Oxford University Press, 1988), which relies upon general cultural knowledge about the improvisatory and resisting practices of African-American musicians.

7. See E. Franklin Frazier, *Black Bourgeoisie* (New York: Free Press, 1957). Frazier's study chronicles an "obsession" for status among the black middle class, an abandonment of "culture" for "society." "The emphasis upon 'social' life or 'society,'" Frazier writes, "is one of the main props of the world of make-believe into which the black bourgeoisie has sought an escape from its inferiority and frustrations in American society. This world of make-believe to be sure, is a reflection of the values of American society, but it lacks the economic basis that would give it roots in the world of reality. In escaping into a world of make-believe, middle-class Negroes have rejected both identification with the Negro and his traditional culture. Through delusions of wealth and power they have sought identification with the white America which continues to reject them. But these delusions leave them frustrated because they are unable to escape from the emptiness and futility of their existence. Gertrude Stein would have been nearer the truth if she had said of the black bourgeoisie what she said of Negroes in general, that they "were not suffering from persecution, they were suffering from nothingness," not because, as she explained, the African has "a very ancient but a very narrow culture." The black bourgeoisie suffers from "nothingness" because when Negroes attain middle-class status, their lives generally lose both content and significance" (238). It is important to note, however, that Jones's reliance upon Frazier is selective. His use of the work of *both* Herskovits and Frazier is ironic, as they were long-time intellectual sparring partners. Frazier thought it was fantasy to place much stock in "recovering" an African past. What is of special interest here is Frazier's critical analysis of the "Negro church." Frazier saw the church as a central institution in the development of a "healthy" African-American culture and impugned it for its failure to develop a critical consciousness and its acceptance of class consciousness. See E. Franklin Frazier, *The Negro Church in America* (New York: Free Press, 1958).

8. Jones, *Blues People*, 174. It should be clear by this point that the experience and practice of black musics is immediately transnational. As both a debunking of sloppy genetics and a retreat from a simplistic "melting pot," black music is (potentially) an intercultural expression of opposition, which finds leadership in the creativity of black Americans, and usefulness in an African—and antimodern—consciousness, in promoting the survival of the destructive effects of modernity on individual health. To return to Jones: "What seems most in need of emphasis here are the *double* forms of assimilation or synthesis taking place between black and white American cultures. On the one hand, the largely artificial "upward" social move, demanded by the white mainstream of all minorities, and the psychological address to that demand made by the black bourgeoisie, whereby all consideration of local culture is abandoned for the social and psychological security of the "main." On the other hand, the *lateral* (exchanging) form of synthesis, whereby difference is used to enrich and broaden, and the value of any form lies in its eventual use. It is this latter form of synthesis (certainly available and actual, to varying degrees, since the first black man came into America) that became so important after World War II. . . . The point is that where one form of synthesis, which was actually assimilation, tended to wipe out one culture and make the other even less vital, the other kind of synthesis gave a local form to a general kind of nonconformity that began to exist in American (Western) society after World War II" (191).

9. And, as with all "New world" spaces, there is usually someone else already there, or someone trampled in the rush to proclaim themselves "king." In other

words, in remembering the experience of a Mary Lou Williams, say, or any number of other African-American women musicians, the process of renewal and revitalization is not always or necessarily democratic.

10. Ralph Ellison, *Shadow and Act* (New York: Vintage, 1964), 248.

11. Ellison, *Shadow and Act,* 253. Larry Neal, in his essay "Ralph Ellison's Zoot Suit" (1966), reprinted in *Visions of a Liberated Future* (New York: Thunder's Mouth, 1989), may have got very close to the truth when he wrote: "What Ellison [really] seems to be doing here is castigating LeRoi Jones for not writing the book that he (Ellison) would have written. . . . Ellison is capable of analyzing the specific ideas in *Blues People*, but he just wanted to write his own essay on the blues" (56).

12. "And Shine Swam On," in Neal, *Visions,* 21–22.

13. In addition to the works discussed below, the following are exemplary: Larry Neal's "The Ethos of the Blues" (1971), in *Visions,* and Albert Murray's *Stomping the Blues* (New York: Vintage, 1976). Also pertinent are the numerous articles that appeared in the brief lives of the "Black Arts" oriented journals *Cricket, Soulbook,* and the politically leftwing *Liberator.* An example from the white left would be Frank Kofsky's *Black Nationalism and the Revolution in Music* (New York: Pathfinder Press, 1970). Ralph Ellison's *Shadow and Act* was made up of his own musical reflections from the fifties and early sixties. Contemporary African-American critics Stanley Crouch (*Notes of a Hanging Judge: Essays and Reviews, 1979–1989* [New York: Oxford University Press, 1989]), Greg Tate (*Flyboy in the Buttermilk* [New York: 1991]), Nelson George (*The Death of Rhythm and Blues* [New York: Dutton, 1989]), and Gerald Early [*Tuxedo Junction* (New York: Ecco Press, 1989]) are greatly influenced by this Jones inspired tradition, as is a white academic like Lawrence Levine (*Black Culture and Black Consciousness* [New York: Oxford University Press, 1978]). American Studies connections in this story deserve more investigation; Ben Sidran's *Black Talk* was originally his American Studies dissertation at the University of Sussex and Charles Keil (*Urban Blues*) went on to teach and have a leadership role in American Studies at SUNY-Buffalo, to say nothing of Levine's connections or that of Neil Leonard, mentioned below. Things are especially entangled given the rise of American jazz criticism in the 1930s, especially in left publications like *New Masses,* and the concomitant rise of American Studies as an institution. Helpful in sorting out some of these ideological questions are John Gennari, "Jazz Criticism: Its Development and Ideologies," *Black American Literature Forum* 25, 3 (1991): 449–523 and Scott DeVeaux, "Constructing the Jazz Tradition: Jazz Historiography," *Black American Literature Forum* 25, 3 (1991): 525–60.

14. Paul Goodman, in the *New York Times Magazine,* February 25, 1968.

15. Charles Keil, *Urban Blues* (Chicago: University of Chicago Press, 1966). On page 185 he writes: "I think it is possible to interpret the soul and solidarity syndrome as a key phase in an incipient movement or perhaps as a complex response to the civil rights movement. This interpretation rests initially on a few broad assertions: American society is in the midst of a revolution, and the crisis is forcing basic cultural readjustments on the part of both blacks and whites; the black masses have only recently been emotionally affected by the current "revolution"; most of those in the ghettos, though they read or hear about it, have yet to receive any concrete benefits from this revolution; Negro men are especially disadvantaged, from almost any point of view, and at the very bottom of the American socio-economic heap; the disc jockeys are much more interested in freedom and self-respect than in integration per se and, perhaps because of their vested ethnic interests, even a little afraid, consciously or unconsciously, of absorption or disappearance in the white mainstream. If assertions of this sort have some validity, then the soul

movement readily takes on a strong nativistic and revitalizing tone. The concept of nativism implies, to this analyst at least, a reaction, an affirmation of the old values in response to the new stresses and conflicts. It may well be that the soul movement represents a retrenchment or retreat."

16. Neal, *Visions*, 113.

17. Neal's essay "Ralph Ellison's Zoot Suit" (1966) begins the cultural nationalist re-evaluation of Ellison, and encourages Black Arts sympathizers to move beyond the critique of the older novelist as "apolitical" or a "snob." Neal reveals and analyses the "folk consciousness" in Ellison's work, and rightly concludes that, while he would like Ellison to be more open to the experimental nationalist ethos, the Black Arts movement and Ellison have a great deal in common.

18. Ben Sidran, *Black Talk* (New York: Holt, Rinehart and Winston, 1971), 159.

19. Sidran may have revealed much about another cultural conversation when he wrote: "Black musicians have pioneered in a contemporary masculinity, and they have remained true to a source of higher values. As such, they have become models for a twentieth-century 'natural man.' Their music has flowed from the belief that the individual can free himself through collective action of the most intuitive sort, and they themselves have both the mobility and the element of surprise so highly prized in twentieth-century America. If Western man has 'lost' his masculinity to the machines and corporate structures he lives to serve, the black musician, whose work is his play and whose orientation is the polar opposite of technological, increases his importance as a social archetype" (158). This vision of a romantic patriarchy is surely oppositional, but still it is African-American antimodernism at its potentially most reactionary.

20. See, in particular, Martin Williams, *The Jazz Tradition* (New York: Oxford University Press, 1970). Important precursors were Marshall Stearns, *The Story of Jazz* (New York: NAL, 1958); Francis Newton (E. J. Hobsbawn), *The Jazz Scene* (London: MacGibbon and Kee, 1959); Neil Leonard, *Jazz and the White Americans* (Chicago: University of Chicago Press, 1962); Nat Hentoff, *The Jazz Life* (New York: Dial, 1961); and Barry Ulanov, *A History of Jazz in America* (New York: Viking, 1952), insofar as they demonstrated some sensitivity to history and cultural issues. Some critics tried to stay clear of the "Jones tradition" by emphasizing musicology (Gunther Schuller, *Early Jazz: Its Roots and Musical Development* [New York: Oxford University Press, 1968]) or by de-emphasizing race (James Lincoln Collier, *The Making of Jazz: A Comprehensive History* [New York: Houghton Mifflin, 1978]).

21. Which is not to say the text is useless, for it is an incredibly useful document in outlining and describing the social implications of the transformation in jazz in the years 1957 to 1967. It is also my sense that Kofsky has some of the same hunches that I wish to pursue. In *his* discussion of *Blues People*, Kofsky notes that "although white radicals seem mostly unaware of it, spokesmen for the culture of the blues people like LeRoi Jones are, through their critique of the barbaric mores and values of white America, making a profound contribution to the eventual reconstruction of society on humanist (or just human) lines" (Kofsky, *Black Nationalism*, 106). Also, to Kofsky's credit, he tended to direct his invective at other white critics. When the jazz criticism establishment decided, seemingly in committee, that Free Jazz was anti-jazz, Kofsky confronted them vigorously and often, and demonstrated that he was as perceptive as any white critic in reading the changing tone of the decade. Most importantly, Kofsky asserted the need for avant-garde musicians, most of whom were black, to have some chance to articulate the importance of their contributions. John Gennari, in his "Jazz Criticism: Its Development and Ideologies," cited in note 24, points out the irony that despite the supposed militancy of *Blues*

People, white leftist critics like Kofsky and Ralph Gleason were much more demanding than they about the relationship between an interpretation of the music and the American social context.

22. See Allen Merriam and Raymond Mack, "The Jazz Community," *Social Forces* 38 (1960): 211–22; Howard S. Becker, *Outsiders* (Glencoe, Ill.: Free Press, 1963); Charles Nanry, "The Occupational Subculture of the Jazz Musician" (Ph.D. diss., Rutgers University, 1970); Edward Harvey, "Social Change and the Jazz Musician," *Social Forces* 46 (1967): 34–42; and Robert Stebbins, "The Jazz Community: The Sociology of a Musical Subculture" (Ph.D. diss., University of Minnesota, 1964).

23. For an account of these conversations see Cecil Brown, "James Brown, Hoodoo and Black Culture," *Black Review* 1 (1971): 180–85; Donald Byrd, "The Meaning of Black Music," *Black Scholar* 3 (Summer 1972): 28–31; Milford Graves and Don Pullen, "Black Music," *Liberator* 7 (January 1967): 20; Errol Green, "Black Music," *Liberator* 8 (April 1968): 12–13; Joe Howard, "The Future of 'Soul' in America," *Black Dialog* 1 (1965): 23–24; LeRoi Jones, *Black Music* (Westport, Conn.: Greenwood Press, 1980) and "The Ban on Black Music," *Black World* (July 1971): 4–11; Ralph Metcalfe, "The Western African Roots of Afro-American Music," *Black Scholar* 1 (June 1970): 16–25; Alvin Morrell, "Notes on the Avant-Garde: A Brief Perspective on Black Music in the United States," *Soulbook* 4 (1966): 234–43; Larry Neal, "The Black Musician in White America," *Negro Digest* (March 1967): 53–57 and "Black Revolution in Music," *Liberator* 5 (September 1965): 14–15; Richard Ralston, "Black Music as History: Explorations into Pan-Africanist Trends in the Culture of the Black Masses," *Pan-African Journal* 6.3 (1972): 263 ff; Charlie Russell, "Has Jazz Lost Its Roots?" *Liberator* 4 (August 1964): 4–7; A.B. Spellman, "Revolution in Sound," *Ebony* (August 1969): 84–89; and Ron Welburn, "The African Music Continuum and the James Brown Band," *UMUM Newsletter* 3.11 (1974): 5–8.

24. Coltrane is, of course, not the only possible emblem of the connection between the discourse of black music and African-American antimodernism. Marvin Gaye was, by the late sixties, combining a pop music sensibility with a form of Christian evangelization. (See Cornel West on Marvin Gaye in his *Prophetic Fragments* [Trenton, N.J.: Africa World Press, 1990].) The culture critic bell hooks has talked about Otis Redding embodying a "spiritual" consciousness within the decade. Aretha Franklin's relationship with the church generally and her father, the Reverend C. L. Franklin specifically, might be profitably explored. The great gospel singer Mahalia Jackson published her autobiography during the sixties, and was active in the civil rights movement. Just about any of the so-called avant-garde could be explored under the rubric of African-American antimodernism; this wealth of choices speaks to the credibility of the discourse of black music as potentially oppositional, and clearly antimodern. The most dramatic example of African-American antimodernism in music might be found in the life and work of Charles Mingus. His autobiography dramatically and effectively confronts questions of authenticity—personal and musical—and articulates the, by now, ritual denunciation of American society. Most powerfully, Mingus imagines a conversation with Fats Navarro, a trumpeter comparable in ability to Miles Davis who died of tuberculosis at age twenty-one, about the inviolability of a moral universe, and the inevitability of "God." See Charles Mingus, *Beneath the Underdog* (New York: Penguin, 1971). Also pertinent is Mingus's ballet *The Black Saint and the Sinner Lady* (1963), which replays the landscaping of a moral universe seen among other African-American antimodernists (including, perhaps, a negative gender typology). The Impulse recording includes liner notes written by Mingus's therapist, and an account of how he was able to survive Bellevue Hospital to be able to complete the composition. Another possi-

bility worth considering would be bandleader Herman Blount, who—in 1957—became Sun Ra, and subsequently organized his Arkestra, and developed a comprehensive mythology surrounding his origins (extraterrestrial). His music playfully (and *substantively*) combines the worlds of black nationalism and space travel.

25. Kalamu Ya Salaam, "The Man Who Walked in Balance," *Coda* 245 (September 1992): 21.

26. There are a number of biographies of Coltrane: Bill Cole, *John Coltrane* (New York: Schirmer, 1976); Brian Priestley, *John Coltrane* (London: Apollo, 1987); C. O. Simpkins, *Coltrane: A Musical Biography* (New York: Herndon House, 1975); J. C. Thomas, *Chasin' the Trane: The Music and Mystique of John Coltrane* (New York: Doubleday, 1975); and the most important, Lewis Porter, *John Coltrane: His Life and Music* (Ann Arbor: University of Michigan Press, 1998) which includes an excellent bibliography. Booklength interpretations of Coltrane's career include Eric Nisenson, *Ascension: John Coltrane and His Quest* (New York: St. Martin's, 1993) and John Fraim, *Spirit Catcher: The Life and Art of John Coltrane* (West Liberty, Ohio: GreatHouse Company, 1996). Coltrane's producer at Impulse Records, Bob Thiele, has written an autobiography, *What a Wonderful World* (New York: Oxford University Press, 1995). Useful sketches and interviews include John Coltrane (with Don DeMichael), "Coltrane on Coltrane," *Downbeat*, September 29, 1960, 26–27; Frank Kofsky's interview included in his *Black Nationalism and the Revolution in Music*; Valerie Wilmer, "Conversation with Coltrane," *Jazz Journal* (December 1962): 2; Richard Turner's "John Coltrane: A Biographical Sketch," *Black Perspective in Music* 3 (1975): 3–16, and the biographical article by Barry Kernfeld in *The Grove Dictionary of Jazz*. Also invaluable are liner notes to the numerous Coltrane albums by Ralph Gleason, Nat Hentoff, Alice Coltrane, LeRoi Jones, A. B. Spellman, and others. For a discography, see Yasuhiro Fujioka, ed., *John Coltrane: A Discography and Musical Biography* (Metuchen, N.J.: Scarecrow Press, 1995).

27. Lawrence Christon, "This Trane Keeps A-Rollin'," *Los Angeles Times* (Calendar) July 12, 1992, 5 ff.

28. Liner notes to John Coltrane, *Giant Steps* (Atlantic LP 1311, 1960).

29. Williams, *Jazz Tradition*, 229.

30. "Improvisation in Jazz," liner notes to Miles Davis, *Kind of Blue* (Columbia LP CK40579, 1959). Martin Williams describes *Kind of Blue*: "Here were 'modal' pieces with harmonic challenges cut to a minimum, and with the soloist allowed to invent on a single chord or scale for sixteen measures, or even as long as he liked" (*Jazz Tradition*, 229). Also on "modes," see note 43 below.

31. Williams, *Jazz Tradition*, 230. Another review provocatively suggested: "Coltrane is not an artist you can listen to casually. You must give him your undivided attention to even begin to appreciate his talent. He emits a stream of musical consciousness that could, I suppose, be likened to some of the writings of James Joyce. He produces music that might be incomprehensible to some listeners, but its value and meaning lie in his compulsion to weave an entire piece of musical cloth almost instantaneously." Charles Hanna, in the *Minneapolis Sunday Tribune*, quoted in Thomas, *Chasin' the Trane*, 134.

32. If the Free Jazz enthusiasts were guilty of an uncritical belief in "progress(ion)," its most virulent critics were most often guilty of a nostalgia that belied a fear of their own financial insecurity. Surveying this ground, what is revealed is a group of nervous professionalists who had no conception of the purpose of the new music and whose status was threatened by their inability to thickly describe the new practice. In Jones's conception of the tradition, this is the "secretive" once again asserting itself to wrest creative if not financial control from the critical

cadré. Or as A. B. Spellman put it (quoted in Jones, *Blues People,* 235), "What does anti-jazz mean and who are these ofays who've appointed themselves as guardians of last year's blues?"

33. See Thiele, *Wonderful World.*

34. Liner notes for *John Coltrane & Johnny Hartman* [MCAD-5661]

35. Thomas, *Chasin' the Trane,* 113.

36. Quoted in Christon, "This Trane," 80.

37. Walter Benjamin, *Illuminations: Essays and Reflections* (New York: Schocken, 1968), 258.

38. Musicological analyses of his oeuvre include Zito Carno, "The Style of John Coltrane," *Jazz Review* 2.9 (1959): 17 and 2.10 (1959): 13; Barry Kernfeld, "Adderly, Coltrane, and Davis at the Twilight of Bebop: The Search for Melodic Coherence (1958–1959)" (Ph.D. diss., Cornell University, 1981); and Lewis Porter, "John Coltrane's Music of 1960 through 1967: Jazz Improvisation as Composition" (Ph.D. diss., Brandeis University, 1983).

39. Neal, *Visions,* 53.

40. "Following Lester Young, Illinois Jacquet, and others, he used 'false' fingerings to extend the tone-color and upper range of his instrument. The same quest led him to rescue from oblivion the soprano saxophone, which soon rivaled the tenor as his principal instrument. On both he learned to leap between extreme registers at seemingly impossible speed, and thus to convey the impression of an overlapping dialogue between two voices. . . . Radical timbres akin to human cries dominate his late improvisations as his concern with tonality and pitch waned" (Kernfeld, "John Coltrane," *Grove Dictionary of Jazz,* 237).

41. "Coltrane's expansion of individual sonority went hand-in-hand with an expansion of group texture. . . . Coltrane went to the forefront of experimental jazz with *Ascension* (1965), which presented a sustained density of dissonant sound previously unknown to jazz. Two alto and three tenor saxophonists, two trumpeters, a pianist, two double bass players, and a drummer played through a scarcely tonal, loosely structured scheme; their collective improvisation and many of their "solos" stressed timbral and registral extremes rather than conventional melody" (Kernfeld, "Coltrane," 237).

42. See Leonard Meyer, *Emotion and Meaning in Music* (Chicago: University of Chicago Press, 1956) and *Style and Music: Theory, History, and Ideology* (Philadelphia: University of Pennsylvania Press, 1989) and Jacques Attali, *Noise: The Political Economy of Music* (Minneapolis: University of Minnesota Press, 1985).

43. Modes are "the scales which dominated European music for 1,100 years (approx. A.D. 400 to A.D. 1500) and strongly influenced composers for another hundred years (up to c.1600). They have since reappeared from time to time in the work of some composers, especially in the 20th century. Throughout that total period of 1,500 years the plainsong of the Church, which is entirely modal, has continued to accustom the ears of fresh generations to the melodic effect of the Modes." See Michael Kennedy, "Modes," in *The Concise Oxford Dictionary of Music,* 3rd ed. (New York: Oxford, 1980), 423–24. And, ironically, the modes are best represented by "white keys" of the piano.

44. John Gennari, "Jazz Criticism," 513. Kofsky's interview (*Black Nationalism,* 221–43) is often a painful experience: "*Kofsky:* I asked you about Malcolm . . . because I've interviewed a number of musicians and the consensus seems to be that the younger musicians talk about political issues . . . that Malcolm talked about . . . and . . . try to express this in the music. Do you find in your own groups . . . that these issues are important and that you talk about them? *Coltrane:* Oh, they're

definitely important; and as I said, the issues are part of what *is* at this time. So naturally, as musicians, we express whatever is. *Kofsky*: Do you make a *conscious* attempt to express these things? *Coltrane*: Well, I tell you for myself, I make a conscious attempt, I think I can truthfully say that in music I make or I have tried to make a conscious attempt to change what I've found, in music. In other words, I've tried to say, "Well, *this* I feel, could be better, in my opinion, so I will try to do this to make it better." This is what I feel that we feel in any situation that we find in our lives, when there's something we think could be better. So it's the same socially, musically, politically, and in any department of our lives" (226–27).

45. Liner notes to *Revised Smithsonian Collection of Classic Jazz*, 1987.

46. *Coltrane Live at Birdland* (MCAD-33109).

47. Neil Leonard's *Jazz: Myth and Religion* (New York: Oxford University Press, 1987) explores in an extended fashion the idea of the "jazz community" as a cult, and the practice of the music as similar to that of an ecstatic religion: "I do not argue that jazz is inherently sacred or that religion lies at its heart, but only that it often stimulates religious or quasi-religious feelings and behavior, and answers needs commonly associated with them. Hopefully the results throw light on the role of music in our lives and on the nature of religiously-linked behavior in this supposedly secular time" (x).

48. Kalamu Ya Salaam, "Man Who Walked in Balance," 23–24.

49. Liner notes to *A Love Supreme* (MCA/Impulse-5660, 1964).

50. Floyd, *Power of Black Music*, 190.

51. Porter, *John Coltrane: His Life and Music*, 242. Porter provides a close musicological analysis of the whole of the suite.

52. Litweiler, *Freedom Principle*, 98–99.

53. See Todd Gitlin, *The Sixties: Years of Hope, Days of Rage* (New York: Bantam, 1987), especially chapter 8.

54. Martin Luther King, Jr., "Nonviolence and Racial Justice," *Christian Century* (February 6 1957): 165–67.

55. Interview in Kenneth B. Clark, ed., *The Negro Protest* (Boston: Beacon Press, 1963), 35–46.

56. See Denis de Rougemont, *Love in the Western World* (New York: Pantheon, 1954).

57. Howard Thurman, *Disciplines of the Spirit* (New York: Harper and Row, 1963).

58. Coltrane also did a benefit for CORE in April of 1964.

59. Liner notes for John Coltrane, *Meditations* [MCAD-39139].

60. See Kevin Gaines's excellent book *Uplifting the Race: Black Leadership, Politics, and Culture in the Twentieth Century* (Chapel Hill: University of North Carolina Press, 1996).

61. The *Chicago Tribune* critic Jack Fuller, quoted in Christon, "This Trane," 80.

62. Quoted in Porter, *John Coltrane*, 275.

63. Ibid.

64. Williams, *Jazz Tradition*, 230–34.

65. Litweiler, *Freedom Principle*, 13–14. Litweiler's summing of late sixties Coltrane is helpful: "For those who respect puritanism, the occasionally expressed critical idea that John Coltrane was a kind of musical puritan is a reasonable conclusion. The rigor and determination of his music are puritan qualities; so is his abandonment of sonic richness for tenor sax power, control, and often beauty. Some puritan values are absent here—for example, his music is not an ennobling experience—but most obviously present throughout his recordings is the primary virtue of courage. His music was spiritual quest long before he explicitly said so in *A Love Supreme*. His cyclic structures of the Sixties are the cycles of his inner life; that is why

he needed to play long solos. They move us so urgently because in hearing him, we recognize our own struggles against complacency, against fears, ever into life's unknowns. Surely the Freest of his recordings, *Interstellar Space*, makes clear for all time what sustains his creative spirit: Now without obstacles of any kind, he nonetheless continues in conflict, endless and exalted. And the conflicts in John Coltrane's music, the inner turmoil that's ongoing in life, are what have communicated more than any other statements in the Free jazz era" (103). Litweiler almost regrets what Coltrane continues to force him to remember: human limits, temporality, and the constraints of history.

66. Thomas, *Chasin' the Trane*, 228.

67. Quoted in Christon, "This Trane," 5.

68. Quoted in Christon, "This Trane," 81.

69. "How Long has Trane Been Gone," quoted in Kimberly Benston, "Performing Blackness: Re/Placing Afro-American Poetry," in Houston Baker and Patricia Redmond, eds., *Afro-American Literary Study in the 1990's* (Chicago: University of Chicago Press, 1989), 176.

70. My interest in Coltrane as representative of some general trends within the decade is not meant to displace or discard his influence as a musical innovator: "Coltrane's impact on his contemporaries was enormous. Countless players imitated his sound on the tenor saxophone, though few could approach his technical mastery. He alone was responsible for recognizing and demonstrating the potential of the soprano saxophone as a modern jazz instrument; by the 1970's most alto and tenor saxophonists doubled on this once archaic instrument. Finally, by selling hundreds of thousands of albums in his final years, he achieved the rare feat of establishing avant-garde jazz, temporarily, as a popular music" (Kernfeld, "John Coltrane," 237).

71. One of the most striking examples is Archie Shepp's introduction to Sidran's *Black Talk*: "I can remember as a young man in my twenties . . . requisitioning the great master's time, which he always gave with infinite grace and aplomb. This of course, would be something less than astounding were it not that Mr. Coltrane's willingness to share his wisdom and profound insights with a younger generation was not exactly the norm among musicians, as is often asserted. . . . Let us consider Mr. Coltrane . . . as "guru.". . . For a moment I thought back to those early days on Columbus Avenue, where the Coltrane family had moved after coming from Philadelphia. . . . The questions themselves were part of a spiritual matrix in which the personality of the master was more important to the relationship than the rhetorical handling of academic whys and wherefores. It transpired more in the spirit of the training of a Yoruba apprentice carver, than in the creation of a conservatory product" (Sidran, *Black Talk*, xii–xv). Or see A. B. Spellman, "Revolution in Sound": "When Ohnedarüth the mystic who was called John Coltrane died July 19 [*sic*], 1967, there was a wave of shock and incredulity in the world of those who are committed to the new black music. It was so generally a feeling of deep personal loss like the death of a close friend that most had never personally met. 'How could Trane be dead,' we asked ourselves, 'when there is so much of him in me?'" (85).

72. Spike Lee's *Mo' Better Blues* was originally to have been entitled *A Love Supreme* and loosely based on Coltrane's biography. This was abandoned after Coltrane's widow objected to the use and portrayal of profanity, sexuality, drinking, etc. in the script. See "Traning the Nineties, or the Present Relevance of John Coltrane's Music of Theophany and Negation," *African American Review* 29.2 (1995): 275–82. As the twenty-fifth anniversary of his death passed, there was a striking reappearance of Coltrane culture. See, for example, Kalamu Ya Salaam's "The Man Who Walked in

Balance"; Darlene Donloe, "Living with the Spirit and Legacy of John Coltrane," *Ebony* 44 (1989): 46 ff; Calvin Reid, "Chasing the Blue Trane," *Art in America* 77 (September 1989): 196–97; Gene Santoro's "Chasin' the Trane"; Edward Strickland, "What Coltrane Wanted," *The Atlantic* 260 (December 1987): 100–102; and Bill Shoemaker and Andrew White, "The Coltrane Legacy," *Downbeat* 53 (1986): 63 ff.

73. Some, but not all, are collected in Sascha Feinstein and Yusef Komunyakaa, *The Jazz Poetry Anthology* (Bloomington: Indiana University Press, 1991). Another concentration of Coltrane material (including the Spellman and Sanchez poems) can be found in Henderson's *Understanding the New Black Poetry*. See also Houston Baker, "Carolina, Coltrane, and Love," *Southern Review* 21 (1985): 855–56; Robert Stepto, "Michael Harper's Extended Tree: John Coltrane and Sterling Brown," *Hollins Critic* 13.3 (1976): 1–16; Gunter Lenz, "Black Poetry and Black Music; History and Tradition: Michael Harper and John Coltrane," in Lenz, ed., *History and Tradition in African-American Culture* (Frankfurt: Campus Verlag, 1984); Sascha Feinstein, "From 'Alabama' to *A Love Supreme*: The Evolution of the John Coltrane Poem," *Southern Review* 32.2 (1996): 315–37; Kimberly Benston, "Late Coltrane: A Re-membering of Orpheus," *Massachusetts Review* 18 (Winter 1977): 770–81.

74. Benston, "Performed Blackness," 176. This is the second occasion in this book in which I have had cause to turn to Benston's seminal essay, and I acknowledge that his thinking about African-American culture, the sixties, and the position of white critics, has been a major influence on my work.

75. Benston, "Performed Blackness," 176–77. Benston goes on to offer an extended and brilliant reading of—perhaps the most important Coltrane poem—A. B. Spellman's "Did John's Music Kill Him?"

76. Response to Benston, "Performed Blackness," 192.

77. "He was a bridge, the most accomplished of the so-called post-bebop musicians to make an extension into what is called the avant garde. . . . He was one of the few older men to demonstrate a sense of responsibility to those coming behind him. He provided a positive image that was greatly needed and stood against the destructive forces that have claimed so many. Having suffered and seen so much himself, he tried to see that others coming along wouldn't have to go through all that" (Archie Shepp, "A View from the Inside," *Music '66/Downbeat Yearbook*, 19–31).

CHAPTER 5

1. Romare Bearden, "Rectangular Structure in My Montage Paintings," *Leonardo* 2 (1969): 18.

2. Ralph Ellison, "The Art of Romare Bearden," *Going to the Territory* (New York: Random House, 1986), 234. This essay on Bearden (originally published in *The Crisis* in 1970) was one of the few sketches Ellison wrote during the sixties—excluding those earlier profiles collected in *Shadow and Act* (1964). It is worth quoting more of Ellison's statement, for it is suggestive of the ways in which "antimodern sentiment" might be more broadly conceived than the ways in which it has been organized in this book:

> For in keeping with the special nature of his search and by the self-imposed "rules of the game," it was necessary that the methods arrived at be such as would allow him to express the tragic predicament of his people without violating his passionate dedication to art as a fundamental and transcendent agency for confronting and revealing the world. . . . To have done this successfully is not only to have added a dimension to the technical resourcefulness of art, but to have modified our way of experiencing reality. It is also to have had a most successful encounter with a troublesome social anachronism

which, while finding its existence in areas lying beyond the special providence of the artist, has nevertheless caused great confusion among many painters of Bearden's social background. . . . What then do I mean by anachronism? I refer to that imbalance in American society which leads to a distorted perception of social reality, to a stubborn blindness to the creative possibilities of cultural diversity, to the prevalence of negative myths, racial stereotypes and dangerous illusions about art, humanity and society. Arising from an initial failure of social justice, this anachronism divides social groups along lines that are no longer tenable while fostering hostility, anxiety and fear; and in the area to which we now address ourselves it has had the damaging effect of alienating many Negro artists from the traditions, techniques, and theories indigenous to the arts through which they aspire to achieve themselves. . . . And while many are convinced that simply to recognize social imbalance is enough to put it to riot, few achieve anything like artistic mastery, and most fail miserably through a single-minded effort to "tell it like it is."

One aspect of the Bearden–Ellison connection that deserves much more attention is their reading of and attraction to the French modernist writer and art historian André Malraux. This may prove to be especially fruitful for investigation because of Malraux's participation in the Resistance in World War II; the influence of Malraux's political art, and the critique of fascism generally, among other aspects of European modernism of interest to Bearden, Ellison, and others, may help to displace the belief that African-American antimodernism (keeping in mind Lears's distinction between literary modernism and modernity) is apolitical.

3. The most important sources currently available on Bearden are Myron Schwartzman, *Romare Bearden: His Life and Art* (New York: Abrams, 1990) and the essays by Mary Schmidt Campbell ("History and the Art of Romare Bearden") and Sharon F. Patton ("Memory and Metaphor: The Art of Romare Bearden, 1940–1987"), included in *Memory and Metaphor: The Art of Romare Bearden, 1940–1987* (New York: Oxford University Press and the Studio Museum in Harlem, 1991), the catalogue to the first major retrospective of Bearden's work since his death in 1987. See also Mary Schmidt Campbell's comprehensive Ph.D. dissertation "Romare Bearden: A Creative Mythology" (Syracuse University, 1982). *Callalloo* 36 (1988) was a special issue devoted to Bearden, and includes memorials by Ellison and others, and, most interestingly, a long poem about Bearden by Michael Harper. Other useful overview essays include Calvin Tomkins, "Putting Something over Something Else," *The New Yorker*, November 8, 1977, 53–58; Avis Berman, "Romare Bearden: 'I Paint Out of the Tradition of the Blues'," *Art News* 79 (December 1980): 60–66; Lowery Sims, "The Unknown Romare Bearden," *Art News* 85 (October 1986): 116–20, My overall perspective in this chapter has been shaped by Sharon Patton's "The Search for Identity, 1950–1987," in *African-American Artists, 1880–1987: Selections from the Evan-Tibbs Collection* (Seattle: University of Washington Press, 1989), 73–113; Richard Powell, *The Blues Aesthetic: Black Culture and Modernism* (Washington, D.C.: Washington Project for the Arts, 1989); David Driskell, *Two Centuries of Black American Art* (New York: Knopf, 1976) and *Africa: Ancestral Legacy* (New York: Abrams, 1990). See also the useful *Romare Bearden as Printmaker*, edited by Gail Gelburd (New York: Council for Creative Projects, 1992); "Romare Bearden: The Unknown American Negro Artist," and "How Effective Is Social Protest Art (Civil Rights)?", both by Jeanne Siegel and included in her *Artwords: Discourse on the 60s and 70s* (Ann Arbor: UMI Research Press, 1985).

4. Romare Bearden, quoted in Jeanne Siegel's "Why Spiral?", 65 *Art News* (September 1966) 49.

5. This is not to suggest that there were no intermediate steps or intermediaries between Picasso and Bearden; many African-American painters and sculptors have struggled with this complex appropriation. If the modernists have turned to "Africa" where can African-American modernists turn? See the art of Sargent Johnson, in particular, and the essays and work included in Driskoll's *Africa: Ancestral Legacy*.

6. The most comprehensive (and sophisticated) study of this nexus of concerns is James Clifford, *The Predicament of Culture: Twentieth-Century Ethnography, Literature, and Art* (Cambridge, Mass.: Harvard University Press, 1988). See also Michel Leiris, "The Discovery of African Art in the West," in *African Art* (New York: Golden Press, 1968); Maurice Nadeau, *The History of Surrealism* (New York: Macmillan, 1965); Michael Pye, "Whose Art Is It Anyway?," *Connoisseur* 217 (March 1987): 78–85; William Rubin, ed., *"Primitivism" in Modern Art: Affinity of the Tribal and the Modern*, 2 vols. (New York: Museum of Modern Art, 1984), and Frank Willet, "Authenticity in African Art," *African Arts* 9.3 (1975): 6–74.

7. Campbell, "History and the Art of Romare Bearden," 7.

8. Campbell, "History," 10.

9. Quoted in Campbell, "History," 9.

10. Campbell, "History," 10–11.

11. Quoted in *Time*, October 23, 1964.

12. Quoted in Avis Berman, "Romare Bearden: 'I Paint Out of the Tradition of the Blues,'" *Art News* 79 (December 1980): 60.

13. The story is told that Bearden was offered a contract by the legendary Connie Mack of the Philadephia Athletics, if the extremely light skinned Bearden could agree to pass for white. Bearden refused.

14. Sharon Patton identifies "306" as the equivalent of a Paris salon, and suggests typical visitors were "Langston Hughes, Claude McKay, William Saroyan, Carl Van Vechten, William Steig, Ralph Ellison, Jack Carter . . . Francisco Lord, Vertis Hayes, Norman Lewis, Jacob Lawrence, Ronald Joseph, Gwendolyn Bennett, Augusta Savage, Aaron Douglas, O. Richard Reid, Frederick Coleman, Ernest Crichlow, Robert Blackburn . . . Sammy Stewart, John Hammond, Andy Razaf . . . and Addison Bates" (Patton, "Memory and Metaphor," 21).

15. Patton, "Memory and Metaphor," 22.

16. Romare Bearden, "The Negro Artist and Modern Art," *Opportunity* 12 (December 1934): 71–72.

17. Bearden, "Negro Artist," 72.

18. Patton, "Memory and Metaphor," 24.

19. We should take seriously, I think, the coincidence of World War II and Bearden's fascination with images and stories of violence, death, and resurrection.

20. Patton, "Memory and Metaphor," 31.

21. Bearden, "Rectangular Structure in My Montage Paintings," 12. The insights that Bearden gained from this "practice," eventually led to his collaboration with painter Carl Holty on a book, *The Painter's Mind: A Study of the Relations of Structure and Space in Painting* (New York: Garland, 1981).

22. Quoted in Charles Childs, "Bearden: Identification and Identity," *Art News* 63 (1964): 24 ff.

23. Very insightful (and comprehensive) on Bearden's work in the 1950s is Matthew S. Witkovsky, "Experience vs. Theory: Romare Bearden and Abstract Ex-

pressionism," *Black American Literature Forum* 23 (Summer 1989): 257–82. In chronicling the sixties transformation the following have been useful: Dore Ashton, "Romare Bearden, Projections," *Quadrum* 17 (1965): 99–110; Charles Childs, "Bearden: Identification and Identity," *Art News* 63 (October 1964): 24, 54, 61; Cathy Aldridge, "Bearden Collages Sold Though Exhibit Goes On," *New York Amsterdam News*, November 4, 1967, 23; John Canaday, "Romare Bearden Focuses on the Negro," *New York Times*, October 14, 1967; Grace Glueck, "Minority Artist Finds a Welcome in a New Showcase," *New York Times*, December 23, 1969, 22 and "A Brueghel from Harlem," February 22, 1970; and Jeanne Siegel, "Why Spiral?", *Art News* 65 (September 1966): 48–51 ff.

24. Campbell, "History," 12–20. It should also be noted that if Bearden was ill at ease with the "social world," he was also increasingly uncomfortable with the direction of American art. Matthew Witkovsky writes that "By around 1950, most Abstract Expressionist artists had resolved the struggle [between formalism and representation] in favor of complete abstraction. All art has subject matter, they claimed, but the potential significance of a fully abstract work transcends any figurative depiction's meaning, because abstract feelings and essences form the basis for universal reality" ("Experience vs. Theory," 268). Witkovsky incorrectly suggests that, in the years 1952–1963, Bearden removed figures from his paintings; although Bearden clearly became "more abstract," he could not make the full commitment because, I suggest, of his attachment to painting as a form of speech—and in need of speaking subjects. As Bearden put it in a letter to Carl Holty in 1950: "It'll be grand when I can get the colors to walk about the picture like free men and not isolated in certain areas like people with smallpox. But to find those controls whereby the colors can act like free men and not exist in a state of anarchy" (Quoted in Schwartzman, *Romare Bearden*, 169).

25. There is a fascinating group interview with Baldwin, Bearden, Alvin Ailey, and Albert Murray—certainly a grouping within which many "antimodern" ideas are shared. See Nelson E. Breen, ed., "To Hear Another Language: A Conversation with Alvin Ailey, James Baldwin, Romare Bearden, and Albert Murray," *Callaloo* 12 (1989): 431–52.

26. Campbell, "Romare Bearden," 170.

27. See Carl Holty papers and Romare Bearden papers, both in the Archives of American Art, Smithsonian Institution, Washington, D.C., for correspondence between the two friends.

28. April J. Paul, "Introduction à la Peinture Moderne Americaine: Six Young Painters of the Samuel Kootz Gallery: An Inferiority Complex in Paris," *Arts* 60.6 (1986): 65–71. Myron Schwartzman notes that Bearden was lucky to have owned most of his own work so that he did not have to suffer the indignity of watching the prices of his work crash quickly.

29. Campbell, "Romare Bearden," 171.

30. See Schwartzman, *Romare Bearden*, 176.

31. By far the most comprehensive account of Bearden's 1950s is to be found in "Sea Breeze: The 1950's" in Schwartzman, *Romare Bearden*.

32. The parallel to Coltrane here is quite striking: "Nanette's influence on Romare's life was profound. The first years of their marriage not only marked his full return to painting, they also resulted in other healthy changes in his life. Nanette got him to stop taking tranquilizers and to stop smoking cigarettes. Most important, she was a stabilizing presence in his life. It was no easy task for Romare to devote his concentration to painting once more, but as Nanette remarked, he was now again "at one with himself." Schwartzman, *Romare Bearden*, 178.

33. Particularly striking for anyone with an interest in dialogic models is this: "From Mr. Wu, Bearden . . . learned about the "open corner" of Chinese landscape painting, usually the right hand corner, that acts as an entranceway for the viewer, who becomes part of the painting by imaginatively completing areas the artist has deliberately left unfinished" (Schwartzman, *Romare Bearden*, 186).

34. Schwartzman, *Romare Bearden*, 179.

35. And, for a brief time, he did work totally in abstraction. As Sharon Patton put it: "For about five years, between the late fifties and early sixties, Bearden experimented with Abstract Expressionist techniques — splashed or dripped paint, variations of the same color, and various approaches to oils, acrylics, and paper. . . . His paintings were nonrepresentational and emphasize the primacy of the two-dimensional picture plane and color. However, Bearden was not interested in the existentialism represented by contemporary American painting or in its aggressive, gestural style." Patton, "Memory and Metaphor," 35. It is also significant that Bearden's paintings — unlike those of other abstractionists — always had titles, often supplied by his wife. We might say that there is always a woman lurking behind the philosophic barriers, whether as in "Blue Lady," or in the contributions of Nanette Bearden.

36. Robert Farris Thomson, *Flash of the Spirit: African & Afro-American Art & Philosophy* (New York: Vintage, 1983), 221–22.

37. This may have been flexible; comments in an article from *Black Dialog* responding to the group's first showing refers to fifteen artists; Sharon Patton suggests twelve; Mary Schmidt Campbell says twenty-four. See also Floyd Coleman, "The Changing Same: Spiral, the Sixties, and African-American Art," in William E. Taylor and Harriet G. Warkel, *A Shared Heritage: Art by Four African Americans* (Bloomington: Indiana University Press and Indianapolis Museum of Art, 1996), 148–58.

38. "Why Spiral?" *Artnews* 65 (September 1966): 48–61 ff.

39. Schwartzman, *Romare Bearden*, 209.

40. See Coleman, 149. The "spiral" is, as we've seen, a recurrent theme in Hayden, Marshall, and Demby, and also appears in the title of an early Coltrane recording.

41. *First Group Showing (Works in Black and White)*, exhibition catalogue (New York: Spiral Gallery, 1965), quoted in Schwartzman, 209.

42. Siegel, "Why Spiral?" 48.

43. Siegel, "Why Spiral?" 50.

44. "I asked Bearden whether he had encountered much in the way of prejudice in trying to show and sell his work to a white market. 'That's a difficult question,' he said, 'and one that every artist would answer differently. To me, so much of the gallery scene has to do with social things. For instance, a lot of artists used to go to the Cedar Bar, you know, to meet Kline or de Kooning, and a lot of them were helped in that way. If the Negro artist isn't involved in that sort of thing . . .' Bearden's voice trailed off. I broke the silence by asking whether the Negro artist *still* wasn't involved in that sort of thing. 'Oh, there's some association now between Negro and white artists in the studios and lofts. A lot of Negroes live in the vicinity now. I think, on the other hand, that the Negro artists who emerged in the thirties were thrown more together.'" (Jay Jacobs, *Art Gallery Magazine* 11 (April 1968): 26–31.

45. Patton, "Memory and Metaphor," 37.

46. On photomontage see: Matthew Teitelbaum, ed., *Montage and Modern Life, 1919–1942* (Cambridge, Mass.: MIT Press, 1992); Dawn Ades, *Photomontage* (London: Thames and Hudson, 1986). On Bearden's "projections," in particular, see Gail Gel-

burd and Thelma Golden, *Romare Bearden in Black-and-White: Photomontage Projections, 1964* (New York: Whitney Museum of American Art, 1997) and the superb "Signifying Identity: Art and Race in Romare Bearden's Projections," *Art Bulletin* 76.3 (1994): 411–26.

47. Ekstrom quoted in Schwartzman, *Romare Bearden*, 212.

48. Bearden's account of the "transformation": "My own inspiration was developing along lines that were extremely personal. What this meant, of course, was my desire to have my expression individually understood. Subject matter, I find, is of no importance, except, of course, when it means a great deal to an artist who can transform it into something personal . . . something universal. If subject were just a matter of race and identity, then one could not have affinities with anything other than one's own culture. What an artist brings to the subject—unless he is totally primitive—is equally important, forming a synthesis out of many years in art and several cultures. . . . I create social images within the work so far as the human condition is social, I create racial identities so far as the subjects are Negro, but I have not created protest images because the world within the collage, if it is authentic, retains the right to speak for itself" (Quoted in Charles Childs, "Bearden: Identification and Identity," *Artnews* 63 [October 1964]: 24–25 ff).

49. Preface to Teitelbaum, *Montage and Modern Life*, 8.

50. Quoted in Hans Richter, *Dada: Art and Anti-Art* (London: Thames and Hudson, 1965), 117.

51. Letter to Michael Gibson, *International Herald Tribune*, June 15, 1975. Quoted in Schwartzman, *Romare Bearden*, 216.

52. "Romare Bearden," *Callaloo* 11.3 (1988): 421.

53. In addition to the Schwartzman and Campbell/Patton texts, Bearden's work has been collected in a number of exhibitions: *Romare Bearden, Oils, Gouaches, Watercolors, Drawings, 1937–1940* (New York: 306 West 141st St., 1940); *New Paintings by Bearden* (New York: Samuel Kootz Gallery, 1944); *Ten Hierographic Paintings by Sgt. Romare Bearden* (Washington, D.C.: The G Place Gallery, 1944); *Bearden: Paintings and Water Colors Inspired by Garcia Lorca's "Lament for a Bullfighter"* (New York: Samuel M. Kootz Gallery, 1946); *Romare Bearden: Paintings and Projections* (Albany, N.Y.: The Art Gallery, SUNY, 1968); *Romare Bearden: The Prevalence of Ritual* (New York: Museum of Modern Art, 1971); Bunch M. Washington, *The Art of Romare Bearden: The Prevalence of Ritual* (New York: Abrams, 1973); Mary Schmidt Campbell, *Mysteries: Women in the Art of Romare Bearden* (Syracuse, N.Y.: Everson Museum of Art of Syracuse and Onondaga County, 1975); *Romare Bearden, 1970–1980* (Charlotte, N.C.: The Mint Museum, 1980); Romare Bearden and Derek Walcott, *The Caribbean Poetry of Derek Walcott and the Art of Romare Bearden* (New York: Farrar, Straus, and Giroux, 1983); *Romare Bearden: Origins and Progressions* (Detroit: The Detroit Institute of the Arts, 1986); and *Romare Bearden, 1911–1988, A Memorial Exhibition* (New York: ACA Galleries, 1988).

54. Quoted in Patton, "Memory and Metaphor," 40.

55. Quoted in Patton, "Memory and Metaphor," 39.

56. "Works of this type require an art history very different from what we have had in the past for contemporary art. Understanding the works of artists who fill their art with history, biography, cultural values, and traditions requires much more than the descriptive rhapsodizing required for work with only a visual content. Bearden's work signaled the need for patient iconographic study; his personal biography, the history of the Black American, the aesthetic traditions on which he draws, all this knowledge is a requirement, as well as the willingness to believe that art in the twentieth century can have a moral center. In many ways this willingness to look

at the visual arts as moral humanistic study may be the greatest challenge the work poses" (Campbell, "History," 17).

57. Berman, "Romare Bearden," 67.

58. This was also a way for Bearden to demonstrate the complexity of his racial identity. For instance, he painted a version of Pieter de Hooch's "The Spinner and the Housemaid," called "Woman in a Harlem Courtyard," because as he put it, he was unwilling "to deny the Harlem where I grew up or the Haarlem of the Dutch masters." See Childs, "Identification and Identity," 25. Bearden's work with musical figures ("Folk Musicians" for instance) always seems to recall Picasso's "Three Musicians."

59. "Inscription at the City of Brass: An Interview with Romare Bearden," *Callaloo* 11.3 (1988): 433.

60. It is important to note that Bearden often gave different works the same title as a way, I think, of emphasizing the centrality of certain themes and enacting a kind of literary ritual through repetition. A second painting entitled "Patchwork Quilt" is dated 1970; it is distinguished from the first by its focus on a reclining nude female figure—a dark black this time—on what is a literal quilt, pieces of joined material on the "canvas."

61. Somewhat less pedantic is Bearden's explanation of the use of space in his collages: "When I begin a work now, I first put down several rectangles of color, some of which, as in a Rembrandt drawing, are of the same proportion as the canvas. I might next paste a photograph (or a piece of paper), perhaps of a head, in the general area where I expect a head to be. . . . I attempt ever more definite statements, superimposing other materials over those I started with. I try to move up and across the surface . . . avoiding deep diagonal thrusts and the kind of arabesque shapes favored by the great Baroque painters. Slanting directions I regard as tilted rectangles, and I try to find some compensating balance for these relative to the horizontal and vertical axes of the canvas. . . . What I'm trying to do is establish a vertical and a horizontal control of the canvas. . . . I like the language to be as classical as possible, but I don't want complete reductionism" (Avis Berman, "Romare Bearden," 63).

62. Hilton Kramer, "Bearden's 'Patchwork Cubism,'" *New York Times*, December 3, 1978.

63. Campbell, *Mysteries*, 1.

64. Campbell, "History," 16.

65. Quoted in Patton, "Memory and Metaphor," 70.

66. Along with *The Painter's Mind* (New York: Crown, 1969), Bearden wrote (with Harry Henderson) *Six Masters of Black American Art* (Garden City, N.Y.: Doubleday, 1972), and was working on a major history of African-American art at the time of his death.

67. Schwartzman, *Romare Bearden*, 217.

68. Bearden interview with Schwartzman, quoted in Schwartzman, *Romare Bearden*, 62.

69. See, for instance, Randy Williams, "The Black Art Institution," *Black Creation Annual* 1974: 60–62. Sharon Patton, in her essay "The Search for Identity," in *African-American Artists: 1880–1987*, writes that "between 1966 and 1973 there were thirty major exhibitions of African-American art. The rest of the 1970's, however, were disappointing. There was less than enthusiastic institutional sponsorship of exhibitions, many galleries and artists groups dissolved, and artists often 'disappeared'" (100).

70. "There were a number of young minority artists out of the whole 'uplift' thrust of the Johnson years who were on scholarships to various colleges, art

schools. Many of these young people had graduated with academic degrees; others had come out of art school and felt that they were ready to paint, and we found there was little outlet for their work.... The other problem was that there were a number of people (especially women), who had majored in Art History, and were anxious to work in the field of art, but who had no experience. So this was the problem we had to face in order to make some disposition toward helping these young people" (Bearden, quoted in Schwartzman, *Romare Bearden*, 223).

71. Campbell, "History," 16.

72. Patton, "Memory and Metaphor," 70.

73. "On Ethnographic Surrealism," in Clifford, *The Predicament of Culture*, 146–47.

74. Bearden and Holty, *Painter's Mind*, 217.

75. Foreword to Schwartzman, *Romare Bearden*, 8.

76. Ibid.

CHAPTER 6

1. Walter Brueggeman, *Hope within History* (Atlanta: John Knox Press, 1987).

2. "C.L.R. James, "On the Origins," *Radical America* 16.3 (1988): 51.

3. Quoted in David Lewis, *W.E.B. Du Bois: Biography of a Race, 1868–1919* (New York: Henry Holt, 1993), 2.

4. W.E.B. Du Bois, *In Battle for Peace* (New York: Masses and Mainstream, 1952).

5. See Herbert Aptheker, ed., *The Correspondence of W.E.B. Du Bois, Volume III: Selections, 1944–1963* (Amherst: University of Massachusetts Press, 1978), 439–40. The letter was subsequently published in *Worker*, November 26, 1961 and *Political Affairs* 42 (October 1963): 31–34.

6. For instance, see the special issue of *The Nation*, December 14, 1998, especially Judith Stein, "History of an Idea," 13–17, and Robin Kelley, "Integration: What's Left?" 17–23.

7. See Eric J. Sundquist, *The Oxford W.E.B. Du Bois Reader* (New York: Oxford University Press, 1996), 624.

8. "The Realities of Africa," in Sundquist, *Du Bois Reader*, 656.

9. "The Future of Africa," in Sundquist, *Du Bois Reader*, 664.

10. "Africa, Colonialism, and Zionism," in Sundquist, *Du Bois Reader*, 639–40.

11. "Whites in Africa after Negro Autonomy," in Sundquist, *Du Bois Reader*, 673.

12. Sacvan Bercovitch, *The American Jeremiad* (Madison: University of Wisconsin Press, 1978). See my discussion of Bercovitch in chapter 1.

13. I propose this comparison much in the same spirit in which I introduced the work of Adorno earlier. In this case, there is much obviously to be gained by thinking through the consonances in the career of Du Bois and Benjamin. The scope of their intellectual interests, their peripatetic life and learning styles, their contested religiosity and Marxism, their provocative relations with women, their resilient attention to the question of the meaning of the twentieth century, their idiosyncratic commitment to allegorization, and, indeed, their shared education in late nineteenth and early twentieth century Germany, are suggestive of the ways in which our understanding of both thinkers might be enhanced by some creative comparative work. But again, and perhaps more importantly, I mean to insist upon the ambition and intellectual accomplishment of black artists and thinkers, and to insist upon recognition of the ways in which black cultural work exists—by necessity—as a kind of homegrown Frankfurt school.

14. W.E.B. Du Bois, *The Autobiography of W.E.B. Du Bois* (New York: International Publishers, 1968).

15. The *Autobiography* does not necessarily constitute the whole of Du Bois's liter-

ary activity in the context of the American sixties. Du Bois also wrote "The Negro People and the United States," *Freedomways* 1 (Spring 1961): 11–19; his letter to Gus Hall, as discussed above, also deserves attention as a sixties document, as might his late 1950s trilogy of novels *The Black Flame*. See Sidney Finkelstein's sympathetic evaluation of the novels: "W.E.B. Du Bois's Trilogy: A Literary Triumph," *Mainstream* 14 (October 1961): 6–16.

16. Worth noting too is the renaissance in black self-representation: Claude Brown, *Manchild in the Promised Land*; Eldridge Cleaver, *Soul on Ice*; Anne Moody, *Coming of Age in Mississippi*; Malcolm X (with Alex Haley), *The Autobiography of Malcolm X*; Gwendolyn Brooks, *Report From Part 1*; and, of course, just about all of James Baldwin's oeuvre. Despite there being significant differences here in terms of cultural generation, nearly all of these texts represent literary commitments quite distinct from that of Du Bois.

17. See Eric J. Sundquist, "W.E.B. Du Bois: Up to Slavery," *Commentary* 82 (December 1986): 62–67—and Eric Lott's later meditation on this essay, "Nation Time," *American Literary History* 7.3 (1995): 555–71; Keith Byerman, *Seizing the Word: History, Art, and Self in the Work of W.E.B. DuBois* (Athens: University of Georgia Press, 1994); Adolph L. Reed, Jr., *W.E.B. Du Bois and American Political Thought: Fabianism and the Color Line* (New York: Oxford University Press, 1997). Useful treatments of Du Bois include: Arnold Rampersad, *The Art and Imagination of W.E.B. Du Bois* (New York: Schocken Books, 1990); David Blight, "W.E.B. Du Bois and the Struggle for American Historical Memory," in Geneviève Fabre and Robert O'Meally, eds., *History and Memory in African-American Culture* (New York: Oxford University Press, 1994); David Levering Lewis, *W.E.B. Du Bois: Biography of a Race, 1868–1919* (New York: Henry Holt, 1993); William Andrews, *Critical Essays on W.E.B. Du Bois* (Boston: G. K. Hall, 1985); and Gerald Horne, *Black & Red: W.E.B. Du Bois and the Afro-American Response to the Cold War, 1944–1963* (Albany, N.Y.: SUNY Press, 1986). On the *Autobiography* see: Eric Sundquist, "Introduction: W.E.B. Du Bois and the Autobiography of Race," in his *Du Bois Reader*; Herbert Aptheker, *The Literary Legacy of W.E.B. Du Bois* (White Plains, N.Y.: Kraus International, 1989); William E. Cain, "W.E.B. Du Bois's *Autobiography* and the Politics of Literature," *Black American Literature Forum* 24.2 (1990): 299–313; and Albert E. Stone, "History and a Final Self: W.E.B. Du Bois and Henry Adams," in his *Autobiographical Occasions and Original Acts: Versions of American Identity from Henry Adams to Nate Shaw* (Philadelphia: University of Pennsylvania Press, 1982).

18. Lott, "Nation Time," 555.

19. See Gilbert Osofsky, "The Master of the Grand Vision," *Saturday Review* (February 24, 1968): 42; Alden Whitman, "End Papers," *New York Times*, April 9, 1968: 45; Richard Kostelanetz, "W.E.B. Du Bois: Perhaps the Most Important Black in American Intellectual History," *Commonweal*, November 1, 1968: 161–62; Truman Nelson, "A Life Style of Conscience," *The Nation*, April 29, 1968: 574–75; Louis Filler, "Review of Du Bois, *Autobiography*," *American Historical Review* 74.1 (1968): 315–16; W. M. Brewer, "Review of Du Bois, *Autobiography*," *Journal of Negro History* 54.1 (1969): 72–75; and Peter Shaw, "The Uses of Autobiography," in *American Scholar* 38 (Winter 1968–69): 136–44. I am using the reprint of Peter Shaw's review included in William Andrews, ed., *Critical Essays on W.E.B. Du Bois*, 48–54.

20. Kostelanetz's "vital center" politics are also on display in his author's note: "Richard Kostelanetz co-authored *The New American Arts* (Horizon) and edited *Beyond Left and Right* (Morrow)."

21. Knight writes: "Each Fall the graves of my grandfathers call me, the brown / hills and red gullies of mississippi send out their electric / messages, galvanizing my genes . . ."

22. Cain, "W.E.B. Du Bois's *Autobiography* and the Politics of Literature," 307.

23. Stone, "History and a Final Self," 36.

24. Walter Benjamin, *Illuminations* (New York: Schocken, 1988), 255.

EPILOGUE

1. Orlando Patterson, "Toward a Future That Has No Past—Reflections on the Fate of Blacks in the Americas," *The Public Interest* 27 (Spring 1972): 25–62.

2. Herbert Marcuse, *One-Dimensional Man* (Boston: Beacon Press, 1964), 253.

3. "Inner City Blues (Make Me Wanna Holler)." Written by Marvin Gaye, James Nyx, Anna Gaye, and Elgie Stover.

4. "Mercy Mercy Me (It's the Ecology)." Written by Marvin Gaye.

5. Stephen Carter, "The Dialectics of Race and Citizenship," *Transition* 56 (1992): 80–99.

6. E. J. Dionne, *Why Americans Hate Politics* (New York: Simon and Schuster, 1992). Carter also discusses Judith Shklar, *American Citizenship: The Quest for Inclusion* (Cambridge, Mass.: Harvard University Press, 1991) and Laurence Tribe and Michael Dorf, *On Reading the Constitution* (Cambridge, Mass.: Harvard University Press, 1992).

7. Carter, "Dialectics," 86.

8. See Shklar, *American Citizenship*: "There is no notion more central in politics than citizenship, and none more variable in history, or contested in theory. In America it has in principle always been democratic, but only in principle. From the first the most radical claims for freedom and political equality were played out in the counterpoint to chattel slavery, the most extreme form of servitude, the consequences of which still haunt us. The equality of political rights, which is the first mark of American citizenship, was proclaimed in the accepted presence of its absolute denial. Its second mark, the overt rejection of hereditary privileges, was no easier to achieve in practice, and for the same reason. Slavery is an inherited condition. In these essays I shall try to show . . . the enormous impact that not merely the institution of black chattel slavery but servitude as an integral part of a modern popular representative republic, dedicated to the "blessings of liberty," has had on the ways Americans think about citizenship" (1). Why should we pay close attention to the contributions of African-American antimodernists?: "The struggle for citizenship in America has . . . been overwhelmingly a demand for inclusion in the polity, an effort to break down excluding barriers to recognition, rather than an aspiration to civic participation as a deeply involving activity" (3). If we object to the "level of public discourse" we may need to direct attention to and reveal those conversations that illustrate this dilemma about "standing."

INDEX